Frontier Settlement in Mexican California

The Híjar-Padrés Colony, and
Its Origins, 1769–1835

C. Alan Hutchinson

New Haven and London, Yale University Press, 1969

Library of Congress catalog card number: 69–15448

Designed by Marvin Howard Simmons,
set in Baskerville type,
and printed in the United States of America by
The Carl Purington Rollins Printing-Office of
the Yale University Press, New Haven, Connecticut.
Distributed in Great Britain, Europe, Asia, and
Africa by Yale University Press Ltd., London; in
Canada by McGill University Press, Montreal; and
in Latin America by Centro Interamericano de Libros
Académicos, Mexico City.

In Memory of
My Mother and Father

Preface

My interest in Hispanic California was first centered upon its Mexican period as an outgrowth of the study of contemporary Mexican history. It became evident, however, that the problems faced by the Mexican government in its Territory of California were, with some exceptions, the same ones that Spain had already faced in its Province of California. Furthermore, it appeared that Mexican policy makers were soon following closely in the footsteps of their Spanish predecessors in dealing with these problems. It is one of the aims of this study, therefore, to trace the background of Mexican policy in California to its Spanish origins. In this way a sense of the continuity of historical development may be brought out.

A major theme which seems to emerge from this investigation is the pressure exerted upon Spanish and Mexican relations with the California Indians by continued fear of Russian, and later American, encroachments upon California. It is not within the scope of this work to attempt to come to any final conclusion as to how realistic the Spanish or Mexican governments were in their belief that the Russians and Americans were dangerous at this period, but simply to record their views and keep them in mind when discussing the gradual changes that their policies toward the California Indians underwent. It has been customary to play down Spain's fear of Russia on the northwest coast and to emphasize her fears of England, but unless due attention is given to this little-known aspect of Spanish foreign policy, it is difficult to understand fully Mexico's evident feelings of insecurity toward Russia on gaining her independence. It is for this reason that Spain's relations with Russia on the northwest coast are dealt with at length in Chapter 1, and Mexico's continued fears about Russian movements in California are taken up chronologically in the remaining chapters.

Perhaps the most baffling problem that Spain and Mexico faced in California was in their relations with the California Indians. It has not been sufficiently emphasized that Spanish policy toward the Indians of New Spain, and indeed of all Spanish America, was undergoing slow but steady change in the latter part of the eighteenth and early years of the nineteenth century. The Enlightenment, with its humanitarianism and utilitarianism, together with a growing anti-mission sentiment, gradually produced an outright demand for the secularization of the California missions on the ground that they were not being sufficiently successful in converting their Indians into Christian, Spanish-speaking farmers able to hold the land for Spain. Yet if the state was increasingly impatient with the Franciscans for their alleged slowness in making civilized men out of the Indians of California, the Franciscans were increasingly reluctant to turn their mission Indians loose to be abused as manual labor while the whites seized the rich mission lands as their own. Controversies arose over the nature of the Indian—whether he was in fact a rational human being or a kind of subspecies. These controversies and changes continued right on into the Mexican period, although by then the Indians were legally the equals of the white men if, in practice, they continued in their servile status. Liberal opinion in Mexico became split between those who wanted integration of the Indian into society at once, with full equality, and those who saw in this a clever way of defrauding the unlettered Indian out of the little he still possessed. These and other problems confronting Spain and Mexico in California were tackled by two important commissions on the Californias, the first organized by the viceregal government of New Spain, the second by the Mexican government. New documentation has made it possible to discuss the personnel and workings of these two commissions in some detail.

Most of the book is concerned with Mexican California, and it attempts to augment the relative lack of recent scholarly work on this period by utilizing fresh source material on the careers of California governors Echeandía, Victoria, and Figueroa. In addition, attention is given to some little-known but important figures, such as Francisco de Paula Tamariz— himself a governor-designate of California neglected by the history books—and Valentín Gómez Farías, a vice-president of Mexico who did more than any other Mexican to settle and develop California. The well-known colonizing expedition of José María Híjar and José María Padrés (which was actually planned and organized by Gómez Farías) is analyzed as a kind of case history of the problems that arose. Long considered an example of Mexican attempts to defraud the Californians, it seems clear that this colony was unjustly dispersed by Governor Figueroa, who, by doing so, helped to pave the way for the eventual take-over of California by the Americans some ten years later. The appendixes contain a number of new documents, not previously available, of importance for both Spanish and Mexican California.

I owe a debt of thanks to more people than I can mention by name here, and I would like them to know that their assistance is gratefully remembered although it is not recorded. First, I should like to thank my wife for her interest in the study and her valuable suggestions. I am indebted to the Wilson Gee Institute for Research in the Social Sciences at the University of Virginia for grants that enabled me to spend a summer in California and continue my research the following summer in other repositories. I have also had financial assistance from the Research Committee of the University of Virginia for travel, the purchase of microfilm, and typing expenses. The American Association for State and Local History gave me a grant which enabled me to work in the Mexican archives, and the American Philosophical Society provided funds that permitted a more extensive exploration of California archives than had been possible previously.

It gives me great pleasure to thank a number of librarians and archivists without whose help the study could not have been done. At the Alderman Library of the University of Virginia, I wish to thank Miss Helena Koiner and her efficient assistants, who cheerfully obtained so many items for me through inter-library loan. At the Bancroft Library of the University of California, I am particularly indebted to Dr. John Barr Tompkins and his able colleagues, whose valuable assistance both in person and by correspondence made it possible for me to undertake this study. At Santa Barbara I greatly appreciated the friendly help of Father Maynard Geiger, O.F.M. I also want to thank Dr. Nettie Lee Benson of the Latin American Collection at the University of Texas, and Dr. Archibald Hanna, Curator of the Beinecke Rare Book and Manuscript Library at Yale University. In Mexico, I am grateful for the friendly assistance given to me by Dr. Rubio Mañé, Director of the Archivo General de la Nación, and by General Benecio López Padilla, Director of the Archivo de Defensa. In addition I wish to thank Dr. Manuel Alcalá, Director of the Biblioteca Nacional, and Dr. Antonio Pompa y Pompa of the Instituto de Antropología e Historia. I also received valuable assistance from Señor Jesús Amaya Topete. In Spain, I am greatly in debt to Dr. José de la Peña, Director of the Archivo General de Indias, and to Dr. Ricardo Magdaleno, Director of the Archivo General de Simancas. I should also like to express my thanks to Teniente de Navío Roberto Barreiro-Meiro of the Museo Naval and Dr. Miguel Bordonau, Director of the Biblioteca Nacional. Finally, I wish to record my appreciation of the services of Mrs. Michael Podtiaguine, who translated numerous documents from the Russian, and Miss Ruth Ritchie, Mrs. Adele Hall, and Miss Frances Lackey, who typed the manuscript.

C. ALAN HUTCHINSON

Charlottesville, Va.

Table of Contents

Abbreviations

Abbreviations

RRAC	Records of the Russian-American Company, National Archives, Washington, D.C.
SBMA	Santa Barbara Mission Archives, Santa Barbara Mission, Santa Barbara, California
SP	Stearns Papers, Huntington Library, San Marino, California
ZAC	Zacatecas State Library, Zacatecas, Mexico

Chapter One

The Russian Lever

When Mexico declared its independence from Spain in 1821, one of its major concerns was the danger it believed to be threatening its distant province of California, and the Mexican government began to search in the old viceregal archives for information on what steps Spain had taken to protect this little-known and isolated region.[1] The Mexicans felt that Spain had been negligent in protecting California from possible invasion by the Russians and attack by the English or Americans, but even a brief examination of the record shows that Spain had spent vast sums of money and exerted considerable energy in her desire to keep foreigners away from an area that she considered essential for the protection of the enormously rich mining region of Mexico proper.

Even in the second half of the eighteenth century Spain looked upon the Pacific Ocean, or South Sea as it was still called, as closed to foreign shipping. California itself was little known until a beginning was made to settle it in 1769, while the northwest coast and the region west of the Great Lakes in the interior were unexplored. Stretched out as she

1. The name California is used throughout in place of Upper or Alta California.

was across the vast distances of the Americas, there is little reason to think that Spain would have been interested in extending her sparsely settled domains into these unknown territories had it not been for disquieting rumors that began to circulate concerning Russian explorations far to the north.[2]

Authoritative information regarding the epoch-making second Russian voyage of exploration under Vitus Bering, which had taken place in 1741, finally appeared in 1758 in the third volume of a work entitled *Sammlung russischer Geschichte* by Gerhard Friedrich Müller, professor of history at the St. Petersburg Academy of Sciences. In addition to its translation into English in 1761 and French in 1766, it prompted the publication of several books on the subject of Russian explorations in the north Pacific, one of them rather alarmingly called *The Muscovites in California*.[3] In actual fact, since the name "California" to a Spaniard of the day meant the entire northwest coast of North America, just as "Florida" had meant the entire Atlantic coast some two hundred years before, the book's title was not so misleading as it now appears. Furthermore, there may even have been some Russians on the coast, for Alexei Chirikov, Bering's second in command, had been obliged to leave fifteen men marooned on shore at about latitude 57 degrees for lack of boats to continue his search for them. When reports were made later in the century that a Spanish expedition had come across blond-headed Indians, the officials of the Russian-American Company began to speculate that Chirikov's men must have started a Russian colony in the area (for an early published report on

2. Stuart R. Tompkins and Max L. Moorhead indicate in their article, "Russia's Approach to America" (*British Columbia Historical Quarterly*, *13* [1949], 59–61), how this information began to appear in print.

3. 9 vols. St. Petersburg, 1732–64; Giuseppe Torrubia, *I Moscoviti nella California* (Rome, 1759); Tompkins and Moorhead, "Russia's Approach," pp. 61–62; James R. Masterson and Helen Brower, "Behring's Successors, 1745–1780," *Pacific Northwest Quarterly*, *38* (1947), 37–38.

these Indians, see Appendix A).[4] Disturbing as the rumored presence of Russian settlements north of California undoubtedly was to Spain, there was also the possibility that her age-old enemy England, then engaged in a life and death struggle with France for colonial dominance in North America and India, might revive her sea raiding in the Pacific. The Spanish authorities were reminded of this possibility by the Jesuit Father Marcos Andrés Burriel in his *Noticia de la California,* which appeared in 1757 under the authorship of Father Miguel Venegas. Father Burriel also warned his readers that if England succeeded in discovering the long-sought Northwest Passage connecting the Atlantic with the Pacific, she might well dominate the commerce of the western coasts of the Americas, long monopolized by Spain. Although the Northwest Passage was not found until the middle of the nineteenth century, it so happened that English attempts to discover it were diverted in the second half of the eighteenth century from the northeast to the northwest coast of America, measurably adding to Spain's concern for this region.[5]

The Spanish government, from 1759 in the capable hands of Charles III, reacted remarkably promptly to the new situation that was beginning to take shape. Plans were made in 1760 for a separate government of the northern frontier provinces of New Spain under the Audiencia of Guadalajara, although they were not put into effect. The following year, after the Family Compact with France was revived and Spain was preparing to join in the Seven Years War as an

4. Frank A. Golder, *Russian Expansion on the Pacific 1641–1850* (Gloucester, Mass., 1960), pp. 186–87. For a full account of this incident, which Golder believed to have occurred at Lisianski Strait, separating Chichagof Island from Yakobi Island and located at approximately 58 degrees N. latitude, see Golder's *Bering's Voyages* (2 vols. New York, 1922, 1925), *1*, 291–97, 311, 315–16, 324, 345–46.

5. Miguel Venegas, *Noticia de la California* (3 vols. Mexico, 1944), *3*, 145; Glyndwr Williams, *The British Search for the Northwest Passage in the Eighteenth Century* (London, 1962), p. 161.

ally of France and Russia against England, an ambassador was sent to St. Petersburg, the first after a lapse of thirty-one years.[6] The Marqués de Almodovar, the new ambassador, was instructed to find out about Russian voyages in the north Pacific, especially the expeditions of Bering and Chirikov.

In a dispatch from St. Petersburg on October 7, 1761, Almodovar, after retelling the story of Bering and Chirikov, said that he thought the danger to Spanish America from the Russian expeditions was at that time "so remote that it scarcely merits consideration." On the other hand, he reported that it had already been suggested in print that the newly discovered regions might be called New Russia because, although Russia had not as yet taken possession of them, she could do so whenever she wanted. He concluded his letter by remarking that he thought the Russian voyages were more likely to increase knowledge of geography than to add to the size of the Russian empire, although in centuries to come things might change.[7]

Even in the eighteenth century, however, change sometimes came with a suddenness that must have surprised men. By the Treaty of Paris in February 1763, England gained Canada from France, putting an end to Franco-Spanish rivalry in the New World but leaving new ways open for English fur traders to penetrate to the northwest coast. The following year the British Admiralty sent out Commodore John Byron on an expedition whose ultimate, although un-

6. Charles Edward Chapman, *The Founding of Spanish California* (New York, 1916), p. 74. Luis Navarro García, in his *Don José de Gálvez y la comandancia general de las Provincias Internas del norte de Nueva España* (Seville, 1964), pp. 90–91, states that the presence of two Dutch ships in the Pacific persuaded the Spanish government to consider separating New Galicia from the control of the viceroyalty in 1750. Tompkins and Moorhead, "Russia's Approach," p. 231.

7. Almodovar to Ricardo Wal [sic], St. Petersburg, 26 Sept./7 Oct., 1761, Archivo General de Indias, Seville, Spain (cited hereafter as AGI), Estado 86, 5M281, items 4–25.

fulfilled, objective was to search for a Northwest Passage on the west coast of America. Also in 1764, the new Spanish ambassador in St. Petersburg, the Vizconde de la Herrería, reported in two dispatches that Russian fur trappers had found beautiful black foxes on some islands off the northwest coast, and the Russian government was now greatly interested in sending out more exploring expeditions in the area.[8] From then on, as the great wealth to be obtained from furs on the northwest coast gradually became apparent, Russian and English interest in the area steadily increased, and Spain was forced to take energetic measures to protect her dominions.

Russia authorized two exploring expeditions in 1764, but only one left; the other was delayed until 1768. On December 1, 1767, the Spanish ambassador reported from Moscow that Russian forces had reached the mainland, although he did not know at what latitude on the coast. Then he relayed the genuinely alarming news that this force had been repulsed by the Indians with a loss of three hundred Russians. In other words, the Russians, if this report was accurate, were now landing relatively large numbers of men on the mainland somewhere north of California. This information was sent to the Marqués de Croix, Viceroy of New Spain, together with orders to alert the new governor of Lower California, Gaspar de Portolá, to possible Russian attacks, which he was to prevent so far as he could. On the same date that these instructions were sent to Croix in New Spain, he and José de Gálvez, then visitor-general, wrote a joint statement to Madrid suggesting the founding of a colony at Monterey. They mentioned that they were omitting a discussion of the danger from England and Russia in their report be-

8. Henry Folmer, *Franco-Spanish Rivalry in North America* (Glendale, 1953), p. 310; Williams, *British Search*, pp. 158–61; Vizconde de la Herrería to Marqués de Grimaldi, St. Petersburg, Mar. 19/30, 1764, and Sept. 7/18, 1764, AGI, Estado 86, 5M281.

cause a military officer, Marshal Antonio Ricardos, had left New Spain to present a full memorial on this matter in 1767.[9] It is apparent that the Spanish government at Madrid and its officials in New Spain had come to the conclusion at the same time that something must be done to avert the danger threatening California. Gálvez' instructions ordered him to confer with Viceroy Croix on forming "settlements in the provinces in suitable places," and the two men discussed at length the matter of making a settlement at Monterey. Madrid duly approved, and the work went forward.[10]

Spain's interest in her own activities in California seems for a time to have abated her fears of Russian encroachments farther north. In 1772, however, the Conde de Lacy, the new Spanish ambassador at St. Petersburg, was ordered to find out with the utmost secrecy whether the Russians were continuing their expeditions or if they had given them up, and how successful they were. He reported he had convincing evidence that news of the Spanish movement north into California in 1769 must have leaked out, perhaps by way of the Russian embassy in Madrid, and the Russian government had been afraid that Spain was about to launch an attack on their possessions in Kamchatka and on the northwest coast. He added that the Russians were keeping their recent discoveries secret, and their maps did not reveal their latest settlements. He managed to get a statement about them from someone who had access to the Russian sealed archives, how-

9. Tompkins and Moorhead, "Russia's Approach," pp. 239, n. 19, 242, n. 24; Herrería to Grimaldi, Moscow, 20/31 Nov. 1767 *sic*, and Julián de Arriaga to Croix, Madrid, Jan. 23, 1768, both AGI, Estado 86, 5M281; Irving Berdine Richman, *California Under Spain and Mexico* (Boston, 1911), pp. 506, 512; Chapman, *Founding*, p. 73.

10. Herbert Ingram Priestley, *José de Gálvez, Visitor-General of New Spain* (Berkeley, 1916), p. 413; Gálvez to Croix, San Blas, May 20, 1768, AGI, Audiencia Guadalajara 417; Navarro García comes to a similar conclusion in his assessment of the motives behind the move to settle California. He stresses, in addition, the influence of the expulsion of the Jesuits from Lower California (*Don José de Gálvez,* pp. 156, 162).

ever, and proceeded to reveal that they had a fur hunting establishment on the American mainland at 64 degrees. The Russians themselves believed the mainland was California, which extended north to 75 degrees. Here for the first time was detailed information regarding the whereabouts of the Russians on the northwest coast, and Ambassador Lacy ended his letter by pointing out that the Russians were now but a "short distance from the King's dominions." He suggested that the matter required careful attention from the government and well-directed measures to oppose Russian advances.[11] In two further dispatches from St. Petersburg in May 1773, Lacy reported that the ambitions of the Russians were so vast they were contemplating an invasion of China with an army of 25,000 men and thinking of sending off at the same time a maritime expedition against Japan. He also revealed that one of the members of the Russian Academy of Sciences had proposed, in a detailed report, that as soon as the Russian war then going on with Turkey was over, a part of the fleet should be sent to Kamchatka so that from there it could begin fresh conquests on the coast. The academician concluded his report with the ominous thought that Russia had more right to America than any other power because America had in the past been settled by immigrants from Siberia.[12]

The Madrid government did not wait for these alarming reports to take action. A month before they were written, the Spanish government instructed Viceroy Antonio Bucareli

11. Lacy to Grimaldi, Oct. 22, 1772, Mar. 19 and Apr. 23, 1773, AGI, Estado 86, 5M282.

12. Lacy to Grimaldi, May 7 and 11, 1773, AGI, Estado 86, 5M283. Lacy mentions that the member of the Academy who made the report was "Haller," presumably the Swiss scientist Victor Albrecht von Haller. But since Haller was not a member of the Russian Academy, Tompkins and Moorhead suggest that it may have been Leonhard Euler, a Swiss mathematician who was an academician ("Russia's Approach," p. 247, n. 33).

of New Spain that he was "to take convenient measures" to find out whether the Russians were continuing their explorations. Russian secretiveness at St. Petersburg now made the Spanish government turn the search for information about Russian activities on the northwest coast over to Viceroy Bucareli, who planned and put into execution an impressive program of maritime exploring expeditions and overland journeys.[13] His objectives were to search for the Russians, claim, without settling, newly discovered northern regions, settle the San Francisco Bay area, and find a way to bring artillery and other heavy equipment by river across the Isthmus of Tehuantepec to avoid the expense of a journey around Cape Horn or from the Philippines. As Bucareli pointed out in one of his dispatches, it was not that the king needed any more territory, for he already had "much more than could be populated in centuries," but it was preferable to have Indians as neighbors rather than Russians.[14]

The Madrid government lost no time in cooperating with their active viceroy, arranging to send him in August 1773 six naval officers who were to serve in the planned exploring expeditions. Before he received this information, Bucareli had already made some preparations for the first maritime expedition under first pilot and brevet Ensign Juan José Pérez Hernández. He had also made preparations for an

13. Dispatch to Viceroy of New Spain, Apr. 11, 1773, AGI, Estado 20, Mexico 1. In a recent study, Bernard E. Bobb deplores what he considers to be the excessive praise heaped upon Bucareli by Chapman for the part Bucareli played in preparing defensive measures for California. Bobb prefers to give most of the credit to José de Gálvez, whom he considers to have pioneered the way in this matter. It would appear that both men deserve due praise, but it should be remembered that they were not alone in realizing the danger to California from Russia, which was very much in the air at Madrid and Mexico at the time (Bernard E. Bobb, *The Viceregency of Antonio María Bucareli in New Spain* [Austin, Texas, 1962], pp. 156–65).

14. Bucareli letter no. 1048, Mexico, July 27, 1773, AGI, Estado 20, 3M707.

overland journey from Tubac, a recently founded garrison point or presidio in Sonora, to Monterey, to be carried out by the experienced frontier officer Juan Bautista de Anza. Bucareli thought of Anza's exploration as necessary to provide a less exposed route for sending forces superior to those the Russians might establish on the coast.[15]

Bucareli instructed Ensign Pérez to take possession in the king's name of all unoccupied land that he discovered. He was to recite a formula in doing so that referred to Pope Alexander VI's famous donation of the Americas to the Catholic Kings in 1493. Pérez was informed that the real intention of the Crown in making these expeditions was to convert the Indians to Christianity. He was on no account to make any actual settlements but was to mark appropriate sites which might be settled later. He was to avoid settlements by foreign powers, but if he ran into one, he was to read to the colonists the sixteenth-century Spanish document known as the Requirement. This called upon its hearers, normally Indians, to acknowledge the Roman Catholic Church as the ruler of the world and the Spanish kings, acting in the name of the Pope, as the lords of the Americas. If this had no effect, the offending inhabitants were to be removed by force. Unfortunately, there is no recorded instance of the reading of the Requirement to Russians on the northwest coast, but it may be readily conjectured that it would have had even less effect on them than it did on the Indians.[16]

There was little delay in putting Bucareli's plans into effect. Anza marched from Tubac on his successful overland expedition to Monterey on January 8, 1774. Ensign Pérez

15. Bucareli to Julián de Arriaga, Mexico, Nov. 26, 1773, Jan. 27, 1774, AGI, Estado 20, 3M708. For details of the Anza expeditions see Herbert E. Bolton, *Anza's California Expeditions* (5 vols. Berkeley, 1930).

16. Bucareli to Arriaga, Nov. 26, 1773, AGI, Estado 20, 3M708; Instructions of Bucareli to Juan Pérez, Dec. 24, 1773, AGI, Estado 20; Dispatch to Viceroy of New Spain, Madrid, Dec. 23, 1773, AGI, Estado 20.

sailed from San Blas on January 24, and Colonel Agustín Crame, a military engineer from Veracruz who had been given the job of reconnoitering routes across the Isthmus of Tehuantepec, reported on January 2, 1774, that not only was a water route over the isthmus possible, but he had found the remains of an old road which had formerly been used to transport artillery from ocean to ocean. Esteban José Martínez, second in command of the Pérez expedition—which in California came to be commonly called "the expedition for Russia"—reported in his diary on July 20 that they had reached 55 degrees, 30 minutes, the region in which Chirikov had lost his men in 1741. Juan Pérez noted on the same day that the Indians were good looking, with white complexions, and most of them had blue eyes. The women were white too and had blond hair. The ships finally reached latitude 55 degrees, 49 minutes, and returned without seeing any foreigners.[17] According to Ambassador Lacy, the Russians learned about the Pérez expedition from an account of it in the *Gazette de Leyde* of March 21, 1775. (For a translation of this account, see Appendix A.) He reported that they were concerned at the news and took pains to try to find out more about it. Later a German naturalist by the name of Peter Simon Pallas, who was working in Russia at this time, asked whether the blond Indians that the Spaniards had encountered might not be descended from Chirikov's boats' crews. This question was to be raised later still by the Russian-American Company.[18]

No sooner had the Pérez expedition returned to San Blas on August 27, 1774, in the frigate *Santiago* than Viceroy

17. Bucareli to Arriaga, Feb. 24, Mar. 27, Nov. 26, 1774, AGI, Estado 20; Chapman, *Founding*, p. 230; Tibesar, *Writings of Junípero Serra*, 2, 73.

18. Lacy to Grimaldi, Apr. 31, 1775, AGI, Estado 86, 5M283; Lacy to Grimaldi, May 1, 1775, AGI, Estado 38; Masterson and Brower, "Behring's," p. 83, n. 164. For a general account of the Pérez expedition see Henry R. Wagner, *Cartography of the Northwest Coast of America* (2 vols. Berkeley, 1937), *1*, 172–74.

Bucareli gave orders for the ship to be prepared for another voyage of exploration. The commander this time was to be First Lieutenant Bruno de Hezeta. Hezeta was ordered not to call at San Diego or Monterey and to try to reach 65 degrees latitude. He sailed on March 16, 1775, from San Blas, and Second Lieutenant Juan Francisco de la Bodega y Quadra, in command of the small schooner *Sonora,* who sailed farther north than Hezeta, reaching 58 degrees, returned to Monterey on October 7. No foreigners were seen, and Bodega went through ceremonial possessive acts up to latitude 57 degrees, 18 minutes, probably by burying bottles containing notices and by erecting large crosses, after the Spanish custom. An important adjunct to Hezeta's expedition was a reconnaissance of San Francisco Bay made by Lieutenant Juan de Ayala on the *San Carlos* in August 1775. This was designed by Bucareli to precede a second journey by Anza, whom he decided to send to San Francisco with sufficient troops to form an escort for two new missions and for protection for the port. Anza left Tubac on this famous second expedition on October 23, 1775, and explored the site of San Francisco at the end of March 1776.

Bucareli planned no further exploring voyages for 1776; instead he wanted to concentrate on supplying the missions and presidios and encouraging them to increase their farming operations. He wanted to hold back further settlements until Monterey could produce its own food and help supply a later establishment farther north. He said he preferred to make communication from Sonora to Monterey safe rather than extend farther along the coast. He wanted to wait until it could be seen how successful these operations were going to be and whether something could be done from New Mexico before doing more about San Francisco, although he realized it was a magnificent port, very suitable for colonization. Bucareli's preference for inland exploration, presumably because it would be safe if the Russians gained control of the coast, may be seen in the unsuccessful attempt of

Fathers Francisco Athanasio Domínguez and Silvestre Vélez de Escalante to travel from New Mexico to Monterey in 1776.[19]

The Spanish government decided meanwhile to do away with the old policy of keeping its voyages on the northwest coast secret and to publish information about them in the *Gazeta de Madrid*. Details of the expedition to California in 1769 and the exploring voyages of 1774 and 1775, together with information about the reconnaissance of San Francisco Bay and the possession of various ports on the coast, "with the agreement and satisfaction of the natives," were given in the *Gazeta* on March 19 and May 14, 1776. (For translations of these accounts, see Appendix B.) The reason for these explorations was attributed to the "pious Catholic zeal" of the king to convert the Indians to Christianity. This publicity was particularly pleasing to the Spanish ambassador in London, who wrote his government that it made clear to the world what Spain's rights were, and thus it would avoid future disputes. Also it came at a very appropriate time, for the Spanish government was aware at this point of the preparations to send Captain James Cook off on his famous third voyage to the northwest coast.[20]

It was probably Spanish fears about Cook's voyage that prompted Madrid to instruct the viceroy on May 20, 1776, to send out another exploring expedition to the northwest coast. This expedition, under Ignacio Arteaga, did not leave San Blas until February 11, 1779. Bodega, one of the commanders of the expedition, reached latitude 61 degrees on the

19. Bucareli to Arriaga, Nov. 26 and Dec. 27, 1774, Mar. 27 and Nov. 26, 1775, AGI, Estado 20; Wagner, *Cartography*, pp. 177, 179; Chapman, *Founding*, pp. 349, 356; Joseph J. Hill, "The Old Spanish Trail," *Hispanic American Historical Review, 4* (1921) 444–73 passim; Herbert E. Bolton, *Pageant in the Wilderness* (Salt Lake City, 1950).

20. AGI, Estado 20, 3M718; Príncipe de Maserano to Grimaldi, London, Apr. 12, 1776, Archivo General de Simancas, Valladolid, Spain (cited hereafter as AGS), Sección Estado.

voyage. The Spaniards had still not actually seen the Russian settlements on the coast but, as it happened, this was to be the last expedition for several years. Spain finally entered the War for American Independence in June 1779, and on April 19, 1780, it was decided that explorations were to cease for the duration.[21]

In the course of the war, Spain feared that England might persuade Russia to join in against her, and in fact the British government did attempt to win over Catherine II by offering her the island of Minorca. Richard Oswald, the English peace commissioner during negotiations between England and her former American colonies, even proposed a plan for an English and Russian attack on California from Kamchatka.[22] Fortunately for Spain, Catherine had her eye on the Crimea, and Russia did not enter the war.

The postwar situation on the northwest coast, however, was to be very different from what it had been. While the war was still going on, William Coxe wrote *An Account of the Russian Discoveries between Asia and America,* in which he revealed the rich profits to be made in furs; John Rickman and William Ellis, in separate narratives of Cook's third expedition, which had returned in August 1780, showed how easily they could be obtained from the Indians of the northwest coast. Half a dozen blue beads, Ellis pointed out, could be bartered for a skin worth as much as a hundred dollars. In the third volume of the official account of Cook's voyage,

21. Wagner, *Cartography,* p. 192; Bodega to José de Gálvez, San Blas, Nov. 28, 1779, AGI, Estado 20, 3M720; Interim Viceroy Mayorga to person unnamed, Mexico, December 1779 (note dated Apr. 19, 1780), AGI, Estado 20, 3M.

22. R. A. Humphrey, "Richard Oswald's Plan for an English and Russian Attack on Spanish America, 1781–1782," *Hispanic American Historical Review, 18* (1938), 95–101. Spain in her turn offered Russia bases in Morocco in exchange for help in recovering Gibraltar (José María Sánchez-Diana, "Relaciones diplomáticas entre Rusia y España en el siglo xviii," *Hispania, 12* [1952], 593, 595).

which came out in 1784, Captain James King wrote that the best sea otter pelts were worth a hundred and twenty dollars each at Canton.

The news of the wealth to be made on the northwest coast now attracted fur traders from England, France, the newly independent United States, and Spain itself. The first trading ship appeared on the coast in 1785; in 1786 there were six; and by 1792 more than twenty were doing a prosperous trade north of Nootka. By 1792, in fact, a trade route from Boston to the northwest coast to Canton and return had been established. What was more, the presence of so many ships sailing in and out of the bays and channels of these coastal waters brought a resurgence of the hope that a Northwest Passage might exist.[23] Because of this the governments of France, England, and Spain sent official exploring expeditions once again to the northwest coast.

The first of these naval exploring voyages to appear was the French expedition under Jean François de Galaup, Comte de La Pérouse, who was instructed to concern himself with the fur trade and to take possession of some point north of the Spanish possessions. He showed an interest in a Northwest Passage while on the coast in 1786. Spurred on by the news of this expedition, the Spanish government ordered the sailing early in 1787 of the first of a new series of exploring voyages. The Spanish authorities had learned that the Russians had established a post at Nootka, and the main objective of the expedition was to find out where the Russians were on the coast. The ships left San Blas on March 8, 1788, under the command of Esteban José Martínez on the *Princesa*, with Gonzalo López de Haro in command of the *San Carlos*. This expedition finally succeeded in getting in touch

23. William Coxe, *Account of the Russian Discoveries* (London, 1787), p. 342; Williams, *British Search*, pp. 214–15; James Cook and James King, *A Voyage to the Pacific Ocean* (2d ed. 3 vols. London, 1785), *3,* 435; Samuel Eliot Morison, *The Maritime History of Massachusetts* (Boston, 1921), p. 50.

with the Russians, and López de Haro found out that they were planning to establish a settlement at Nootka.[24]

Following a suggestion made by Esteban José Martínez, Viceroy Manuel Antonio Flores reacted to this information by authorizing Martínez to occupy Nootka and garrison it. It was planned that missionaries were to be sent later to convert the Indians. Martínez duly sailed for Nootka, which he reached early in May 1789. Foreign merchant ships entered the sound, but they turned out to be English rather than Russian; Martínez seized them and thus brought on the long drawn-out and dangerous incident with England known as the Nootka Sound Controversy.[25] The final agreement in 1794 provided that both sides were to leave the region unsettled, an outcome which aroused Russian interest in it once more. For Spain, however, the incident had a sobering effect which helped to turn her interests from exploration to consolidation of her California possessions.

The situation of the Russians on the northwest coast was also vitally affected by postwar developments in the region. In the first place, there had been a disastrous reduction in the number of fur-bearing animals in the areas in which the Russian fur trappers hunted, and the former rich profits were gone. Furthermore, cutthroat competition for the trade that still remained gradually eliminated all but the strongest fur trading companies. In 1788, Gregory Ivanovich Shelikov, the head of one of the largest of these companies, suggested consolidation and the formation of a monopoly concern under imperial protection. Nothing came of this at the time, however, because Russia was engaged in war with Turkey and Sweden and also needed English support in increasingly

24. Wagner, *Cartography*, pp. 199, 202; López de Haro to Esteban José Martínez, on board packetboat *San Carlos*, July 4, 1788, AGI, Estado 20, 3M722.

25. Wagner, *Cartography*, pp. 214–18; Williams, *British Search*, p. 227. The standard work on the subject is William Ray Manning, *The Nootka Sound Controversy* (Washington, D.C., 1905), pp. 279–478.

hostile relations with revolutionary France. On the other hand, there was concern in Russia that Cook's third voyage presaged English attempts to seize areas preempted by Russians, and in 1787 Shelikov's men were instructed to raise Russian imperial emblems at certain localities visited by an English ship and secretly to bury in the ground iron tablets on which were written in copper letters, "Land under Russian Domain." Shelikov himself urged his men in 1786 to expand their fur hunting activities as far south as the Spanish settlements in California at 40 degrees, distributing medals with the Russian imperial arms to Indian chiefs on the way.[26]

While waiting for a more favorable moment to press his pleas for consolidation of Russian fur trading interests under the aegis of his own company, Shelikov urged Catherine to order the Synod of the Greek Orthodox Church to concern itself with converting the Indians of the area to Christianity. Finally, in 1797, when Russia's friendly relations with England had cooled because of English opposition to further Russian penetration of Turkey, a consolidation of the two largest fur trading companies was achieved which led to the formation in 1799 of the Russian-American Company. In addition to a monopoly of all fur trading on the coast and in the Aleutians from 55 degrees to the Bering Strait, it was given the right to explore and settle as Russian possessions lands both north and south of 55 degrees. In the view of a modern Russian historian, Russian expansion on the coast was now to be surreptitiously promoted by the government-protected Russian-American Company.[27]

At the time of the unexpected and painful Spanish confrontation with England at Nootka Sound, Spain's fears on the northwest coast were mainly of Russia. Viceroy Flores had

26. S. B. Okun, *The Russian-American Company* (Cambridge, Mass., 1951), pp. 20–21, 36, 141; Clarence B. Andrews, "Russian Plans for American Dominion," *Washington Historical Quarterly, 18* (1927), 83–84.

27. Okun, *Russian-American Company*, pp. 30, 52.

reported to Madrid in 1788 that the country to the north of California was being rapidly occupied by Russians, and in 1789, at the time that the confrontation was taking place, he was writing in his instructions to his successor, the Conde de Revilla Gigedo, that the Russians had establishments on the northern coasts of California and were trying to expand them. He reported that further explorations of the coast were being made, and the special objective of the present one was to prevent the Russians from occupying Nootka. Spain was still claiming to possess all the coast up to 61 degrees, "beyond Prince William's Sound," in 1790, and the Russian government was reported by the Spanish ambassador in Paris to have assured Madrid "of the purity of its intentions" with regard to this boundary.[28] Several more Spanish exploring expeditions sailed along the coast to report back the whereabouts of Russian settlements and to search for the elusive Northwest Passage, then enjoying a brief period of international interest.[29] But by 1793, on the eve of the final settlement of the Nootka Sound Controversy, Viceroy Revilla Gigedo wrote his government that he thought Nootka Sound should be surrendered to the English. In his instructions prepared for his successor, the Marqués de Branciforte, in 1794, he repeated his opinion that Spain should claim no farther than the Strait of Juan de Fuca, because he thought that the Russians could become more dangerous neighbors than the English. It would take the English longer than the Russians to organize an attack on Spanish territories in the area, and

28. Flores to Antonio Valdés, Mexico, Nov. 26, 1788, AGI, Estado 20, 3M721; Flores to Revilla Gigedo, Mexico, Aug. 26, 1789, *Instrucciones que los virreyes de Nueva España dejaron a sus sucesores* (Mexico, 1867), p. 125; Robert Greenhow, *The History of Oregon and California* (Boston, 1844), p. 425.

29. These Spanish expeditions included the following: Fidalgo (1790); Eliza (1791); Malaspina (1789); Galiano Valdés (1792); Eliza-Martínez y Zayas (1793). The British expedition of Vancouver (1792) temporarily scotched the idea of a Northwest Passage.

in his view it would be very difficult for them to hurt Spain there.[30]

Three years later, in his own instructions to his successor, Branciforte stated that he thought California could withstand attacks by English corsairs but not a full-scale invasion because of the difficulty of garrisoning it with a sufficiently large army. If California were conquered, he warned, it would be extremely difficult to recapture, and the enemy would intercept Spanish trade with the Philippines and South America and perhaps, with the help of rebel Indians, even raid the rich mining areas of New Mexico and Sonora. He did not say who the enemy might be, but it is likely he was thinking of the Russians. Branciforte's successor as viceroy was Miguel José de Azanza, who had been one of José de Gálvez' secretaries and had some practical experience of Sonora and California; he had also been in the Spanish embassy in Russia in 1783 and 1784.[31]

30. Manning, *Nootka Sound Controversy*, p. 469; *Instrucción reservada que el Conde de Revilla Gigedo dió a su sucesor en el mando Marqués de Branciforte* (Mexico, 1831), p. 179.

31. *Instrucciones que los virreyes de Nueva España dejaron a sus sucesores* (Mexico, 1867), p. 139; Sánchez-Diana, "Relaciones," pp. 599, 602. Greenhow and Manning stress Spain's fear of Russia on the northwest coast. Some writers consider England more dangerous to Spanish interests. Chapman states that, in spite of the large number of documents on Spain's fear of Russia, Spain was "not much afraid" of Russia. He thinks Spain should have been much more concerned about England (*Founding*, p. 217). John Walton Caughey, in his *California* (New York, 1940), considers the Russian threat an excuse for Gálvez to begin his northward movement (pp. 119–20). Wagner believes that the Spanish expedition of 1789 to Nootka Sound was directed as much at the English as the Russians and asserts that "the Spaniards were not particularly afraid of the Russians but they were desperately afraid of the English" (*Cartography*, p. 215). Bobb appears to agree with Caughey (*Viceregency to Bucareli*, p. 158). Bancroft discusses Russian activities in California in great detail in separate chapters in his *History of California* and in his *History of Alaska* without laying any particular emphasis on their threat to Spain. Richman contents himself with a brief mention of Spain's fear

Whether the Spanish government under the new King Charles IV appointed Azanza to be viceroy of New Spain because of his combination of knowledge of California and Russia is not known, but it is at least clear that his tenure of office began a period of extreme danger for California. This was due to the Napoleonic wars, in the course of which Russia veered from alliance with England against France to alliance with France against England and back again. Spain, no longer a major power, was tossed about in the gigantic struggle at first on the side of France against England and Russia, then allied with England and Russia against France. One of the most dangerous periods of the wars for California seemed to be the first one, from 1798 to 1807, during most of which Russia was allied with England, and Spain feared an attack by both of them on California.

The War of the Second Coalition, uniting England, Russia, Austria, Naples, Portugal, and the Ottoman Empire against France and Spain, began in December 1798, but it was not until a year later, on December 20, 1799, that Viceroy Azanza sent a dispatch to Madrid saying news had reached New Spain that it had begun. His first thought was the danger that California would face if the Russians decided to invade from Kamchatka. He said he was aware of the difficulties presented by such a project, but Russia was a country that would try anything, and it had long wanted to establish colonies in California. He thought the danger a real one; he had not yet received a dispatch from Madrid which was to confirm his fears. The government at Madrid had learned that the British ambassador at Vienna had just given the Russian ambassador

---

of Russia (*California under Spain and Mexico*, pp. 65–66). Perhaps the Spanish government did not think that England would do more than raid her Pacific coast possessions. In the case of Russia, on the other hand, Spain feared a possible invasion based either on Kamchatka or the Russian settlements north of California. There had been a threat of a Russian-English alliance during the War for American Independence; this threat was to materialize during the Napoleonic wars.

to the Austrian court a plan for an invasion of California from Kamchatka supported by the Russian establishments on the northwest coast. The Russian ambassador had sent it to Emperor Paul by special messenger; the king advised Azanza to be on his guard.

As we have seen, Azanza already was on the alert; the difficulty was that there was very little he could do. He informed Madrid that there were only 740 Spanish males of all ages in both the Californias, that long distances separated the Californias from those provinces of New Spain which could provide assistance, and that the few troops available in the viceroyalty would have to be used in other more important places where the danger was more acute. There could be no thought of defending California by a permanent force. He suggested that the government should send six frigates to the Pacific to be based at Acapulco; these would be sufficient to protect California from the very limited naval forces that the Russians could muster or that their English allies would be willing to lend them. They could also help to keep the Pacific clear of the pirates who were infesting it. In spite of the obvious difficulties involved, Humboldt later reported that some plans were made in Mexico at this time to "prepare a maritime expedition in the ports of San Blas and Monterey against the Russian colonies in America." In California itself there was a revival of interest in opening overland communication with New Mexico and Sonora.[32]

As a matter of fact, there was, in all probability, little likelihood of a joint Russian-British invasion of California in

32. Azanza to Mariano Luis de Urquijo, Mexico, Dec. 20, 1799, AGI, Estado 28; dispatch to Viceroy of New Spain, San Lorenzo, Dec. 11, 1799, Biblioteca Nacional, Mexico City, Mexico (cited hereafter as BN); Azanza to Urquijo, Dec. 20, 1799, AGI, Estado 28; Alexander von Humboldt, *Essai politique sur le royaume de la Nouvelle Espagne* (5 vols. Paris, 1811), 2, 499; *Instrucción reservada que dió el virrey don Miguel José de Azanza a su sucesor don Félix Berenguer de Marquina* (Mexico, 1960), p. 74.

1799 because Russia withdrew from the coalition with England even before the news reached New Spain that the war had begun. It is true that after the assassination of Paul I in March 1801, and the succession of his son Alexander as tsar, there was a reconciliation with England following a period of coolness. But the Treaty of Amiens which was announced in California at the end of the year, brought a general, if temporary, ending to the wars in May 1802.

Invasion, for the time being, seemed unlikely, but nonetheless the authorities continued to be concerned. Viceroy Félix Berenguer de Marquina, in his instructions of January 1, 1803, to his successor, José de Iturrigaray, remarked that the late war had caused great fear that California would be invaded and seized by the enemy and that this danger remained in case war broke out again, for it was impossible to send or maintain a sufficiently large force there to protect it. That Viceroy Marquina's fears were warranted is confirmed by reports that the newly formed Russian-American Company sent secret orders to its able manager Alexander Baranov in 1802 to push his settlements south down the northwest coast. Baranov's dreams of a greater Russia on the Pacific coast, furthermore, appear to tally with Count Nikolai Petrovich Rumiantsev's dispatches in 1803, in which the Russian-American Company's settlements on the coast are regarded as bases from which to extend Russian influence as far as the East Indies.

While the authorities in New Spain were aware of the Russian menace to California, they were also mindful of the presence of other powers on the northwest coast. As early as 1789, Viceroy Flores reported to his successor that the newly independent "American colonists" seemed to be wanting to establish themselves on the northern coast of California. In 1803 the enterprising New England sea captain Joseph O'Cain made a contract with Baranov, who was anxious to find new hunting grounds for sea otter on the California coast, by which O'Cain was to supply the ships and Baranov was to provide the Aleut hunters and equipment for joint hunting ventures. For Baranov it was a temporary partnership until he could provide his own ships; for the Californians it was yet another illegal intrusion. O'Cain began his hunting at San Diego in December 1803, adding to Spain's suspicions about the Americans.[33]

Meanwhile in Europe, after a brief respite, Napoleon began the war again in May 1803. In January 1805, Russia and England, together with Austria and Sweden, entered a third coalition against France and Spain, and the war's tempo quickened. On October 21, 1805, the British fleet smashed the combined fleets of France and Spain at Trafalgar, but six weeks later Napoleon crushed the Russians with a brilliant victory at Austerlitz. The Russians were to suffer yet another costly defeat at the hands of Napoleon at Friedland in June 1807 before Tsar Alexander, at his famous meeting with Napoleon on a raft in the Niemen River near Tilsit, agreed to make a treaty with France. Russia emerged from Tilsit the ally of France against England, although on Russia's side, at any rate, it was to be what has been called "a war fought with folded arms."

In 1806, while Russia was still an ally of England, her interest in the northwest coast became apparent once more. One of the men who accompanied Russian navigators Lieutenant Commanders I. F. Krusenstern and Y. F. Lisyansky in 1803 on what was to be the first Russian round the world voyage was Nikolai Petrovich Rezanov, the tsar's chamberlain and a high official of the Russian-American Company. He was at Sitka, the seat of government of Russia's American

---

33. *Instrucciones* (Mexico, 1867), p. 211; Adele Ogden, "Russian Sea-Otter and Seal Hunting on the California Coast," *The Russians in California* (San Francisco, 1933), pp. 30–31; Mairin Mitchell, *The Maritime History of Russia* (London, 1949), p. 229; A. E. Sokol, "Russian Expansion and Exploration in the Pacific," *American Slavic and East European Review, 11* (1952), 94–95; *Instrucciones* (Mexico, 1867), p. 125; Bancroft, *California, 2,* 32.

possessions, in 1806, and a month before he left for a visit to California to purchase urgently needed provisions, he wrote a secret letter to the company. In this he recommended that the company establish a settlement on the Columbia River as a stepping-stone to San Francisco Bay. He felt that settlers could be attracted to the future establishment on the Columbia, and in ten years the Russians would be strong enough "to make use of any favorable turn in European politics to include the coast of California in the Russian possessions." The Spaniards were "very weak in these countries," he observed, and if the company had been strong enough in 1798, when war had been declared between Russia and Spain, "it would have been very easy to seize a piece of California from 34 degrees to Santa Barbara" without New Spain's being able to send assistance overland because of the terrain. On the other hand, Rezanov pleased the Californians by telling them that on his return to St. Petersburg he would propose to the tsar that he be sent to Madrid as Ambassador Extraordinary. Rezanov would then press for trade between the Spanish and Russian settlements. "He expects his proposals to be approved," wrote Father José Señán, "and if they are, this Province will benefit greatly."[34]

The outlook for California was at this unpropitious stage when a new and dramatic move in the war in Europe in 1808 once more reversed the ephemeral alliances of the times. Napoleon sent an army of 100,000 men into Spain in March, causing a popular uprising against the French and bringing swift support from British forces under Wellington. Meanwhile, although Tsar Alexander outwardly refurbished the Franco-Russian alliance at the Congress of Erfurt in September, Russia sent no troops to assist Napoleon and became in

34. N. Nozikov, *Russian Voyages Round the World* (London, 1940), p. 3; Rezanov to Russian-American Company, New Archangel, Feb. 15, 1806, in Bancroft, *California*, 2, 80, n. 29; *The Letters of José Señán, O. F. M. Mission San Buenaventura 1796–1823*, ed. Lesley Byrd Simpson (San Francisco, 1962), p. 18.

fact but a nominal and unwilling ally. With the swift growth of a national movement in Spain against French occupation, led by provincial councils or juntas which took over after Napoleon's removal of Charles IV and Ferdinand VII in favor of his brother Joseph as king of Spain, the "favorable turn in European politics" which Rezanov had been awaiting to advance into California was fast approaching. Even before it had arrived, however, Baranov started to put Rezanov's plans into effect by sending out an expedition to establish a settlement on the Columbia River in October 1808. This attempt failed; the ship was wrecked and most of the men were captured by Indians. A second expedition left on October 26 to try to find a base in California north of San Francisco Bay from which sea otter could be hunted without having to share the profits with Yankee ship captains. This expedition, under Ivan Kuskov, reached Bodega Bay in January 1809 and remained there for nearly eight months, exploring the country and establishing friendly relations with the Indians. Kuskov reported favorably on the Bodega Bay region, pointing out that it was not occupied by any European power. The Russian-American Company petitioned the tsar to persuade Spain to permit it to trade with the Spanish colonies in California and also asked for permission to make a settlement on the coast itself.

As it happened, the Russian government had already made overtures at Madrid to establish trade with California, but the negotiations took place in March 1808, when Charles IV abdicated from the throne. The following month he and his son Ferdinand were prisoners of Napoleon in France. The attempt to open trade relations with California by negotiation with Madrid was abandoned. Nonetheless the tsar replied to the Russian-American Company's further petition by allowing them to arrange trade relations as best they could. In answer to the company's request for permission to found a settlement, the tsar authorized them to proceed on their own account and assured them of protection when "occasion should require it." With this imperial encouragement, on March 15, 1810, the directors of the Russian-American Company drew up a proclamation "to our friends and neighbors the noble and brave Spaniards, inhabitants of the Californias," in which they announced that they were going to send them a shipload of merchandise needed in California to exchange for grain, tallow, cattle, "and other productions which there abound." The proclamation said nothing about making a settlement, but the brief sentence justifying the move was phrased in such a way that this objective could be implied. "The actual condition of Europe in general," the directors explained, "and of Spain in particular gives rise to the presumption that there is today no impediment to the admission of the Russians to the coast, especially since their object serves the interests of both parties."[35] This proclamation was not delivered to the Californians until about March 1812, but, as will be seen, the situation was even more satisfactory to the Russians then than it had been in 1810.

Governor Joaquín de Arrillaga of California soon became aware of a Russian ship anchored at Bodega; he reported to Viceroy Pedro Garibay on March 31, 1809, that he had caught three deserters who had escaped from the vessel because they were hungry. Garibay also reported that on March 26 a party of seventeen Aleut hunters had disembarked from their *bidarkas*, or kayaks, in San Francisco Bay and had attacked a force sent to apprehend them. The leather-jacketed soldiers were forced to fire upon them, killing four and taking prisoner two who were wounded; the rest escaped.[36] Such were the immediate results of the presence of the new "friends and neighbors."

For some sixty years the authorities in old and New Spain had been afraid of the day when the Russians would become

---

35. Ogden, "Russian Sea-Otter," pp. 38–40; Bancroft, *California*, 2, 79–82, 295–96, n. 2.

36. Garibay to Martín de Garay, Mexico, July 16, 1809, BN; Garibay calls the ship the *Neva*, which is probably an error.

their neighbors to the north. That day had now arrived, and it so happened that neither old Spain nor New Spain was going to be able to do much about it. Already by 1809 New Spain was beginning to feel the powerful influences of the Napoleonic invasion of the mother country. A revolutionary movement was uncovered at Valladolid (modern Morelia) in December of that year, and early on the morning of September 16, 1810, the parish priest of Dolores, Miguel Hidalgo y Costilla, was to raise aloft the banner of Our Lady of Guadalupe, the Indian Virgin, and begin the harsh eleven-year war ending in Mexico's independence from Spain. The favorable moment that Rezanov had spoken of was now at hand, and the Russian-American Company—after December 15, 1811, increasingly a government enterprise—made the most of its opportunity.[37]

The government of Spain, in the hands of a regency since the deposition of its monarchs, not only confronted the French menace at home but from 1810 on saw its far-flung empire rising against it. England had become its welcome ally; Russia in 1811 had still to show its colors. Francisco de Zea Bermúdez, the Spanish envoy at St. Petersburg, informed the tsar's government on November 12, 1811, that the regency ardently desired to reestablish friendly relations between the two countries. Early the following year his efforts in this direction were put to a test by the Venezuelan deputation in London, who, he learned, were trying to get Russia to acknowledge the independence of Venezuela. Perhaps Francisco de Miranda, the famous precursor of the movement for independence, who had been in Russia, where he was friendly with the former Empress Catherine the Great, was behind this move.[38] The French ambassador at St. Petersburg had made

37. Anatole G. Mazour, "The Russian-American Company: Private or Government Enterprise?" *Pacific Historical Review, 13* (1944), 170–71.

38. For a discussion of the role that Catherine may have had in mind for Miranda in Russian expansion in North America, see Joseph O. Baylen and Dorothy Woodward, "Francisco de Miranda in Russia," *The Americas, 6* (April 1950), 431–49.

the most of this affair to discredit Spain's strength and unity at the imperial court, but although Zea Bermúdez reported that if the matter came before the Council of State it was likely to be accepted, he managed to persuade the tsar and the council to oppose it. In March 1812, Zea Bermúdez proposed a treaty of alliance between Spain and Russia against France and added that the regency would provide His Imperial Majesty with three million pesos in silver as soon as possible and would discuss a further loan when circumstances permitted.[39] There is no evidence that Zea Bermúdez offered any other inducement to the Russians at this point, although Captain Pedro Canel Acevedo, a military officer from Asturias who had traveled in California, seems to have suggested, in secret testimony to the Spanish Cortes in 1811, that certain commercial favors be granted to the Russians at Nootka together with further undisclosed recommendations. He expected that Nootka might become a second St. Petersburg with Spanish help, his main point being that Spain had more than any other country to offer Russia in order to persuade it to become a perpetual ally.[40]

Zea Bermúdez' efforts were finally rewarded on July 8, 1812, when he signed a treaty with Russia which provided that the Russian emperor was to recognize the Spanish Cortes meeting at Cádiz and its recently formulated constitution as legitimate. Also it provided that commercial relations between the two countries were to be reestablished and extended.[41] Further details of the alliance were to be worked out later; in the meantime, each country was to help the other against the common enemy. At the very time that the treaty was being signed, Napoleon was beginning his mam-

39. Francisco de Zea Bermúdez dispatches, St. Petersburg, Nov. 12, 1811, Feb. 7 and Mar. 29, 1812, AGS, Sección Estado.

40. Pedro Canel Acevedo, *Reflexiones críticas sobre la constitución española, cortes nacionales y estado de la presente guerra* (Oviedo, n.d.), pp. 49, 195.

41. Treaty with Russia made at Velikie Luki, July 8, 1812, AGS, Sección Estado.

moth invasion of Russia, which was to bring him by September into Moscow, only to be forced into disastrous retreat in October; in Spain the French were retreating. Apart from the obvious relief to Spain from the French invasion of Russia, little seems to have been done under the treaty. Spain did send about four hundred pounds of Havana cigars to Russia on a British vessel in September 1812, however, and Russia sent 2,032 men of the Imperial Guard of Alexander to Spain under Lieutenant Colonel Alexander O'Donnell in August 1813.[42]

Once friendly relations between Spain and Russia were formally established, it might have been expected that the long fear of a Russian invasion of California would finally disappear. It was precisely at this time, however, that the invasion occurred. Early in 1812 Baranov, who apparently feared American landings south of the Columbia,[43] sent Kuskov on the *Chirikov* to Bodega Bay with ninety-five Russians and about eighty Aleuts with their bidarkas. Landing about March, they built a wooden fort on a bluff overlooking the ocean some eighteen miles above Bodega Bay; it was officially dedicated and named Ross on September 10. José Argüello, the commander of the garrison at San Francisco, noticed bidarkas in the bay in July and sent Ensign Gabriel Moraga to investigate the information the Indians gave him that a ship was on the beach north of Bodega. Moraga inspected the fort shortly before it was dedicated, and Russian sources report that he promised to use his influence in favor of Kuskov's desire to trade with the Californians for

42. All weights and measures are converted into American equivalents according to the tables in Manuel Carrera Stampa, "The Evolution of Weights and Measures in New Spain," *Hispanic American Historical Review*, 29 (February 1949), 2–24; Cádiz, Sept. 19, 1812, AGS, Sección Estado, E8216; Eusebio de Bardari to Conde de Fernán-Núñez, St. Petersburg, Aug. 10, 1813, AGS, Sección Estado.

43. Records of the Russian-American Company, letters received by the Governors General, National Archives, Washington, D.C. (cited hereafter as RRAC), Company Report, August 1817.

grain, meat, and tallow. On his return from Ross, Moraga reported in person to Governor Arrillaga.

Governor Arrillaga was in something of a quandary. The previous May he had written the first of a series of letters to the viceroy pointing out the difficult position of his troops, who had not received their supplies since the insurrection had begun in Mexico two years before. The missions were likewise unable to obtain their supplies; California was beginning to feel the severe pinch of the war in Mexico. Trade with the Russian settlement at Ross presented an unexpected way out of Governor Arrillaga's problems, but it was, of course, illegal, as was the settlement itself. Moraga went back to Ross on a second visit late in January 1813 and talked about trade with Kuskov. Kuskov showed him the 1810 proclamation by the directors of the Russian-American Company, inviting the Californians to trade with the company. According to Russian sources, Arrillaga consented to this, pending the approval of the viceroy, and Kuskov sent off $14,000 worth of goods, which were exchanged for breadstuffs.[44]

Viceroy Calleja first heard the news of the landing at Bodega from José de la Cruz, commander of the troops in New Galicia. Calleja at once sent out instructions to him and to the military authorities in the western Interior Provinces and the naval base at San Blas, as well as to the governors of Sonora and Lower California. On July 9, 1813, Calleja wrote Governor Arrillaga ordering him to keep a close watch on the newcomers and to try to find out their plans. He said he did not fear an attack by Russia, because of the friendly relations of that country with Spain, but the intruders might be Americans who had designs on California. Calleja's letter to Arrillaga crossed with one from Arrillaga to him, written

44. For a discussion of confusion in local nomenclature in this region, see Clinton R. Edwards, "Wandering Toponyms: El Puerto de la Bodega and Bodega Bay," *Pacific Historical Review, 33* (1964), 253–72; Bancroft, *California, 2,* 199, 297, 301, 302.

after the return of Moraga from his second visit to Ross. Realizing now that it was Russians he was dealing with, Calleja wrote to Arrillaga again on August 3 enclosing a copy of the treaty between Spain and Russia. Calleja ordered Arrillaga to inform Kuskov that the occupation of Spanish territory by the Russian-American Company was a violation of the treaty. Kuskov was to be requested to remove his settlement before Calleja notified the government in Spain. On September 5, 1813, Calleja sent a dispatch to Madrid in which he reported that an expedition of foreigners, apparently Russians, had established a fort at the port of Bodega, close to San Francisco, with thirteen pieces of artillery. He concluded his dispatch to the minister of state by saying that until he received orders he would keep a close eye on developments and would take what action was necessary while preserving, on his part, the friendly relations existing between Spain and Russia.[45]

Obviously embarrassed by the news, the Spanish regency replied through its minister of state on February 4, 1814. First the dispatch pointed out that Governor Arrillaga's reference, in one of his letters forwarded with the viceroy's, to a ship stranded on the beach might mean that the Russians had been forced to put in at Bodega. For this reason there could not be complete certainty that the Russians had deliberately planned to build their establishment. On the other hand, the fact that the Russians were in great need of provisions furnished perhaps the best method of making them leave; for if they were not given food unless they came to the presidio at San Francisco, they could be disarmed and returned to their own country by the first available ship. The minister added, however, that his department knew that the Russians were anxious to establish trade between their American establishments and the Spanish settlements in California. He thought a trade such as this unobjectionable,

45. Calleja to Ministro de Estado, Sept. 5, 1813, BN; Bancroft, *California*, 2, 302–03.

given the isolation of the area and the close friendship of the two countries. The regency, he said, felt that Calleja should "wink at" this trade, provided it was limited to Upper California and not Lower and provided it included only farm products and goods belonging to the local inhabitants. The minister concluded his dispatch by saying that the regency hoped that Calleja's zeal, prudence, and keen judgment would enable him to manage the affair with the necessary delicacy so that the Russians would evacuate Ross without affecting the friendship between Spain and Russia.[46]

What Calleja thought of these disjointed and contradictory orders is not revealed, but perhaps fortunately for him King Ferdinand VII was restored to the Spanish throne in March 1814. Ferdinand returned to Madrid in May and proceeded to dissolve the liberal Cortes and annul the Constitution of 1812, setting the political clock back to March 1808, when Napoleon had sent his legions into Spain. On February 22, 1815, Calleja wrote to the new government, sending with his letter a copy of the above-mentioned instructions from the regency. After calling attention to the fact that these instructions differed from previous orders, he asked that the king be informed that in spite of them he would continue as before until he received fresh instructions from His Majesty.

Almost a year later Madrid finally sent out the new royal orders. Calleja was to do his duty as viceroy in the defense of California without waiting for special orders from the government. In this way, if political circumstances made it convenient to do so, the king could disapprove of the viceroy's conduct, while the viceroy himself would always be "in a good position." The dispatch concluded with the usual references to Calleja's zeal and prudence and the delicacy of the affair. Calleja's own policy, which his new instructions permitted him to follow, was one of moderation, which he ad-

46. José Lugardo to Viceroy of New Spain, Madrid, Feb. 4, 1814, AGI, Provincias Internas, 23. There is another copy of the letter in the BN.

mitted was forced on him by the complete lack of money and men in California and by having only three decrepit ships at San Blas, so badly needing repairs that they could hardly sail up the coast.[47]

In California Colonel Arrillaga, the governor, died on July 24, 1814. He was replaced by Captain Pablo Vicente Sola, a fifty-four-year-old Spanish officer of grenadiers, who had been fighting against the rebels in Mexico under Lieutenant Colonel Torquato Trujillo. Sola arrived in California in August 1815 and took over from José Argüello, who had been acting as interim governor.[48] He issued several warnings to the Russians to keep away from Spanish territory, and in September, when some crew members of the brig *Ilmen* landed near San Francisco Bay, he had them arrested, sending the two leaders to San Blas and making the others work on the fortifications at Monterey.[49]

Calleja, unable to pursue a more vigorous policy, "making a virtue out of necessity," as he put it, ordered the prisoners returned before the Russian governor complained to him about the matter. Also off the coast of California in 1815 was the *Suvarov*, sent by the Russian-American Company with trade goods for California and provided with another proclamation to the Californians dated July 13, 1813, written in Spanish and Russian, pointing out the mutual advantages of trade. The *Suvarov* called at San Francisco on August 20

47. Pedro Cevallos to Viceroy of New Spain, Madrid, Jan. 22, 1816, Archivo General de la Nación, Mexico City (cited hereafter as AGN), Provincias Internas, *23*, 13; Calleja to Ministro de Estado, Feb. 22, 1815, May 6, 1816, BN.

48. Hojas de servicio of Vicente Pablo Sola [sic], Archivo de Defensa, Mexico (cited hereafter as AD); *Gaceta extraordinaria del gobierno de México,* June 8, 1811. The authorities are divided on whether the governor's name should be spelled Sola or Solá; the writer follows the Mexican sources, Bancroft, Hittell, and Richman in spelling the name Sola.

49. Calleja to Minister of State, May 6, 1816, BN; Bancroft recounts a somewhat different version of this affair *(California, 2, 307–08).*

without revealing the real objectives of her visit. The governor (it is not clear whether it was Argüello or Sola) provided the ship with food, wood, and water as requested. According to Russian sources, the ship sold her cargo to the Californians; the Spanish documents do not mention this, understandably enough, but Viceroy Calleja did approve a deal apparently made with a previous ship by which the Russians supplied 2,826 pesos worth of cloth for clothing the troops and their families in exchange for grain. In spite of the fact that the troops had not received their supplies for six years, and Calleja could not forward them or the mission supplies because of lack of funds, dangerous conditions on the roads in Mexico, and lack of shipping, he nontheless gave orders that there was to be no trade with the Russians. Sola continually urged the viceroy to find a way to get the supplies for the year 1811, then awaiting transportation at Acapulco, sent north. Early in 1815 the viceroy arranged for funds for these purchases to be made available at the royal treasury in Guadalajara instead of at Mexico City, but they were not forthcoming.[50]

In spite of the obvious difficulties confronting him, there is some evidence that Calleja was making plans in 1816 to use guns instead of talk on the Russians, who refused to move from Bodega unless authorized to do so from St. Petersburg. José de la Cruz, the comandante of New Galicia, had asked Manila two years before for considerable supplies of muskets, ammunition, and artillery, some of which were sent to California with the first supply ship to get through in October 1816. At the end of June, Calleja wrote to the governor of California informing him what steps he was to take if the Russians persisted in their refusal to leave Bodega. At the same time Calleja called upon the neighboring prov-

50. Calleja to Minister of State, May 6, 1816, BN; Bancroft, *California*, 2, 306; Sola to Viceroy, May 5, 1816, AGN, Provincias Internas, *23*, 86, 96, 101.

inces of Lower California, Sonora, and the western Interior Provinces to be prepared to render assistance.[51]

That nothing came of these preparations may have been partly due to news that a naval expedition composed of Buenos Aires insurgents was at large in the Pacific. It had lately attacked Callao and Guayaquil and was said to be intending to invade California. This expedition, under Hippolyte Bouchard, did not actually attack California until 1818, but it caused a flurry of defense activity there in 1816.[52] It was also at this time that the Spanish ambassador in London reported that the Cuban José Alvarez de Toledo, at that time a rebel leader, was about to come to England on his way to Russia, where he was to offer the crown of independent Mexico to the Archduke Constantine, brother of the tsar, provided he accepted the new constitution proclaimed by the independent Mexican Congress of Chilpancingo at Apatzingán in 1814. The Spanish government, which had received the same information from Paris, took the matter seriously and instructed its ambassador in London to point out to the British government the consequences of Mexico's falling into the hands of Russia, Britain's enemy, instead of remaining under friendly Spain. It was reported a few years later in a New York newspaper that Toledo had approached the tsar with a plan to cede California to Russia—one of many rumors of the kind that shortly became current.[53]

With the coming of a new viceroy, Juan Ruiz de Apodaca —a distinguished naval officer who had been Spanish ambassador in London and Governor-General of Cuba—in September 1816, a more vigorous policy against the Russians

51. Calleja to Minister of State, May 6, 1816, BN; José de Gardoqui to José de la Cruz, Manila, Dec. 27, 1814, and Sola to Viceroy, Nov. 6, 1816, AGN, Provincias Internas, 23, 33, 116.

52. Sola to Viceroy, July 3, 1816, AGN, Provincias Internas, 23, 96.

53. Pedro Cevallos to Conde de Fernán Núñez, AGS, Sección Estado, E8177; Ambassador at London to Pedro Cevallos, Sept. 1, 1816, AGS, Sección Estado; Gaceta del Gobierno Imperial de México, Aug. 15, 1822.

seemed to be in the making. Before the new instructions had arrived in New Spain, however, Governor Sola found himself confronted by a delegation from another Russian round the world exploring expedition under Lieutenant Otto von Kotzebue of the Russian navy, which arrived at San Francisco in October 1816. Sola seized the opportunity to complain about the presence of the Russian-American Company at Bodega, whereupon Kotzebue sat down with Sola and some of his officers for a conference. In the course of the conference Sola related how the viceroy of New Spain had written to Kuskov, by way of Governors Arrillaga and Argüello, ordering him to leave Bodega because it belonged to the king of Spain, as did all the coast up to the Strait of Fuca at 54 degrees. Kuskov, he went on, had replied by word of mouth, without putting anything on paper, that he was not going to leave, on the pretext that he had sent the viceroy's communications to Baranov, who would send them to St. Petersburg where they would reach the tsar; whatever the tsar decided Baranov and Kuskov would do. At this point Kotzebue asked Sola to provide a messenger to summon Kuskov to the conference. This was done, and on October 26 the meeting reconvened. After being questioned about his remaining at Bodega, Kuskov replied that he had indeed been there five years and that he would leave when Baranov, who had sent him there, ordered him to do so. Sola then once again asked Kotzebue if he could order Kuskov to leave, but he replied that he did not have sufficient authority to do so. He volunteered, however, to write to the tsar informing him of the actions of Baranov and Kuskov and to send him a copy of the written report of the conference signed by everyone who was present at it. He felt sure that as soon as this information reached the tsar, who maintained an intimate alliance with Ferdinand VII, he would come to a wise and just conclusion. The conference ended on October 28, with Sola taking two copies of the record of the meeting to send to the viceroy, and Kotzebue taking two to send to St. Petersburg. According to the interpreter at the conference, Adelbert von Chamisso, Kotzebue duly sent off his report, but although it reached St. Petersburg, it was filed in one of the government departments without being shown to the tsar. Chamisso also revealed that at the very moment the report was being sealed in the conference room at the presidio, Kuskov, with Kotzebue's knowledge, was sending out two boats to hunt otter in San Francisco Bay. Perhaps the Russians did not take the matter very seriously.[54]

In his report to the viceroy dated January 2, 1817, Sola stated that he needed two hundred more infantry and four field guns with skilled artillerymen simply to protect the province, which was threatened by the Americans as well as by the Russians. It would take large reinforcements, he said, to remove the Russians.

Meanwhile the Russian-American Company persuaded its government once more to negotiate with Madrid for permission to trade with California. The Spanish government seized the opportunity to ask the Russians some pointed questions about their settlement at Bodega. By what right, they wanted to know, had the Russians established a settlement on Spanish territory and built a fort there? It was not a fort, was the reply, but simply a fence against the savages. Becoming increasingly impatient, on February 10, 1817, the Spanish government prepared but did not issue a confidential order authorizing the viceroy to remove the Russians by force, although he was not to insist on a complete cessation of trade between the Russian-American Company and the Californians. It was also decided to protest formally to the Russian government, and on April 27, 1817, Zea Bermúdez outlined to Foreign Minister Nesselrode the friendly gestures which

54. August C. Mahr, *The Visit of the "Rurik" to San Francisco in 1816* (Stanford, 1932), pp. 48–49, 116–20. It should be noted that the English translation provided with the original Spanish report of the conference is not reliable. See also Otto von Kotzebue, *A Voyage of Discovery* (3 vols. London, 1821), *3*, 38–51.

had been made to the Russians by the Spanish authorities in California. He was sorry to have to point out, he said, that the Russian settlers had paid no attention to these moves, which he was sure was due to the obstinacy and greed of some of the merchants. The king of Spain was confident, Zea Bermúdez reported, that the tsar would issue orders which would result in the departure of the Russians.[55]

The tsar's government now called upon the company for a report in answer to Zea Bermúdez. After stating misleadingly that the Spaniards had not protested against their occupation of Bodega, the company said that the Spaniards claimed all the territory north of San Francisco, even beyond the Columbia, although they never had occupied it or conquered the local Indians. Although it was close to California, they went on, the Russian settlement at Bodega could never be dangerous to Spanish possessions and might even protect them against their enemies. If the Russians were not there, they said, the Americans undoubtedly would be. That the company felt itself on shaky ground in this matter, however, is revealed by a dispatch it sent to its agents on the northwest coast admitting that Ross was situated too close to Spanish eyes.

When the Spanish government apparently became convinced that its diplomatic negotiations with the Russians were not going to bring about their removal from Ross, it sent its confidential order to remove them by force to Viceroy Apodaca on June 23, 1817. Apodaca forwarded the order to Sola and asked him to suggest effective means by which the royal instructions could be carried out. Sola had himself just finished complaining once again to an envoy sent to him by Baranov about the Russian settlement at Bodega. In a letter to Baranov, Sola questioned whether the tsar had actually given the company permission to found the settlement, since

55. Bancroft, California, 2, 214–15; H. Q. to Governor General, Aug. 14, 1817, RRAC; Apodaca to Ministro de Estado, October 1817, AGI, Estado 32; Zea Bermúdez to Nesselrode, Apr. 15/27, 1817, RRAC.

this authorization would naturally have been sent to Madrid and from there to Mexico and California. He also pointed out that there had been ample time to get a reply from St. Petersburg on the matter, showing that he was not misled by Kuskov's excuses.[56] In his reply to Apodaca's letter enclosing the confidential royal order to remove the Russians by force, Sola said he thought a surprise attack might succeed if he had two warships, three hundred infantry with four field guns, and artillerymen. This force would have to be completely equipped and armed and provided with ammunition. The provincial government, he emphasized, had no funds to pay for the expedition and could provide only food; the troops then in California had not been paid for eight years. He suggested that the field guns and some of the attacking force go by sea and that the remainder and the cavalry go by land. He concluded by proposing that when his forces were in position at Ross he should send Kuskov an order to leave. Then, if Kuskov replied as he had done in the past, he would order his men to seize the fort; he thought Kuskov might be sent to San Blas or Acapulco. He approved of the attack; in his view there was no other way to get the Russians out, for, he thought, if they were to keep waiting for orders from the emperor in St. Petersburg, the matter "could go on for a very long time."[57]

Viceroy Apodaca forwarded Sola's dispatch to Madrid in due course with his approval; he suggested that it would be desirable to send four ships and five hundred men rather than Sola's proposed three ships and three hundred men. With a larger force before him, Apodaca reasoned, the enemy commander who surrendered would have a better excuse for his action than if he was confronted by a small one. But Apodaca had to admit at once that he did not have the neces-

56. Aug. 14, 1817, RRAC; Apodaca to Ministro de Estado, October 1817, AGI, Estado 32; Sola to Apodaca, Apr. 3, 1818, AGI, Estado 32, M568, items 15–20; Bancroft, *California*, 2, 313–14.

57. Sola to Apodaca, Apr. 3, 1818, AGI, Estado 32, M568.

sary five hundred men available, "at least while there are bands of rebels to fight in this kingdom." As for ships, there was one poor brig at San Blas and two other ships that were unserviceable, and no funds to equip and repair them. Confronted with revolution in all its American possessions, Spain was in no position to send the necessary reinforcements to California; the expedition never did sail.[58]

In Spain itself Ferdinand VII maintained intimate relations with Tsar Alexander, apparently feeling that with his powerful legitimist support the dangerous situation confronting Spain in its American possessions would be overcome. The strongly anglophobe Dmitrii Pavlovich Tatischev, Russian ambassador at Madrid, who had become a dominant influence in Ferdinand's powerful kitchen cabinet, was engaged in farfetched schemes by which Russia, in return for mediation in the Americas, might receive compensation in territorial cessions by Spain. According to the American minister at Madrid, these included not only Majorca or Minorca but also unlikely regions such as Texas or Louisiana. Rumors of Russian atempts to obtain Mediterranean bases reached the British press in April 1817, and the Spanish ambassador in London reported in June that the British government thought that Spain was to seize Portugal with Russian support, while Russia was to get Minorca from Spain.[59]

Behind the cloud of rumor there actually were secret negotiations in process between Spain and Russia. It appears

---

58. Apodaca to Ministro de Estado, Sept. 30, 1818, AGI, Estado 32, 4M568, items 11–14. Another copy of the letter is in the BN.

59. Tatischev has been described as "the virtual foreign minister of Spain" (Andrei A. Lobanov-Rostovsky, *Russia and Europe 1789–1825* [Durham, N.C., 1947], pp. 389–90); George W. Erving to John Q. Adams, Madrid, Apr. 6, 1817, in William R. Manning, ed., *Diplomatic Correspondence of the United States Concerning the Independence of the Latin American Nations* (3 vols. New York, 1925), *3*, 1933–34; dispatch from London, June 17, 1817, AGS, Sección Estado; John Howes Gleason, *The Genesis of Russophobia in Great Britain* (Cambridge, Mass., 1950), p. 42.

that Ferdinand asked Alexander for permission to build warships in Russian shipyards in order to speed up plans to subdue the revolted colonies in the Americas; Alexander countered by offering to sell him a Russian fleet of five ships of the line and three frigates. Tatischev and the Spanish minister of war, Francisco de Eguía, signed the secret treaty at Madrid on August 11, 1817. It provided that Spain was to give Russia a down payment of £400,000 sterling, which England was to grant Spain in February 1818 as a result of a treaty between England and Spain to suppress the slave trade in the Spanish possessions. Spain was to pay the remaining 13,600,000 rubles by March 1, 1818, although this was later amended to December 1820. The Spanish ambassador at London was instructed to inform the British government that the purchase of the ships had been a private deal and was not to be considered in any way as a political matter. Pierre de Polética, the Russian minister to the United States, later assured John Quincy Adams that Alexander had no intention of taking sides with Spain in her quarrel with her colonies when he sold Ferdinand the fleet.[60]

The Russian fleet duly arrived at Cádiz on February 21, 1818, but the ships were soon found to be unseaworthy and provided no additional threat against the Spanish colonies. The secrecy surrounding the deal, however, provided the basis for a fresh flood of rumor which now increasingly singled out the Californias as the territory to be ceded to Russia for her assistance in subduing Spain's revolted colonies. Other rumors pictured Spain as granting the Balearics to Russia, the Canaries to Holland, Cuba to England, and Puerto Rico, Santo Domingo, and the Philippines to France

60. Manuel de Saraleguí y Medina, *Un negocio escandaloso en tiempos de Fernando VII* (Madrid, 1904), pp. 119–26; Dexter Perkins, "Russia and the Spanish Colonies, 1817–1818," *American Historical Review, 28* (1923), 657, n. 4; José Pizarro to Duque de San Carlos, Oct. 28, 1817, AGS, Sección Estado, E8177; John Quincy Adams, *Memoirs*, ed. C. F. Adams (12 vols. Philadelphia, 1874–77), *4*, 381.

in return for funds with which to prosecute the war against her colonies.[61]

By the latter part of 1818 these reports were widespread in California itself. "It is being said openly throughout the Province," reported Father Señán, "that Spain is ceding this country to the Russians." He added that letters from Guadalajara were saying the same thing and that the crew of a Peruvian ship stated it was common knowledge in Lima that Spain had sold California and Minorca to Russia three years before. These rumors were widely reported in the American press and were corroborated by the on-the-spot dispatch of J. B. Prevost, who wrote to Secretary of State John Quincy Adams from Monterey on November 11, 1818, foretelling an early Russian seizure of San Francisco Bay and eventual Russian occupation of all California. As it happened, a brief eleven days after Prevost made his report, Monterey was attacked and captured from the sea by foreign invaders, but they were the long-expected insurgents from Buenos Aires under Captain Hippolyte Bouchard, not Russians.[62]

In spite of the growing rumors that Russia was to be given Spanish territory in the Americas in return for assistance against the revolting Spanish colonies, there is no evidence that any such territory was offered by Spain. In fact, as far as California was concerned, what evidence there is shows that Spain merely instructed the governors of the province to provide an official welcome for visiting Russian ships on world cruises. At the very time he was presumably negotiating with Ambassador Tatischev, Minister of War Eguía sent a dispatch to Viceroy Apodaca urging vigilance in California

61. *Niles Weekly Register, 13* (Jan. 3, 1818), 297; *16* (Mar. 20, May 29, July 24, 1819), 78, 237, 361–62; *17* (Dec. 11, 1819), 232; John C. Hildt, *Early Diplomatic Negotiations of the United States with Russia* (Baltimore, 1906), p. 142.

62. 17th Congress, 2d Session, no. 536, American State Papers, Miscellaneous, 2, 1009; *The Letters of Señán,* p. 108; Bancroft, *California, 2,* 220–49.

and an attitude of "prevention is better than cure" toward any foreign ships in the region. These intrusions were to be resisted, Eguía ordered, but "all possible urbane explanations" were to be used first. The Spanish government could not believe, Eguía continued, that the friendly Russian court had authorized these moves, which undoubtedly were being done without the knowledge of the emperor.[63]

With the coming of 1821 and Mexican independence from Spain, the Russian-American Company showed no sign of removing its colony at Ross. Indeed, in March 1821 the Russian government asked the company whether it could supply flour not only for its own settlements but for Russian government employees in Kamchatka. Despite the difficulty of buying grain in California, the company reminded the government of the benefits of obtaining the right to trade with New Spain.

Thinking Mexicans were by this time already beginning to ponder for themselves the threat of Russia on the northwest coast. Was it not possible that Spain might cede California to Russia in the same way that she had granted her rights to the northwest coast above 42 degrees in 1819 to the United States? Some members of the Council of the Russian-American Company, who wanted to expand Russian territory to include San Francisco Bay, were anxious to persuade Spain to do exactly that. Others, who pointed out that Spain had lost control of Mexico, felt that such a cession would be valueless. The tsar agreed with them. But Mexican fears of a possible Spanish reconquest during her early years of independence made these possibilities seem probable and helped to prolong the fear of Russian advance against California.[64]

63. Eguía to Viceroy of New Spain, June 30, 1818, BN; Conde de Venadito to Ministro de Guerra, Jan. 31, 1821, BN.

64. Company to Count Dmitrii Alexandrovich, Minister of Finance, Mar. 8, 1821, RRAC; Okun, *Russian-American Company*, p. 132; Carlos María Bustamante, "Medidas para la pacificación de la América mexicana," MS of 1820, Bancroft Library, University of California, Berkeley (cited hereafter as BL), chap. 18.

Chapter Two

Mission Indians and Colonists

Spain was well aware that if she was to save California, and perhaps all of New Spain, from the threat of Russian or other foreign encroachment, she must colonize it. From 1769 until Mexico became independent in 1821, Spain never ceased in her endeavors to populate and develop California. The task turned out to be an uphill one which Spain was never able to complete, and all of the problems it involved, together with some new ones, passed on to Mexico when she took possession of her inheritance.

When Visitor-General José de Gálvez arrived in Lower California in 1768, he began to make plans for occupying the Monterey area. He and Viceroy Croix had in mind setting up a presidio at Monterey, providing colonists and, above all, extending the line of missions from Lower California into the new region. For some seventy years the Jesuits had run the missions of Lower California, and on their expulsion in 1767, Franciscans from the College of San Fernando in Mexico City took their places. The Jesuits had succeeded in occupying Lower California for Spain after Spanish attempts to colonize it had failed; furthermore, they had done it with a minimum of cost to the Spanish treasury, for they had raised their own money, known as the Pious Fund for the Californias, for the project. With his mind constantly aware of the necessity for economy in government, yet at the same time convinced of the need for a northern advance, Gálvez naturally turned to the same means that had been used in Lower California.

From the Spanish point of view, in fact, everything pointed to the suitability of the mission as the spearhead of northern advance. Indians in large numbers were known to inhabit northern California; congregating them into missions would not only provide for their conversion to Christianity but would also eventually, it was hoped, turn them into loyal subjects of the king. With vast areas of the Americas beckoning the few Spanish settlers coming to the New World, an institution like the mission, which seemed able to transform wild Indians into dark-hued Spanish farmers, was to be welcomed with open arms. In addition to these advantages the missions became farms providing, with Indian labor, large numbers of cattle and quantities of grain which could be used to help establish more colonies farther up the coast. There were, of course, possible difficulties; the Indians, for example, might not be sufficiently docile to labor in the missions. This, fortunately for the Spaniards, was not the case. On the other hand it is clear that the objectives of the missionaries and of the government that urged them on were not entirely the same. The major purpose of the missionaries, if not their only one, was to convert the pagan Indians to Christianity and thereby save their souls in the next world. The government was thinking of using mission Indian labor to help establish new settlements in an isolated region of a vast empire now threatened by foreign powers. It might be expected that with these different objectives royal officials and missionary fathers would not always be in agreement, and they were not.[1]

Some idea of the conflict which was to arise between the

[1]. For a discussion of the social and political function of the mission, see Herbert E. Bolton, "The Mission as a Frontier Institution in the Spanish American Colonies," *American Historical Review*, 23 (1917), 42–61.

government, now keenly interested in occupying California, and the missionaries may be seen with the arrival of the dynamic Gálvez in Lower California. While he was in Mexico City, he and Viceroy Croix had heard that the missions in Lower California were in a wretched state, and he made it his first duty to look into this matter. He sent out questionnaires to the new Franciscan missionaries, headed by the intrepid Father Junípero Serra, asking them about the customs of the Indians, their progress in education, their civil government, how much property they had, and many other questions.[2] With most of the replies still not received but with some additional information from other sources, Gálvez arrived at the conclusion that the Jesuits had grossly neglected their missions in the southern region of Lower California. Impressing upon the viceroy the fact that he was not exaggerating, Gálvez said that the Jesuits had deliberately set out to make California as poor as they had said it was; they had destroyed it instead of developing it. As a result the government had to continue to spend money on it while the Jesuits used their Pious Fund for other purposes. If Lower California had been in other hands, it would, he felt, have been a rich land. When the Jesuits were expelled, the wealth of the missions was already in a well-advanced stage of destruction. Then soldier-commissioners were put in charge of the mission temporalities, and these men, having no other models but the former missionaries, continued their destructive work. "There is no doubt," concluded Gálvez, "that if I had arrived two months later than I did, I should not have found more than a sad memory of the missions."[3]

2. Gálvez to Croix, Sept. 8, 1768, AGI, Guadalajara 416, 2M930. For an invaluable survey of the period and career of Father Serra, see Maynard J. Geiger, *The Life and Times of Fray Junípero Serra* (2 vols. Washington, D.C., 1959) and Antonine Tibesar, ed., *Writings of Junípero Serra* (3 vols. Washington, D.C., 1955–56).

3. Gálvez to Croix, Sept. 8, 1768, AGI, Guadalajara 416. For a scholarly treatment of this subject, see Peter Masten Dunne, S.J., *Black Robes in Lower California* (Berkeley, 1952), pp. 406–12.

Gálvez' anti-Jesuit attitude was the result of the long campaign that had been waged against the Society which had ended in its expulsion from all Spanish dominions. It is not surprising that a prominent government official should at this point make the Jesuits the scapegoat for whatever ills he found in Lower California.

The fact was, however, that the Jesuits knew much more about Lower California than Gálvez, who had been there only four months when he optimistically forecast that it would soon be able to support itself without requiring an annual subvention from the royal treasury; indeed he went further, prophesying that it would not be long before it began to pay back into the treasury the large sums that had been spent on it. Gálvez closed his letter to Croix by reassuring him that the missions were now in the hands of the Franciscans, who would not deviate an iota from their vow of poverty, and that the Pious Fund for the Californias, which was now in government hands, had more than enough money with which to extend the missions far to the north.

Gálvez not only criticized the Jesuits for their supposedly erroneous views about the poverty of Lower California; he also found fault with their handling of the Indians. In his opinion the mission Indians were living the same "irrational and barbarous kind of life" that they did before they were converted.[4] The missions, he found, were simply large farms or haciendas where the missionaries and some servants or soldiers had their lodging. The Indians wandered about in

4. Gálvez to Croix, Sept. 8, 1768, AGI, Guadalajara 416. Priestley appears to think that California was considered wealthy at this time (*José de Gálvez*, p. 211, n. 37). See, however, the Jesuit Father Johann Jakob Baegert's remarks in his *Observations in Lower California* (Berkeley, 1952), p. 48, where he states: "First, it [Lower California] is of all the countries of the globe one of the poorest. . . . The aridity of California and the consequent lack of agriculture, trades, and work bring with them the constant idleness, the continuous roving about of the native Californians, and their lack of clothing and housing." See also Andrés Burriel [Miguel Venegas], *Noticia de California, 1,* 42–43.

the surrounding country, generally naked, in search of their food, just as they had always done. The Indians, he went on, regarded their work in the missions with horror; they hated agriculture, fled from religious instruction, and looked upon society as the greatest of their woes. His explanation for this state of affairs was that the Jesuits had exploited them by forcing them to work in turns on the missions, several of which did not even provide them with food for their pains. To make things worse, Gálvez continued, no Indian was permitted to own property or to pass on property to his children, so that there was no chance of any of them alleviating in this way "the insupportable slavery under which they all groaned."[5] In another letter Gálvez referred to the lack of civilization of the mission Indians and their scanty instruction, and as a final indictment of the Jesuits, he produced figures drawn from his recent interrogatory showing that there had been a tremendous loss of life in the missions. Assuming, he said, that a few years before the southern region of Lower California had contained 30,000 Indians and that the northern Indian villages contained an equal number, it was horrifying that only 7,149 of this large number of Indians remained alive. The Jesuits, he said, "have almost extinguished the population of this Province."[6]

After such a wholesale denunciation of the missions under the Jesuits, it is remarkable that Gálvez was willing to go ahead with a mission plan for the future settlement of the Monterey area. The villains in his piece, however, were the

5. Gálvez to Croix, Nov. 23, 1768, AGI, Guadalajara 416, 2M932.

6. Gálvez to Croix, Dec. 6, 1768, AGI, Guadalajara 416, 2M932. Father Baegert estimated that in 1767 the fifteen missions of Lower California contained 12,000 Indians (Observations, p. 54); according to the calculations of Professor S. F. Cook, at least 20,000 mission Indians died from diseases up to 1773. Cook estimates that between 25 and 40 percent of the population decline in Lower California may be directly attributed to epidemic disease (Sherburne F. Cook, The Extent and Significance of Disease among the Indians of Baja California 1697–1773 [Berkeley, 1937], pp. 35–36).

Jesuits, not the missions as such. All that was necessary, in his view, were some reforms, and all would be well under the Franciscan regime. Urged on, as he put it, with "sentiment and humanity," the basic forces behind concern for the oppressed and lowly in the eighteenth century, Gálvez decided first of all to feed and clothe the Indians, making use of the resources of the Pious Fund. If the Indians became accustomed to wearing clothes, he pointed out, they would in due course be ashamed to appear stark naked, and they would therefore acquire a need which they did not then have. Since the Indians embarrassed the white men by declining to work because they did not want money, having nothing they desired to buy, Gálvez was aiming in this instance not only at their modesty but at making them into consumers. In a regulation he issued to all of the Franciscans, Gálvez ordered that all Indians were to be made to live at a fixed domicile in a well-planned town. They were to work in the fields and be given their own property, which they would be permitted to cultivate; they were to feed themselves with the produce they raised. Unless the Indians were brought together in towns of this kind, Gálvez felt, they could never be civilized, and in this he echoed traditional Spanish policy. Finally, all of the Indians, either as individuals or as groups, were to be supported by the missions to which they belonged. In a word, Gálvez concluded, in that part of California that had been conquered, there were to be no Indians who did not live in towns in a civilized fashion and who did not support themselves and dress like rational persons. Furthermore, it was important that these improvements be made as soon as possible, for a group of six French academicians and two Spanish naval officers accompanying them were due to arrive shortly in California for astronomical observations. These visitors were likely to travel all over Lower California and would publish accounts of their work; it was highly desirable for the honor of the government and of the Franciscans that they should not describe the greatest and most pious monarch in the world as lord, in Lower California, of deserts, with brutish, vagabond Indians as his vassals.[7]

While Gálvez made it clear in his instructions to the Franciscans that the Indians must lead the kind of life that a rational or civilized person led, he did not say whether he thought they could actually become civilized persons or whether he simply had in mind making them appear to be rational. From the point of view of the missionaries the point was a crucial one. If the California Indians were as well endowed mentally as other people, or—what would amount to the same thing—if they were considered to be the equals of other men, then the missionaries would be expected to civilize them in the course of time. On the other hand, if the Indians were not the equals intellectually of the white man, the government could hardly complain if the missionaries were unable to raise them to the level of the white man's civilization. This whole question had, of course, already been discussed at length in the sixteenth century, when the Dominican Father Bartolomé de Las Casas, in a long-fought struggle in defense of the Indians, strenuously upheld the view that the Indians were just as much men as the Spaniards. In 1537 Pope Paul III had issued his famous pronouncement that the Indians were "truly men" and "capable of understanding the Catholic faith."[8]

Father Luis Sales, one of the Dominicans who took over the missions of Lower California from the Franciscans in 1772, was reminded of the old controversy as he went about his daily tasks with the Indians. For him, however, the original debate had been concerned with the rationality of the

7. Gálvez to Croix, Nov. 23 and Dec. 6, 1768, AGI. The expedition Gálvez referred to was that led by the Abbé Jean Chappe d'Auteroche, which arrived in 1769. The original account is in Jean Chappe d'Auteroche, *Voyage en Californie* (Paris, 1772). It was edited by Jean Dominique Cassini.

8. Lewis Hanke, *The Spanish Struggle for Justice in the Conquest of America* (Philadelphia, 1949), p. 73.

Indians of New Spain proper. What, he asked himself, would learned men say about the California Indians, "who are supposed to be the most savage?"[9] If Father Sales had been a regular reader of the philosophical writings of France and England, he would have known that the eighteenth-century intellectuals had become very much interested in the problem of the nature of primitive man and especially of the American Indian.

In spite of the current fashion of the noble savage, it has to be admitted that neither the travelers of the first half of the century, who helped to spark the revival of interest in the Americas, nor the philosophers who learnedly discussed the American Indians in their studies could find much to praise about them. There were, of course, exceptions to the frequently critical estimates of the Red Man; Jean Jacques Rousseau even had the temerity to assert that primitive man was better than his civilized counterpart in Europe.[10] But many of the philosophers would probably have agreed with the verdict of Pierre Bouguer, the French scientist who had traveled to Ecuador in 1735 with a party of astronomers, when he wrote:

> [the Indians] are all extremely indolent, they are stupid, they squat for days in the same place, without moving, or speaking a single word. . . . One often does not know what kind of motive to suggest to them when one wants to persuade them to perform some service. It is vain to offer them money, they answer that they are not hungry.[11]

In 1768, when Gálvez was issuing his instructions about the Indians of Lower California, Cornelis de Pauw published

9. Luis Sales, *Noticias de la provincia de Californias, 1794* (Madrid, 1960), p. 32.

10. In his *Discours sur l'inégalité*, which first appeared in 1755.

11. *La figure de la terre, determinée par les observations* (Paris, 1749), p. cii.

his *Philosophical Researches on the Americans,* in which he maintained that the Indians were superior to animals only because they had the use of their hands and their tongues, but they were "inferior to the least of the Europeans." Furthermore, during the almost three centuries since the discovery of America, Indians had been constantly brought to Europe, where they had been exposed to every kind of culture, but in spite of this not one had managed to make a name for himself in the sciences, the arts, or the professions. It is true that Buffon, the distinguished naturalist, who did not himself think very highly of the Indians, could not agree with de Pauw, whom he accused of selecting his evidence to fit his prejudices, but many of the learned men of the day discounted the ability of the Indians.[12]

In eighteenth-century Spain, where the American Indians attracted a great deal of attention, as they did in other European countries, the theme of the noble savage found little favor with many writers whose epic poems had to provide the old heroic conquistadores with foes worthy of their mettle. The Indians they described were likely to be cunning, fierce, and cruel. In fact the nature of the American Indian became inextricably intertwined with the nature of the Spaniard. The more rational and human the Indian was made to appear, the more brutal and savage his Spanish opponent looked. Father Benito Jerónimo Feijóo solved the problem in the modern fashion by putting the conquest

12. M. de P[auw], *Recherches philosophiques sur les Américains* (3 vols. London, 1771), *2,* 130; Buffon, *Oeuvres completes* (26 vols. Paris, 1828), *10,* 465, and *11,* 79. Other unfavorable verdicts may be found in Antonio de Ulloa, *Noticias americanas* (Buenos Aires, 1944), pp. 244, 246, 248–49, 252–54, 258; William Robertson, *Works* (8 vols. Oxford, 1825), *6,* 243–386; Charles Marie de La Condamine, *Viaje a la América meridional* (Buenos Aires, 1942), pp. 42–43. More favorable views may be found in Antoine Joseph Pernety, *Dissertation sur L'Amérique et les Américains contre les Recherches philosophiques de M. de P.* (Berlin, 1770). For a masterly discussion of this whole question see Antonello Gerbi, *La Disputa del nuevo mundo* (Mexico, 1960).

into its proper historical epoch. American writers increasing-ly took up the cudgels for the Indians as the century pro-gressed. A sonnet published in Mexico in 1778 described them as human beings like anybody else, and a Jesuit from Paraguay bitterly denounced Juan Bautista Muñoz's official *History of the New World* in 1797 as but an abstract of de Pauw and Robertson, citing as his proof the evidence brought forward by Thomas Jefferson in his *Notes on the State of Virginia,* where he resolutely defends the American Indian against his detractors.[13]

The Indians of Lower California had, if possible, an even worse reputation than those of the rest of the Americas. Most of the philosophers failed to make any distinction between the Indians of one region and those of another, and Father Andrés Burriel, in his well-known work on California, began his unfavorable remarks on the Indians with the words: "The basic characteristics of the Californians, as well as of all other Indians, are stupidity and insensibility; want of knowledge and reflection, inconstancy, impetuosity, and blindness of appetite, laziness and abhorrence of all labour and fatigue; an incessant love of puerile and brutal pleasure and amuse-ment." But Father Burriel concluded his indictment by making it clear that the Indians of Lower California were a shade worse than their peers, "for even in the roughest moun-tains and the least frequented corners of this part of the world [Europe], there are no people so little cultivated, so lacking in appearance and so feeble in soul and body, as the unhappy Californians." Father Johann Jakob Baegert, who had spent seventeen years in Lower California before being removed in 1768, stated that as a general rule the California

13. Anthony Tudisco, "The Land, People, and Problems of America in Eighteenth-Century Spanish Literature," *The Americas, 12* (1956), 367, 376; Joseph Joaquín Granados y Gálvez, *Tardes americanas* (Mexico, 1778), p. 13; Francisco Iturri, *Carta crítica sobre la historia de América del Sr. Don Juan Bautista Muñoz* (Puebla, Mexico, 1820), p. 25; Thomas Jefferson, *Notes on the State of Virginia* (New York, 1964), pp. 55–66.

Indians were "stupid, awkward, rude, unclean, insolent, ungrateful, mendacious, thievish, abominably lazy, great talkers to their end, and naive and childlike so far as intelligence and actions are concerned." On the other hand Father Baegert held that the Californians, like all other Indians, were "human beings, true children of Adam, as we are." "They are endowed," he continued, "with reason and understanding like other people, and I think that, if in their early childhood they were sent to Europe . . . they would go as far as any European in mores, virtues, in all arts and sciences." He also contended that in one respect, at least, they had the advantage over the Europeans: "I wish to state with full assurance and without fear of contradiction that, as far as this earthly life is concerned, they are incomparably happier than those of Adam's children who live in Europe and upon the blessed soil of Germany, even those who appear to be living on the very pinnacle of temporal bliss."[14]

Father Baegert's more optimistic account of the California Indians was distinctly the exception to the rule; Father Sales, the Dominican, could see no such promise in his California charges. He found them "half rational," although he admitted that there were exceptions to this. "I am of the opinion," he wrote, "that perhaps in the whole world there is no nation so poor, so unhappy and so lacking in intellectual qualities as these [Indians]."[15]

Trying to make the Indians live like white men so that they might settle California for Spain was not only a vexing problem, it was a major cause of friction between the missionaries and government officials in the Californias. Father Sales reveals how this occurred in one case. Gálvez had ordered that the Indians were to be given possessions of their own, presumably as a stimulus to make them work for themselves. One of the early governors, Sales does not say which, in an apparent attempt to carry out Gálvez' intentions, issued

14. Venegas, *Noticia, 1,* 71, 72–73; Baegert, *Observations,* pp. 49, 80.
15. Sales, *Noticias,* pp. 31–32.

a decree "ordering that all the Indians of all classes and conditions that there were should have absolute and individual control over the property and utensils of the missions and that these should be divided up among them." Sales says that the governor was "thinking of making the Indians happy." From the point of view of Sales, the whole idea was ridiculous. "Anyone who thoroughly understands the condition of the Indians," he wrote, "will easily understand the fatal consequences of this decision." No sooner was the order published, Sales continued, than the cattle and farms belonging to the missions began to be destroyed.[16]

Confronted with situations that they thought impossible, the missionaries could and did make use of the standard device of "I obey but do not comply," whereby viceroys put off enacting legislation made in Spain that they could not enforce. That they did this in Lower California when it came to enforcing Gálvez' regulations is revealed in a long complaint drawn up by Felipe de Neve in 1774, shortly before he became governor. He stated that although Gálvez had ordered that at each mission the boundaries of the new town which was to be founded, together with crop lands and commons, were to be marked out, this had nowhere been done because it was not in accordance with the ideas of the missionaries. In Neve's view the Franciscans and Dominicans were going the same way as the Jesuits. They wanted to be entirely independent of the royal officials so that they could accumulate all the cattle and crops produced on the missions as their own, in addition to their stipends. Jumping to the conclusion that the desire of the missionaries to hold themselves aloof from royal officers was due to greed, Neve argued that the viceroy should give control of all mission crops, cattle, and hides to the governor, who should then establish the towns planned by Gálvez. Neve thought the harvests could be greatly increased if this were done, and the con-

16. Ibid., p. 94.

siderable surplus that would be available could be used to help the new settlements at Monterey and San Diego.[17]

That there was more to the matter than one man's unfavorable impression of missionary activities, however, is revealed by a number of proposals put forward at this time to modify the missions in some way. In addition to the economy which was so prominent a part of Gálvez' ideas, the suggestions show that the authorities either did not believe what the missionaries were telling them about the limited capabilities of the Indians or felt that the missionaries would be likely to try to make themselves too independent of the government unless they were made completely dependent on their stipends. A suggestion was made in 1772 that new methods of dealing with the Indians should include reviving Bishop Vasco de Quiroga's Indian towns in Michoacán; the Franciscans answered that the California Indians were not sufficiently civilized to respond to this scheme. In 1776 a former Franciscan missionary in Sonora, Father Antonio de los Reyes, presented a proposal to change the organization and management of the Franciscan missions in the area of the recently formed Interior Provinces, which included the Californias. His suggested changes, which were based on his own brief experience in Sonora, amounted to making missionaries in these areas less dependent on their missionary colleges and provinces by creating custodies or minor provinces within them. The proposal was adopted by the Council of the Indies and the crown in 1782, but it proved impractical and was abolished in 1791.[18]

When it was decided to establish missions on the Colorado River in 1780, another new plan was devised. Towns for Spanish settlers were to be set up, with small squads of soldiers to protect them. Franciscan Fathers were to act both as priests for the Spaniards and as missionaries among the sur-

17. Ruth Lapham Butler, "A Statement by Phelipe de Neve," *Hispanic American Historical Review*, 22 (1942), 357–60.

18. Richman, *California*, p. 145; Geiger, *Life of Serra*, 2, 343–66.

rounding Indians; the Indians were not to be required to live in mission communities but could obtain lands and live in the towns with the Spaniards. The missionaries were not to have control of temporalities. Whether the new system would have worked in California cannot be said. It was tried out under unfavorable conditions on the Colorado and ended in disaster; the Yuma Indians destroyed two towns and massacred the inhabitants in 1781, thus cutting off overland connections between Sonora and California.[19]

In California, meanwhile, it had been decided to establish three more missions among the Chumash Indians in the Santa Barbara Channel area. In his plans for these missions, Viceroy Martín de Mayorga revealed that Neve's ideas on removing the temporalities from the missionaries were now going to be put into effect. But the Franciscan Fathers who were to take over the new missions refused to do so under these conditions. The College of San Fernando sent a letter explaining why the missionaries needed temporalities. They said their experience had shown that the Indians could be won over only by giving them presents. Unless the missionary could himself distribute gifts to reward his Indians, progress in conversion would be impossible. As if in answer to Neve's bitter attack of 1774, the letter continued by saying that Governor Neve had warned his men not to take the side of the friars, perform services for them, or bring back mission Indians who had escaped. As a result, the soldiers disregarded the teachings of the Fathers and by their bad behavior toward the Indians, especially the women, undid their missionary work.

Plans for establishing two new missions in the channel area at San Buenaventura and Santa Barbara were delayed by the Yuma massacre, but they went forward again in 1782. Governor Neve issued instructions for the presidio com-

19. Bancroft, *California*, *1*, 357–62. For a good modern discussion of these Indians, see Jack D. Forbes, *Warriors of the Colorado* (Norman, Okla., 1965), pp. 185–86, 201–05.

mander which showed that the authorities had not been swayed by the pleas of the missionaries. In the new missions the Indians were to continue to live in their Indian villages; they were not to be required to live in mission communities, and the missionaries were to have no temporalities to control. There appears to have been no immediate demonstration by the Franciscans against the new system, but a succession of petty bickerings between the missionaries and the lay authorities revealed that their different objectives made cooperation between them difficult. In spite of the government's instructions, the new missions soon became communities of Indians raising crops and herding cattle which were disposed of by the missionaries in the traditional fashion.[20]

While the practical affairs of the missions went on as before, new signs of a radical change in attitude toward the Indians began to appear on the horizon. In 1779 there appeared a posthumous book by Bernardo Ward, an Irishman who had held high office in Spain, entitled *Proyecto económico*. In it he suggested that England and France were dealing more successfully with their Indians, and at much less expense, than Spain. The key to their success, he held, was that they made no attempt to conquer or subject the Indians in any way but simply tried to provide them with things they wanted by trading with them. The Indian way of life should not be scorned, he said, and if they were treated with kindness and encouraged in friendly fashion to work, they would settle down and become useful vassals of the Crown. He proposed that the Indians be given land of their own and full right to possess the fruits of their work. To those who argued that the Indians were not capable of working in this way, he replied that he doubted whether this was true, but even if it were, they might still be made into useful laborers. On the missions Ward limited himself to remarking that since the

20. Bancroft, *California, 1*, 374–75, 381.

Spanish church was so rich, he thought that part of the expense of running them should be borne by the American bishoprics.[21]

Ward's combination of humanitarianism with utilitarianism in dealing with the Indians was to prove increasingly attractive to a government overburdened with expenses; and although there is no direct evidence that it had an immediate effect on California, possibly some of its recommendations did influence Neve in those parts of his instructions dealing in general with Indian relations. Neve gave orders that there was to be as little interference as possible with the Indians' life in their native villages. Soldiers were forbidden to enter them, unless under orders, on pain of severe punishment. The Indians were to be civilized by example and gradually led to become vassals of the king; they were not to be made Christians by force. Trade with them was to be encouraged by fairness. It is probable, however, that these ideas were in the air at the time rather than having their origin in any one book.[22] On the other hand, there were also warning signals that a change in attitude toward the Indian was badly needed: in 1780 the Inca leader Tupac Amaru started a major civil war against the Spaniards in the Andes, which was only put down in 1781 after bloody fighting; and closer to home, there was the Yuma massacre on the Colorado that same year.

Spanish mission policy, at any rate, was absolved of all charges of cruelty by the distinguished French explorer La

21. Bernardo Ward, *Proyecto económico* (Madrid, 1787), pp. 15–16, 50, 83–84, 86–88, 90, 213. In 1789 José del Campillo y Cosío in his *Nuevo sistema de gobierno económico para la América* repeated in identical terms those portions of Ward's work dealing with the Americas. For a brief discussion of the unresolved charges of plagiarism see C. Alan Hutchinson, "The Mexican Government and the Mission Indians of Upper California," *The Americas, 21* (1965), 345, n. 43.

22. Navarro García sees a general slackening off of missionary fervor on the frontier at this time *(Gálvez, pp. 421–22).*

Pérouse, who visited California in 1786. He spoke approvingly of the "wise and pious conduct" of the missionary fathers and of their success in converting the Indians. He also had high words of praise for Felipe de Neve, whom he described as wanting more civil liberty for the Indians. Yet La Pérouse did find some faults in the mission system: the condition of the Indians on the missions reminded him of one of the more humanely run slave plantations in the French colonies. After stating that the missionaries, either because of prejudice or because of their experience, were convinced that "reason is almost never developed" in the Indians, he asked whether it might not be possible, in spite of the obvious difficulties, to persuade a few Indian families of the advantages of a society based on the rights of man. He thought that giving the Indians land of their own to cultivate might provide the stimulus for farm or other work. He did not think the mission regime, with its emphasis on rewards in the next life, was well suited to lifting the Indians out of their state of ignorance.[23]

Difficult as it was to civilize the California Indians, the constant fear of Russian or other foreign encroachment spurred Spain on to occupy the country. The first and most obvious way to do this, of course, was to persuade settlers to come to California; but it proved almost as hard to accomplish this as to make the Indians into Spanish farmers. To begin with, not just anyone would make a suitable immigrant. Gálvez wanted people who were "useful, capable of farming [California's] lands and making use of its wealth of minerals, grain and other fruits and also able to bear arms to protect their homes should the occasion arise."[24] On the other hand, the missionaries understandably wanted the

23. *The First French Expedition to California. La Pérouse in 1786* (Los Angeles, 1959), pp. 55–56, 64, 66, 75, 133.

24. "Diario histórico de los viages de mar y tierra," AGI, Estado 43 (Guadalajara), 5M259.

settlers to be good Christians who would make acceptable models for their Indian neophytes. Both the lay authorities and the missionaries liked the idea of having plenty of artisans—blacksmiths, carpenters, masons, bakers, and members of other trades and professions—men who knew how to get skilled jobs done.

In practice, most of the men who came out were soldiers for the presidios. At first there were no women—a circumstance which made some of the Indians think that the Spaniards were the offspring of mules. This had come about because, as Father Junípero Serra explained, "mules were the only members of the female gender they saw among us." It also led to ill feeling with the Indians when some of the soldiers went on so-called "hunting" expeditions and took to lassoing native women to take their pleasure of them. Father Serra insisted that the soldiers should be of good character, and at least some of them should be married men with their families. He wanted two families to live at each mission so the wives could help to instruct the Indian women.[25]

Peopling California was slow and unsteady; half of those who came on the original expeditions of 1769 died, leaving only 126 men. Fernando de Rivera y Moncada brought some 51 persons—married soldiers with their families, including some unmarried women and bachelors—to Monterey in 1774. Juan Bautista de Anza, on his second expedition in 1775, brought with him 30 married soldiers, 29 of whom brought their wives with them. Included with 136 members of the soldiers' families were some 17 settlers. The total number of persons on the expedition was 240.[26]

The first town or pueblo founded in California was San José, which was established in 1777 near the mission of Santa Clara. The heads of families here were 5 colonists and 9

25. Tibesar, *Writings of Serra*, 2, 67, 203; Chapman, *Founding*, p. 324.

26. Caughey, *California*, p. 128; Ruth Staff, "Settlement in Alta California Before 1800" (M.A. thesis, University of California, 1931), 34–35; Chapman, *Founding*, pp. 347–48.

soldiers; the total population was 66. Unfortunately the boundaries between the town and the mission were not clear and trouble arose between the two. That it was more than a matter of boundaries, however, is made clear by Father Lasuén. The townspeople of San José, he reported in 1787, made use of the Santa Clara mission Indians "indiscriminately for all their house and field work. They are an immense hindrance to the conversion of the pagans, for they give them bad example, they scandalize them, and they actually persuade them not to become Christians, lest they would themselves suffer the loss of free labor."[27] The site of the town was poor, and it developed slowly. In 1790 it had 78 settlers of whom 28 were listed as Spaniards, and of the remainder approximately 8 were Indians, 28 mestizos, 8 mulattoes, and 1 was European. Thirteen of the men were farmers, 4 were artisans.[28]

In June 1779, when there were eight missions containing 1,749 Christian Indians, Governor Neve drew up his "Regulations for Governing the Province of the Californias," a landmark in the history of colonizing the province. Towns of *gente de razón,* or rational persons (i.e. persons who spoke Spanish and lived as Spaniards did), Neve stated, were necessary to increase the production of agricultural produce, cattle, and other branches of industry, so that they could supply the presidios with food and horses without their having to rely on the slow, wasteful, and risky bringing in of these items from New Spain. The town of San José had been founded with this in mind, and another, to be settled from Sonora and

27. Finbar Kenneally, *Writings of Fermín Francisco de Lasuén* (2 vols. Washington, D.C., 1965), *1,* 168. For a detailed discussion of the San José-Santa Clara problem see Geiger, *Life of Serra, 2,* 191–201. Navarro García, in a reference to the founding of San José, sees California's main problem at this time as antagonism between the royal authorities and the missionaries *(Gálvez,* p. 397). See also Oscar Osburn Winther, "The Story of San José, 1777–1869," California Historical Society *Quarterly, 14* (1935), 3–27, 147–74.
28. The totals do not tally. Staff, "Settlement," pp. 80, 82.

Sinaloa, was to be established.[29] Every settler was to receive a lot in the new town and four pieces of crop land outside it, each of about eight acres. Two of these eight-acre fields were to be irrigable and two not. It was calculated that it normally required about eight acres to seed about two and a half bushels (one *fanega*) of corn. Both the land and the house on the town lot could be passed on to the settlers' descendants. The acreage could not be split up or alienated in any way, nor could it be mortgaged or endangered by making it the basis for a loan. The settlers were to be exempt from taxes for five years. Holding of these grants of land was conditional upon the settler and his descendants' providing two horses, a saddle, gun, and other weapons, to be paid for by them. The settler was to be ready to defend his district or go wherever the governor ordered him in an emergency. He was also to receive some farm animals, which he was to pay for in due course in mules and horses.[30] These regulations for colonizing California were not superseded until it became a Mexican territory.

The new town to be founded mentioned in Neve's regulations was Los Angeles. Rivera y Moncada recruited settlers for it in Sonora and Sinaloa in 1780 and 1781. He contracted them to remain for a ten-year period; they were to be paid ten pesos a month for the first three years and were to receive

29. *Reglamento para el gobierno de la provincia de Californias* (San Francisco, 1929), p. 42. The authorities appear to be divided in their interpretation of the term *gente de razón*. Lesley Byrd Simpson explains it as meaning "whites" or "civilized people" (*Letters of Señán*, pp. vii, 9, n. 1). Edward H. Spicer, in his *Cycles of Conquest* (Tucson, Ariz., 1962), p. 301, refers to it as meaning "upper class people of Spanish descent." Jack D. Forbes (*Warriors of the Colorado*, p. 345) thinks of the term as meaning "someone who behaved rationally by being a Catholic and speaking Spanish." From its use in Spanish and Mexican California it is clear that it did not simply mean non-Indian. On the other hand it does not seem to have been applied to mission Indians whether they were Roman Catholics and spoke Spanish or not.

30. *Reglamento*, pp. 43–46, 50.

rations valued at one real a day for ten years. Rivera was supposed to recruit 24 heads of families, but he only managed to get 13, and of these 11 reached California. They consisted of 22 adults, made up of 2 Spaniards, 8 Indians, 1 coyote (a variously defined mixture of Indian and mestizo), 8 mulattoes, 2 Negroes, 1 mestizo, and 22 children. They included farmers, a shoemaker, a cowherd, a mason, a tailor, and others without trades. They founded Los Angeles on September 4, 1781, and it became the most successful of the Spanish towns; by 1790 it contained 141 people.[31]

The third of the early Spanish towns to be founded was Branciforte, established in 1797 as a *villa,* which put it more under military discipline. It was planned to make Branciforte a better town than San José and Los Angeles; the settlers were to be robust farmers from cool or temperate climates, masons, tailors, hatters, shoemakers, and even fishermen to engage in whaling. Discharged soldiers were welcomed. But the results were even more disappointing than they had been for the two previous towns. Nine settlers, recruited in Guadalajara mainly from vagabonds and criminals, arrived in 1797. They were poverty-stricken, poorly clad, and ill with venereal disease. They were given the inducements in Neve's Regulation together with a donation of from twenty to twenty-five pesos. For their first two years they were to receive an annual salary of 116 pesos; for the following three years this was to be reduced to sixty-six pesos. They were given the necessary tools, implements, and seeds, and each settler received three cows. Governor Borica ordered an officer to instruct them in agriculture, treat them kindly, and try to get them to work. It is said that in 1798 Governor Borica even ordered that the amount of clothing each settler's wife had be reported to him, so if they needed more it should be provided. The paternalism lavished upon Branciforte, however, did not pay

31. Staff, "Settlement," p. 84. See also Thomas Workman Temple, Jr., "Se Fundaron un Pueblo de Españoles," *Annual Publications,* Historical Society of Southern California, *15* (1931), 69–98.

off. The settlers became a scandal in California for their immorality; they did not raise enough food to feed themselves, and they hated what they looked upon as their exile from Guadalajara. The town was a failure.[32]

In the increasingly frustrating situation presented by mission Indians and low caliber colonists, who did not seem able to settle down and become hard-working subjects, a new hope appeared after the end of war in 1783. Captain Cook's third voyage to the northwest coast had revealed the money to be made by trading trinkets with the coastal Indians for sea otter furs and selling them at high prices in Canton. Vicente Basadre y Varela, whose background is uncertain, although he appears to have traveled in the Americas since 1777, suggested that New Spain might trade California sea otters at Canton for mercury, which it needed in large amounts for processing its silver ores. The Crown took up the idea, and at least three shipments of pelts were sent to China, to the considerable benefit of the royal treasury but with little appreciable gain for California.[33] Ciriaco González Carvajal, Intendant of the Philippines, scenting rich profits, brought forward another scheme which might have helped to solve California's problems. Possibly influenced by Bernardo Ward's new views on how to deal with the Indians, González Carvajal proposed in 1786 that Spain should trade in sea otter skins with the coastal Indians, who were to be treated with the utmost humanity and kindness. His plan made no mention of establishing missions, but he thought that more presidios should be set up and colonists brought in from the Philippines. The settlers he had in mind, however, were convicts and prostitutes who, he thought, might settle

32. Caughey, *California*, p. 179; Staff, "Settlement," pp. 90–94; Florian [Francis] Guest, O.F.M. "The Establishment of the Villa de Branciforte," *California Historical Society Quarterly, 41* (1962), 29–50.

33. Basadre to Príncipe de la Paz, May 1, 1797, AGI, Estado 40. For a full account of Spanish interest in the trade see Adele Ogden, *The California Sea Otter Trade* (Berkeley, 1941).

down successfully in the new environment and become good citizens. Bearing in mind the factors which in those days made poverty-stricken women into prostitutes and the minor crimes which made a man into a convict, there may have been more to his plan than would appear on the surface. In any case, he pointed to the success of the English establishments at Botany Bay to support his plea. He also suggested that convicts who were sent to die in Africa or to the fortress at Veracruz, where yellow fever killed them off, might be diverted to the northwest coast. He drew the line at admitting hardened antisocial criminals, whom he thought it would be better to exterminate.[34]

Nothing came of González Carvajal's suggestions, although they may have influenced the authorities in New Spain to permit the sending of convicts to California. Three convicts with shackled feet arrived in Monterey in 1791; twenty-two more came out in 1798, several of them artisans; and in succeeding years, both under Spain and Mexico, the authorities continued to send them, in spite of protests from California, since they were unable to persuade anyone else to go. Distinguished naval officers, who had firsthand experience with the sea otter trade, continued to recommend that Spain should take part in it, if only to lessen the profits the foreigners were making out of it. Malaspina even proposed to devote one of the volumes of the work that he was never permitted to write to explaining how this trade would help to promote the prosperity of California, so that it would cease to be a burden to the Crown.[35]

34. Ciriaco González Carvajal to José de Gálvez, June 20, 1786, AGI, Guadalajara 4921.

35. Staff, "Settlement," p. 46; Pedro de Novo y Colson, *Viaje político-científico alrededor del mundo por las corbetas Descubierta y Atrevida* (2d ed. Madrid, 1885), p. 372. Donald C. Cutter, in his *Malaspina in California* (San Francisco, 1960), appears to come to the conclusion (pp. 68–69) that Malaspina reported adversely on the otter trade, but see also the authoritative work by Adele Ogden cited in n. 33 above, in which Malaspina is described as enthusiastic over the trade. Among the other

In spite of the constant setbacks, demand for colonists continued to come from the officials, who never ceased to be worried about California's security from foreign attack. Governor Pedro Fages strongly urged further colonization in 1785 on the ground that as a result of the increasing numbers of Indians in the missions, they could not be depended on to furnish sufficient grain for the presidios. While little or nothing was accomplished in this respect at the time, the missions began to come in for increasingly harsh criticism. One of the most radical statements of this kind was prepared by Captain Nicolás Soler, Inspector General of presidios, in November 1787; in his view it was time that the mission Indians were released from the missions, since they were now ready for civilized life. He even proposed that Spaniards be given land on the missions and that Indians be allowed to settle in the Spanish town lands. There should be no further stationing of troops at missions or in towns. The results of these fundamental changes, he thought, would be to attract the non-Christian Indians toward the life of their converted fellows, with a consequent easing of the task of the missionaries. These remarkable proposals were far ahead of their time; indeed it was not until 1833 that the Mexican government produced similar ones that even then were considered too advanced. The replies that Fages gave Soler, to the effect that the Indians were not ready to become citizens, and that the Laws of the Indies were opposed to allowing Spaniards to settle on mission lands since these were eventually to belong to the Indians, were the very answers that the opponents of the Mexican legislation put forward in 1833.[36]

A few years after Governor Fages' complaint about the possibility of the missions' not being able to supply the presidios with sufficient grain, the situation changed radical-

---

naval officers who recommended the trade were Bodega y Quadra, Cayetano Valdés, Dionisio Alcalá-Galiano, Juan Vernacci, and Secundino de Salamanca.

36. Bancroft, *California*, *1*, 395, 396, n. 14, 449.

ly. In 1792 José Longinos Martínez, the botanist, noted that in the few years preceding his visit the missions had made an effort to sow more grain, and their harvests had been so great that they did not know what to do with their surplus. Longinos felt that industrious farmers from Catalonia would in a few years make California flourish, and he deplored the ideas of those who wanted to send criminals to populate it. He pointed to the strides that had been taken by the Chumash Indians of the Santa Barbara Channel area who, he said, had "sucked in the maxims of civilization and have kept them." "There are plenty of people in this land," he asserted. "What is needed is someone to teach them."[37]

The new-found productive capacity of the missions was, however, to bring fresh problems in its train. The abundance of cattle and grain that he saw on the missions suggested to the English explorer George Vancouver that some strong maritime power, interested in the fur trade on the coast, might well use these supplies to establish itself in California. In a description of California published in 1808, the American William Shaler went even further. Spain, in his view, had smoothed the way for an invader by stocking California with cattle and horses and teaching the Indians agriculture and the useful arts. California's defenseless inhabitants, he thought, would not oppose an invader who treated them well, secured their liberty and property, and gave them free trade. "In a word," he concluded, "[the Spaniards] have done everything that could be done to render California an object worthy the attention of the great maritime powers." Furthermore, he thought that California would be easy to capture

37. Father Junípero Serra referred to the Santa Barbara Channel Indians in 1775 as "these interesting and gifted gentiles" (Tibesar, *Writings of Serra*, 2, 349). The Chumash were generally regarded as superior by the Spaniards. See Campbell Grant, *The Rock Paintings of the Chumash* (Berkeley, 1965), pp. vii-viii, 8–73. Lesley Byrd Simpson, trans., *California in 1792: The Expedition of José Longinos Martínez* (San Marino, Calif., 1938), p. 32.

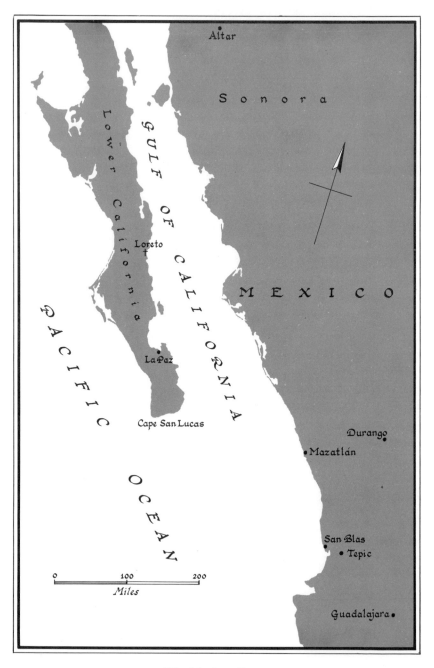

The Mexican Coast

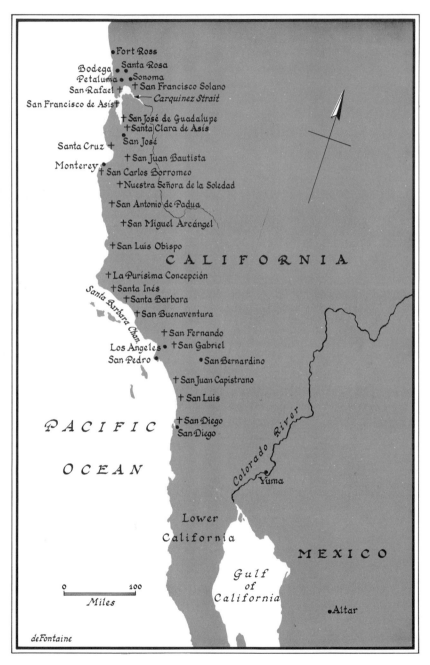

Missions on the California Coast

and to hold.[38] It is true that Malaspina continued to regard the missions as "so many vigilant guards on the great extent of our boundaries" confronting rival European powers, but it is evident that they were but signs of legal possession and not fortresses to prevent invasion, as later became clear when a test case occurred.

Malaspina and Vancouver also differed in their opinion of the missions, although they both praised the missionaries. For Malaspina the missions had brought a better life to the Indians by ending their fratricidal wars, by providing them with better food, and by teaching them the Christian religion; California had become a land of peace. Vancouver thought that the mission Indians were as uncivilized as ever: "they are certainly a race of the most miserable beings I ever saw, possessing the faculty of human reason," he wrote.[39]

That there was beginning to be a certain impatience with the slowness of the missions in making civilized men out of the Indians at this time is revealed on several occasions. In a report he made in 1794, Miguel Costanzó, a well-known military engineer and architect in New Spain, remarked, "Some missions have been for a hundred years in charge of friars and presidial guards. The remedy is to introduce *gente de razón* among the natives from the beginning. . . . They should be settled near the missions and mingle with the natives. Thus the missions will become towns in twenty-five or thirty years."[40] And in a letter written in 1796, Governor

38. George Vancouver, *A Voyage of Discovery to the North Pacific Ocean and Round the World* (3 vols. London, 1798), 2, 502–03; William Shaler, *Journal of a Voyage between China and the North-Western Coast of America* (Claremont, Calif., 1935), pp. 76–78.

39. Novo y Colson, *Viaje*, pp. xxvi, 447; Vancouver, *Voyage*, 2, 12.

40. For a useful summary of the career of Costanzó see J. A. Calderón Quijano, "Ingenieros militares en Nueva España," *Anuario de Estudios Americanos*, 6 (1949), 31–36; Bancroft, *California*, 1, 602–03. Navarro García points out that Teodoro de Croix, Antonio de Bonilla, and other leaders felt that the missionaries were forgetting to make their neophytes into normal men of Spanish culture (*Gálvez*, p. 422).

Diego Borica said that according to the laws, mission Indians were to be free after ten years. "But," he added, "those of New California at the rate they are advancing will not reach the goal in ten centuries; the reason, God knows, and men know something about it."[41]

Whatever he meant by this cryptic remark, there were others who felt they knew what the reason was. Viceroy Revilla Gigedo, in confidential instructions prepared for his successor in 1794, remarked that all classes in New Spain were improving their position in society except the Indians. He felt that it would be a difficult and lengthy process for them to improve themselves because their customs and habits prevented them from having any desire to do so. As an example of the problem he had in mind, he cited the case of the Crown's desire to provide the Indians with their own towns by grants of 180 square yards of land, or however much they might need to provide for themselves. But in spite of the opportunity, very few Indians were taking advantage of it. Since he had been viceroy, scarcely twelve Indian towns had been founded. The Indians, he went on, preferred work like cutting trees or making charcoal, which would give them immediate benefits, to agriculture, which required a period of waiting before the fruits were ready.[42]

41. Father Lasuén put forward the missionaries' view of the law in 1779 to Felipe de Neve as follows: "We are apostolic missionaries bound by papal bulls to depart from the missions as soon as we recognize that the neophytes, whom we have brought together by our missionary efforts, are sufficiently instructed in the divine law, and sufficiently competent to care for the economic welfare of their families and for the political government of their pueblos. When that stage is reached, they may then come under the jurisdiction of the parish priests sent by the bishops to whose care they are to be entrusted. As for us, we then return to our college; or we look for other Indians to take under instruction, beginning at their level of intelligence and continuing the training until they can exercise average discretion" (Kenneally, *Writings of Lasuén, 1,* 76); Bancroft, *California, 1,* 580.

42. Revillagigedo, *Instrucción reservada,* pp. 34 (item 150), 102 (items 407–81).

Probing further into what the authorities obviously considered a baffling problem, Manuel Abad y Queipo, Bishop of Michoacán, revealed some of its causes. Admitting that the Indians clung to their ancient customs, Abad y Queipo suggested that this was because they lived a life of enforced segregation from the Spaniards and the other racial groups in New Spain who could help them. Their color, ignorance, and poverty kept them apart from the rest of society, as did their language. In addition, the law prevented them from intermarrying or forming attachments with other groups. To make things even worse, the bishop continued, in an ill-advised effort to protect the Indians, they were not permitted to borrow more than trifling sums or to make business contracts. This deprived them, in his opinion, of any chance of improving their training or bettering themselves. Treated as if they were children, they had sunk into an apathetic, indifferent class. Abad y Queipo's cure for this situation was to integrate the Indians into the mainstream of society: destroy the segregation of the Indian towns by permitting non-Indians to buy land and settle in them, and in general, treat the Indians like other men. Views remarkably similar to those of Abad y Queipo are now being persuasively advanced by modern anthropologists.[43] The distinguished scientist and world traveler, Alexander von Humboldt, who was in New Spain in 1803, strongly backed the views of Abad y Queipo, and went further than the bishop could have done by accusing the creole landowners of wanting to keep the Indians in their degraded state for their own selfish reasons.[44] To the landowners' arguments that if the Indians

43. "Escritos del Obispo . . . Don Manuel Abad Queipo," in José María Luis Mora, *Obras sueltas* (2 vols. Paris, 1837), *1*, 55–56, 60, 69; Margaret Mead, *New Lives for Old* (New York, 1956), pp. 442–45.

44. He attributes the famous *Representation to the King* of 1799, however, to Fray Antonio de San Miguel (Humboldt, *Political Essay, 1*, 189, n.). Juan A. Ortega y Medina states that Fray Antonio de San Miguel "influenced" Abad y Queipo in drawing it up. Alejandro de Humboldt, *Ensayo político sobre el reino de la Nueva España*, ed. J. A. Ortega y Medina (Mexico, 1966), p. 229, n. 115.

were granted more liberty and permitted to enjoy the rights of man they would turn against the whites, Humboldt retorted that he had heard those who were opposed to freeing the serfs in Russia and other parts of Europe advance the same arguments. Humboldt warned his readers of the danger that so many of the eighteenth-century philosophers had fallen into of summarily passing judgment "on the moral or intellectual dispositions of nations from which we are separated by the multiplied obstacles which result from a difference in language and a difference of manners and customs." Finally, Humboldt added urgency to his plea for better treatment of the Indians: "It is therefore of the greatest importance, even for the security of the European families established for ages in the continent of the new world, that they should interest themselves in the Indians, and rescue them from their present barbarous, abject, and miserable condition."[45]

When foreign critics castigated the Spaniards for continuing to abuse the Indians in the way that the early conquistadors had done in the sixteenth century, however, they were not hard to refute. And when charges of cruelty were leveled against the missionaries in California, Governor José Joaquín de Arrillaga did not hesitate to exonerate them in his 1804 report.[46] It was not that the bad old days that Las Casas had described with both eloquence and exaggeration were returning; the complaint now was that the missions were taking too long to civilize their Indians. Governor Arrillaga reported to Viceroy Félix Berenguer de Marquina that the Indians on

45. Humboldt, *Political Essay, 1,* 171, 199–200, 203.

46. See Martín Fernández de Navarrete's reply to the charges of Charles Pierre Claret Fleurieu in *Relación del viage hecho por las goletas Sutil y Mexicana en el año de 1792* (Madrid, 1802), pp. v-vi, cxxxviii-cxxxix, cxlvi. Fleurieu criticized the Spanish advance to Monterey as a "usurpation" and a "project of iniquity" which the Spaniards tried to justify by associating God with it (*A Voyage Round the World* [2 vols. London, 1801], *1,* lvii). See also Bancroft, *California, 2,* 27, 163.

the coast in California were all subject to the missions, but he added, "if it comes to civilization, they still have far to go." He attributed this situation to a lack of sufficient efforts to civilize the Indians or to teach them the arts and too little interest in their comfort and culture. They still did not possess any property of their own, he pointed out; everything belonged to the community. In his opinion, this showed how backward they were. Nor did the governor approve of the methods used by the missionaries in converting the Indians, although he did not specify what he objected to. This did not mean, however, that the authorities were beginning to think that the missions were no longer serving a useful purpose. Viceroy Marqués de Branciforte, who was an enthusiastic promoter of colonization, also wanted to found new missions which, in his own words, "should be situated on frontiers or places close to villages of Indians who are restless or unwilling to embrace Religion." In his instructions to his successor, Azanza, Branciforte revealed what lay behind his thinking on this matter: he warned that a foreign foe might find allies among the unconverted California Indians or the rebel Yumas or the many other tribes of barbarians near the provinces of Sonora and New Mexico.[47]

The point of view of the Franciscan missionaries on the problem of civilizing the California Indians at about this time is perhaps best put by Father Lasuén. He admits, first of all, that "the greatest problem of the missionary" is "how to transform a savage race such as these [Indians] into a society that is human, Christian, civil, and industrious." "This can be accomplished," he continues, "only by 'denatu-

47. Arrillaga to Marquina, Dec. 7, 1801, AGN, Californias, *17*, 348; Branciforte to Príncipe de la Paz, June 26, 1796, AGI, Estado 25; *Instrucciones* (Mexico, 1867), p. 139. Some observers see a radical change in Spanish policy toward hostile tribes during this period, with missions giving way to reservations near frontier outposts. See Joseph F. Park, "Spanish Indian Policy in Northern Mexico, 1765–1810," *Arizona and the West, 4* (1962), 344.

ralizing' them. It is easy to see what an arduous task this is, for it requires them to act against nature." He felt, however, that the task was being accomplished: "it is being done successfully by means of patience, and by an unrelenting effort to make them realize that they are men."[48] Differences of opinion between the missionaries and the lay authorities on how long it should take to civilize the California Indians helped to promote misunderstandings between them, but often smaller, more practical matters caused friction.

An instance of this occurred in 1800 when Felipe de Goicoechea, comandante of the presidio at Santa Barbara, answered a set of fifteen questions about Indians at the mission there. After the comandante had written down his answers, Father Estevan Tapis, at the mission, in his turn answered the questionnaire and sometimes commented on the comandante's replies. Most of the eleven questions on the existing manuscript were factual ones, which the comandante and Father Tapis answered with little or no difference of opinion in their views. There were others, however, on which they either disagreed completely or did not entirely agree with each other.

One of the questions was whether the Indians were instructed in the "precise principal mysteries of our religion" before they were baptized. The comandante answered that the fathers instructed the pagan Indians for a week or so before they were baptized, but he did not know whether they emerged "with the necessary light about the articles of our religion" or not.[49] Father Tapis replied to this that in the view of the missionaries, "when an adult is baptized he is by then sufficiently instructed in the precise and principal

48. Kenneally, *Writings of Lasuén*, 2, 202.

49. On this question Father Lasuén stated in 1801: "It will happen but rarely that anyone is baptized after no more than a week of instruction. Fifteen, twenty, and thirty or more days are devoted to it, depending on what they observe of their aptitude and other circumstances" (Kenneally, *Writings of Lasuén*, 2, 200).

mysteries." Another question asked what the Indians were given to eat and whether it was sufficient to keep them going on the work they had to do. The comandante answered by saying flatly that the Indians did not get enough to eat to "resist the fatigues" of the work they were given. Father Tapis, after objecting to the comandante's use of the word "fatigues," replied that the Indians did get enough to eat and that they managed to feed their hens from the leftovers they had.

It is in their answers to two questions involving the Indians' labor, however, that the different opinions of the missionary father and the comandante may most clearly be seen. In his answer to one of these questions, Goicoechea summed up his thoughts by saying that the amount of work the Indians did, bearing in mind their food, clothing, and other factors (which he did not mention) should be moderated. He also thought that Indians doing piecework labored too long, and he commented that he was "moved with compassion" on the subject. In his reply, Father Tapis explained in detail exactly how much work certain jobs required. An Indian at the mission made forty adobe bricks a day, but he frequently did not have to work on Saturday because he had already made his weekly quota of bricks by Friday. Governor Arrillaga had ordered in 1793 that the daily quota of bricks was to be fifty, so that when Sergeant José María Ortega asked for Indians in 1794 to make bricks for a house outside the mission, he was permitted to use Indian labor on condition that each Indian should not make more than fifty bricks. He agreed to this condition, and the Indians made fifty bricks, but it turned out that the sergeant had increased the size of each brick. Father Tapis then turned to tile making. On the mission sixteen Indians made five hundred tiles a day, but in 1795 Comandante Goicoechea forced ten Indians to make five hundred tiles a day when they were working on the presidio, with the raw materials for the tiles farther off than they were on the mission. After they had worked four days at this rate, the Indians complained to the fathers that their hands and arms hurt. The missionaries were shocked but thought that the Indians were fooling them and advised them to continue to work. The next day, a Friday, they made 525 tiles, whereupon the comandante, on his Saturday visit to the mission, was asked about the matter. He said that this was the amount the soldiers used to make. The missionaries then suggested that ten soldiers and ten mission Indians be set to making tiles for a day, so that it could be determined who made the most. The comandante opposed this idea, however, and told the fathers that he did not need the Indians anymore because he had enough tiles.

The second question on which there was a sharp difference of opinion between the comandante and the father missionary was whether the missionaries allowed their Indians to have contact with gente de razón and whether they were punished if they went to the presidio, even when they had permission to leave the mission. Emphasizing his words, the comandante answered this by saying that at Santa Barbara the mission Indians were not allowed to associate with gente de razón and were punished if they did so, even if they had permission to leave the mission. He said he thought this a strange policy between people of the same nation, and it meant in practice that the Indian was prevented from making something extra for himself by working outside the mission. It also meant, he said, that it would take the Indians longer to become civilized. Father Tapis replied that Indians who worked for gente de razón when they had permission to leave the mission were not punished. He said that sometimes the missionary fathers did not allow Indians to work for gente de razón because they worked them too hard. Sergeant Ortega, he remarked, had given an Indian one day to make a pair of shoes, whereas on the mission they were given two days, and as a result the Indian complained and quit the work. Indians had been asked to work the grindstones, and when they got back at night their hands were covered with blisters. They were not sent anymore.[50]

Even after noting that Comandante Goicoechea did not have the advantage of commenting in his turn on Father Tapis' remarks, it is evident that the missionaries at Santa Barbara and the other missions were playing their traditional role of protecting the Indians against the tendency of some of the gente de razón to exploit them. On the other hand, the comandante's remark linking the mission Indians with his own men as belonging to the same nation shows that some of the ideals of the eighteenth-century philosophers were beginning to percolate down to lower levels. Furthermore, the accepted view of the Indians' basic inferiority was slowly to be challenged by a growing realization that if in the past he had built magnificent temples and pyramids possibly he had it in him to rise again. Buffon seems to have changed his earlier views on the Indians when he learned about the many fine ruined cities they had built. In New Spain, José Antonio Alzate became very much interested in Mexico's pre-Hispanic past and described former Indian civilizations in glowing colors to the point of toning down such unfavorable items as human sacrifice. Alzate became indignant at writers who brushed aside the Indians as stupid.[51]

While the situation on the missions continued along traditional lines, with the usual friction between the missionaries and the authorities, new efforts were made to offset Russian and other foreign encroachments by colonizing California. An attempt to occupy Bodega in 1793 failed, however, and although there was a good deal of discussion about a project of a certain militia lieutenant from Manila named Luis Pérez de Tagle to establish a colony of Filipinos in the area, nothing came of it. The viceroys in their instructions to

50. "Preguntas y Respuestas," Oct. 30, 1800, Santa Barbara Mission Archives (cited hereafter as SBMA), 390.

51. W. F. Cody, "An Index to the Periodicals published by José Antonio Alzate y Ramírez," *Hispanic American Historical Review, 33* (1953), 446.

their successors mentioned the desirability of populating California, but their accounts of what they had accomplished in the matter reveal how little was actually being done. Viceroy Azanza, for example, mentioned that his contribution had been to send twenty-one orphan children, boys and girls, to California from Mexico City. Marquina merely remarked about the need for colonization and mentioned the Tagle proposal.[52] On the other hand, a report by Father Salazar in 1796, at a time when there was considerable interest in colonizing California in New Spain, criticized the inhabitants of the recently established towns for colonists. They were lazy, Father Salazar said, more interested in gambling and playing the guitar than in working their land or educating their children. The young men grew up unrestrained and wandered among the Indian villages setting a bad example that would soon end in disaster. The pagan Indians did most of the work, took most of the crop, and were so well off that they were not interested in being converted and living at the missions.[53] Father Señán confirmed these strictures, but he added that there were good reasons for excusing the settlers in large part. They looked upon their work as useless, he explained, because they could get nothing for their grain at the presidios, which had no surplus farm implements, household utensils, or cloth to barter for it. And even if they were paid in cash there was nothing they could buy with their money, so they gambled it away. Nonetheless it looked as if the balance of the scales was about to turn: the despised Indian was beginning to appear in a more favorable light, and at the same time, the gente de razón were being depicted in highly unflattering terms.

That the world was to be turned upside down was shortly made clear by Napoleon's invasion of Spain in 1808 and by

52. Bancroft, *California, 1*, 515–17; Arrillaga to Marquina, Dec. 7, 1801, AGN, Californias, *17*, 348–51; *Instrucción reservada* (Mexico, 1960), p. 74; *Instrucciones* (Mexico, 1867), p. 211.

53. Bancroft, *California, 1*, 603–04; *Letters of Señán*, pp. 2–3.

Hidalgo's Grito de Dolores in New Spain in 1810. Out of the turbulence in Spain came legislation that was to make the Indian the equal of the white man, at least on paper, while in New Spain, Father Hidalgo, the Indian-loving priest of Dolores, urged his listeners to recover the lands that the hated Spaniards had stolen from their forefathers three hundred years before. A few years earlier the Inquisition had declared a book to be seditious because it contained "general principles on the equality and liberty of all men."[54] Now the Indians of New Spain, led by a priest, were to bear the main brunt of a war that was to defeat their former conquerors. That it was to take another hundred years before the Mexican Indian managed to achieve something of the promised equality for himself merely showed that the social results of the war were far harder to achieve than the political. At the time, however, both in Spain and in New Spain, liberals spoke of the rights of man as belonging to all, Indians included.

Legislation in favor of the Indian appeared rapidly in Spain: on May 26, 1810, he was freed from paying tribute; on October 15, 1810, he was included in a decree giving equal rights to all natives of Spain and the Americas; on February 9, 1811, he was permitted to raise any crop or engage in any business or profession he wanted, on equal terms with all other men. The liberal Spanish Constitution of 1812 declared that the Indian was to be considered a Spaniard and a citizen; by a decree of November 9, 1812, he was to be granted land, and those American colleges which provided scholarships for students were to reserve some for Indians. On September 8, 1813, it was decreed that the Indian, along with all other men, could not be punished by whipping.[55]

54. Monelisa Lina Pérez-Marchand, *Dos etapas ideológicas del siglo xviii en México* (Mexico, 1945), p. 123.

55. Manuel Dublán y José María Lozano, *Legislación mexicana* (52 vols. Mexico, 1876–1910), *1*, 331–32, 336, 340–41, 396, 425–26; the Spanish Constitution of 1812, Title 1, chap. 11, art. 5, and Title 11, chap. 4, art. 18.

Shortly after this flood of belated legislation recognizing the equality of man, the government at Madrid decided to make some inquiries regarding the general population of the Americas, and in particular the Indians. The questions touched on a multitude of matters concerning the Indians: their origin, their languages, their virtues and vices, their beverages, food, how much they paid for their land, and many more. Presumably, now that the Indian was to be equated with the Spaniard, it seemed a good idea to learn more about him. The questionnaire in due course reached California and was filled out by the missionaries.[56] One of the questions asked whether the Indians liked or disliked the Europeans and Americans. A majority of the replies, after pointing out that Indians did not distinguish between Spaniards and creoles, said they were indifferent toward them. In another question, the authorities wanted to know whether the Indians' moral and political state at that time showed any improvement over what contemporary historians said it had been some twenty years after the conquest. The answers to this question were as vague as the question itself, but by asking it the authorities seemed to be planning future moves against the missions. More revealing in some ways than their answers about the mission Indians were a few remarks by the missionaries about the white or non-Indian settlers in California. Father José María de Zalvidea of San Gabriel remarked that the pagan Indians, both men and women, worked in the fields and also as cooks, water carriers, and in other domestic services. This, he said, was one of the strongest reasons why the "people who are called rational" were so fond of doing nothing. And Father Ramón Olbes of Santa Barbara stated bluntly that "the people who are

56. Father Maynard Geiger has published the text of the questionnaire and the replies of some of the missionaries in a series of articles in *The Americas*: 5 (1949), 474–90; 6 (1950), 467–86; *10* (1953), 211–27; *12* (1955), 77–84. See also Zephyrin Engelhardt, *The Missions and Missionaries of California* (2d ed. 2 vols. Santa Barbara, 1929–30), 2, 569–600.

called rational in this province are so lazy and fond of idleness that they do not know how to do anything except ride horseback; they hold that any kind of work is dishonorable and it appears to them that only Indians should do the work; and so they ask for Indians to perform even the most essential services for them such as cooking, washing, and working in their gardens."[57] Similar situations arose in areas where Negro slaves performed the manual work, such as the Old South in the United States or Brazil during the Empire.

A strong movement now set in against the missions in the Americas. Canel Acevedo published an extravagant attack on the California missionaries in which he said that there was hardly a missionary returning to Mexico after fifteen years in California who did not bring back with him a fortune of 50,000 pesos, which he had made in trade or as a smuggler with foreign ships. To add to the injury, Canel Acevedo pictured the returned missionary as spending his ill-gotten gains on women in Mexico City. He assured his readers that this was not an infrequent occurrence and that he was not maligning the missionaries. Later in his book, however, he admitted that there had been some "very great and virtuous" men among the missionaries, like Father Antonio Margil or Father Junípero Serra. Canel Acevedo moved to less shaky ground in his attack when he criticized the length of time some of the missions had been in existence without being made into parishes. He also referred to the startling loss of life on the missions due to venereal and other diseases.[58]

Another attack on the California missions was drawn up by Francisco de Paula Tamariz y Moure, a Spanish naval officer who had visited California while serving as captain of one of the supply ships from San Blas, where he was stationed from 1805 to 1808. An English naval officer who met

57. Ciriaco González Carvajal, Ministro de Ultramar, "Interrogatorio," Oct. 6, 1812, SBMA, document 630.
58. Canel Acevedo, *Reflexiones*, pp. 126–28.

him in 1825, when Tamariz was fifty-three, described him as "a little vivacious, elderly man, a native of Andalusia . . . lame of one leg . . . excessively loquacious . . . [and provided with an] ever fertile imagination." Tamariz seems to have drawn up his report on California, which was to be of fundamental importance in the determination of both Spanish and Mexican policy toward the province, in 1812, when he was in Mexico City. He sent it to both Viceroy Venegas and his successor, Viceroy Calleja, without eliciting any known response. On his return to Cadiz late in 1813, he sent it to the authorities once more, letting them know that he would like to be governor of California. The three-man Spanish Council of Regency, which was in charge during the enforced absence of Ferdinand VII in France, refused to consider his plan, but nothing daunted, he sent it again to the new government established when Ferdinand returned to Madrid in May 1814. Here at last his neglected memorial, now entitled "On Improving the System of Government in Upper California," attracted favorable attention.[59]

Written at a time when the Mexican rebel leader José María Morelos was beginning to exert strength in the Acapulco area, Tamariz' memorial endeavored to show that the missionaries ran California in their own interests, without considering the interests of the settlers or of New Spain as a whole. California was sufficiently wealthy, if properly developed, he thought, to send food and other supplies to the needy viceregal government, but the missionaries were interested only in producing enough for their own needs. He accused the fathers of inducing the Indians into the missions to exploit them as manual workers; the missionaries did not know the Indians' language, and indeed he labeled them

59. R. W. H. Hardy, R.N., *Travels in the Interior of Mexico* (London, 1829), pp. 16–17; Francisco de Tamariz y Moure, Expediente de nobleza, Archivo-Museo Don Alvaro de Bazán, El Viso del Marqués, Ciudad Real, Spain (cited hereafter as AM), caja 43; his memorial is printed in *Las Misiones de la Alta California*, (2 vols. Mexico, 1914), 2, 89–117.

"so-called missionaries," alleging that they were simply *curas,* or parish priests. The missionaries, he felt, were harsh to the Indians, and their Indian policy hurt the colonists, for they would not allow pagan Indians to work in the towns, so that the settlers were forced to have recourse to mission Indians for their necessary manual labor. But the missionaries forced the settlers to pay two silver reales a day for mission Indians, which was ridiculous, he felt, in a region where "the natives do not know the value of money." Furthermore, it meant that most years the settlers did not sow any crops because they could not afford to pay such wages. His solution to the problem was to secularize the missions but to keep the Indians working on the land in the same way that the missionaries had done. The government would then benefit from the sale of the former mission products, while the missionaries would become parish priests with control only over religious matters. He conceded that administering the new system would be more expensive, for majordomos and other overseers would have to be paid, but he pointed out that the government would not have to pay stipends to the missionaries, and the increase in crops would benefit both California and New Spain.

Tamariz' arguments were probably more accurate as reflections of the settlers' complaints against the missionaries than as a realistic appraisal of the causes of California's underdevelopment. Anti-clericalism, however, had gained a strong foothold in Spain, as it did in New Spain, and to blame the missionaries for all the economic ills of California did not seem incongruous. It may be noted also that Tamariz had a poor opinion of the California Indians: they were "sad, lazy, abandoned by nature, and thieves by custom," but on the other hand, they could be managed easily, being "docile and easy to persuade with gentle treatment."[60] Again, his new system of development depended on Indian labor, and

60. *Misiones,* 2, 90–92, 94–96, 99, 102–03, 106–07.

it may be presumed that under the paid administrators the Indians' wages would be kept down to a level that would be approved by the settlers.

That Tamariz' memorial was in tune with his times is evident from the fact that shortly before he returned to Spain in December 1813, the Cortes, meeting at Cádiz, passed a general law secularizing all missions. The proposal had been presented to the Cortes on September 4 and 7, 1813, by a four-man committee on overseas affairs; it became law on September 13, 1813.[61] The law provided that all missions in overseas provinces which had been in existence ten years were to be immediately turned over to the secular clergy "without any excuse or pretext of any kind." The missionaries who left these establishments were to apply for permission to establish new missions in other unsettled regions. The missionaries were also to cease immediately their administration of the haciendas of the Indians, who were to select individuals from among themselves, through their town councils and with the assistance of the superior political chief, to run the former missions. The decree further stated that mission lands were to be distributed as private property according to a previous land-grant decree passed on January 4, 1813. This had provided that uncultivated, unsurveyed land and state-owned land was to be distributed with full possession and boundaries duly marked, so that its owners might fence it and use it in any way they wished. Residents of towns, whose jurisdiction included the land to be granted, were to have priority in obtaining it. Applying this last provision to the missions would mean that the mission Indians would have priority in obtaining the lands of their former missions, but it also implied that other persons might obtain this land after the former mission Indians had obtained their share of it.[62] This important decree secularizing the

61. *Diario de las discusiones y actas de las Cortes,* 22 (Cádiz, 1813).

62. Francisco de la Maza, *Código de colonización y terrenos baldíos* (Mexico, 1893), pp. 152–53; Dublán y Lozano, *Legislación, 1,* 397–99.

missions was to be the basis for all future moves in this direction in California until 1833.

The Tamariz memorial interested the Madrid government in reform in California. On July 5, 1814, the authorities sent Tamariz' statement to Viceroy Calleja. With it came instructions to appoint a junta or commission of five or seven men in Mexico City to examine the memorial, agree upon the most appropriate means whereby the abuses it outlined, if they actually existed, might be corrected, and suggest what might be done to improve the government of California in order to increase its population and enable it to prosper.[63] Calleja decided that the commission should consist of seven men and a secretary without vote. On July 28, 1815, he appointed Antonio Torres Torija, a distinguished lawyer from Puebla who was then an honorary judge of the Audiencia of Guadalajara, president of the commission. The remaining members, selected with the help of the Consulado of Mexico City, were Gonzalo López de Haro, the naval officer who had been in command of the *San Carlos* in the 1788 expedition which had finally succeeded in getting in touch with the Russians; Nicolás Carrión, a high official in the Tribunal of Accounts; Captain Juan Ignacio González Vértiz; Captain Joaquín Cortina González, who was almoner of the College of San Fernando; Lieutenant Juan Manuel de la Lama; and Juan Lorenzo de Antepara, a Mexico City merchant. The first secretary of the commission was Manuel González de Ibarra, then a clerk in the Tribunal of Accounts. González de Ibarra was shortly replaced as secretary by Tomás de Suria, a former engraver in the mint who became an auditor of payments in the accounting office. Suria had gone on the Malaspina expedition to the northwest coast as an official artist and had had some experience in California.[64]

63. *Misiones, 2,* 111–12.

64. Calleja to Torres Torija, July 28, 1815, Frederick W. Beinecke Collection, Yale University Library, New Haven, Conn. (cited hereafter as BC); José Mariano Beristain de Souza, *Biblioteca hispano-americano*

According to Tamariz, who returned to New Spain in 1816 to take over a position in the treasury at Chihuahua, the first meeting of the commission was presided over by Viceroy Calleja. But little or nothing seems to have been accomplished until the new viceroy, Juan Ruiz de Apodaca, arrived in August 1816. With Apodaca in the chair, the commission met in the Viceregal Palace on July 5, 1817, and Secretary Suria read a summary of Tamariz' memorial, which he followed with some observations of his own. Anxious to tone down Tamariz' indictment of the missionary fathers in order not to alarm them, Suria nonetheless favored secularization of the missions. On the economic side, he felt that freedom of trade would bring prosperity, which would in turn attract immigrants to California. Among the other business transacted at this meeting, it was decided that President Torres Torija should write a letter to Father Juan Calzada, guardian of the College of San Fernando, asking why the Franciscan missions had not been made into parishes, since they had been in existence some forty years. For some reason this letter was not sent until February 8, 1818.[65]

Father Calzada's answer was that the Indians were far from ready for the change, and the bishop of Sonora, whose diocese included the missions in California, pointed out that there were not enough secular priests to take over from the missionaries. As a matter of fact, the College of San Fernando had proposed late in 1817 to cede nine of the California missions to the Franciscan College of Missions

---

septentrional (3d ed. 5 vols. Mexico, n.d.), 5, 40–41; Justino Fernández, *Tomás de Suria y su viaje con Malaspina* (Mexico, 1939), p. 107; Henry R. Wagner, "Journal of Tomás de Suria of his Voyage with Malaspina to the Northwest Coast of America in 1791," *Pacific Historical Review*, 5 (1936), 236.

65. Tamariz to Viceroy Conde del Venadito, Nov. 20, 1820, BC; Junta de California, BL transcript, Secretaría de Gobernación, legajo 1830–34, pt. 3.

at Orizaba because of a shortage of fathers in its own college.[66]

Although busy with his duties at Chihuahua, Tamariz did not forget about his California project; but he was never able to find out on his visits to Mexico City what the commission was doing about it. On one occasion when Tamariz visited his office, Torres Torija showed him a pile of commission papers on his desk and spoke about the need for "time and patience." The slow monotony of the commission's pace was enlivened briefly, however, when one of its members, Captain Joaquín Cortina González, sent Father Juan Rivas, a Dominican who was the supply officer in Mexico City for the missions of Lower California, a copy of Tamariz' report for his comments. Father Rivas' reply was an indignant rebuttal of virtually everything in the report. He even had an explanation for Tamariz' unfriendly attitude toward the Franciscans: he said that Tamariz and the chaplain of his ship, Father José María Afanador, had been seducing Indian women at Missions San Buenaventura and San Juan Capistrano. Father Rivas also seized the opportunity to blast the colonists in California, whom Tamariz had praised, as being for the most part vicious and lazy. According to Suria, the commission on the Californias continued with its labors until the death of its president, Antonio Torres Torija—the date of whose decease is not known—when its activities were suspended. It was to be revived again, however, when Mexico took over after winning its independence in 1821.[67]

That California during the closing years of Spanish rule had reached a stage of economic stagnation and general discontent is amply confirmed. Travelers reported that its

66. Hutchinson, "Mexican Government," pp. 340–41. The statement on p. 340 of this article that the diocese of the Bishop of Durango included the California missions is an error. It should read Bishop of Sonora. SBMA, document 697; AGN, Californias, 45, 174.

67. Tamariz to Conde del Venadito, Nov. 20, 1820, BC; Misiones, 2, 155–56, 190–91; AGN, Californias, 45, 174.

commerce was nonexistent and that everyone was reduced to a subsistence level. There were reports of the discontent of the troops, who had not received their pay since the beginning of the war in 1810, and even the missionaries were beginning to lose their patience. As for the mission Indians, officials at the Royal Tribunal of Accounts in Mexico City complained that the missionaries had not made them into "useful vassals of the King," while Governor Sola sent a bitter dispatch to Viceroy Conde de Venadito complaining that when Monterey was attacked by Bouchard's Argentine rebels the Indians, far from helping to resist the invaders, had fled to the hills. Russian visitors to California on a round the world expedition in 1816 criticized the missionaries for not trying hard enough to civilize the Indians. "I have never seen [a mission Indian] laugh," one of the members of the expedition wrote, "I have never seen one look one in the face. They look as though they are interested in nothing."[68]

In Mexico the Indians' stock was steadily rising. Insurgent leaders like Hidalgo, Morelos, and later Iturbide went on record in favor of the Indian. The rebel Constitution of Apatzingán in 1814 gave the Indians citizenship, and a leading Mexican intellectual praised Las Casas in 1816 as "a tireless agent of the Indians." There was also a new sensitivity toward the Indians' point of view. In 1817 Viceroy Apodaca received an anonymous letter protesting against a move to permit a play called "The Conquest of Mexico" to be staged in Mexico City, on the ground that the lower classes (in other words, the Indians) would be aroused by the word "conquest." The play had, in fact, been banned for this very reason—because of what Apodaca called the "foreign philosophism adopted by some of our modernists against the old heroic Spaniards who loved their King and their

68. Carlos María García report, Sept. 28, 1818, AGI, Estado 32, 4M568, items 26–29; AGN, Californias, 17, 217–19; Conde del Venadito to Primer Secretario de Estado, Mar. 31, 1819, AGI, Estado 33, Mexico 14; Mahr, Visit of the "Rurik," pp. 33, 61, 99.

Country." Apodaca agreed that the play should be banned, not because it might arouse trouble—he did not think it would—but because he was told it was dull and not worth showing.[69]

When the Spanish Constitution of 1812, which had been annulled on Ferdinand VII's return to the throne in 1814, was once more proclaimed in Mexico on May 31, 1820, the Indian was restored to his position of equality with the white man. Proclamation of the Constitution was soon followed by a flood of pamphlets informing the Indians of their new status. "The name Indian has gone now," one of them announced. "We are all Spaniards," said another. "Any man whatever country he is from," began another in words that sound familiar today, "and whatever his color, should be esteemed or despised according to whether his works do credit or discredit to the excellence of his being, without any other consideration except this one having any influence on the matter."[70]

For the California missionaries, however, the new changes and unexpected pressures that accompanied them were anything but satisfactory. It is true that Governor Sola officially praised them for the horses and other supplies they had furnished when the rebels under Bouchard attacked Monterey; they also received a letter of commendation from Father Juan Buenaventura Bestard, the Franciscan Comisario General of the Indies in Spain. Father Bestard praised them for having kept their flock faithful to the king thus far in the civil war in New Spain, and he did not doubt that they would continue to do so, for, he added, "Your Reverences will inform them that it is impossible for a man who is unfaithful to the King to be faithful to God." Most of the missionaries

69. Hutchinson, "Mexican government," p. 340; Constitution of Apatzingán, chap. 3, art. 13; Lewis Hanke and Manuel Giménez Fernández, *Bartolomé de Las Casas* (Santiago, Chile, 1954), item 584; Apodaca to Ministro de Estado, October 1817, AGI, Estado 31, Mexico 12.

70. *La Chanfaina se-quita* (Mexico, 1820); *La Malinche de la constitución* (Mexico, 1820); *Parabién de los indios* (Mexico, 1820).

in California were to take this injunction literally and find themselves after independence in difficulties with the Mexican government.[71]

Gratifying to the Franciscans as these dispatches may have been, their general position in California was becoming highly unsatisfactory. Their new difficulties seem to have started with Governor Sola's taking of the oath to the Constitution of 1812 in October 1820. It was followed by publication of the secularization decree of September 13, 1813, on January 20, 1821.[72] On February 7 Father Guardian Baldomero López wrote to Father Mariano Payeras, president of the California missions, giving instructions that if the bishop of Sonora came to California, it would be to take over the missions in accordance with the secularization decree. Father López said he did not think the bishop could actually secularize the missions because he did not have enough clergy to take over, and the Franciscans would be asked to continue. In his view, this gave the order an opportunity to show its disinterestedness and willingness to work; he felt they should not consent to continue unless the government urgently asked them to do so, and then only if the government agreed to fulfill its commitments and to provide the means for founding new missions in the Tulare region or wherever the Father President in California thought best. In the remainder of his letter, Father López described the reprehensible activities of the reformers, whose "heated imaginations" had made them into visionaries without vision, and who had decreed the suppression of the monasteries, the military orders, the hospital orders, and other regular orders except for the overseas missionaries. All convents belonging to the same order were to be joined together so that no city would have more than one of each.[73]

71. Sola statement, July 6, 1819, SBMA, document 765; Bestard to Missionaries, Aug. 29, 1818, SBMA, document 735.

72. Bancroft, *California*, 2, 265, 431.

73. López to Mariano Payeras, Feb. 7, 1821, SBMA, document 827.

The effect of these new and revolutionary changes was not slow in making itself felt in far-off California. Shortly after he had taken the oath to the Constitution of 1812, Governor Sola began to press for changes which he had previously favored but had done nothing to put into effect. After informing Father Payeras that he regarded the missionaries as administrators of haciendas belonging to the Indians, Sola demanded that in future the fathers were to be held strictly accountable for all the sales of mission products to ships. They must render to him the original invoices and other bills for these transactions. Furthermore, they were to provide him with full information about their resources. He also thought that the conversion of the missions into parishes had been delayed overly long, and he began a policy of immediately releasing the most capable Indians to establish two new towns, one in the north, one in the south, or to add Indian sections to already founded non-Indian towns. Father Payeras reported to his college that Governor Sola's changes were unacceptable. He said it had taken him five hours to persuade the governor not to enforce his requirement that the originals of all mission accounts be sent to him for that year and until the viceroy handed down a decision on the matter. Since, so far as he knew, the governor had not asked any other exporter to hand over his documents, Father Payeras was convinced that Sola had been too ready to believe what he suspected or what someone had told him. Payeras admitted that if one were to ask many of the non-Indian settlers how much property such and such a mission had, the answer would come without hesitation that it owned immense wealth in land and buildings and that its coffers were filled with money. People who answered like that, went on Father Payeras, did not realize that each mission had some one thousand Indian neophytes in it, and when their property was concentrated at one point it looked like a fortune. He recalled a story told about La Pérouse and Father Lasuén. La Pérouse asked how much Father Lasuén had harvested from his mission; Lasuén told him; La Pérouse thereupon asked him how many Indians were in the mission. On being informed, La Pérouse calculated how much each of them would have and then replied in bad Spanish, "Mucho poco, Señor."

Father Payeras pointed out that since 1810 the missions had assisted the settlers and the troops with food, clothes, and money amounting to about 500,000 pesos. All this had been done without elaborate written accounts, just on the good word of the missionaries, whose economy and frugality had been responsible for the successful management of the missions. But now Sola wanted to treat the missionaries like clerks or cashiers who were to be responsible for their accounts. If this were done, Father Payeras prophesied, within two years the missionaries would be in difficulties and would be made to look like criminals, no matter how hard they struggled with the mountain of paper work. Payeras had told Sola that he could not do this. The missionaries, he said, were old, tired, and ailing; they were buried in these isolated regions without the possibility of relief and without resources, and they might even be weary of their work by this time. Governor Sola replied by suggesting that if they were tired the missionaries should give up their control of the temporalities, to which Father Payeras answered that the king had charged them to take care of the temporalities and had not asked any accounting from them but their word as religious. If the temporalities were handed over to an official, he went on, the resulting divided responsibility would be likely to cause friction, and the work of the missions would be slowed down. Furthermore, many of the missions were beginning a new spiritual conquest of the Tulares region in the interior, and non-Christian Indians were coming in large numbers to be baptized. This was a time when the missionaries needed the temporalities, and this was what they were for. The Indians with whom the missionaries dealt were not rational civilized persons like those whom the

Apostles baptized, but so rough and animal-like "that it is necessary to teach them how to be people." To domesticate and tame them, he said, required "bread in the hand, clothing, and exquisite patience, and above all the gentle yoke of the gospel."

There is a bitter taste to Father Payeras' letter because it is clear he thought that Governor Sola was simply anxious to get hold of the wealth of the missions for his own purposes. Father Payeras deplored the governor's experiment in secularizing certain more advanced Indians from the missions. These Indians, he said, were the right hand of the missionaries on whom they depended to keep the missions going. Now, in the name of equality, the Indian who had behaved well at the mission—and who was supposedly as free and as much the master of his own actions as a Spaniard—was to be assigned by the authorities against his will to some town, perhaps far from his relatives and his tribe, where people spoke another language. Father Payeras suggested that if they wanted to found towns, all they needed to do was change the names of the mission communities and they would have them, for the missions, he admitted, were not designed to last forever. If the missions were secularized, he proposed that the missionaries advance farther into the frontier regions to the north or the east or even follow the northwest coast into the lands held by foreigners at Bodega or on the Columbia River, for he knew that the Indians there wanted the Franciscans to provide missions for them.[74]

When Mexico officially declared its independence from Spain on September 28, 1821, California was still largely unsettled, while the danger from the Russians at Bodega had greatly increased. Mutual distrust between the military and the missionaries had grown worse, and a new egalitarian attitude toward the Indians on the missions promised future trouble. Governor Sola had already begun the process of

74. Mariano Payeras to College of San Fernando, June 18, 1821, SBMA, document 833.

secularization, which was to be the major problem of the Mexican period of California history. In addition, another serious complication was to arise which had been absent from the period of Spanish control: Spaniards themselves were soon to be considered foreign enemies on Mexican soil, and at first virtually all the missionaries were Spaniards. These difficulties, together with a number of others equally new, faced Mexico as she took over from Spain on the California frontier.

Chapter Three

Mexico Takes Over

When Mexico won her independence from Spain, it did not take her statesmen long to discover that a number of pressing problems confronted them in the distant province of California, of which the most dangerous, in their view, was the presence of the Russian settlement at Ross. Carlos María Bustamante, the future congressman from Oaxaca, writing from his prison at Veracruz in 1819, had already noted the formidable increase of Russian power after the defeat of Napoleon; and William Davis Robinson, the American who had fought for the insurgents in the war for independence, reported in January 1821, before independence was won: "There is no circumstance which has excited more indignation among the Mexican people, than that of the Russians having made an establishment at Badoga Point [Bodega], and if the Mexican revolutionists had succeeded in their struggle for independence, one of the first acts of the new government would have been the expulsion of the Russians from that post."[1]

The possible dangers resulting from the Russian settlement in California were emphasized in the United States early in 1821, as a result of a congressional inquiry into the

1. Bustamante, "Medidas," BL; *Niles Register* (Mar. 10, 1821), p. 24.

desirability of occupying the Columbia River, and American newspapers carried further warnings about the strength of the Russian base at Bodega. In France, a book attributed to Comte Beaumont de Brivazac appeared in 1822. Entitled *Europe and its Colonies,* it described Russia as a horrendous monster, slowly but surely devouring other countries. One of the areas threatened by this monster, the author believed, was the northwest coast of America. According to Brivazac, Spain had secretly ceded California to Russia.[2]

In Mexico, William Davis Robinson's prophecy of immediate concern with Russian encroachment became a fact almost at once. Some two weeks after the provisional governing junta, whose president was the victorious General Agustín de Iturbide, declared Mexico's independence from Spain on September 28, 1821, Tadeo Ortiz de Ayala, a prominent revolutionary figure from Jalisco, dedicated his *Summary of the Statistics of the Mexican Empire* to Iturbide. In this influential little book, Ortiz pointed out that the Russians at Bodega were but seventy-eight miles (thirty *leguas)* from the magnificent port of San Francisco, and their presence there might be due to some secret agreement with Spain. Among his suggestions for dealing with this problem was one to reopen communication by land between California and Sonora, and California and New Mexico.[3] Other more urgent warnings came from Colonel José Antonio de Andrade, the interim superior political chief of New Galicia, who stressed the desire of both the Russians and the Americans to expand on the northwest coast and lamented the unprepared state of the neglected California garrison to cope with any attack. Colonel Andrade thought that the Russians

2. 16th Congress, 2d Session, no. 497, American State Papers, Miscellaneous, 2 (Washington, D.C., 1834), pp. 631, 633; *National Intelligencer* (Jan. 25, 1821); *Niles Register* (Mar. 10, 1821); Beaumont de Brivazac, *L'Europe et ses colonies* (2 vols. Paris, 1822), *1, 3, 29.*

3. Tadeo Ortiz de Ayala, *Resumen de la estadistica del imperio mexicano* (Mexico, 1822), p. 98.

would seek to take advantage of what they might suppose was an agitated and disorganized period for Mexico, following its independence, by moving against California. He also remarked that Spain had been on the point of making a treaty with Russia to cede California to that country when negotiations were proceeding for the delivery of Russian warships. In her present greatly weakened state, Colonel Andrade went on, Spain might find it advantageous to make that cession.[4]

Mexican forebodings about the insecurity of California were finally brought together by a three-man Committee on Foreign Relations appointed by the governing junta and headed by the distinguished lawyer Juan Francisco de Azcárate.[5] On December 29, 1821, shortly before the new Congress, which was to take the place of the governing junta, convened, the Azcárate committee presented its important report on foreign policy. Its section on Russia began: "This great power which extending its arms over Europe and Asia seems to be going to dominate the old world, has also very advanced designs on the new." In the committee's view, however, this "political colossus," which was such a dangerous neighbor, faced imminent foreign problems in Europe and domestic problems within its own enormous expanse which were likely to distract its attention from its distant California colony. Unable to provide the necessary force to protect this colony, the committee thought, Russia would readily agree to make a boundary treaty with the Mexican Empire. The committee felt that Mexico should endeavor to persuade the Russians to withdraw, not only from Bodega but also from any other settlement they had on the coast south of the Columbia River. If this could be done, the

4. Andrade to Agustín de Iturbide, Oct. 22, 1821, AGN, Provincias Internas, 23, 131, 133–34; Manuel Cambre, *Gobiernos y gobernantes de Jalisco* (Guadalajara, 1910), p. 4.

5. The other members of the committee were Count Casa de Heras Soto and José Sánchez Enciso.

committee pointed out, the United States possessions on the Columbia would provide a bulwark of defense between the Mexican Empire and the Russians. The committee urged that this be done as soon as possible.[6]

That the Mexican government took the recommendations of the Azcárate committee seriously is revealed by the instructions it provided for Canon Agustín Fernández de San Vicente, of the cathedral at Durango, who, as will be seen, went as a commissioner to California in 1822 to persuade the missionaries to accept the new Mexican Empire. The government ordered the canon to find out how dangerous were the Russian and American establishments on the northwest coast, to discover whether the Americans had moved south from the Columbia to San Francisco Bay, and to report what the strength of the Russians was at Bodega. So varied was the information on these matters the canon picked up in Monterey that he decided to go overland to Bodega and Ross to find out what was happening. Although he found that they were held by a handful of soldiers and a few Indians, he was informed that the Russian establishments on the northwest coast could not survive without the meat and grain of California. "They are almost reduced to seal meat," he reported, "and have little even of that." Since Rezanov's visit to California in 1806, he added, this was well known in Monterey. He was convinced that the Russians had designs on California, but since their forces were weak, if the Mexican government took prompt action he did not doubt that it could maintain its boundary line. If, however, nothing was done, he stated categorically, "We shall lose the precious and fertile Province of California, the western key to our continent." According to Russian foreign office sources, the canon demanded while he was in Ross that the Russians produce documents showing their right to the territory they

6. Juan Francisco de Azcárate, *Un programa de política internacional* (Mexico, 1932), pp. 22, 24.

occupied. When these were not forthcoming, he stated that Ross was Mexican territory, and the Russians must evacuate it within six months. When he returned to Mexico in 1823, he brought with him three Russian deserters, so that they might confirm Russian designs on California.[7]

It is clear from other developments that the Russian government was certainly interested in strengthening its position on the northwest coast at this time. A first indication of its plans may be seen in the tsar's famous *ukase* of September 4/16, 1821, which forbade all foreign ships from trading, fishing, or even landing on the northwest coast from 51 degrees to the Bering Strait. A second ukase of September 13/25, 1821, continued the exclusive privileges of the Russian-American Company for twenty years and extended the area of its monopoly south from the existing point at parallel 55 to parallel 51.[8] In justification of this move to the south, the Russian minister at Washington, Pierre de Polética, tried to impress Secretary of State John Quincy Adams by stating that in 1789 López de Haro in the *San Carlos* had found 462 descendants of the men left on the coast by Alexei Chirikov in 1741. A major difficulty about this story is that Polética claimed these Russian colonists had been found in latitudes 48 and 49, whereas Chirikov had marooned his men on shore at about latitude 57 degrees.[9]

At the same time that the Russian minister in Washington was referring to the supposed descendants of Chirikov's

7. Agustín Fernández de San Vicente Report to José Ygnacio García Illueca, Apr. 12, 1823 (copy), BC; AGN, Provincias Internas, 23, 142; Okun, *Russian-American Company*, pp. 133–34.

8. According to the Julian Calendar in use in Russia the date was Sept. 4, 1821; by the Gregorian Calendar Sept. 16, 1821. For the text of the ukase of Sept. 4/16, 1821, see 58th Congress, 2d Session, Senate Document no. 162. *Alaskan Boundary Tribunal, 1* (Washington, D.C., 1904), pt. 2, pp. 9–10.

9. Ibid., Appendix, p. 38. See above, p. 2; this discrepancy had already been pointed out. Henry Middleton, U.S. Minister to Russia, duly informed Secretary Adams of this in 1823 in his *Confidential Memorial* (ibid., Appendix, p. 60).

crews, the Russian-American Company at St. Petersburg was giving instructions to its manager on the northwest coast to try to find this lost colony. As for Ross, the company informed its representatives that its California colony had been started in 1812 with the tsar's permission. The land had been bought from the Indians, and it had not been previously colonized by any European country or by the United States. Spain, the company officials concluded, had no ownership rights to Ross. It might appear from this correspondence that the company was unaware that Mexico had succeeded to Spain's former position in California, but in fact they knew of this. On April 28, 1822, they informed their manager, M. F. Muraviev, that Spanish power in America, both north and south of the equator, had gone, and with it had also gone Spanish laws forbidding foreigners to trade in those areas.[10]

While attention in Mexico was now to be centered upon the rise of Iturbide to emperor in May 1822 and his rapid decline and exile in March 1823, the stage was being prepared in Washington for a confrontation between the United States and Russia over the northwest coast. The new Mexican foreign minister under the interim government known as the Supreme Executive Power, which followed Iturbide's fall, was Lucas Alamán, an unusually able and experienced man. From his residence in Philadelphia, Colonel José Anastasio Torrens, the Mexican chargé d'affaires, informed Alamán in June 1823 of rumors that the Russians were planning to seize everything they could on the northwest coast in order to dominate the Pacific and monopolize trade with India. On November 22, 1823, after being instructed by Alamán to find out more about Russian moves in the California area, Torrens reported that it was being said Spain had ceded the Californias to Russia before Mexico had become independent and before the Spanish treaty of 1819

10. Headquarters to M. F. Muraviev, Mar. 3, Apr. 28, July 18, 1822, RRAC.

with the United States, by which the United States had fallen heir to Spanish claims on the northwest coast from 42 degrees to 50 degrees. Torrens felt that in view of the influence that Russia then had at Madrid, it might be claimed that such a treaty had been made. He thought that the interest the Russian legation was taking in Mexican affairs confirmed his suspicions.[11]

While Torrens, unable from lack of funds even to travel to Washington to present his credentials to President Monroe, was forced to play an observer's role on the sidelines, Secretary of State Adams busied himself with the affairs of Russia on the northwest coast. In a letter to a Boston correspondent on July 15, 1823, Adams asked, "But what right has Russia to any colonial footing on the *Continent* of North America? Has she any that we are bound to recognize? And is it not time for the American *nations* to inform the Sovereigns of Europe that the American continents are no longer open to the settlement of *new* Russian colonies?"[12]

Isolated as he was from diplomatic negotiations that deeply concerned his country, Torrens was nonetheless able to keep well abreast of developments. He reported to Alamán on November 22 that he had been assured the President of the United States had protested to Russia that he would not permit any European nation to establish itself on the American continent, and the President would speak of this in his message at the opening of Congress the following month.[13]

11. José A. Torrens to Secretario de Relaciones, June 21, 1823, in Enrique Santibañez, ed., *La Diplomacia mexicana* (2 vols. Mexico, 1910–12), 2, 12, 26–27, 50.

12. Italics by Adams; J. Q. Adams to James Lloyd, July 15, 1823, Adams Letterbook, May 1825, pp. 240–42, reel 147, microfilm, Alderman Library, University of Virginia. The letter is reproduced in Samuel Flagg Bemis, *John Quincy Adams and the Foundations of American Foreign Policy* (New York, 1949), p. 515, n. 13.

13. Santibañez, *Diplomacia*, p. 50. Actually Adams had protested to the Russian minister, Baron Tuyll, on July 17, 1823. John Quincy Adams, *Memoirs, 6,* 163.

Four days after Torrens reported to his government on the noncolonization principle, which was indeed to be included in President Monroe's famous message, Secretary Adams explained at a cabinet meeting that if the Holy Alliance actually did invade Latin America, they would divide it among themselves and colonize it. Russia, Adams thought, might take California, Peru, and Chile, while France took Mexico and England seized Cuba. "I thought," noted Adams in his memoirs, "we could not too soon take our stand to repel it."[14]

Another method of partitioning the former Spanish-American Empire was being rumored in Mexico at this time: England was to get Peru and Buenos Aires, France was to receive Colombia, and Spain was to take Mexico. Perhaps significantly, it agreed with the plan mentioned by Adams on only one point: Russia was to have California.[15] While rumors such as these were in circulation, Lieutenant Dimitry Zavalishin, a Russian naval officer, arrived in California in September 1823 and proceeded to try to put them into practice. He wanted to make San Francisco a Russian naval base and to colonize with Russians the area between San Francisco and the American settlement at the Columbia River. He hoped to be able to persuade officials of the government in California to declare their independence of Mexico, after which Russians would be invited to come in as settlers, and eventually California would come under the rule of Russia. With its base at San Francisco, a Russian fleet would be able to dominate the Pacific, control trade with China, and restrain the influence of the United States and England. Unable to make any headway with California government officials, Zavalishin, according to his own account of his career in California, tried to win over some of the missionaries by posing

14. Adams, *Memoirs, 6, 207*.

15. Carlos María Bustamante, *Diario histórico de México* (Zacatecas, 1896), p. 568.

as an enemy of the Masons (the source of all' evil according to certain conservative circles in Mexico at the time) and a supporter of monarchy. Zavalishin recorded that Father José Altimira, a padre at the newest and most northern of the missions, San Francisco Solano, listened with interest to his description of a mythical Military Order of Restoration, supposedly under the auspices of the tsar, which was to help the missionaries. It is of interest that according to his plans the Russian-American Company was to pledge itself not to molest the missions and was to permit them to retain their "Indian laborers." About the time that Zavalishin was beginning to think his subversive techniques were having some effect, he was suddenly recalled to Russia. On his return to St. Petersburg, the Russian-American Company became enthusiastic about his plans for improving the operations of the company and offered him the position of manager of the Ross colony. The necessary approval of the tsar, who was reported as saying at about this time that he "was much too busy with Greece to worry about the Spanish Colonies," was not forthcoming, however. Zavalishin's final suggestion that Russia annex California was turned down.[16]

It may perhaps be assumed that President Monroe's message of December 3, 1823, played its part in persuading the Russian government against backing wild schemes such as Zavalishin's. At all events, Torrens forwarded the text of the message to his government on December 6, with the remark that it was "very satisfactory." He added that the noncolonization principle in the message, which he cited, would form the basis for the future boundary negotiations between Russia and the United States on the northwest coast. Torrens would undoubtedly also have approved of the text of the treaty between the United States and Russia, signed on April

16. Lobanov-Rostovsky, *Russia and Europe*, p. 402; Okun *Russian-American Company*, pp. 111, 134–39; Anatole G. Mazour, "Dimitry Zavalishin: Dreamer of a Russian-American Empire," *Pacific Historical Review*, 5 (1936), 26–37.

5/17, 1824, which stated in article three that Russia would not from that date form an establishment on the northwest coast south of 54 degrees, 40 minutes. On the other hand, the Russian foreign minister, Count Nesselrode, considered that Ross was situated too far south to be part of the northwest coast, and therefore the provision not to form new establishments did not apply to the Ross colony. As far as Russia was concerned, she was still free to expand in California.[17]

Dangerous as Russian proximity to Mexico's settlements in California appeared to be, nothing could be done on the diplomatic level to promote the security of the area until Russia recognized Mexican independence. That she was unlikely to do so until Spain took this step was also clear. Successive Mexican governments, therefore, began to devote themselves to the difficult task so long undertaken by Spain: strengthening California by populating it and developing it commercially.

Before this could be begun, however, a great deal of necessary information about California had to be collected and digested. Few people in Mexico knew anything about California, and communication with the authorities there was incredibly slow; as late as March 8, 1822, José Manuel de Herrera, minister of foreign affairs, whose department took charge of civil affairs in California, had not received a single dispatch from that province. To make the situation more difficult, rumors and conflicting reports from ships' captains soon began to flood Mexico City. According to one account, Governor Sola, a Spaniard, had been completely opposed to Mexican independence, although it was argued that he would do nothing to stop it.[18] Disquieting information also began to

17. Santibañez, *Diplomacia*, p. 67; *Alaskan Boundary Tribunal, 1,* Appendix, pp. 11, 74, 168.

18. *Memoria presentada al Soberano Congreso por el Secretario de Relaciones* (Mexico, 1822), p. 7; Gonzalo Ulloa to Pedro Celestino Negrete, San Blas, Jan. 1, 1822, Andrade to Supremo Consejo de Regencia, Dec. 10, 1821, AGN, Provincias Internas, *23,* 119, 133–34.

come in about the Spanish Franciscan missionaries. According to some, they were ready to hand over the missions to parish priests in accordance with the law of September 13, 1813; according to others, they were strongly opposed to Mexican independence. Another report from a ship's captain said that Governor José Argüello of Lower California had refused to proclaim Mexican independence there because he knew that the Spanish missionaries were opposed to it, and their influence with the garrison and the people was very great. On the other hand, Captain José Bandini, father of the well-known figure in Mexican California, Juan Bandini, apparently thought that the missionaries would take the oath to independence because the Spanish Cortes had deprived them of their temporalities.[19]

Most of the reports coming in about the attitude of the missionaries seem to have portrayed them as opposing Mexican independence, however, and on March 13, 1822, Iturbide wrote Herrera, the minister of foreign affairs, asking him to call the attention of the regency to the "conduct of the missionary Fathers which demands, in my opinion, a prompt remedy." Herrera now busied himself writing to Father José Gasol, guardian of the College of San Fernando in Mexico City, and to Father Bernardo, Bishop of Sonora, in whose diocese the missions were. Before he received a reply from the bishop, who said that so far as he knew everyone in California, including the missionaries, was in favor of "our glorious independence," Herrera wrote him again, saying that he had confirmation of his previous letter stating that the missionaries in both Californias were in opposition to Mexican independence. In his reply, Father José Gasol explained in some detail how the mission system worked and why so many of the missionaries, who had been deprived for years of even such essentials as beeswax for their candles, were discontented and wanted to leave the missions. "The common

19. Captain Juan Gómez to Nicolás de la Gándara, Feb. [date illegible], 1822; Gonzalo Ulloa to Iturbide, Feb. 21, 1822, AGN, Californias, *45,* 2-3, 25; Un particular, n.d., AGN, Provincias Internas, *23,* 126.

enemy," went on Father Gasol, was attacking the missionaries, hoping thereby to seize the mission temporalities, which were essential if they were to survive.[20]

With the mission problem revealing more complex difficulties at every step, the government decided on April 10, 1822, to send a commissioner to both Californias to inform the missionaries about the "true state of the Empire," and to try to win over the inhabitants to the idea of independence. The man selected for this post, as has been seen, was Canon Agustín Fernández de San Vicente of Durango, whose bishop, Juan Francisco de Castañiza Larrea—who was also Marqués de Castañiza—had attracted the favorable attention of Iturbide. Canon Fernández, a genial, rosy-cheeked ecclesiastic, allegedly too fond of the gaming table, wine, and women, arrived at Loreto with the news of the accession to the throne of Emperor Agustín I.[21] Accompanying him as chaplain of his ship was the notorious Father José María Afanador, whose visit to California some years before with Tamariz had caused such scandal. It may have been Father Afanador, in fact, who was responsible for the immorality commonly attached to the canon's visit by the Californians.

It immediately became obvious to the canon that the most pressing problem in Lower California was not whether the whites recognized Mexican independence, but whether the Indians could be prevented from leaving the missions. He reported to Minister of Relations Herrera on July 9, from Loreto, that the mission Indians were continually petitioning him to free them from the control of the missionaries.[22] The

20. Iturbide to Secretario de Relaciones, Mar. 13, 1822, AGN, Californias, *45;* Herrera to Bishop of Sonora, Apr. 27, 1822, Bishop of Sonora to Herrera, Apr. 26, 1822, AGN, Provincias Internas, *23,* 155, 186; José Gasol to Herrera, Mar. 21, 1822, AGN, Californias, *45,* 18.

21. Vicente de P. Andrade, *Noticias biográficas sobre los ilustrísimos prelados de Sonora, de Sinaloa y de Durango* (3d ed. Mexico, 1899), pp. 266–67; Herrera to Canon Fernández, Apr. 10 and 25, 1822, AGN, Provincias Internas, *23,* 142, 171; Bancroft, *California, 2,* 469.

22. Fernández de San Vicente to Secretario de Relaciones, July 9, 1822, AGN, Californias, *45.* This letter is reproduced in Spanish and in English

situation seemed to him dangerous, and on July 27 he issued provisional regulations for mission government in Lower California. These were to be in force until the Imperial Constituent Congress passed upon the matter. It would appear from article one of these regulations that the mission Indians had already learned from a ship's captain that they were now citizens of Mexico and that they had abused their new-found liberty by showing disrespect toward the missionaries. At all events, the canon's regulations were designed to restore some of the authority of the missionaries without, however, depriving the Indians of their new citizenship. The difficulties that such a project brought with it may be seen in the contradictory nature of several of the regulations. Article three, for example, gave the missionaries, who were to control the mission temporalities, the right to assign the new citizens their work on the missions; while article four provided that if these new citizens wished to better their position by moving somewhere else, they were to be permitted to do so. Instructions that were later compiled for commissioners who were to reside on the missions provided that the commissioner was to explain to the Indians that "the civil liberty that they enjoy, consists in being men who are useful to the Republic.[23] At some time in the future, continued these instructions, the Indians might be considered worthy of taking any job that they deserved, "according to their capacity, conduct and merit." Living a civilized life really meant, the Indians were told, working at some job; indeed, if they did not work they would lose their citizenship.[24]

---

translation in Herbert E. Bolton, "The Iturbide Revolution in the Californias," *Hispanic American Historical Review*, 2 (1919), 226–31.

23. The word "republic" here is presumably used in its Latin sense of "commonwealth," since Mexico was an empire.

24. The reglamento manuscript is document 888 in SBMA; it is printed in Maza, *Código de colonización*, pp. 164–66. The instructions are in Maza, pp. 166–69.

It is apparent that when it came to the crucial matter of Indian labor, the white man was a better talker than performer. As it was, however, the canon's regulations went too far for at least one of the missionaries. Father José Pineda complained that the regulations were "all in favor of the Indians," who could leave one mission and go to another if they wanted and were to be paid for their work as well as fed. His conclusion was that the missions would suffer a tremendous upheaval, and after admitting that he had no right to say anything, he added: "It can be seen that the Commissioner does not know what Indians are; if he did he would not have left such regulations."[25]

Once more the familiar problem about the nature of the Indian was brought to the fore. Under Spain the authorities had hoped that the mission Indians could be civilized and made into useful members of society. Liberal opinion in Mexico now regarded them as fellow citizens and brothers, who only needed education and encouragement to make themselves part of the new society.[26] But resistance to these theories was strong, and whenever the Indians did not appear to behave in the way that their liberal supporters hoped and believed they would, their theories lost ground. The problem was to continue to be a major one for Mexico as it had been for Spain.

Canon Fernández arrived at Monterey on September 26 and immediately became involved in mission affairs there. At a conference on October 8 with Governor Sola and a number of missionaries and other government officials, he decided that there should be no immediate enforcement of secularization, as the law of September 13, 1813, had decreed, but that instead mission Indians capable of supporting themselves

25. José Pineda to Captain Guerra, Oct. 3, 1822, De la Guerra, "Documentos para la historia de California," BL, *6*, 86.

26. For statements of these views see Carlos María Bustamante, "Medidas," BL, *1*; Ortiz de Ayala, *Resumen*, p. 30.

might leave their missions and take their share of the property, if they obtained the permission of the local military commander and missionary father. This was but a continuation of the secularization measures already initiated by Governor Sola. The canon did go beyond this, however, in his recommendation that the missions should establish elementary schools in which the Indians should be taught to read and write.

After organizing the new government of California under a provincial deputation and a political chief or governor in accordance with the Spanish Constitution of 1812, which was then in effect in Mexico, Canon Fernández returned to Mexico on the brig *San Carlos* with former Governor Sola, now elected California's deputy in the Mexican Congress. They reached San Blas around the middle of January 1823.[27] The canon had encountered no difficulty over the matter of Mexican independence, and he had made some stopgap provisional regulations to deal with the complicated mission situation. There remained two other important matters that demanded attention in California and in other areas of Mexico—colonization and trade—and they were being eagerly tackled by others.

Mexico emerged from its long war of independence with a boundless euphoria and limitless optimism for the future. The new magic of free trade would change her deserts into great cities; foreign settlers would pour into the country and strengthen its frontiers against possible encroachments from the north. There were ready answers for the doubting Thomases: these things were actually happening in the United States; and had not the distinguished Alexander von Humboldt pointed the way in his *Political Essay on the Kingdom of New Spain?* Humboldt had indeed reminded the

27. Zephyrin Engelhardt, *Missions and Missionaries of California* (4 vols. San Francisco, 1908–15), *3,* 152, 154; Bancroft, *California,* 2, 461–62, 471.

Mexicans of the need to strengthen California by colonizing it, and he had also suggested once more how California might utilize its wealth in sea otter and beaver furs, which might be traded profitably in China for mercury. Continuing on from there, Tadeo Ortiz suggested creating a company that would trade in California furs, pearls, and the abalone shells so desired by the Indians of the northwest coast. Perhaps taking a hint from Humboldt's favorable comparison between British success in settling Australia and Spain's failure to populate California, Ortiz recommended once more that convicts be sent north as colonists.[28]

The first authoritative discussion of the colonization of California, however, was made by the Azcárate committee, which candidly stated that it must be undertaken at once to offset the dangers of Russian encroachment. The committee's solution to this old problem was ingenious, and may have been suggested to them by some remarks made in the United States Congress at the beginning of 1821 about the ease of securing Chinese to colonize the Columbia River area. At any rate, the committee came out strongly for colonizing California with Chinese. Where else, the committee asked, could settlers be found? What European family would be willing to circle the globe to reach California? And who would be willing to cross 1,300 miles (five hundred leagues) of land (this was the committee's highly inaccurate estimation of the distance overland from sea to sea at the latitudes of California) merely to get to California? The small numbers who might go to California from Mexico, the committee considered, would barely be able to keep off the weak attempts of the Russians to invade, at a time when they were fully occupied with their European problems. What would happen when they could devote their full time to this region? In the committee's view, Chinese settlement would follow naturally once

28. Bustamante, "Medidas," BL, xviii; Humboldt, *Political Essays*, 2, 348; 3, 286; 4, 88, 367; Ortiz de Ayala, *Resumen*, p. 99.

trade with China, which it highly recommended, became well established.[29]

Shortly after the Azcárate committee presented its report, the new Imperial Constituent Congress met and appointed a Committee on Colonization. One of its original members was Valentín Gómez Farías, a physician from Jalisco who had entered politics as a representative from Zacatecas and who was to do more than any other Mexican to colonize California. Although this committee met several times during 1822, most of its work concerned Texas, which was considered in even greater danger than California. Before a general colonization law could be worked out, the Congress was dissolved by Iturbide on October 31, 1822. Its successor, a rump congress of deputies selected from the previous body and called the Instituent National Junta, issued a colonization decree on January 4, 1823, which provided regulations for the distribution of land to foreign colonists. After the collapse of Iturbide, however, this decree ceased to be recognized, and the new constituent Congress, established under the interim government of the Supreme Executive Power, passed the unfinished business over to its Committee on Colonization. After urgings from Foreign Minister Alamán, who reminded the deputies that in the case of California the foreign colonists might be Asiatics and that convicts from Mexico might be sent there, the Congress finally issued a colonization law on August 18, 1824.[30]

This law, however, did no more than provide guidelines for the states, into which the Mexican Republic was now

29. Azcárate, *Programa*, p. 39. For a discussion of the bringing of Chinese to the northwest coast in 1788 see Manning, *Nootka Sound Controversy*, pp. 289–90; American State Papers, Miscellaneous, 2, 633.

30. Comisión de colonización, 1822, pp. 186–92, Archivo de la Cámara de Diputados, Mexico City (cited hereafter as ACD); *Actas del congreso constituyente Mexicano* (4 vols. Mexico, 1822–23), *1*, 26, 33, 41, 48, 53, 83; *2*, 1, 7, 12, 24; *Memoria que el Secretario de estado presenta* (Mexico, 1823), p. 33; *El Aguila Mexicana* (Aug. 1, 1924).

divided by the Federal Constitution of 1824, to prepare their own colonization regulations. Under the new constitution the Californias were divided into the two territories of Lower California and Upper California, and according to the colonization law, the federal government would at some future time provide colonization regulations for the territories. As will be seen, this did not actually happen until 1828, but in the meantime some of the principles laid down in the law of 1824 were of considerable interest in California. One of these was the statement in article two that privately owned land or land owned by a corporation or a pueblo could not be colonized. This meant that mission lands were exempt from colonization. Again, article nine gave Mexican citizens the preference over foreigners in the distribution of land and further stated that no distinction whatever was to be made between one citizen and another, except for individual merit or services to the country or, where these factors were equal, residence within the area to be colonized. Since the Constitution of 1824 made the Indians citizens equal in every way to the white man, this provision of the colonization law meant that the mission Indians, and perhaps even the non-Christian Indians, might be granted lands of their own.[31]

When a committee of the Territorial Deputation set to work in California on a territorial colonization regulation in accord with the colonization law of 1824, its recommendations touched on some of the points mentioned above. It stated that California still had land not owned by missions or private individuals that could be used for crops, although not for pasturing cattle. It recommended that irrigable lands that the missions were not cultivating be given to individuals for this purpose. It added it "could not doubt" that lands occupied by the pagan Indians in the interior also belonged to the nation and that the Indians themselves were members

31. Maza, *Código de colonización*, pp. 191–93; a translation of the law may be found in Executive Document no. 17, 31st Congress, 1st Session, serial no. 573, pp. 139–40.

of the nation, although living apart from it because they "lacked civilization." These interior lands should be opened to settlement, the committee believed, and the Indians persuaded by the obvious advantages they saw to settle down themselves. Missions, the committee considered, were not likely to attract the Indians, since Indians in them were separated from their own country, deprived of their liberty, and forced to work. The committee felt that the Indians might be won over to civilized life more easily if they were approached first in their own villages. There they might be more inclined to adopt Mexican customs and manners.[32]

These ideas on how to civilize the Indians, which go back to the writings of Bernardo Ward or José del Campillo, were being increasingly mentioned in Mexico at this time by men whose views on other matters had little in common. Prominent members of the various colonization committees, such as Gómez Farías and Lorenzo de Zavala, thought in this way, as did Ortiz de Ayala.[33] Others, like Congressman José San Martín from Oaxaca, launched bitter public attacks on the missions in which, he said, "religion is almost entirely unknown and humanity is totally outraged." Lucas Alamán, in his report to Congress of November 8, 1823, remarked, "If the mission system may be held to be the most convenient way to withdraw savages who roam the forests without any idea of religion or intellectual culture, from their barbarism, it cannot serve more than to establish the first principles of society but not to lead men to its perfection." The government, went on Alamán, believed that if the California mission Indians were given land of their own to cultivate, together with the

32. Juan Bandini, "Documentos para la historia de California," BL, pt. 1, p. 35.

33. The ideas of Bernardo Ward on trade were being explained in the *Gaceta Diaria de México* in June 1825. *Actas del congreso constituyente mexicano, 3,* 48; Juan A. Mateos, *Historia parlamentaria de los congresos mexicanos* (25 vols. Mexico, 1877–1912), *1,* 812–14; 2, 25–45; 3, 46–52, 52–67; Ortiz de Ayala, *Resumen,* p. 30.

necessary means to do so, and if foreign colonists were established there, the territory would move rapidly forward. Giving urgency to Alamán's desire to take a "new look" at the situation in the Californias, as he put it, was a serious revolt of mission Indians that occurred early in 1824 in three of the southern missions. Minister of War Manuel de Mier y Terán reported that it had almost become a general mission revolt and that some Indian deserters from the missions were putting themselves at the head of pagan Indians in their attacks on the whites.[34] The military authorities in California blamed the missionaries for keeping their Indians in "a state akin to that of slavery," while the point of view of the missionaries, as expressed by Father Baldomero López, guardian of the College of San Fernando, was that the military and the Territorial Deputation were to blame because they were responsible for the extra and unpaid work the Indians were forced to perform. With the Russian bear at the door such problems must be solved.[35]

In order to consider carefully the many problems involved in the major changes contemplated in the Californias, the Supreme Executive Power, at the request of Minister of War Mier y Terán, decided to appoint a Commission on the Californias, a direct successor of the first commission, to make a thorough study of all aspects of the matter. The commission was to keep in touch with the government through the minister of relations, Lucas Alamán, by reporting every week on its work.[36]

34. José San Martín, *Memoria y proposiciones sobre las Californias* (Mexico, 1943), p. 12. There is a translation by Henry R. Wagner (San Francisco, 1945). *Memoria* (1823), p. 33; *Memoria* del Secretario de Guerra (Mexico, 1825), p. 20.

35. Theodore H. Hittell, *History of California* (4 vols. San Francisco, 1885–97), 2, 77; Engelhardt, *Missions, 3,* 210.

36. D [Diez Bonilla?] to Mier y Terán, Aug. 9, 1824, BC. There is a doctoral dissertation entitled "The Junta de Fomento de Californias 1824–1827" by Keld John Reynolds, University of Southern California, 1945.

Between July 12, 1824, when it first met at the home of
Colonel José María Tornel, and the end of August 1827,
when it was ready to disband, some twenty men had been
members of this important body, which was officially known
as the Commission for the Development of the Californias.
Its normal meetings seem to have been on Thursday morn-
ings, although when it was extremely busy early in 1825 it
met on any weekday. It divided its work between three standing committees and when necessary created additional committees. It followed parliamentary rules at its sessions, which
were held in a room in the former Viceregal Palace, called at
this time the National Palace. About the middle of January
1825, the commission had to move to the national archives
for its sessions, since the new Federal Congress took over its
former meeting place for its chamber.[37]

Three of the members of this new commission had been in
the first one. These men were Manuel González Ibarra, Francisco de Paula Tamariz, and Tomás Suria. Suria had been
the last secretary of the earlier commission and ended by
having the same position in the new body. Tamariz, who was
probably the most active member of the new commission,
returned to New Spain in 1816 with a position at the Chihuahua treasury. He joined Iturbide in 1821 and became
comptroller general of the insurgent army until he sailed as
a minor member of the first Mexican legation to the United
States in 1822. On March 6, 1823, Tamariz asked Iturbide to
make him governor of Upper and Lower California. Iturbide
duly appointed him to this post on March 8, but his own fall
from power prevented Tamariz from taking office. Tamariz
frequently warned the commission members of the dangers
of the Russian establishment near San Francisco Bay. Just
before the second commission ended its career, its president

37. Diez Bonilla to Mier y Terán, July 14, 1824, BC; Mier y Terán to
Sola, July 8, 1824, AD, caja 381, Cancelados D/iii/4/6052; AGN, Californias, *18*.

recommended that Tamariz be made governor of California, but the authorities took no action on the matter.[38] Some of the other distinguished men on the commission included Father Servando Teresa de Mier; Juan Francisco de Azcárate; Carlos María Bustamante; Juan José Espinosa de los Monteros, often regarded as the leading lawyer in Mexico at this time; José Mariano Almanza, a prominent Veracruz merchant; Pablo Vicente Sola, former governor of California, whose election to represent the territory was rejected on the grounds that he had committed atrocities during the war for Mexican independence; Ignacio Cubas, archivist of the national archives; Isidro Ignacio Icaza, the first director of the National Museum of Archaeology, History and Ethnography; and Tomás Salgado, a prominent lawyer who later became governor of Michoacán and president of the Supreme Court.[39]

The government issued instructions to the commission on July 17, 1824, to consider certain California questions, among which it recommended that the missions be given priority. The commission devoted itself to this difficult matter from

38. AGN, Californias, *45*, 35–37, 174; AD, Expediente xi/iii/2–710; Tamariz to Junta, May 26, Sept. 12, 1825, BC; Santibañez, *Diplomacia, 1,* 71.

39. Bustamante, *Diario,* p. 427. The remaining members included General Mariano Diez Bonilla, the first president and first appointed member of the Commission; Colonel José Ignacio Ormaechea, paymaster of the California presidio garrisons; Mariano Domínguez, a lawyer, who was the son of Miguel Domínguez, husband of the famous Corregidora of Querétaro. His father had been a substitute member of the Supreme Executive Power and in 1824 was president of the Supreme Court. Diego García Conde, formerly governor intendant of Durango, was director of the corps of engineers, and his brother, Alejo García Conde, had been comandante general of the Western Interior Provinces. Pedro Dionisio de Cárdenas was a Veracruz merchant, and Francisco Fagoaga, a learned member of the wealthy family of that name. Francisco Cortina Gónzalez was apparently a relative of Captain Joaquín Cortina González of the earlier commission.

then until April 1825, only interrupting its deliberations when the government asked it to examine preliminary instructions that had been prepared for the first governor to be sent out to California. Even here the major preoccupation of the commission was the missions.[40]

Inspired by the humanitarian movement of eighteenth-century Spain, the commission disapproved of the mission method of civilizing pagan Indians. In its view, the Spanish concept of spiritual conquest, whereby troops were used to help gather non-Christian Indians into the fold, was not in accord with the methods for converting the heathen laid down by Jesus Christ and applied by His Apostles. Conversion should be brought about by persuasion, the commission believed, and it may be surmised that the famous Dominican Father Bartolomé de Las Casas, whose treatise *The Only Method of Attracting All People to the True Faith* is a classic exposition of this viewpoint, was in their minds. At all events, one of their members, Father Servando Teresa de Mier, was a Las Casas enthusiast. Indeed Las Casas was a popular figure at this time in Mexico, the government itself

---

40. The instructions are not available nor are the documents of the Commission. The major reports of the Commission were published by Tamariz in 1827 under the title *Colección de los principales trabajos en que se ha ocupado la junta nombrada para meditar y proponer al supremo gobierno los medios más necesarios para promover el progreso de la cultura y civilización de los territorios de la alta y de la baja California.* Within this collection there was a *Dictamen* on the government's instructions to the new governor of California, a plan for the organization of the missions, colonization plans for foreigners and for Mexicans, and a proposed bill to organize the government of the Californias. In addition, Tamariz was mainly responsible for three more pamphlets within the collection dealing with California trade. There is a translation of these reports, with an introduction and notes, by Keld J. Reynolds entitled "Principal Actions of the California Junta De Fomento, 1825–1827," California Historical Society *Quarterly,* 24 (December 1945), 289–320; 25 (March, June, September, December, 1946), 57–78, 149–68, 267–78, 347–67.

accepting a portrait of the great Protector of the Indians at ceremonies in the Chamber of Deputies and the Senate in April 1825.[41]

Not only did the commission deplore the principles that they conceived lay behind the mission method, they felt that it was ineffective, since in their view, pagan Indians would not want to become mission neophytes. When a non-Christian Indian entered a mission, the commission argued, he left his home and suddenly had to live an entirely different kind of life, which forced him to change his habits and customs, his morals, and his religion. He became in their view a monk, without any of the advantages that they saw in this vocation for those who had devoted their lives to it. While the Indians were being made into religious rather than into ordinary members of society, the commission held that the missionaries, who had charge of the temporalities of the mission estates and who sold their products to foreign merchants, were overly immersed in commercial affairs and unable to devote sufficient time to the religious needs of their charges. The missions, then, were not good either for the Indians or for the Franciscan missionaries. Their object in pursuing this line of reasoning was to justify one of their major recommendations, which was that the government should take over the mission temporalities.[42] Behind their arguments for this move there were undoubtedly other reasons of which, perhaps, the most persuasive was the fact that the missions had been able to support not only themselves but the troops and many of the whites in California for some thirteen years without receiving any help from Mexico. That this had been done at the expense of the mission Indian, who had to do the work, and would presumably have to continue to labor in

41. Hutchinson, "The Mexican Government," *The Americas, 21*, no. 4, 345–46; Lewis Hanke and Giménez Fernández, *Bartolomé de Las Casas* (Chile, 1954), p. 262; *Plan para el arreglo de las misiones* (part of the *Colección* mentioned above in n. 40), pp. 6–71.

42. *Plan para el arreglo de las misiones,* pp. 6–7, 10; *Dictamen,* pp. 7–8.

the future if similar results were to be obtained, they did not appear to understand.

In presenting their own view of how best to civilize the pagan Indians, the commission first avowed that they distrusted the views of European authors like Father Venegas (actually Father Burriel) who had such poor opinions of the California Indians. They felt that more information was needed about the abilities of these Indians. At least they were docile enough, the commission pointed out, so that large numbers of them had been subjected to living a monastic kind of life. If they were treated in more kindly fashion and attracted by trade and friendly relations toward society, including giving them things they needed and wanted, they could be civilized more easily than by the mission method. As for the Indians actually living on the missions, the commission proposed that those who had been Christians for many years should, in accordance with the secularization law of 1813, become in the course of time simply the parishioners of their former missionary fathers. This should be done slowly, because the mission Indians were still very backward. Following Alamán and other Mexican thinkers of the day, they looked upon ownership of land as the most powerful means of promoting industry and self-reliance in the Indians and suggested that Christian Indians on the missions should have priority in its distribution. On the other hand, they did not think that land should be given to every Indian regardless of his ability to cultivate it and make a living from it. They suggested that the new governor should find out how many were able to do this and give them as much as they could cultivate from the common lands of the missions, taking care to leave the missions sufficient land so that they could continue to support those of their neophytes who were not yet ready to leave and start out on their own.[43]

The next assignment they undertook was to prepare a set

43. *Plan para . . . las misiones,* p. 7; *Dictamen,* pp. 6, 9–13.

of regulations for foreign colonization in California that would implement the general law of August 18, 1824. Article two of these proposed regulations stated that mission lands belonged to the mission Indians and to Mexicans resident in California and could only be distributed between these two groups. This proposal went beyond the general opinion in California, which was that mission lands belonged only to mission Indians. In their succeeding set of regulations for the colonization of California by Mexicans, the commission stated that Christian Indians who could run their own affairs were to have priority in the division of mission land and were to receive as much as they could cultivate. They also provided that those settlers who had received grants of land under Governor Neve's regulations of 1779 were to keep them, while those who had not been granted land and did not have any were to receive as much as they could cultivate. And while they emphasized that nothing was so important for the development and security of California as settlement by Mexicans, they insisted that it must be done without damaging the interests of the mission Indians or the Mexican residents already there. It will be seen that the commission's findings on missions and mission Indians had considerable influence on Mexican policy in California.[44]

In other respects the commission was not so successful.[45] One of the greatest needs for Mexican California was a set of

44. *Plan de colonización extrangera; Plan de colonización de nacionales*, p. 3. arts. 4, 7, 8.

45. Tamariz was mainly responsible for some prolix and grandiose reports, endorsed by the Commission, for trade with Asia through a monopoly concern to be called the Asiatic-Mexican Company. His ideas lacked practicality and bore no fruit, although they may have influenced the men who founded the Cosmopolitan Company in 1834. Tamariz' reports are entitled: *Plan político mercantil para el más pronto fomento de las Californias; Proyecto para el establecimiento de una compañia de comercio directo con el Asia; Proyecto de reglamento en grande para el establecimiento de la Compañia Asiático-Mexicana*. All these form part of the *Colección* mentioned above in n. 40.

laws for its internal administration. The commission pointed this out in its first report on January 3, 1825, but in spite of reminders by Lucas Alamán and every other foreign minister, and despite the fact that the commission produced a lengthy proposal on the matter in 1827, the Mexican Congress was never able to complete an organic law for the territory. The government of California, therefore, continued under the Spanish system, provided by the Spanish Constitution of 1812, of a Provincial, or in the case of Mexican California, a Territorial Deputation, a political chief, known as a governor, and town councils. The duties of these bodies were given in detail in the Spanish law of June 23, 1813, and this continued to be one of the cornerstones of California law during the Mexican period.[46] Spanish law not considered to be clearly in opposition to the new Mexican republican system, in fact, continued in effect in Mexico until new legislation took its place. In practice, this meant that Spanish laws were only in force in respect to some of their articles, the remainder being considered repugnant to the new Mexican system. In addition, some parts of the country upheld Spanish laws which were not considered in effect in others. Legal problems brought about by confusion of this kind proved to be a severe handicap to effective action in Mexican California. On occasion a law was considered to be valid if it suited the governor and invalid if it did not suit him.[47]

Under the Mexican Constitution of 1824 and the Acta Constitutiva, the Californias formed two territories immedi-

46. *Dictamen*, p. 4; Alamán, *Memoria* (1825); *Iniciativa de ley*. The law of June 23, 1813, is in Dublán y Lozano, *Legislación mexicana*, *I*, 413–25.

47. In 1829 a Mexican lawyer published a list of Spanish laws "not totally opposed to independence and the [new] form of government adopted" which, in part, had been or were in effect somewhere in the Republic. He listed in his collection the secularization law of Sept. 13, 1813. *Colección de los decretos y órdenes de las Cortes de España que se reputan vigentes en la República de los Estados Unidos Mexicanos* (Mexico, 1829), pp. i–iv, 106–07.

ately subject to the federal government, and the federal Congress acted as their legislature. They were each represented in the Chamber of Deputies by a representative with voice but no vote. Administratively, the political chief or governor of California reported to the Ministry of Internal and Foreign Relations, which was reorganized in 1826 so that the second section of the Internal Department took care of colonization, land division, and missions in California. Since the governors were generally also military men, they reported to the minister of war; in addition, the minister of justice and ecclesiastical affairs concerned himself with mission affairs.[48]

The Mexican governors and Territorial Deputations of California were severely handicapped by the lack of an organic law for the territory and by the confusion resulting from the necessity of trying to follow laws designed for the monarchy in Spain and for the Mexican Republic at the same time. The Mexican government was also from the first overwhelmed by problems of its own, which included a perennially drastic shortage of funds in the treasury and the pressing need to organize and establish a workable government, confronted as it was by ever increasing lawlessness. Successive Mexican congresses had little time to attend to far-off California, no matter how pressing its affairs seemed to be; and the months that it sometimes took the mail to reach Monterey from Mexico City and vice versa made California more like an overseas colony of Mexico than an integral part of the republic. In addition, the old problems of security for the territory from Russian and American threats, the need for colonization, and the backwardness of the mission Indians appeared no less difficult than before. Indeed, the steady growth of a strong anti-Spanish sentiment in Mexico made things worse in California.

The new republican government in Mexico made its first appointment for California on March 17, 1824, when General

48. *Reglamento interior de la Secretaría de Estado y del despacho de relaciones interiores y exteriores* (Mexico, 1826).

Juan José Miñón was made comandante general, or military commander, of California and Lower California. Circumstances in Mexico prevented him from going to his post, however, and the appointment ended on July 15, 1825.[49] According to the law of June 23, 1813, the offices of military commander and political chief, or governor, were to be kept separate, unless disorder or foreign danger made it necessary to combine them temporarily. Whether it was intended to make General Miñón also the political chief of California before he left is not known. General Miñón was replaced by José María Echeandía, a tall, thin, chestnut-haired, thirty-seven-year-old native of Mexico City.[50] Minister of War Gómez Pedraza sent him his orders as military commander of the Californias on January 31, 1825, and on February 12 Minister of Foreign Relations Alamán appointed him political chief of both Californias. At the time of these appointments, Echeandía was a lieutenant colonel in the Corps of Engineers who described himself as being commander of the corps and "chief of studies in its academies." During 1823 and 1824 he had commanded the army engineers in Veracruz in the campaign against the Spanish occupied fort of Ulúa. He had become ill with fever there—possibly malaria—and returned to Mexico City, where he had been elected a member of the Provincial Deputation of Mexico. In November 1824, President Victoria selected Echeandía to survey the boundaries of the newly organized Federal District, and he was at work on this when he was appointed to California.[51]

It would appear that Echeandía was not overly pleased at

---

49. AD, expediente xi/iii/2-471/Cancelados; Bancroft is in error in stating that Miñón did not accept the position (Bancroft, *California, 3*, 8).

50. The last name is sometimes spelled Echandía and sometimes preceded by "de."

51. AD, expediente xi/iii/5–1926/Cancelados; Angustias de la Guerra Ord, *Occurrences in Hispanic California*, trans. and ed. Francis Price and William H. Ellison (Washington, D.C., 1956), p. 12; AD, expediente xi/iii/5–1926.

the prospect of going to such a distant territory. He seems to have had an eye on the position of Director General of Engineers, then held by the ailing General Diego García Conde, who was a member of the Commission on the Californias. Echeandía had suggested to Iturbide in 1821 the organization of a company of engineers and had been permitted to form one. He commanded it during the siege of Mexico City. He was proud of his part in founding the future Corps of Engineers, and after his return from California he continued to have an interest in the teaching of scientific subjects in the Military College. He later called himself a professor of architecture, and in a book published in 1832, Tadeo Ortiz de Ayala refers to him as an intelligent architect who would have done honor to Mexico if he had been encouraged. Ortiz says that he could not make a living as an architect and that circumstances made him enter the army.[52] Since for Echeandía going to California also meant leaving his wife, Mariana Salcedo, and his four daughters in Mexico City, there would appear to be little reason, other than the need to earn his living, why he should have wanted to go.

Echeandía's original instructions from the minister of war and the minister of relations are not available, although Hittell summarizes from the old California archives the major points in them: Echeandía, in accordance with the duties of a political chief in the law of June 23, 1813, was directed to prepare a census and collect statistics on California. Following the recommendations of the Commission on the Californias, he was to report on the abilities of the Indians and to state which Indians were capable of farming land on their own. These were to receive lots from the common lands of their mission, although the mission was not to lose so much land that it could not continue to support its neophytes. He

52. Miguel A. Sánchez Lamego, *Apuntes para la historia del arma de ingenieros en México* (5 vols. Mexico, 1943–49), *1*, 12–13; AD, expediente xi/iii/5–1926; Tadeo Ortiz de Ayala, *México considerado como nación independiente y libre* (2 vols. Guadalajara, 1952), *1*, 153.

was to look into the relationship between pagan and mission Indians and the friars, and between these Indians and the government. He was to make recommendations for improving the conditions of the Indians. He was also instructed to keep watch on the Americans and the Russians. That the commission's remarks on the original draft of Echeandía's instructions influenced the government in preparing the final wording handed to Echeandía is shown by the citations that he later made to Governor Figueroa. Both of his quotations from his instructions—concerning making the missionaries into parish priests and distributing mission land to certain Indians—reproduce verbatim the wording of the commission.[53] It is of interest that the commission's comments on the original draft of the government's instructions show that they contained articles on other matters not mentioned by Hittell. These included orders to prevent the missionaries from interfering with the temporal affairs of the missions or from abusing the mission Indians. According to the commission, the original draft also referred to the opposition of the missionaries to making grants of land or to setting up haciendas. Whether these anti-missionary provisions remained in the final version of the instructions is not clear, although, since Hittell was no friend of the missionaries, it is unlikely that he would have omitted them if he had seen them. The instructions prepared for Echeandía by Minister of War Gómez Pedraza criticized both the missionaries and the military in California. He concluded by saying, "The President wants these abuses to be reformed but this reform is more a work of policy than of authority." "It is important," Pedraza went on, "not to oppose openly the missionaries' system," because their influence was such that if they were aroused they could cause worse trouble. At the same time, it was necessary to continue steadily to cut down the arbitrary ways in which

53. Hittell, *History*, 2, 82–83; Echeandía to Figueroa, Mar. 19, 1833, BL, State Papers, 2; *Dictamen*, pp. 9, 13.

the Indians of California were being oppressed so that they might experience the advantages of the "liberal system." This must be done prudently and slowly, however, so that Indian customs should not degenerate, as they might, into licentiousness.[54]

Before leaving Mexico City for Acapulco around the middle of February 1825, Echeandía selected six young officers from the Corps of Engineers to accompany him to California. The four most prominent of these were Lieutenants Mariano Alcocer and José María Padrés and Second Lieutenants Agustín Zamorano and Romualdo Pacheco. Echeandía sailed on the *Morelos* from Acapulco in March, but as a result of bad weather, damage to the vessel, and poor navigation, the ship had to put in at San Blas sometime late in April. While the *Morelos* was being repaired, Echeandía went inland to the more healthy town of Tepic. Here he learned that General Diego García Conde had resigned as director general of the Corps of Engineers, and he promptly applied for the post. President Victoria refused to accept his resignation from his position in California, however, and Echeandía continued on in the *Nieves* to Loreto, Lower California, which he reached on June 22. He remained in Loreto organizing the administration of Lower California until October 4, when he set out overland for San Diego, which he reached, after a difficult journey, at the end of the month. No sooner had he arrived than he wrote President Victoria saying that his health was broken because of the "cruelty of the climate of this Territory." He added that if he had not recovered in six months' time he wanted to return to Mexico.[55]

54. *Dictamen*, p. 7; Gómez Pedraza to Echeandía, Jan. 31, 1825, AD, expediente xi/iii/5–1926. Gómez Pedraza uses the word "people" instead of "Indian" in his letter; nonetheless he seems to be referring to the mission Indians.

55. The two other officers were: Second Lieutenants Andrés Navas and Miguel García Lobato. It is not certain whether they actually went to

From the first, Governor Echeandía must have found himself immersed in the two most difficult questions of the day in California: the dissatisfaction of both the missionaries and the Indians. The Indians on the southern missions had just ended a serious revolt against the white man, while the missionaries, almost all of whom were Spaniards, did not look with favor upon taking an oath to the republic of Mexico, whose independence the king of Spain had not yet recognized. Echeandía had a meeting with some of the southern mission fathers in April 1826, which was inconclusive as far as persuading the missionaries to take the oath. He also consulted them, however, on mission problems, and as a result of this and other conferences and of a trip to the southern missions by Lieutenant Pacheco, Echeandía worked out a secularization program which he announced on July 25, 1826. This program followed the precedents already set in California by Governor Sola and Canon Agustín Fernández de San Vicente. It permitted mission Indians who wanted to leave their missions to do so, provided they had been Christians for fifteen years or since their childhood, and provided they could earn their living. They also had to be married or not minors. The procedure was to be that Indians should petition the commanding officer of the presidio, either orally or in writing, that they wanted to leave their missions. This officer was then to obtain information about them from their mission father, and if they met the required provisions the presidio commander was to decide whether they could leave their missions. They and their families were to be allowed to go where they wanted "like a member of the Mexican nation."[56] That some

California or not. AD, expediente xi/iii/5–1926. Departmental Records, 5, 154; BL, Superior Government State Papers, Decrees and Dispatches, 3, 11; Bancroft, *California, 3*, 9.

56. Bancroft, *California, 3*, 91, 102; Echeandía to Comandantes of San Diego, Santa Barbara, Monterey, and the Father Prefect, July 25, 1826, AGN, Californias, *18*.

Indians were already living off their missions, with or without authorization, is revealed by Echeandía's final order that the comandantes were to question these Indians and either allow them to remain as they were or have them returned to their missions in accordance with his secularization plan.

According to Echeandía, many Indians petitioned him to leave their missions, and indeed the records contain several petitions in broken Spanish. One of these joint petitions from the mission of San Buenaventura begins, "Although we are Indians prostrated at your feet we earnestly beg your worship to Attend to this Entreaty which we are making." Very seldom does the voice of the Indian himself come through as it does here; almost invariably the white man speaks or writes for the Indian. This particular group of petitioners was composed of masons, tile makers, carpenters, muleteers, soap makers and vaqueros—in other words, those who had learned trades on the mission and thought they could make a living by themselves. Echeandía consulted Father Narciso Durán, president of the California missions, about this group. Father Durán advised that if, on investigation, it was found that their petition and the promises they made were genuine, Echeandía might try some of them out to see whether they did what they said they could do. He pointed out, however, that these Indians were the most useful Indians in the mission, and if all of them were released the mission might no longer be able to support itself. Perhaps, he said, it would be necessary to release all the Indians at San Buenaventura if these petitioners were freed.[57]

It soon became clear that the missionaries were opposed to Echeandía's plan. Father Francisco González de Ibarra put it this way:

57. For a unique description of mission life by a young Indian boy see Minna and Gordon Hewes, "Indian Life and Customs at Mission San Luis Rey," *The Americas, 9* (1952), 87–106; San Buenaventura, Oct. 23, 1826, and Narciso Durán to Echeandía, San José, Feb. 16, 1827, AGN, Californias, *18*.

[The Indians] are being told that they are free, but in fact they are simply being deceived. . . . Some are leaving their missions, some are going off into the woods, some are going to work for [the whites], the so-called people of reason. As a result of this the crops cannot be sown at the regular time and even those that are sown are lost, for there is no one to harvest them. And the Indians who have gone off, because of their little knowledge, will slowly but surely lose their lands and become slaves.

According to this point of view, the white men would exploit the neophytes who left their missions. Father Francisco Suñer, who was in charge at San Buenaventura, put forward another point of view in later correspondence with Echeandía. The Indians on his mission, he said, were by no means ready to earn their own living. If those who wanted to leave were permitted to do so, they would either become servants of the white men or would do nothing. Since idleness was the mother of all vices, they would become robbers and outlaws who would destroy cattle. Instead of being useful to California they would ruin it. What was more, the Indian should not always be trusted: "Sometimes he comes dressed in sheep's clothing but within he is a rapacious wolf; his voice is that of Jacob and his hands are those of Esau. Not all Indians are like this but there are many who are, who bless what they would like to curse and kiss the hand that they would like to burn."[58]

That Echeandía's experiment in secularization did not work well is attested to by Captain F. W. Beechey, a British naval officer who was in California at the time that Echeandía's program was begun in 1826 and who returned in 1827 and observed the results. The mission Indians who were released, he reported, behaved like schoolboys out of school.

58. "Informe de las misiones de California, 1826," *Boletín* del archivo general de la nación, *30* (1959), 252; Francisco Suñer to Echeandía, Dec. 19, 1828, AGN, Californias, *18*.

They committed every excess, gambled away all their possessions, and were either taken back on the missions or punished
for their crimes by being put to hard labor in shackles. Echeandía seems to have hoped that the Indians who were freed
from the missions under his plan would identify themselves in
time with the whites and would finally be considered exactly
the same as "rational settlers." In the course of 1827 he
became convinced that his program would not work, however, and at the end of 1828 he produced an entirely new
one.[59]

In Echeandía's opinion, the weakness of his original proposal of 1826 was that when it was put into practice not all
the Indians who could have left the missions did so, and those
who left ran into difficulties and received no protection.
It had been bad both for the Indians and for the missions
which were to be towns.[60] His new proposal of 1828, which
he sent to the government in Mexico, provided that all the
missions, excepting the new establishments of San Rafael and
San Francisco Solano, were to be converted into towns within
five years. These new towns, formed from the missions,
were to be settled by the former mission Indians and any
other Mexicans who wished to reside in them. Each family
of mission Indians, or of Indians who had left the mission
with permission, was to be given a house lot of 225 feet
square (75x75 *varas*) and a farm plot of about eight acres
(200x200 varas). They were also to receive a generous number
of farm animals, together with the necessary farm tools.
They were not to be allowed to dispose of their new possessions for five years, after which time, the regulation runs,
they would have acquired sufficient knowledge of the value

59. F. W. Beechey, *Narrative of a Voyage to the Pacific* (2 vols. London, 1831), 2, 320; Echeandía to Minister of Relations, Dec. 6, 1826, and
Echeandía to Comandante of San Diego, BL Departmental Records, *5*,
95, 183–84.

60. Echeandía "Ley sobre administración de misiones," Jan. 6, 1831,
BL, Departmental Records, *9*, 66–78.

of their property so that presumably they would want to keep it. The mission church and the house of the missionary, who was now to be the chaplain, were to continue to be used in this way. The other mission buildings were to be made into facilities such as schools, jails, quarters for the town council, hospitals, and so forth. Undistributed land and cattle, vineyards, orchards, mills, and other similar items were to be put in charge of an administrator, who was to be under the town council and the Territorial Deputation. A similar arrangement was to be put into practice in Lower California. The former missionaries were to be permitted to remain as parish priests or to leave and establish new missions at some other point in the interior.[61]

Echeandía heard nothing from the government in Mexico about his plan, probably because the government was itself involved in a series of *pronunciamientos*. These unseated the newly elected President Gómez Pedraza in December 1828 and installed Vicente Guerrero as president on April 1, 1829, only to depose him and elevate his vice-president, Anastasio Bustamante, to power on January 1, 1830. In California, according to Echeandía, the missionaries were reluctant to go ahead with his proposals, possibly because they thought that one of the succession of governments in Mexico would annul them.[62] By the middle of 1830, however, when the political scene in Mexico had settled down, Echeandía submitted his 1828 plan to the Territorial Deputation, which approved it, with minor changes, in August 1830. Echeandía then sent this new version, sometimes called the plan of 1830, to Mexico for approval. It was still not sufficiently detailed however, to provide a practical guide to the way in which the new towns should be set up. In its 1828 version the plan itself called for the formation by the territorial government of another set of regulations to do this; and

61. Echeandía to Minister of Relations, Dec. 11, 1828, AGN, Californias, *18*.
62. Echeandía to Figueroa, Mar. 19, 1833, BL, State Papers, 2.

either Echeandía or the Territorial Deputation added to his original plan instructions for the appointment of police commissioners whose duties and salaries it gave, together with those of the administrators already mentioned in his original project. In addition, the number of missions which were to be converted into towns was limited in the beginning to two: San Gabriel and San Carlos. The only other major change—probably suggested by Echeandía, who consistently showed an interest in educating the mission Indians—was the additional of several articles providing for the establishment of two schools, one at San Gabriel and one at San Carlos, where mission Indians, carefully selected according to their ability, were to learn reading, writing, and arithmetic. Echeandía issued these regulations as his secularization decree of January 6, 1831.[63]

In his report to the Congress dated January 5, 1831, Minister of Relations Alamán, once more in power, referred to Echeandía's 1828 plan in favorable terms. It seemed to him very practicable for those missions which were far enough advanced to be made into towns. He said that it would be passed on to the Congress and recommended that it be considered by that body in conjunction with the plan drawn up for the missions by the Commission on the Californias. Alamán opposed the decree of January 6, 1831, however, on the ground that it did not follow strictly enough the secularization law of September 13, 1813.[64]

Father Durán, in a report written on December 31, 1831, found Echeandía's secularization proposals completely unacceptable. Even Echeandía's provisions for educating the Indians drew his fire. Father Durán's theme was that the white people in California lived lives of ease at the expense of the Indians. "If there is anything to do," he wrote, "the

63. Echeandía, "Ley sobre administración de misiones," Jan. 6, 1831, BL; Bancroft, *California, 3*, 302, 305–06.

64. *Memoria de la Secretaría de Estado* (Mexico, 1831), p. 33; Echeandía to Figueroa, Mar. 19, 1833, BL, State Papers.

Indian has to do it; if he fails to do it, nothing will be done."
Teachers could not be found to instruct the whites, he
pointed out, let alone the Indians. He wanted the whites to
show by their example how the Indians should live, not
live at their expense. In a final attack on those responsible
for the plan, he said that general opinion in California had
it that a conspiracy was afoot:

> Now what all believe is, that, under the specious pretext
> of this Plan, there was a secret project of a general
> plunder of the mission property in return for the said
> enormous sacrifice of about a million dollars in drafts
> against the nation, by selling and converting into cash
> everything possible. This the leaders intended to take
> along out of the country in order to enjoy it in foreign
> lands.[65]

Father Durán's charge of a conspiracy against mission
property by certain members of the Territorial Deputation
was answered by an equally unsupported countercharge that
the missionaries were using their wealth and influence to
plot against the federal system of government, break Mexican
laws, corrupt officials, and generally make themselves hated
by intelligent citizens. Some friars, the Deputation alleged,
had fled to Spain with gold and silver belonging to the missions. It is true that Father Antonio Ripoll and Father José
Altimira, who, it will be remembered, had listened to the
siren song of the Russian officer Zavalishin, fled to Spain
without leave on an American ship. But it has not been
proven that they took mission funds with them.[66]

It is evident that a new bitterness had worsened the relations between the Spanish missionaries and the authorities
in California. This situation was probably due in part to
a wave of hysteria against Spaniards in Mexico, which reached
its height in 1829 when Spain foolishly decided to try to

65. Engelhardt, *Missions, 3,* 398, 401.
66. Bancroft, *California, 3,* 93–94, 313.

reconquer her former colony. Mexico's long and bloody war for independence left little room for good feelings between the former enemies; and what little possibility of reconciliation there was soon vanished when Mexicans discovered that Spaniards who had joined Iturbide's movement at the end of the war were rewarded with good government jobs, which they would have liked to have themselves. Were Spaniards to continue to have the old priority over creoles that they had enjoyed under Spain? Mexican feeling against these officeholders erupted in 1824 in a revolt by General José María Lobato.

Spain, meanwhile, refused to recognize Mexican independence, and irritation and fear of Spanish monarchist plots reached a crescendo in 1827 on the discovery of a conspiracy by Father Arenas to restore Spanish rule. The inevitable outcome of constant newspaper attacks on Spaniards in Mexico was a series of state and federal laws to expel them. As it happened, one of the strongest advocates of legislation to remove all Spaniards was Lieutenant José María Padrés, who had sailed for Lower California with Echeandía in 1825.

Padrés, who was to play a prominent role in California affairs, was a thirty-year-old engineer officer from Puebla, described by a visiting Englishman as "a short, dark, phlegmatic-looking man." Bright, ambitious, and interested in a variety of scientific subjects, Padrés was dissatisfied with his position at Loreto, where he had stayed while Echeandía went on to San Diego. In 1827 Padrés found himself back in Mexico City, the newly elected deputy to the Congress from Lower California.[67] In the course of that year Padrés showed himself to be a militant Mexican nationalist and played a prominent part in the Chamber of Deputies in drawing up the federal law of December 20, 1827, exiling all Spaniards, with some exceptions, until Spain recognized Mexican inde-

67. Hardy, *Travels in the Interior of Mexico*, p. 240; AD, expediente D/iii/716/Cancelados, caja 532.

pendence. In California, Governor Echeandía was reluctant to apply this law even to those Spanish Franciscans who refused to take the oath to the Mexican constitution, on the ground that Mexican substitutes must take their places before they could leave.[68] Severe criticism of Echeandía for his failure to expel the Spanish missionaries from California soon began to come in to the government, and shortly thereafter the officials of the Corps of Engineers were asked to report on the career of Padrés. On July 17, 1828, Minister of War Gómez Pedraza ordered Governor Echeandía to turn over his military command in California to Padrés and return to Mexico City.[69]

On March 20, 1829, while Padrés was waiting at Tepic, out of the reach of the fevers of San Blas, for shipping to take him to California, a more stringent law expelling the Spaniards was passed. This one gave Spanish residents of the Californias three months to leave the republic. Padrés immediately wrote the government that it would require troops and Mexican missionaries to take the place of the Spaniards before this law could be put into effect in California. Because of the political convulsions in Mexico, Padrés' letter did not receive the attention of the new minister of relations, Alamán, until October 1830. By that time Vice-President Bustamante had already authorized the dispatch to California of ten Mexican friars from the Franciscan College of Guadalupe at Zacatecas, who had given up their Tarahumara missions. The Mexican government was in such financial difficulties, however, that the friars had to wait for two

68. The Law of Dec. 20, 1827, may be found in Dublán y Lozano, *Legislación mexicana*, 2, 47–48; the part played by Padrés is briefly recorded in *El Sol* (Mexico City). See, for example, the issues of Nov. 30, 1827, Jan. 8 and 10, 1828, and June 7, 1828; Engelhardt, *Missions*, 3, 267–68.

69. Secretario de Hacienda to Secretario de Guerra, Apr. 1 and 8, 1828, AGN, Californias, *18;* AD, expediente D/iii/716; Gómez Pedraza to Echeandía, BL, Superior Government State Papers, p. 45.

more years before they received the necessary travel money. Padrés himself did not arrive at San Diego until July 1, 1830, where his reputation as an opponent of the missionaries and exiler of Spaniards had undoubtedly preceded him.[70] It should perhaps be added that despite Spain's attempt to invade Mexico at Tampico in July 1829, the Spanish missionaries were not exiled from California. There simply was no one to take their places. As one contemporary put it, the new generation of Mexican youth, no longer limited to the priesthood and the bar, now interested itself in other careers.[71]

Mexican missionaries were admittedly hard to find: Mexican colonists willing to go to California were no less scarce. The government was finally able to issue regulations for the colonization of the territories on November 21, 1828, and while these were a step in the right direction, they bypassed the important question of what to do about mission lands by merely stating that they could not be colonized until it was determined whether mission lands were to belong to mission Indians and Mexican settlers or not.[72] Settlers were not forthcoming unless they were shipped out as convicts. These continued to come in spite of protests from the Californians. Even supposedly informed persons in Mexico, such as Carlos María Bustamante, who was a member of the Commission on the Californias, did not hesitate to recommend sending prostitutes or political opponents to California. In 1828, Valentín Gómez Farías advised sending a military colony to California, and the following year Juan Francisco

70. Dublán y Lozano, *Legislación*, 2, 98; Padrés to Minister of Relations, Mar. 30, 1829, Alamán to Minister of Justice, Oct. 4, 1830, Minister of Justice to Alamán, Oct. 8, 1830, AGN, Misiones, *24*, 116, 117, 118.

71. *Memoria que leyó el secretario de estado y del despacho . . . de justicia y negocios eclesiásticos* (Mexico, 1825), p. 20. It may be noted that both Tomás Suria and Francisco de Paula Tamariz were excused from complying with the law of Mar. 20, 1829 (BL, Papeles varios, *34*).

72. Maza, *Código de colonización*, p. 240.

de Azcárate prepared a report on the need for such a colony to contain Russian advances toward San Francisco Bay. [73]

The Californians wanted hard-working immigrants, but it is evident that they themselves were anything but industrious. Captain José Bandini reported in 1828 that most of them did nothing. Their days were spent in dancing, riding, and gambling. They had neither profession nor trade, and few had as much as an elementary education. Behind this sad state of affairs, which is amply confirmed by reports from the missionaries, lay the fact that the Californians were seldom without Indians to do their work, and there was a shortage of land which might be obtained with full property rights. Bandini also reveals something of the fears of the merchants of the Los Angeles area that the territorial authorities in Monterey would try to limit foreign shipping to Monterey. According to Bandini, such a move would ruin California, for the missions with the most tallow and hides were in the south, from 80 to 170 leagues (208 to 442 miles) from Monterey. The roads were good, he said, but some of the hills were too steep for carriages, and bags of tallow would not travel so far; nor would mules carry a sufficient load of hides to make it worthwhile to send them such a distance. These were the economic realities behind the successive moves to make Los Angeles the capital and open the southern ports to foreign trade. They helped to split the territory politically into a northern and southern region. [74]

It was fortunate for Mexico that during Echeandía's difficult administration as governor of California Russia showed no aggressive tendencies toward the region. In fact, Russian

73. Bancroft, unbound notes on immigration and colonization, 1773–1833, BL; Bustamante, "Diario," May 31, 1826, Oct. 7, 1827, Zacatecas State Library, Zacatecas, Mexico (cited hereafter as ZAC); El Sol (Mexico City, June 6, 1828); Azcárate Report, Nov. 23, 1829, BL, Colonización y terrenos baldíos, Fomento, legajo 2, expediente 52.

74. José Bandini, A Description of California in 1828 (Berkeley, 1951), pp. 35, 38. This volume contains the original Spanish as well as an English translation. The translation is not reliable.

energies were fully taken up with a succession of domestic and foreign troubles that included the Decembrist uprising on December 13, 1825, shortly after the death of Tsar Alexander I, a war with Persia that lasted from 1826 to 1828, a war with Turkey from 1828 to 1829, and the Polish Revolution of 1830–31. Diplomatically, Mexico had no direct relations with Russia, but United States Minister Poinsett reported in March 1826 that the Mexican government did not fear the designs of the Holy Alliance because they felt that the United States and England would keep a watch on moves from that quarter. In his message at the opening of the Congress on January 1, 1826, in fact, President Victoria had said that the government did not find any threats against the independence of the Latin American countries in the conduct of the tsar.[75] Even after Poinsett was obliged, by congressional pressure in the United States, to reinterpret his rendering of President Monroe's message of December 1823 to the Mexican government, so that it should be clearly understood that a President of the United States could not pledge that country to defend Latin America against foreign attack unless Congress gave its sanction, the Mexican government showed no sign of worry. In May 1826 President Victoria admitted that "Monroe's memorable promise" was "not sustained by the present government of the United States of the north"; on the other hand, as the Mexican officials with whom Poinsett discussed the matter put it in another connection, "it was so obviously to the interest of the United States to assist in defending the Americas against the attack of United Europe."[76]

Prior to this the United States had embarked on a project to persuade Spain to recognize the independence of her former colonies in return for a guarantee that Cuba and

75. Poinsett to Henry Clay, Mar. 8, 1826, Manning, *Diplomatic Correspondence of the United States, 3*, 1654; *Un siglo de relaciones internacionales de México* (Mexico, 1935), p. 8.

76. *Un siglo de relaciones*, p. 11; Poinsett to Clay, May 6, 1826, Manning *Diplomatic Correspondence, 3*, 1657–58.

Puerto Rico should remain in Spanish hands. The United States asked Russia to use its influence with Spain to promote this move and duly informed Mexico of what was afoot in May 1825. Since Mexico was actively preparing an attack on Cuba at that point, in conjunction with Colombia, this news was unwelcome, but it probably did not escape the attention of the Mexican Ministry of Foreign Affairs that if Russia should succeed in persuading Spain to recognize the independence of Mexico, Mexico might have a better chance of persuading Russia to do the same.[77]

In spite of some indications that the new government of Tsar Nicholas I would go further in persuading Spain to recognize the independence of her former colonies, nothing was accomplished in that direction. In California, the Russian-American Company was equally anxious for the Russian government itself to recognize Mexican independence so that the trade in grain with California, which the company urgently needed, might be increased. By March 1828, the company's headquarters in St. Petersburg had come to the conclusion that it was useless to hope for such a development which, as the managers put it, was "so important for us and so insignificant for the Empire."[78]

The company was, indeed, increasingly discouraged about its colony at Ross. It could not be made to produce sufficient grain, and it was more and more difficult to obtain grain from California except in small amounts. To make things even worse, foreign traders were supplying California with its needs, and it was difficult for the company to sell its goods there.[79] Governor Echeandía continued to be sus-

77. Pablo Obregón to Henry Clay, Washington, D.C., Jan. 4, 1826, Poinsett to Clay, Mar. 8, 1826, Manning, *Diplomatic Correspondence, 3,* 1645, 1653–54.

78. Alexander H. Everett to Henry Clay, Madrid, Apr. 4, 1828, Manning, *Diplomatic Correspondence, 3,* 2153; Manager to Headquarters, Mar. 23, 1828, RRAC.

79. Statement by the Company, Mar. 23, 1828, Apr. 15, 1827, Apr. 10, 1839, RRAC.

picious of Russian attempts to trade and asked his government for a coast guard vessel as a protection against them. In his opinion, urbanity was not enough to avoid their trickery. When the government authorized him to build a fort on the northern frontier of California, Echeandía was obliged to reply that he lacked the means to do so, although he did send an officer to select a site for a barracks for a military guard to be stationed at the mission of San Rafael.

Governor Echeandía actually had more trouble with American trappers than he did with the Russians, for it was during his administration that they first began to cross the Rockies in a thin trickle that was soon to grow into a steady stream. Echeandía put Jedediah Smith in jail in 1827, and when the news was spread in Mexico at the end of that year that the Americans had seized the port of San Francisco, he reported that although this was not so, it was a well-known fact that they wanted California and would take it if they could. He thought defense measures against them had better be taken.[80]

By the end of 1830, when Echeandía's governorship was over, Mexico had been in charge of California for nine years; yet in spite of elaborate plans and constant efforts to adapt them to the local situation, things had not gone well. When in 1828 it looked as if the cumbersome machinery of the Mexican Congress was about to provide the long-needed legislation for California, a series of convulsions paralyzed its efforts. In California itself the mission problem was unsolved; nor were the twin promoters of development, colonization and commerce, further along. Danger from Russia seemed on the wane, but the approach of the Americans overland, instead of by sea as heretofore, now appeared as another threat. If California was to be saved, new and radical measures would have to be tried.

80. Echeandía to Minister of War, Mar. 8, 1827, BL, Departmental Records 5, 175; Bancroft, *California*, 3, 115; Hittell, *History*, 2, 104.

Chapter Four

California and the Reformers

Colonel Manuel Victoria, the new governor of California, was a tall, lean infantry officer from the little town of Tecpan, some fifty-five miles northwest of Acapulco. In February 1829, while temporarily in command of a battalion of the Mexico City garrison, he had requested an appointment in Lower California for reasons of health. The authorities made him governor of Lower California on February 26, 1829, and about a year later, on March 8, 1830, he was appointed governor of California. He arrived at Santa Barbara overland from Loreto on December 31, 1830, and took his oath of office on January 31, 1831. On the ground that Echeandía had not fulfilled his instructions, the government repeated the main points of these to Victoria. After restoring order, Victoria was to send information back to Mexico on the population of California, its public lands, and Indians; he was to pay particular attention to the education, enfranchisement, and civilization of the mission Indians. In this respect it was suggested that he arrange for the sending of some of the more promising Indian youths to Mexico City, at mission expense, to be trained as teachers.[1]

1. AD, expediente xi/iii/4–6580; Alfred Robinson, *Life in California* (New York, 1846), p. 98; Bancroft, *California, 3*, 182; Hittell, *History, 2*, 125–26.

While the government's policy toward secularization of the missions was not changed, it became evident that the Bustamante administration was not going to push for the removal of the Spanish Franciscan missionaries, in spite of the laws on the books. President Bustamante let this be made known through Henry Virmond in October 1829, and it was possibly this evidence of a more sympathetic attitude on the part of the Mexican government that made the California missionaries look upon Governor Victoria's arrival as a heaven-sent blessing. Supported at home by "the army, the church, and the wealthy classes of the community," as the British minister reported, the Bustamante regime attempted to improve the administration of the rural estates belonging to the Pious Fund of the Californias, so that it might forward at least some of the stipends of the missionaries.[2] On the other hand, Lucas Alamán, the minister of relations, who was once more in charge of California affairs, was anxious to find out which of the missions could sustain themselves without having recourse to these funds, which were strictly limited in amount. Confronted with reluctance on the part of the missionaries to reveal their financial affairs, however, Alamán announced to the Congress in 1831 that since the missions had supported not only themselves but also the troops in California for so long, this showed that many of them could now maintain themselves without any help from the government or from the Pious Fund. In the future, he suggested, Pious Fund money should go only to the poorer missions.[3]

Governor Victoria immediately found himself plunged

2. Henry Virmond to Captain Guerra, De la Guerra, "Documentos," BL, 6, 145–46; Pakenham to Palmerston, June 3, 1834, F.O. 50/84. Public Record Office, London, England (cited hereafter as PRO).

3. José María Guzmán to Alamán, Sept. 18, 1830, AGN, Misiones, 24, 307; Alamán to Guzmán, Sept. 22, 1830, AGN, Misiones, 24, 311; Juan Rodríguez de San Miguel, Segundo cuaderno de interesantes documentos relativos a los bienes del fondo piadoso de misiones (Mexico, 1845), p. 25.

into the thick of mission problems. Alamán had sent him Padrés' letter of March 30, 1829, blaming the Spanish missionaries for much of the troublemaking in California, and Victoria began to look into the matter. He was convinced, after talking with the missionaries, that it was Padrés who was the troublemaker, not the Spanish missionaries. He sent Padrés, who was assistant military inspector for the territory, to San Francisco with orders to inspect the troops there, although his real objective was to get him away from Monterey. In March 1831, Victoria went up to San Francisco himself and met Padrés, subsequently taking him on an inspection trip of the frontier posts facing the Russian settlements. In spite of his feelings against Padrés, he then unaccountably sent him to Bodega to ascertain the strength of the Russian forces. Later, Victoria complained that Padrés had told the Russians that the Californians were in a miserable state and that Victoria was a despot, while the missionaries were fanatics who abused the Indians. He does not reveal how he found out what Padrés allegedly said to the Russians.[4]

Victoria began to think that Padrés was the origin of all his increasing difficulties with the Californians. It was Padrés, he felt, who had persuaded Echeandía to remain on in California in the hope that Vicente Guerrero, who had been removed from the presidency by Bustamante, would return to power. If that happened, perhaps Victoria could be removed on the ground that the government that had appointed him was no longer in existence. It was Padrés, he was convinced, who had really drawn up Echeandía's secularization plan of January 6, 1831. This, in Victoria's view, was nothing more than a gigantic plot to rob the missions and divide the spoils with some of the disgruntled Californians, who were Padrés' fellow conspirators. According to Victoria's service record of his administration in California, he was

4. Engelhardt, *Missions, 3,* 357–58; Hittell, *History, 2,* 135.

engaged in a successful campaign to defend mission property from rebels eager to seize it for themselves.[5]

That the missionaries concurred with Victoria's opinion of Padrés, if they had not suggested it in the first place, is revealed by Father Durán's letter to Vice-President Bustamante of August 17, 1831, in which he branded Padrés as a man who had come to California to uphold the dogma "that there is no Hell." "Would human justice," Father Durán asked, "be very sure of the obedience and fidelity of subjects [of the state] once the fear of the justice of God has been removed?" Father Durán also said that Padrés was suspected of being an organizer of Masonry, which was against the law forbidding such societies. He concluded his letter by imploring the vice-president to have Padrés removed from California. In spite of the fact that Governor Victoria added to the already heavy catalogue of Padrés' sins by saying that he was the author of alarming and subversive rumors that had helped to make California disloyal to Mexico, the government did not recall Padrés. Victoria finally took the law into his own hands and ordered Padrés to leave for San Blas in October 1831. He sailed on November 8 on the *Margarita*, eager to tell the government about the iniquities of Victoria's administration.[6]

There is no doubt that Governor Victoria succeeded in making enemies of many of the men of influence in California by refusing to call together the Territorial Deputation, which he knew would oppose him. Instead, he ran the government in dictatorial fashion, meting out severe justice in a way which aroused many against him. Men like Pío Pico, Mariano Guadalupe Vallejo, Joaquín Ortega, Antonio María Osío, and Santiago Argüello, all of whom signed a statement

5. Victoria to Ministro de Relaciones, Sept. 21, 1831, BL, Departmental Records, *9*, 150–52; AD, expediente xi/iii/4–6580.

6. Narciso Durán to Bustamante, Aug. 17, 1831, BL, Archivo de Guerra transcript; Victoria to Ministro de Relaciones, Sept. 21, 1831, BL, Departmental Records, p. 147; Bancroft, *California, 3*, 197, n. 32, 383.

against him, sought to blacken him by associating him with the hated Spaniards, who were then providing a useful scapegoat for the frustrations Mexico was experiencing. California was being held back, these men said, by "the old maxims and customs of our oppressors [the Spaniards]." Many Spaniards who were "public enemies" of the Mexican system of government were in California. Relying on the ignorance of the people, they went on, these men were constantly working to destroy learning and knowledge, which were fundamental for the preservation of society. The governors who had come to California had succumbed to the influence of the Spanish missionary fathers who, because of the mission wealth they controlled and the fanaticism of the people, still had a certain influence with most of the inhabitants. Meanwhile, the unfortunate mission Indians were no farther along than they had been at the time of the conquest. Those who were sufficiently intelligent to realize their natural rights were whipped until they changed their views.[7] It will be seen that these same feelings against the clergy, the military, and the wealthy were beginning to make themselves felt in Mexico, where they were eventually to unseat the Bustamante administration which had relied on these very classes for support.

In California, as in Mexico, there was a movement afoot to bring to life some of the democratic promises of the Constitution of 1824. Carlos Antonio Carrillo, California's representative in the Mexican Congress in 1831, pointed to the need for public education in California, as well as for the long-desired organic law for the territory and the separation of the military command from the civil governorship. It is true that in September 1831 Carlos Antonio Carrillo delivered an address to the Chamber of Deputies on the Pious Fund, which has been described as a "warm espousal of the cause of the missions" by a man who was "an ardent admirer

7. Pío Pico et al, San Diego, Feb. 24, 1832, BL, Legislative Records, *1*, 265.

of the friars" and who "was determined to stop secularization if he could." The fact, however, that two years later,
in 1833, Carlos Antonio Carrillo was one of the leaders in
the Territorial Deputation who persuaded the reluctant
Governor Figueroa to secularize the missions makes it necessary to reexamine his speech. His theme is that public opinion
in California would be opposed to a move to sell property
belonging to the Pious Fund or the property of the missions
themselves, since the missions provided the funds to support
the troops in California and keep the territory going financially. "The idea that the missions should be given the mortal
blow," he says, "may drive the inhabitants to a despair so
deep that it is not easy to calculate. And just as a son detests
and curses the hand which ruined his father, depriving him
of his well-being and his inheritance, so these territories,
when they contemplate their inevitable ruin through the law
mentioned, will make the supreme powers of the Federation
the object of their hatred." It will be recalled that at this date
no final decision by the federal government had been made
on the question of the ownership of mission lands, although
the mission Indians and the white settlers in California were
presumed to have title to them. Carlos Antonio Carrillo
would appear to be more concerned with how mission property would be divided up than with supporting the missions
as such. Carrillo goes on, however, to propose the founding of
more missions in the north to offset the advances of the
Russians and the Americans. In an apparent reference to the
United States, he says that one country has a "settled maxim
. . . to recognize no other right to lands than that of occupation." Then, after pointing out that apparently Mexico is
unable to send colonists and does not have the strength to
protect California by other means, he suggests that there is no
choice but to create more missions to occupy the region, as
they had in the past. Here again the speaker is not exactly
enthusiastic, and he hardly mentions the mission Indians,
whose conversion was the main objective of the missions, ex-

cept to remark that the wealth of the missions is the product of the labor of "the unhappy neophytes." If Carrillo was indeed more concerned with preventing mission lands from going to non-Californians, his speech in 1831 is more understandable, and his position more in line with the men who were later to be his colleagues in secularizing the missions when non-Californians were an apparent threat to mission property.[8]

It is easy to assume, along with the Californians, that Victoria had simply taken over the cause of the friars as his own. There is no doubt that, in his own mind, he was engaged in battling to prevent Padrés and his men from acquiring the mission properties for themselves, but this does not mean that he entirely approved of the missions or that he wanted to keep things exactly as they were. His instructions had ordered him to pay particular attention to public lands and colonization, and in his report on these matters he mentioned that all coastal lands up to the northernmost mission of San Francisco Solano were occupied, the best being in mission hands. Bearing in mind that the regulations for colonizing the territories passed in 1828 stipulated minimum acreages for each colonist (article fourteen), he pointed out that if the mission lands were distributed to the mission Indians, there would not be enough land to provide each Indian with the required minimum. On the other hand, he said there was no doubt that if the chain of missions was moved to some other region, a great deal of good land would be available for distribution. But he could not proceed to assign these lands until the government provided the necessary legislation. He did want to make some grants, however, to make sure the troops could be maintained, so they would not be forever having to run to the missions for help. He added that he had pointed out in previous dispatches the fatal results of this. Statements

8. Carlos Antonio Carrillo to Deputation, July 21, 1831, BL, Departmental State Papers, 3; Herbert I. Priestley, trans. and ed., *Exposition Addressed to the Chamber of Deputies of the Union by Don Carlos Antonio Carrillo* (San Francisco, 1938), pp. x, xvi, 6–11.

like this one show that Victoria did not regard mission property as sacrosanct or the missions as beyond criticism. In another report, Victoria praised the friars for the promising development of their vineyards and other agricultural crops and pointed out that it was the mission Indians who did the work that made this possible. The Indians, he said, "have always been and still are the only working people in the country." At the same time he dwelt on the fearful ravages of venereal disease among the mission Indians and their need for better medical attention and food. In modern times this last matter has been investigated by Professors A. L. Kroeber and S. F. Cook, who have shown that those California Indian tribes who were completely missionized either became entirely extinct or almost disappeared.[9]

Like Echeandía before him, Victoria had been ordered to gather information about the Russians and Americans, and his reports show that he was duly suspicious of these foreigners. He thought the American beaver hunters were particularly dangerous. He refused to allow the Russians to hunt in San Francisco Bay, although they gave him presents. Nonetheless, he preferred the Russians to the Americans: "The Russian colonists," he said, "are good people, very different from the North Americans." He recommended that the government pay particular attention to the security of California and send additional forces to guard against attack. Convicts or persons with bad habits should not be sent out as colonists. California was a vast, fertile country of great natural wealth, he said, and the government should bear in mind that its wealth excited envy.[10]

9. Victoria to Minister of Relations, May 6 and June 7, 1831, BL, Departmental Records, *9*, 126, 134, 137–39; A. L. Kroeber, *Handbook of the Indians of California* (Washington, D.C., 1925), p. 888; Sherburne F. Cook, *The Conflict Between the California Indian and the White Civilization. I. The Indian versus the Spanish Mission*, Ibero-Americana, *21* (Berkeley, 1943), pp. 3–12.

10. Victoria to Minister of Relations, Apr. 13, June 7, 1831, BL, Departmental Records, *9*, 122, 140.

Governor Victoria was clearly not devoid of good sense when dealing with some of California's pressing problems, but his lack of political ability soon arrayed against him many influential Californians. He was convinced that he was standing guard, virtually alone, over mission lands which his foes were intent on seizing for themselves, but his regime ended on a comic opera battlefield on December 5, 1831, near Los Angeles. Here, with fourteen men, Victoria bravely dispersed and put to flight a large number of rebels, according to his own account of the affair. Victoria himself was wounded five times, the most serious of his wounds being a lance thrust that entered his right side and went through his chest. In this "miserable state," as he says, the only thing to do was to make for the nearest mission, which was San Gabriel. On December 9 Victoria had an interview with Echeandía at the mission and asked to be sent to Mexico. He finally sailed on January 17, 1832, having among his fellow passengers two young mission Indian boys, Pablo Tac and Agapito Amamix, who were on their way to Rome, and Father Antonio Peyri, who had decided to leave with the governor.[11]

The ousting of Governor Victoria had been preceded, in accordance with the accepted Mexican custom of the day, by the issuance of a *plan* or pronouncement at San Diego on November 29, 1831, setting forth the objectives of the rebels. It was apparently drawn up by Juan Bandini and signed by him, Pío Pico, and José Antonio Carrillo, brother of the California representative in the Chamber of Deputies. According to an addition made to this plan on December 1, 1831, former governor Echeandía was to assume temporarily both the civil governorship and military command of the territory—although the original pronouncement called for separation of these commands, and the Territorial Deputa-

11. AD, expediente xi/iii/4–6580; Bancroft, *California*, 3, 210; Minna and Gordon Hewes, "Indian Life and Customs at Mission San Luis Rey," *The Americas, 9* (1952), 88.

tion was to appoint two men to these posts. The Deputation met on January 10, 1832, at Los Angeles and quickly became involved in a controversy with Echeandía, who had excused himself from attending its sessions. In accordance with an old law passed in 1822, it appointed its senior officer, Pío Pico, to be civil governor or political chief of California, whereupon Echeandía objected.

Disagreement between Echeandía and the Deputation might have gone farther than it did if it had not been for a movement against both of them at Monterey, headed by Captain Agustín Zamorano, who issued a statement against the plan of San Diego. After an unsuccessful attempt at an invasion, during which Echeandía called together and armed large numbers of mission and non-Christian Indians, Zamorano agreed to a settlement by which he was to remain military commander of the region from San Fernando north, while Echeandía had military control of the south. For lack of a better claimant, Echeandía has generally been accorded the title of civil governor until the arrival of his successor, although he was not so recognized by the Deputation.[12]

Perhaps the most significant development of this period of interregnum was a growing restiveness on the part of the mission Indians. Captain Zamorano noted the serious nature of this in a letter to the minister of war of November 16, 1832, in which he said that he had armed forces at Santa Barbara, Monterey, and San Francisco, but he could not order them to unite, since the Indians in those areas were hoping for just such a move to attack and destroy their missions, which they "abominated with the most deadly resentment." He said there had been an attempted revolt at one of the missions near San Francisco, but it had been put down, although the leaders fled to the forests, where they joined the pagan Indians and fortified themselves. Former mission

---

12. Bancroft, *California*, 3, 202–04, n. 39, 232; Hittell, *History*, 2, 143–46, 152.

Indians from San José and Santa Clara had built a fort in the forest where they were collecting livestock and especially horses stolen from the missions and ranchos in the area, which they had almost stripped of cattle. He added he had heard that the Indians in the south in Echeandía's domain were in a no less dangerous mood.[13]

That all was not well in the south was confirmed two days later, when on November 18 Echeandía issued supplementary regulations for the inauguration of his secularization program of January 6, 1831. It will be recalled that according to this program two missions were to be converted into towns, and certain other missions were to be prepared for the change by the appointment of the necessary officials. Perhaps because some of the missions were now out of his reach, Echeandía apparently modified his plan so that it referred to San Gabriel, one of the missions which he had originally determined to make into a town, together with San Juan Capistrano, San Diego, and San Luis Rey. From the preamble to his new regulations it is apparent that Echeandía had already begun his program of secularization in these, or possibly more, of the southern missions, and that the Indians were delighted and had hoisted him onto their shoulders when he visited the missions. On the other hand the missionaries and the new majordomos reported that the Indians (presumably those still on the missions) refused to work and were insubordinate. Echeandía attributed this development to discontent on the part of the Indians with the amount of clothing they were receiving and to general dissatisfaction because "they do not enjoy all the fruits of the labor which they perform." Father Durán, taking an entirely different view, felt that it showed the experiment had failed, and the Indian "big boys" should be sent back to school.[14]

13. Zamorano to Minister of War, Nov. 16, 1832, BL, Archivo de Guerra transcript.

14. Bancroft states that the new regulations were sent to all the southern missions (*California*, *3*, 314, n. 22); Engelhardt states that they went

That Echeandía may have been worried at the way in which his program was working out may be seen in the fact that the only major change provided by his new supplementary regulations was to make it more difficult for a mission Indian to leave his mission and obtain his share of its property. By the decree of January 6, 1831, all Indians of the two missions to be made into towns who were over twenty-five, or over eighteen if married, were to have a right to their share of its lands. By the new regulations, an Indian would have to have been on the mission ten years and be married, or a widower with minor children, to get his share of the property. All other mission Indians were to continue to work on the mission. This retrenchment is not reflected, however, by the language of the preamble, which harked back to the strong anti-mission tones of the Commission on the Californias and drew forth indignant counterblasts from Father Durán. Father Durán alleged that Echeandía was keeping his position in California through the support of the Indians, whom he had promised to release from their missions. Commenting on the fact that Echeandía had armed the Indians and reminding his readers of the Indian raids in northern California, Father Durán prophesied that unless the Indians were kept under control, before many years had passed the whites would have serious trouble on their hands.[15]

In Mexico City, meanwhile, the Bustamante government was confronted with what must have been two diametrically opposed accounts of the events in California, supplied by former Governor Victoria and José María Padrés; it accepted the version of Victoria and rejected that of Padrés. On April 17, 1832, it appointed General José Figueroa inspector and comandante general of California, and on May 9 it made

---

to the four mentioned above and to the president of the missions, who was at San José (Missions, 3, 418); see also Missions, 3, 433.

15. Articles 1 and 6. Bancroft, California, 3, 314, n. 23; Engelhardt, Missions, 3, 422–41.

him governor as well, presumably feeling that the recent disturbances in the territory made it necessary to continue the joint civil-military command, despite the wishes of the Californians.[16]

General Figueroa was a man of forty, short, dark-skinned, and proud of his Indian blood. He was from Jonacatepec, near Cuautla, in the present state of Morelos. He had had a distinguished career in the war of independence, fighting from the beginning against the Spaniards in the ranks of well-known leaders such as José María Morelos and Vicente Guerrero. He had represented Guerrero at a famous meeting with Iturbide in 1821, the outcome of which was Guerrero's decision to join Iturbide in what were to be the final successful campaigns of the war. After Iturbide's fall from power, General Figueroa came to terms with the new government and was made comandante general of Cuernavaca in 1823. He became a member of the congress of the state of Mexico in 1824 and seems to have taken some part in drawing up an organic law for the state. President Victoria appointed him comandante general of the state of Sonora and Sinaloa at the end of 1824, however, and he moved north in the spring of 1825.

After an expedition to the Colorado River, during which he provided valuable assistance in reopening the old Anza Road, closed since 1781, General Figueroa found himself involved in serious Yaqui and Mayo Indian revolts led by the able Yaqui leader Juan Banderas. After eighteen months of fighting which was said to have cost three thousand lives, Figueroa put the revolt down, although he was criticized for being too indulgent toward the Indians in the course of the struggle. The state of Sonora recognized his services by making him a citizen of the state in 1828 and renaming the presidio of Altar Villa de Figueroa.[17]

16. AD, expediente xi/iii/2–257; Bancroft, *California*, 3, 235.
17. George William Beattie, "Reopening the Anza Road," *Pacific Historical Review*, 2 (1933), 63–64; L. J. Bean and W. M. Mason, *The Romero*

General Figueroa was an old comrade-in-arms and friend of Vicente Guerrero, and when Vice-President Bustamante issued his pronouncement against President Guerrero in December 1829, Figueroa remained loyal to Guerrero. Within a short time, however, Bustamante's movement won general acceptance. Figueroa made peace with the new regime early in 1830 and was appointed a substitute judge in the Supreme Tribunal of War and Marine, a position he kept until he was appointed governor of California in the spring of 1832.[18] Governor Figueroa's distinguished career as a soldier, his practical experience as governor of Sonora, and his knowledge of Indians and sympathy for them, together with his experience in the state legislature of Mexico and the military supreme court, made him undoubtedly the best prepared of the Mexican governors of California. The Californians themselves considered him later as their best governor, and there is virtual unanimity among historians supporting this view. General Figueroa's private life, on the other hand, shows that he had his weaknesses: he was overly fond of gambling, and the 3,300 pesos he owed the state of Sonora when he left it may well have originated in his having to pay off gambling debts. He also owed money to various individuals in Sonora and Sinalo. He abandoned his wife, María Francisca Gutiérrez, shortly after marrying her, and the government was finally forced to subtract a modest amount from his salary so that she and their infant son, Manuel María Figueroa, should not starve. Later lawsuits against the estate of General Figueroa reveal that he had two illegitimate children, Rómu-

Expeditions (Palm Springs, Calif., 1962), pp. 73–80; Bustamante, "Diario," Nov. 4, 1826, ZAC; Pinart, "Documentos para la historia de Sonora," BL, *I–II*, 138; Ignacio Zúñiga, *Rápida ojeada al estado de Sonora* (Mexico, 1835), pp. 9, 42; Spicer, *Cycles of Conquest*, pp. 61–64; Francisco P. Troncoso, *Las guerras con las tribus yaqui y mayo* (Mexico, 1905), p. 50.

18. AD, expediente xi/iii/2–257; Bancroft, *California, 3,* 234, n. 23.

lo Figueroa, who lived in Cuernavaca, and María Jesús Figueroa, who may have remained in California.[19]

Minister of Relations Alamán, who had a high regard for General Figueroa, wrote him on May 17 and gave him a detailed briefing on the current situation in California. Alamán's account of the recent troubles was based on Victoria's views of the controversy. On the same day the senior official in the Ministry of Relations, José María Ortiz Monasterio, sent Figueroa his instructions. After restoring order and rebuilding confidence in the Mexican government, Figueroa was ordered to provide the usual statistical information about California. He was directed to distribute lots from mission lands of a size that competent mission Indians would be able to cultivate, so that they would achieve a desire to work and would continue to acquire property. On the other hand, lands that were necessary for such purposes as supporting the church or providing for schools and other common needs were to be kept intact. In this way, the instructions stated, the missionary system would be gradually replaced by another better suited to the needs of the territory, while the influence of the missionaries would be diminished until they attended to spiritual duties only. Finally, the missions would be secularized; but all this was to be done prudently and tactfully so as not to cause dissatisfaction among the missionaries. Indeed, the governor was to take care to preserve the best relations with these men, to the most influential of whom Vice-President Bustamante was writing personal letters which Figueroa was to take with him.[20] There was nothing new in these instructions, as may

19. AD, expediente xi/iii/2–257; José María Mendoza, "Reclamación contra el Gral. Figueroa," BL, Departmental State Papers, 77, 455; Rancho Los Alamitos Court Case no. 290, BL Collection of Land Cases, pp. 203–07; John Temple to Abel Stearns, Dec. 21, 1857, Stearns Papers, Huntington Library (cited hereafter as SP); Bancroft, *California*, 3, 297.

20. Alamán to Figueroa, May 17, 1832, BL, Superior Government State Papers, Decrees and Dispatches, 8, 66, 86; Bancroft, *California*, 3, 235, n. 23.

be seen by comparing them with those given to Echeandía and to Victoria. They agreed with the recommendations of the Commission on the Californias and with Alamán's own previous statements to Congress. Nor is there any conflict between these instructions and Alamán's letter to Figueroa describing recent events in California.[21]

Figueroa was also ordered to proceed with colonization, which was to be achieved by all possible methods but also with due care. He was informed the government had heard that many foreigners who had gone to California had not been allowed to settle there. Figueroa was therefore instructed to grant them lands in accordance with the colonization law of 1824 and the territorial colonization regulations of 1828, but he was not to allow Russian or American families to make up more than a third of the population. Convicts who had served their time in California were also to be given their own land. Finally, Figueroa was especially urged to increase the population around the new presidio at San Rafael, and he was to try to found new towns at sites that he believed either the Russians or Americans were thinking of seizing. Like Echeandía and Victoria before him, he was ordered to keep a close watch on the Russians and Americans.

Rather better informed and supplied than his predecessors, Figueroa sailed from Acapulco on the *Catalina* on July 17, 1832. He and his men landed first at Cape San Lucas, at the southern tip of Lower California, while the ship went on to San Blas and Mazatlán to take on further supplies and the long-awaited ten Mexican friars from the College at

21. It should be noted that Bancroft points out that the instructions signed by Ortiz Monasterio, whom he mistakenly refers to as Minister of Relations, "go practically much further toward secularization" than Alamán's letter to Figueroa of the same date *(California, 3, 325)*. This has apparently led Geary to state in error that there were two sets of instructions for Figueroa that were contradictory to each other (Gerald J. Geary, *Secularization of the California Missions* [Washington, D.C., 1934], pp. 132–33).

Zacatecas. Unfortunately, when the vessel reached Cape San Lucas again, most of Figueroa's troops and the ship's crew revolted and sailed away, leaving Figueroa and the friars stranded. The occasion for this was a new movement against Bustamante, headed by General Santa Anna, which was eventually to topple Bustamante and bring in Santa Anna as president, with Valentín Gómez Farías, now one of the federalist leaders of the northern states, as vice-president. Figueroa and his company went by land up to La Paz, where they again met the *Catalina* and sailed once more, reaching Monterey on January 14 or 15, 1833.[22]

The core of the new movement against Vice-President Bustamante was a body of northern and western federalist states, including Zacatecas and Jalisco, whose leaders wanted by constitutional means to amend and enforce the Constitution of 1824. Behind this was a growing distrust of the wealthy, the military, and the upper clergy, who had all supported the Bustamante regime. Gómez Farías now emerged as one of the strong-minded leaders of this group. Unfortunately, these men of principle were obliged by political circumstances to team up with the military forces of General Santa Anna, who demonstrated throughout his long career that was so disastrous for Mexico a complete lack of principle and an equally complete absorption in running the country as if it belonged to him. The Bustamante regime fought back against this unlikely combination but finally lost early in December 1832.

It had been arranged that the victorious forces were to reinstall former President Gómez Pedraza until new elections could be held in March 1833. The new government of Gómez Pedraza took prompt action on some matters that concerned California: on January 16, 1833, new regulations were issued for the enforcement of the 1829 law expelling Spaniards from

22. BL, Superior Government State Papers, Decrees and Dispatches, *8*, 88–89; Bancroft, *California, 3*, 236–38.

the country, and on January 23 an order revoked a decree of the previous administration to sell real estate in Mexico City belonging to the Pious Fund of the Californias. Instead, this property was to be rented and the revenue collected and used for California purposes.[23] The results of the March elections, which surprised nobody, made Santa Anna, who was resting at his estate near Jalapa, president, and Gómez Farías, who had accepted the unpopular job of presiding over the customarily empty federal treasury, vice-president.

When President-elect Santa Anna explained that he could not come up to Mexico City to take the oath of office because he could not get his boots on "due to past irritations," many were suspicious that he was planning some move against the new, democratically minded wing of the Federalist Party, headed by Farías. Some of the more ardent spirits among the reformers were scaring wealthy landowners, the military, and the church by talking about dividing up the big estates, giving the surplus to the poor, and creating state militias to offset the power of the army, and by criticizing the clergy and calling for religious tolerance.[24] Attempts to calm the rising fears of those affected by these pronouncements were vain, and as time went by the opposition looked increasingly to the absent Santa Anna for relief.

Meanwhile Gómez Farías, who was above all a man of action, made ready to take the oath of office as vice-president and acting chief executive on April 1. Church bells rang and cannon roared as he took his seat in the large hall of the Exchange, dressed in "republican black," as befitted the first civilian to take charge of the country since it became independent. Carlos María Bustamante, an incorrigible opponent

23. Dublán y Lozano, *Legislación*, 2, 476–77, 479.

24. Santa Anna to VGF, Mar. 16, 1833, Farías Papers, University of Texas Latin American Collection (cited hereafter as FP); Bustamante, "Diario," Mar. 23, 1833, ZAC; *La Antorcha* (Apr. 2, 1833); Juan Suárez y Navarro, *Historia de México y del General Santa Anna* (2 vols. Mexico, 1850–51), 2, 82–83.

of the new regime who refused to attend the opening ceremonies, recorded, from ill-disposed witnesses of the event,
that Gómez Farías "looked like the majordomo of a baker's
shop." These same "scoffing bystanders," as Bustamante himself called his sources of information, "noted the horrible
faces of a large number of the deputies, who revealed their
base lineage and ignoble manners a whole crossbow shot
away." That the elections seemed to have reached down into
the Mexican social classes of the time and produced a new,
less polished and more uncouth type of deputy, obnoxious
to the former ruling group, is confirmed by other contemporaries.[25] The situation may perhaps be compared to the
influx of rough westerners when Andrew Jackson took over
the presidency in the United States.

After taking the oath, Farías made a speech to the Congress
and people of Mexico on the aims of his administration. It
was brief and devoid of the frills so dear to the orators of
the day. He began by calling for action rather than words:
"There have been enough false assurances: the people must
feel and experience the good, their lot must be improved."
This in turn called for the passage of laws putting the pre-
cepts of the Constitution into effect, for "respect and observ-
ance of the social pact is not enough for the people's welfare."
He called for legislation to reform the department of the
treasury and to protect primary education, which he said
was essential "if the republic wants good parents, good
children and good citizens who will know and do their
duty." Justice in Mexico was in a lamentable state, he pointed
out, because the country had no adequate code of laws. "Our
bulky codes," he said, "are filled with laws made for an absolute monarchy, a constitutional monarchy, a colony, an
independent nation, a central government and a federal
republic." Such a jumble of legislation, he went on, "makes

25. Bustamante, "Diario," Apr. 1, 1833, ZAC; Bocanegra, *Memorias*, 2,
418–19.

lawsuits endless and confounds justice." No less urgent than
the matters he had touched upon, he said, was the colonization "of immense lands which await the hand of the farmer
to enrich our country with innumerable and precious products. They will provide subsistence and comfort for many
families who, submerged in misery and perhaps involuntarily
idle, are useless or harmful to their country."[26] Colonization,
he went on, would preserve "the integrity of Mexican territory, covering with population its almost deserted frontiers."

With Santa Anna still showing no sign of wishing to come
up to Mexico City and take the helm, the Farías government
began to produce its proposals for new legislation. "The
Farías administration," remarked José María Luis Mora,
one of its intellectual mentors, was one "in which little was
said but much was attempted." The first of a series of bills
dealing with colonization was put before the Chamber of
Deputies on April 13 by Miguel Ramos Arizpe, minister of
ecclesiastical affairs. This bill was to secularize the missions
of Upper and Lower California, a move which the government felt must come before colonization could be undertaken. Ramos Arizpe addressed the Chamber on the need for
the bill: "A long time ago and even from the time of the Spanish government," he began, "there had been serious thoughts
of changing the system of administration of the missions and
towns of the Territories of both Californias." The reasons
for this, he went on, were not simply social factors, such as
their population or the state of their civilization, but "principally political circumstances and the necessity of setting
on foot the improvement and development that those important areas of Mexico call for because of their position and
their resources." The people of those areas, he continued,
being careful not to call them Indians, had been up until then
under the exclusive and almost patriarchal government of
the religious of the College of San Fernando. These people

26. *El Telégrafo* (Apr. 2, 1833).

"have not yet known nor have they therefore begun to participate in the civil rights or share the joys of liberty and property that our federal pact guaranteed for all Mexicans." Most of the missionaries had always been Spaniards, he said, and almost all of them refused to take the oath for independence or to swear to the Constitution. For this reason the Mexican government had paid particular attention to them. An effort had been made to remove them as quickly as possible, replacing them with Mexican missionaries, in whose political conduct the government had more confidence. It had not been possible to secularize the missions because of lack of clergy in the bishopric of Sonora, and the second expedient of replacing the missionaries with Mexican friars had been partly accomplished after much effort and expense with the recent sending of missionaries from the College of Guadalupe at Zacatecas to take over half of the missions. "But this method," he went on, "even if it were completed for all of the missions, which would be difficult if not impossible in the future, because of the lack of regular clergy, would never be enough to cause the civil administration of the people to thrive." For that reason, he concluded, the government "had become convinced of the absolute necessity and convenience of resorting to the secularization of the missions."[27]

The bill which Ramos Arizpe introduced to the deputies consisted of fifteen articles. It began by stating that the government would proceed to secularize the missions of Upper and Lower California at an opportune time.[28] A parish was to be established at each of the missions in which a parish priest of the secular clergy was to serve at a stated stipend.

27. Mora, *Obras sueltas, 1,* cxcvii; *El Telégrafo* (Apr. 24, 1833).
28. The words "at an opportune time" were later dropped. For a recent bibliography on the subject of mission secularization and a call for further investigation see Manuel P. Servín, "The Secularization of the California Missions: A Reappraisal," *Southern California Quarterly, 47* (1965), 133–49.

The parish priest was not to charge for his services. The former mission chapels were to be the parish churches, and the government would have a cemetery constructed for each parish outside the town. The government would provide an annual sum for the expenses of the parish. The parish priest was to be given the most suitable of the permanent buildings on the mission, the others being made into a town council meeting house, an elementary school, and public buildings or workshops. In order to provide promptly and efficiently for the spiritual necessities of both Californias, a vicar forane was to be established in the capital of northern California, whose jurisdiction was to extend to both Californias. The vicar was not to charge for his needs, which were to be met by a stipend. When the new parish priests had been appointed, the government was to provide for them and their relatives a free sea passage to California, and in addition, a sum for their travel by land, according to the distance traversed and the number of persons involved. The government was to pay the cost of the return journey of the missionaries to Mexico. The government was to meet the expenses involved in the bill by levying upon the resources of the Pious Fund of the Californias.

The Chamber of Deputies received this bill on Saturday, April 13, and turned it over to its Committee on the District and Territories on Monday, April 15. This committee consisted of three men—José María Berriel, Manuel Lozano, and Pedro Anaya—and they kept the bill for nearly a month, returning it, with their amendments, to the Chamber of Deputies on May 9. The changes the committee made to the bill amounted to the insertion of an extra article and an addition to an existing article. The number of articles was kept the same, however, by joining two original ones together. The new article (article eleven) stated that no custom was to be introduced obliging the inhabitants of the Californias to make offerings, no matter how pious, even if they were said to be necessary. And neither the passage of time nor the consent of the citizens was to alter this prohibition. General discussion of the bill took place on June 3 and again on June 25, when, by a vote of twenty-seven to sixteen, it was decided to vote on each article separately. Debate began the following day, June 26, on each article and continued on the following two days, a Thursday and Friday. It was taken up again on Monday, July 1, when the last article was approved. Most of the votes were unanimous, and only one minor change in wording was made in the revised bill presented by the committee. The records for the bill's passage through the Senate are not available, but the Ministry of Ecclesiastical Relations reported on August 17 that the Congress had approved it, and Vice-President Farías duly signed it into law on that day.[29]

The bill securalizing the California missions did not appear to arouse greatly the wrath of the opposition during its passage through the Congress or when it was enacted into law, perhaps because they were aiming most of their weapons at the information leaking out about another bill, which provided that the power of patronage over the church resided in the Mexican nation.[30] It had long been accepted that the Spanish law of September 13, 1813, secularizing all the missions in Mexico was to be put into effect. Indeed, it seems to have been an oversight that this law was not specifically annulled in the new Mexican legislation. This oversight was corrected, however, in the more important and more controversial bill on colonizing the former mission lands that was sent to the Chamber of Deputies on April 16, 1833, three days after the bill on secularization was first introduced. The secularization law had said nothing about the important question of what was to be done with the vast lands, herds

29. *El Telégrafo* (Apr. 27, May 21, June 9, 30, July 2, 4, 5, 6, Aug. 19, 1833); "The Secularization of the Missions," Historical Society of Southern California, *Annual* (1934), pp. 66–73. The law is listed in Dublán y Lozano, *Legislación*, 2, 548–49.

30. *Destierro de los sacerdotes*, May 22, 1833.

of cattle, vineyards, orchards, and other possessions of the missions. The new bill was designed to regulate this most important aspect of the mission problem. It is a bill that has been ignored by the historians of California, perhaps because it never became law. But it is nonetheless important because of the insight it gives into the aims of the Farías government in this crucial matter, and because Governor Figueroa and the authorities in California knew about it and took appropriate action to guard against its application in that area.

The minister of relations, Bernardo González Angulo, who had been appointed during the brief tenure of office of President Gómez Pedraza, introduced the bill with a speech in which he said that Vice-President Gómez Farías' attention had been particularly drawn to the subject of missions, especially those in the Californias, because of

> the large sums allocated for their development, the fertility and wealth of both of them, especially Upper California, and also because they have been neglected, to a certain extent, by both the Spanish government and by the national governments since we obtained our independence. As a result of this those Mexicans who live there under a happy sky with fertile land which abundantly rewards the man who works hard with his hands, with good ports, diving for exquisite pearls, fishing for sea otter, seals, and whales, not to speak of other kinds of industry, have scarcely been able to populate its coasts. And the recently converted Indians on the missions still suffer the vices of idolatry without having tasted all the benefits that civil life provides.

The government, he continued, had been looking into these problems "and others more serious that the present situation of both Californias might give rise to"—an allusion to the danger from foreign encroachments—it had sought the advice of people who could provide true and exact information, and it had consulted the papers, documents, and dispatches on the important affairs of the missions to bring light on a question that was considered of the greatest importance. It had done this with the intention of considering whatever permanent sensible measures might be able radically to remove the problems in these territories and bring them the advantages they now lacked. This situation was due, he said, to the "almost complete lack of active interest" generally shown in that part of the republic. If only a little more attention had been paid to the Californias, a little more care taken to see that the laws were obeyed, it would have been enough to enable them to increase their population considerably and raise their production of goods for the nation's commerce and industry. Unfortunately, he continued, this had not been the case, "in spite of the measures taken by the Spanish Cortes on the secularization of missions, ours continue just the same as the colonial administration left them." This, he felt, was opposed to both reason and justice. It was also illegal, and while it continued, "it cannot be expected that those countries will be happy or that they will reach that state of prosperity that the wealth they contain holds before them."

González Angulo continued his speech with a brief review of the history of the missions, a short statistical summary of the economic geography of both Californias, and a reference to the individuals whose charitable bequests gave rise to the pious funds supporting the missions. The missions themselves had been poorly run, he went on, for the missionaries had been left in control of mission property, and thus it was inevitable that there should occur what had now taken place. The influence of the missionaries had slowed down the development of industry and the benefits that it could produce when encouraged and protected by an enlightened administration. Perhaps these problems would have been overcome by then if the law passed by the Spanish Cortes on September 13, 1813, had been put into effect, but although there did not appear to have been any legal reason preventing this, it had not been done. "It seems," he went on, "that too much toleration has been shown in this matter." What was more, this law, which might have solved the problem if it had been applied when it was passed, would not suffice today: "Another remedy, then, must be found, one that is more positive and more efficient. No room must be left for greed, bad faith, or the maneuvers and stratagems that are at hand and are used when it is desired to avoid complying with a decision."

González Angulo closed his remarks by saying "His Excellency the Vice-President, after having meditated upon what would be most appropriate for the happiness and prosperity of both Californias, orders me to make the following proposals for a law." The bill, in forty articles, followed: Article one stated that lands belonging to the missions and other vacant lands were to be divided among the following groups: first, Indian families in those territories; second, residents of the territories who did not own land or who, if they did own land, had less than this law gave to each family; third, the military who garrisoned those territories; fourth, Mexican families who went to reside in them; fifth, foreign families who went on their own to live there; sixth, *empresarios,* or colonization promoters, and the families they took there; seventh and last, convicts who, having finished their terms, wished to reside there.[31]

Changes were made to this important article, both by the Committee on Colonization of the Chamber of Deputies, of which Deputies Juan Gutiérrez Solano, Antonio José Valdés, Manuel Carrillo, and Vicente Prieto were members, and by the Chamber itself when the bill was being debated. The most interesting change was made by the Committee on Colonization, which put the military who garrisoned the Californias directly after the Indians in the order of priority in which the lands should be divided up, non-landowning

31. *El Telégrafo* (Apr. 22, 1833).

residents coming third. One of the reasons for this is indicated in the addition of the words, "and who are in arrears in their pay," in the sentence dealing with the military. At the end of the article the committee added that the owners should receive their titles to these lands, the titles for the Indians being paid by the Pious Fund, while the others were to pay at cost.[32] During debate on this article in the Chamber of Deputies, Espinosa de los Monteros proposed three further additions. One of these was that the words "precisely in the following order" be inserted just before the list of groups to receive land; another limited mission lands that could be divided among foreign settlers to lands belonging to missions which were at least thirty miles from the boundary; and the third was the addition of a sentence at the end of the article running as follows: "This division is understood to be without prejudice for what is needed and determined by law for the expenses of worship and spiritual administration." His reference was to article two of the secularization bill, which endowed the new parishes to be established in the missions with a sum of from 1,000 to 2,500 pesos a year. At the date that he made these proposals, the secularization bill was still in committee, but it was to be presented to the Chamber in a few days. Espinosa de los Monteros' amendments to the bill were quickly approved by the committee and passed by the Chamber forty-seven to one.[33]

The passage of this article was a notable event in the history of Mexican colonization legislation, since if the bill as a whole had been approved, it would have annulled article two of the colonization law of August 18, 1824, which limited foreign colonization to lands which were neither privately

32. Mateos, *Historia, 8,* Session of Mar. 30, 1833, p. 272; *El Telégrafo* (May 16, 1833).

33. The colonization law of Aug. 18, 1824, limited colonization by foreigners to areas sixty miles from a foreign country and thirty miles from the coast, unless previous approval had been given by the Supreme Executive Power. *El Telégrafo* (May 17, 1833).

owned nor owned by a corporation. It would also have
superseded article seventeen of the regulations for the colonization of the territories of November 21, 1828, which stated
that mission lands were not to be colonized until it had
been decided whether they were to be the property of the
mission Indians and Mexican settlers. This decision had now
been made. These two groups were to get priority, but the
military and other settlers from both Mexico and abroad
were also to have their share. The bill never became law, of
course, but it was duly noted in the newspapers by Governor
Figueroa in California and no doubt stiffened his decision
to oppose the colony sent out later by Farías to settle mission
lands.

No attempt will be made here to comment on all of the
forty articles in the bill introduced by the government (for
a translation of the bill see Appendix C); instead, certain
matters of interest will be pointed out. In article four, for
example, it is stated that the lands were to be granted with
complete title deeds. Land in the Californias was generally
granted only on a provisional basis, so that settlers were
insecure as far as their rights to the land were concerned.
In article five the Indians were prohibited from disposing
of the land given them until after five years, and even then
they could only sell those parts of their land that they had
cultivated and that presumably they were therefore least
interested in selling. It is sometimes mentioned that the new
policy of the liberals in Mexico toward the Indians, based
on equality with the white man, meant in fact that the less
sophisticated Indian would be swindled by the whites. Although there is no doubt that this bill was the work of liberals who approved of equality and integration, the Indian
was nevertheless given protection which the whites did not
receive. This very point came up in the course of debate on
the bill in the Chamber of Deputies. Deputy Escudero proposed that article five be amended to read that Indians and
other colonists as well should not be allowed to sell their

lands for five years. It was the last business to be discussed that day, and the Chamber recessed at 8:00 P.M. The following morning, Escudero withdrew his proposal, but it was taken up by Deputy Riveroll. When a vote was taken, it was narrowly defeated twenty-four to twenty-two, one of the closest votes in the entire debate.[34] Evidently the Chamber was almost equally split in its opinion on the matter of whether Indians should be given a status of complete equality or should still be given some protection. What the view of Farías' government was on this point it is difficult to say with precision, but José María Luis Mora, the highly trusted adviser and counselor of Farías, regarded Father Bartolomé de Las Casas and others who had fought for the Indian as being in reality his enemies, although their motives were of the best. He pointed out that these men, for one reason or another, were convinced that the Indians left to themselves could not equal the whites, and they wanted legislation "to compensate for the supposed superiority of the whites." This was proof, to Mora, that they believed the Indians to be inferior.[35] On the other hand, Rodríguez Puebla, one of the distinguished liberals of the day, who was of Indian blood, wanted to preserve the privileges enjoyed by the Indians in order to help them along. In his view distinguishing between Indian and non-Indian was not opposed to democratic equality. He pointed out that in fact true equality required that the laws should assist all according to their needs. In other words, according to Rodríguez Puebla, the Indians were culturally deprived or sócially disadvantaged, as modern terminology puts it, and needed assistance. According to Mora, the Farías administration, like the governments which preceded it, was opposed to these

34. *El Telégrafo* (May 16, 17, 1833). It is to be noted that the May 17 issue of *El Telégrafo* records that the amendment passed by a vote of 24 to 22 but *El Telégrafo* of May 22 corrected this.

35. *El Indicador de la Federación Mexicana* (Mexico City, Dec. 4, 1833).

ideas and wanted to integrate the Indian into the general mass of the people. The Farías government, Mora summed up, "did not recognize in its actions the distinction between non-Indian and Indian but substituted for that the distinction between rich and poor."[36] A learned Mexican judge of the day was inclined to doubt whether this attitude worked for the benefit of the Indians, and recent writers in Mexico disapprove in stronger terms.[37] In this bill, at any rate, the Farías government took a middle road, giving the Indian a helping hand and some protection while otherwise equating him with the white man.

This tendency of the administration to favor the Indian comes out also in articles eight and nine, which divided up among the mission Indians the cattle belonging to the missions. Any cattle that remained after this had been done were to be distributed among the Californian settlers, the military, the convicts, and families from Mexico. The Chamber of Deputies, however, outdid the government by doubling the number of cattle the Indians were to receive and further stating that the whites were to be given only half the number given to each Indian family. Under article eleven, which made certain provisions in the colonization law for Texas of April 6, 1830, applicable also to the Californias, Mexican families who volunteered to go to the Californias as colonists would be helped by the government to undertake the journey and given their means of sustenance for a year as well as land and implements. Article nineteen of the bill went even beyond this by saying that sea and land transportation for

36. Luis Chávez Orozco, *Las Instituciones democráticas de los indigenas mexicanos en la época colonial* (Mexico, 1943), p. 39; Mora, *Revista Politica,* p. cclxiii.

37. Manuel de la Peña y Peña, *Lecciones de práctica forense* (4 vols. Mexico, 1835–39), *1,* 251; Josefina Muriel de la Torre, *Hospitales de la Nueva Espana* (2 vols. Mexico, 1960), *2,* 286; Moisés Gonzales Navarro, "Instituciones indígenas en México independiente," in Alfonso Caso et al., *Métodos y resultados de la política indigenista en México* (Mexico, 1954), pp. 116–17.

Mexican and foreign families would be paid by the government. On the other hand, if a grantee had not cultivated his lands within five years at least sufficiently to support his family, he would lose them without fail. There was no discussion on this article, so presumably it did not occur to anyone that the Indian might be the one to suffer here.

The actual division of the lands, property, and implements granted by the bill was to be made by a director and subordinate commissioners. The government was to appoint these men and provide the necessary regulations and instructions. The director was also to establish immediately free primary schools in all towns and missions with a population of more than two hundred persons; the government was to pay the salaries of the schoolteachers. The cost of putting the proposed law into effect was not sidetracked. These expenses and others needed to develop the arts and sciences, agriculture, and all kinds of industry in both Californias were to come first from revenue from the estates, capital, and rent making up the Pious Fund of the Californias, secondly from any property remaining after division among the various settlers according to the bill, and thirdly from 50 percent of the revenue from the maritime custom houses of both territories and all of the revenue from internal custom houses in each territory. This fund was to be known as the Development Fund of the Californias and was to be under the direction of the commission then managing the Pious Fund.[38] Until the Development Fund was organized, the government was to meet the expenses of putting this law into effect using the money it owed the Pious Fund. The government was

38. *El Telégrafo* (May 17, 19, 20, 1833); Articles 18 and 25–31. An economic commission to direct the Pious Fund was established on June 27, 1832. It consisted of four men: Juan José Espinosa de los Monteros, Epigmenio José Villanueva, and Manuel González de Ibarra, with Ignacio de Cubas as secretary (AGN, Californias, *1*, 255 verso). It may be noted that three of these men, Espinosa de los Monteros, Ibarra, and Cubas, had been members of the second Commission on the Californias.

authorized to spend up to 100,000 pesos of this money sponsoring immigrants from foreign countries to develop the new
colonies.[39] The government was also authorized to spend
up to 20,000 pesos a year from the fund to help win over the
chiefs and old men of the Indian tribes in the interior of
the Californias. The original article drawn up by the administration began by stating that the government would "try to
attract to the social order by every means in its power all the
tribes of Indians." The committee changed this to read "by
every *gentle* means in its power," showing once again its concern with humanitarian measures. The committee withdrew
the last four articles of the bill, recasting them into a final
article thirty-seven, which annulled both the Spanish law
of September 13, 1813, and article six of the law of May 25,
1832, which had stated that money from the renting of rural
property of the Pious Fund was to be deposited in the treasury
and to be used only for the missions.[40] On April 17 or 18
the bill went to the Chamber of Deputies' Committee on
Colonization, which reported out its revision to the deputies
on April 30.[41] Debate began on May 2 and lasted for a week,
with final approval of the bill by the Chamber being completed on May 9. On May 10 it went to the Senate, which
received it "with satisfaction" and passed it on to its committee on colonization. From here on it disappeared from
view, apparently never emerging from the Senate. The government continued to keep an eye on it, for on May 20, the
day before the Congress recessed, Carlos García, the new
minister of relations, referred to it as "worthy of the preferred attention of the Legislative Power."

39. Articles 34 and 35. *El Telégrafo* (May 20, 1833) states that article
35, which had been revised by the committee, failed to pass by a vote of
24 to 23, while Mateos states that it passed. Mateos is probably correct,
for there is no mention of further revision of the article (Mateos, *Historia, 8,* 360).

40. *El Telégrafo* (May 20, 21, 1833).

41. Mateos *(Historia, 8,* 311) says April 17; *El Telégrafo* (May 2) says
April 18.

One of the major stumbling blocks of an active administration such as that headed by Farías was the crowded schedule of the two houses of Congress. Vital legislation could be stalled for years simply because the Chamber of Deputies or Senate had not been able to get to it. Carlos García provided an example of this on the same day that he reminded the Congress of the desirability of passing the colonization law, when he complained about the government's being hamstrung by the lack of an organic law for the district and territories. "In most cases," he said, "the government could not use the Spanish laws," which were all that existed.[42] Yet the need for such a law had been seen for years, every minister of relations having recommended it to Congress. Such interminable delays in the working of democratic forms of government gave added strength to the forces aiming at a dictatorship under such willing military leaders as General Santa Anna.

In this case, however, the Senate can hardly be blamed for lack of diligence in California affairs, for even the energetic Vice-President Farías found himself almost overcome with difficulties which would have quickly broken the spirit of a less determined man. On May 26 a revolt broke out at Morelia (then Valladolid) in the state of Michoacán, whose *plan,* or manifesto, stated that the garrison there would "uphold at all costs the religion of Jesus Christ and the rights and privileges of the clergy and the army which are threatened by intrusive authorities." The leader whom the rebels proclaimed was none other than the president of the republic, General Santa Anna. Santa Anna had apparently recovered sufficiently from his "past irritations" to take over the government in Mexico City on May 16, but he left again at the head of an army to put down the revolt on June 2, leaving Farías once more in charge of the government. So little confidence did Santa Anna inspire that many people thought he

42. *El Telégrafo* (May 15, 21, June 6, Aug. 14, 16, 1833).

was actually in league with the rebel leader in Morelia.[43] In Mexico City Farías faced the problems of keeping the government running and the garrisons loyal. Even before he had time to face his foes here, another and still more serious piece of news arrived. The long-dreaded Asiatic cholera which had been wreaking havoc in Europe struck the port of Tampico on May 24. The government newspaper, *El Telégrafo*, printed the news that those who were attacked scarcely lasted six hours.[44] The day following the publication of this disquieting news, June 8, the Mexico City garrison joined the rebels and attacked the Farías government, which had only a few civic militia to protect it. To make matters worse, Farías had to announce that President Santa Anna had been taken prisoner by his own officers in an apparent attempt to persuade him to join the revolution. The foxy Santa Anna made no announcements himself, perhaps waiting for what must have seemed the inevitable fall of Farías. But Farías fought off the rebellious garrisons with his handful of supporters and kept the government going.

Some of the leading clergy then joined the fray. The dean and chapter of the cathedral in Mexico City issued on May 14 a clarion call to repentance because of the approaching epidemic of cholera. "Sin is the origin of all calamities that plague the earth," they reminded their readers, as they proceeded to link up the wickedness of those who attacked the church with the horrors of possible death in the approaching epidemic. Again, on the same fatal day of June 8 when Farías battled alone against his foes, the bishop of Puebla published a pastoral letter in which he referred to the onslaughts of cholera that the Mexicans had read about in Havana as "a crack of the terrible whip with which the justice of our celestial Father chastises before our eyes our

43. Bustamante, "Diario," May 29, 1833, ZAC.
44. For a discussion of the epidemic of cholera in Mexico at this time see C. Alan Hutchinson, "The Asiatic Cholera Epidemic of 1833 in Mexico," *Bulletin of the History of Medicine, 32* (1958), 1–23, 152–63.

other brothers so that we may endeavor in good time to disarm and appease him."[45] "Does not the scorn with which the truths and venerable practices of religion are spoken of in conversations deserve punishment without any excuse whatsoever?" the bishop asked, "and does not the liberty with which the young, and even women, read heretical and obscene books and newspapers, which attack fundamental dogmas and ridicule the most holy institutions of the church, deserve to be punished?" The clergy in Mexico, as in California, were clearly more than a match for their critics.

The cholera epidemic did not strike Mexico City until August 6, but between then and September 11, when it was considered to be almost over, the city council estimated that some 10,332 persons, most of them of the poorer classes, had died out of a total of nearly 50,000 who had contracted the disease. This did not include, of course, fatalities in other parts of the country, which had also been ravaged by the epidemic. Added to the horrors of cholera was the civil war which continued on into 1834.[46]

The government's view of the civil war was put forward in an editorial in *El Telégrafo* on July 8:

> [it has been said many times] and we shall not weary of repeating it, the present war is one between rich and poor; between aristocrats or nobles and the people; between those privileged classes who dreamt that they were born to be served by everyone else, and honest, hardworking citizens, whom they want to enslave, so as to make use of their services, while they live in idleness. Finally, it is a war in which the Spaniards are fighting, if not in person, then through perverted Mexicans

45. *Nos el Dean y Cabildo gobernador de esta santa iglesia metropolitana de Méjico* (pamphlet, Mexico, May 14, 1833); *Pastoral que el Illm. Sr. Dr. D. Francisco Pablo Vázquez obispo de la Puebla de Los Angeles dirige a sus diocesanos con motivo de la peste que amenaza* (pamphlet, Puebla, Mexico, 1833).

46. Hutchinson, "Asiatic Cholera," pp. 153, 160.

whom they have turned against the Americans. One must keep one's eyes open and not be deceived: every Mexican who dies on one side or the other is a victory for the Spaniards.[47]

The realities of war and pestilence were grim, but neither side showed any disposition to give way. On the fateful Saturday, June 8, the Congress gave the government the power "to dictate all measures it judges convenient to reestablish order and consolidate federal institutions." These special powers were to be used only in the Federal District and the territories (such as California), in frontier or coastal areas, or in states where plans opposed to state or federal constitutions had been issued. These special powers were to last for four months, but on October 6, 1833, they were extended for another four months, being finally annulled on November 30, 1833, when the situation looked better for the government.[48]

Under the storm and stress to which it was subjected, it would not be surprising to find that the Farías government did little if anything to put into effect its ambitious plans for the colonization of California. In spite of its tremendous domestic difficulties, however, the government did more than any previous Mexican government had done to promote colonization in California and to develop the territory economically. Farías was determined to try to preserve Mexican territory from the possibilities of American or Russian seizure, and the information that was coming into the government about the danger from these countries may have been the main reason spurring the administration on to put its ideas into action.

On April 1, 1833, the War Department sent Farías a statement about California in which it spoke of the "extremely critical" situation it was in because of the domestic troubles

47. *El Telégrafo* (July 8, 1833).
48. Dublán y Lozano, *Legislación*, 2, 532–33, 560, 641.

there and of the threat from the Russians and Americans.[49] It was probably about the time that he became vice-president that Farías asked José María Guzmán, guardian of the College of San Fernando, who was also his personal chaplain, to send him a report on the situation in California, together with some statistical information. In his reply, Father Guzmán stated, "It is indisputable that [the North Americans] need and desire a safe port on this Ocean, and there is no doubt at all that whenever any political disturbance occurs they will keep without risk the safest and most beautiful port in the Universe [San Francisco]."[50] If these warnings were not impressive enough, Tadeo Ortiz' book, *"Mexico Considered as an Independent and Free Nation,"* which he had published while he was Mexican consul at Bordeaux in 1832, became available in at least one bookstore in Mexico City in May 1833. In this impressive work, Tadeo Ortiz, who had devoted a good deal of his life to promoting colonization in various parts of Mexico, again and again drove home warnings about the dangers facing California from the Russians and the Americans. It is likely that the Farías government read and took note of Ortiz' warnings, for in August they appointed him director of colonization in the even more crucial region of Texas. Also about the time that the government began to put its ideas about colonization in California into effect, its newspaper, *El Telégrafo,* remarked in an editorial that Russia had long coveted the riches of California, which would "fall into its power if it continued as it had done up to now in the most lamentable abandonment." "It is well to know," continued the paper, "that Spain by a secret Treaty ceded the Californias to Russia and that that formidable Empire has colonies established near them, that Russian war ships have appeared, doubtless making observations in prep-

49. Apr. 1, 1833, BL, Archivo de Guerra transcript.
50. *Breve noticia que da al Supremo gobierno del actual estado del territorio de la alta California y medios que propone para la ilustración y comercio en aquel país* (Mexico, 1833).

aration for an invasion which would have the worst results for the Republic." Further Russian activity in California had, in fact, come to the attention of the British minister in Mexico who wrote to Lord Palmerston about it, saying that he did not think, as the governor of California had reported to his government, that the Russians, who had allegedly tried to establish themselves on land belonging to the mission of San Francisco, were acting under orders from their government. They were more likely, in his view, to be hunters or fishermen. He admitted, on the other hand, "At this moment if any number even of private adventurers were to attempt a settlement in that remote district, the Government would have great difficulty in finding means to eject them."[51]

In actual fact the Russian-American Company had been dissatisfied for some time with the limited production of food possible at Ross. Baron F. P. Wrangel, a vice-admiral in the Russian navy and a high-ranking member of the company who became governor of its American possessions in 1830, confirmed the unprofitable nature of the company's endeavors at Ross. He suggested that the site of the colony be moved and the Mexican government be asked to cede, in exchange for recognition by Russia, the north bank of San Francisco Bay and other flat land suitable for agriculture between there and Ross. Wrangel admitted that foreigners in California would try to arouse the Mexican government against such a proposal, and he thought that the Russian government itself might oppose the move. The company agreed with his views on Ross and his expansion plans and thought that the Mexican government might be willing to make the necessary cessions if the Russian government were willing to recognize it. But the company managers did not know how the Russian government felt about this, and because of the

51. *El Telégrafo* (May 9, July 16, 1833); Tadeo Ortiz, *México considerado*, 2, 104, 181, 190, 203. Gómez Farías to Department of Hacienda, Aug. 14 [?], 1833, Museo Nacional, Mexico City, legajo 51-7-57-11. Pakenham to Palmerston, Aug. 9, 1833, F.O. 50/80a, PRO.

situation in Europe, they did not wish to bother the government by inquiring. They also did not think that the Mexicans would do more than threaten to remove them from Ross.

Shortly after Governor Figueroa arrived in California he wrote Baron Wrangel, presumably on the orders of the new administration in Mexico, informing him that the Mexican government wished to enter into friendly relations with St. Petersburg. Baron Wrangel wanted to make good use of this opportunity, but the company failed to persuade the tsar's government to take any action on the matter.[52] The Mexican government was making plans at this time to try to get into touch with the Russians by other means. The British minister reported on October 5, 1833, that a new Mexican minister was about to leave for Prussia with instructions "to take advantage of any opportunity that may offer to enter into communication with the Government of Russia for the purpose of endeavoring to induce that Power to recognize the independence of Mexico."[53]

In spite of overwhelming difficulties caused by the epidemic of cholera and armed revolt at home, the Farías administration energetically tackled California's major mission and colonization problems. In the diplomatic field, it also attempted to go to the root of the recurring threat of Russian encroachment by trying to get in touch with the tsar's government. It failed to solve any of these problems, as will be seen, but under the circumstances, it is remarkable that it managed to do anything.

52. Headquarters to Wrangel, Mar. 31, 1832, RRAC; Okun, *Russian–American Company*, p. 146.
53. Pakenham to Palmerston, Oct. 5, 1833, F.O. 50/80a, PRO.

Chapter Five

The Gómez Farías Colony

The first clear indication that the Farías administration was putting into effect its colonization plans for California appeared in an editorial of *El Telégrafo* on July 16, 1833. This said that since the Congress had not completed the laws begun on secularization and colonization of the missions of the Californias, "Señor Farías has made use of the extraordinary powers with which he is invested to provide sizeable funds so that employees charged with working for the prosperity and development of that country, and families who at present have engaged to go there and colonize it will be able to do so." The reason for granting special powers to the federal government was to enable it to reestablish order and consolidate federal institutions; the special powers were to be used in the territories and frontier or coastal areas. California qualified as a territory and also as a frontier and coastal area, and Farías, by a loose construction of the law, interpreted it to include strengthening California by colonization. The editorial also mentioned that Farías was at that time working on plans for a shipyard in one of the California ports, "a measure which will begin to create a national mercantile marine in the South Sea."[1]

1. *El Telégrafo* (July 16, 1833). The editorial actually mentioned only the law on secularization as follows: "las leyes sobre secularización."

It appears from this editorial that Farías was afraid of lengthy delay in the passage of both the law secularizing California missions, which actually did pass both chambers in August, and the law colonizing mission lands, which did not emerge from the Senate. He therefore determined to go ahead, using his special powers, with preparations for sending a colony out to California. Actually, the government newspaper may have been somewhat premature in implying that Farías had provided the funds for the transportation of the colony and government employees to California, for negotiations to do this continued for some time. But he had begun to select men for the undertaking. On July 12 the minister of war, José Joaquín de Herrera, sent a letter to Assistant Inspector José María Padrés, informing him that on orders from the vice-president he was to be sent to Upper California to become comandante general of the troops there if General Figueroa, the actual political chief and comandante general, "continued to be ill and wished to retire." Figueroa had written to Mexico on March 25, 1833, saying that he wished to resign his position for reasons of health.[2]

After he was ordered back to Mexico from California by Governor Victoria, Padrés had sailed for San Blas on November 8, 1831, and had gone inland to Tepic. Here on January 6, 1832, he wrote the Ministry of War asking for his retirement. His reasons for this were that his ill health had become chronic and made him completely unable to continue on active service. He did not say exactly what the nature of his ill health was, but it is known that he suffered from a severe case of venereal disease when he was in Lower California in 1826, and his troubles may have been connected with that.

Since the word "laws" must presumably refer to two or more laws it seems likely that through a printer's error the words "y colonización" have been omitted after "secularización."

2. Herrera to Figueroa, July 12, 1833, BL, State Papers, 2, 205; Figueroa to Minister of War, BL, Departmental State Papers, 2.

He eventually arrived in Mexico City in June 1832 and took up the question of his retirement in person with the authorities. He ran into a snag in the matter, however, for the Ministry of War informed him that it could not retire him until the Congress had determined what rank his position of assistant inspector carried with it. During the remainder of 1832, while he was waiting for Congress to act, Padrés made use of his time by seeking to improve his health, which became somewhat better. At the beginning of 1833, he again pressed for an answer to his request but was told that the situation was the same as it had been before. The Ministry of War then called upon him to work in its offices, and from there he went to the office of the director of the Military College of the Corps of Engineers, in which Echeandía was interested. While he was in this position, the government ordered him to prepare plans for the defense of the northernmost region of California against the Russians at Ross. It was probably in the course of this work that he came to the attention of Vice-President Gómez Farías, who was himself deeply interested in preserving this area from a possible Russian attack. At all events, Farías suggested to him that he go back to California and proceed to put his own plans for the region into effect. Padrés reported that he "respectfully resisted" the idea several times on the ground that his health was poor and that he had a large family, but Farías insisted and Padrés at length consented.[3]

In splitting up the military and political commands in the territory, Farías was following the desires of the new representative from California, Juan Bandini, who had sailed from San Diego for his new post sometime in May 1833 and possibly had had an opportunity to put his views before the vice-president. In July, Governor Figueroa sent a confidential warning to the minister of relations that Bandini represented a clique who wanted to separate the military and civil

3. AD, expediente D/iii–5/716.

commands as a means to further their aims of separating California from Mexico. They also wanted, he said, to give the political command to a Californian, and Figueroa did not think there were any Californians "even tolerably qualified for the office."[4] The Farías government apparently paid no attention to this warning; it is to be noted, however, that Padrés was to become comandante general only if Figueroa wished to resign.

Padrés was informed of his appointment on Friday, July 12. On the following Monday, July 15, Carlos García, the minister of relations, wrote José María Híjar that the vice-president was relieving General Figueroa of his post as governor of California and was appointing him to the position with a salary of 4,000 pesos for that post "and for that of Director of the Colony of that territory."[5] José María Híjar was a member of an old and distinguished Guadalajara family, who had long been a member of the state congress of Jalisco. In 1832, he was secretary to the congress and ran unsuccessfully in the elections for governor of the state.[6] Also in 1832, Híjar had represented Jalisco at a meeting of representatives of federalist-minded states at Lagos to draw up an agreement to call upon Gómez Pedraza to return to the presidency. When Gómez Pedraza took over the presidency, he called together in Mexico City what was known as a "private council," composed of two representatives from each state, to advise him on important matters. Híjar was one of the representatives on this council from Jalisco. In the course of his work on the council, Híjar had occasion to get in touch with Gómez Farías, who had just been appointed minister of the treasury.

4. Bancroft, *California*, *3*, 260, n. 38; George Tays, "Revolutionary California" (Ph.D. Dissertation, University of California, 1932), p. 283.

5. Lombardo to Figueroa, Apr. 11, 1834, BL, State Papers, Missions and Colonization, 2, 117.

6. Sometimes the name includes "de" before Híjar. For a genealogy of the early branches of the family see Jesús Amaya, *Los conquistadores Fernández de Híjar y Bracamonte* (Guadalajara, 1952), pp. 97–100.

It is probable, since Farías was also from Guadalajara and had represented Jalisco in the federal congress, that Híjar and Farías knew each other previous to this meeting in 1832. Híjar was forty years old in 1833, and a young man who saw him at close quarters for a considerable length of time when he was in Monterey in 1834 described him as being of medium height, with blue eyes, chestnut-colored hair and beard heavily streaked with gray, and a calm, good-looking face. He said Híjar was fond of music and had some facility as a composer. He also remarked upon his good education and his kindly disposition.[7]

It may be noted that General Figueroa was given no loophole by which he could avoid handing over his civilian post as governor to Híjar, who was to occupy also the new position of director of the colony. This is clearly a reference to the new position outlined in the bill for colonizing mission land, which was still being considered by the Senate. What the duties of the director of the colony might be were outlined on July 16 in a further letter from García to Híjar, in which he said that the vice-president had appointed him to the post,

> putting confidence in the zeal which you have shown for public service, being assured that in undertaking this commission you will take the greatest care both as to the distribution of lands that are to be given to the colonists and as to the localities in which they are situated, so that the private interests of the colonists may be reconciled with the general interests of the Republic. The new establishments which are formed will in this way fulfill the objectives of the Supreme Government, which are none other than providing for the population and pro-

7. *Diario de las sesiones del congreso de Jalisco* (Guadalajara, 1825), *1*, 7; Juan Suárez y Navarro, *Historia*, *1*, 333–34, *2*, 81; Bocanegra, *Memorias*, *2*, 372; Híjar to Ministro de Relaciones, Jan. 30, 1835, BL, Colonización y terrenos baldíos, Fomento, legajo 6, expediente 173; Estevan de la Torre, "Reminiscencias" (dictated May 1877 for Bancroft), BL, p. 50.

gress of a country recommendable for its climate and its varied products, so that it may be protected from the designs that some foreign nations, principally the Russians established further north, may have on it.

Híjar's total salary was to be 4,000 pesos, which was to be made up of 3,000 pesos for the position of political chief and 1,000 for that of director of colonization. Híjar was also authorized to appoint a reliable person, to be approved by the government, to be the secretary for the colonization commission, with an annual salary of 1,500 pesos. Finally, García said the vice-president had given orders that the families who were to colonize California were to be paid three reales a day per person for the journey over land, the government paying the passage by sea, and that in Mexico City each family was to be given a single lump sum of ten pesos, so that they might equip themselves with what was most essential.[8] On July 17 Híjar presented an estimate of expenses which he said he needed to begin work on the colonizing expedition. His estimate included scientific instruments such as a theodolite, two graphometers, two barometers, a sextant, two chronometers, coastal charts, log tables, and astronomical tables, together with estimates of the expenses involved in taking six elementary schoolteachers and their families (calculated at five persons per family) to California. Added to this were estimates for lodging the families and stabling the horses during the trip, forage for thirty horses and fifteen mules, the cost of the horses, saddles, and mules, and the daily wages of two muleteers, including the purchase of two further horses for two commissioners, whose expenses for the trip were also included. The total cost of the expedition was estimated at 6,985 pesos.[9]

8. García to Híjar, July 16, 1833. BL, State Papers, Missions and Colonization, 2, 207–09. The sum to be given the colonists was later raised to four reales per day for adults and two reales for children under four.

9. José María Híjar, "Presupuesto para marcha y colonización en Californias," BL, Departmental State Papers, *1*, 165.

The vice-president approved this estimate and gave orders that the sum of 6,985 pesos be paid to Híjar. On July 20 the Commission on the Pious Fund of the Californias wrote that they would pay it. Ten days later 5,154 pesos, 4 reales, 3 cuartillos belonging to the Pious Fund in the treasury was ordered to be paid to Híjar. Whether Híjar actually received these funds at this time is not known, but the opposition began to spread the rumor that Farías was trying to get hold of Pious Fund money for civil war expenses. "All that is needed is that they be called *Pious*," lamented Carlos María Bustamante, "for them to be the object of persecution by men who detest anything that is said to be connected with Catholic worship."[10] There is no evidence for this rumor, but no doubt many people believed it. Pamphlets were coming out in May that accused the government of planning to destroy completely the army and "degrade, vilify and if possible annihilate both [secular and regular] clergy, tear down the pious establishments and introduce into the country every sect, religion and belief, deprive all honest men of their positions and their property and raise up the most perverse and immoral of men."[11]

In the midst of difficulties such as these, California affairs were now about to be brought more specifically to the government's attention with the formal taking of the oath by Juan Bandini, deputy for California, on July 23 in the Chamber of Deputies. A week after he had taken his seat, Bandini presented a bill to remove civil power from the military chief, who had combined both civil and military authority up until then.[12] "The Supreme Government," read part of article one of his bill, "will appoint the person who is to take over the office of Political Chief." The Farías administration, using its special powers, had already appointed Híjar political chief

10. J. M. Mendoza to Subcomisario, Nov. 28, 1833, BL, Departmental State Papers, *1*, 163; Anon. to Junta of Pious Fund, Aug. 2, 1833, AGN, Californias, *23*, no. 24; Bustamante, "Diario," July 14, 1833, ZAC.

11. *El Mono* (Mexico City, May 11, 1833).

12. *El Telégrafo* (Aug. 11, 13, 1833).

and made an effort to separate military from civil power in California. But the decree would undoubtedly be given extra strength if Congress passed a law on the matter. Also, Bandini's bill moved the capital of the territory from Monterey to Los Angeles and stated that the Territorial Deputation would, with the agreement of the governor, proceed immediately to draw up its own constitution, which was to be sent to the Congress in Mexico for approval. The bill provided further for a new method of selecting the governor. The California electoral committees, which selected the deputies to the Congress, were to propose three men for the position to the government, which was to appoint one. What was more, to be eligible for the office of governor, the candidate would have to be able to comply with the laws in the constitution and later laws regarding the office of deputy. In effect this would mean that the governor would be a Californian. At this very time, Governor Figueroa was sending in his warning about the motives of Bandini and the "clique of conceited and ignorant men" in San Diego who, he alleged, were plotting to separate California from Mexico. While there is no evidence that they were plotting in this way, it is clear that they wanted to get rid of Figueroa as governor. Perhaps this sufficiently explains Figueroa's obvious enmity toward them. They were also clearly opposed to Monterey and wanted to make their own section of the territory the dominant one. Bandini's bill was sent by the Chamber to the special committee on the district, to which Bandini himself was appointed on July 30. Unfortunately for Bandini, Asiatic cholera invaded Mexico City on August 6, and the Congress closed its sessions because of it on August 14.[13] Congress apparently did not reconvene until the end of September, and the special committee on the district failed to report out Bandini's bill.

13. Tays, "Revolutionary California," p. 283; *El Telégrafo* (Aug. 16, 1833); Hutchinson, "Asiatic Cholera," p. 155.

Bandini, however, continued to propose further legislation. On October 2 a first reading of a bill of his to give the deputy representing California a vote in Congress took place. He gave as his reasons for this that California then had more inhabitants than the Constitution required for this privilege.[14] This bill was read a second time on October 5, when it was sent to the Committee on Constitutional Matters, from which it also apparently failed to emerge. On October 16 he presented a bill to permit the ports of San Francisco and San Diego to engage in foreign commerce. Article two of this bill provided that Monterey, Santa Barbara, and San Pedro were to "remain lesser ports for national coastwise traffic." Because of this, the bill stipulated that the customs office at Monterey was to be moved to San Francisco, and the San Diego customs house was to become a permanent one and have its staff increased in number. Again, nothing seems to have been done about this proposal. Perhaps by this time, however, residents of Monterey had become convinced that Bandini was not representing them.

Bandini continued his active, if unsuccessful, legislative career during the remainder of October, but in November his persistent efforts were finally to be rewarded. On November 7 he presented the following bill:

14. *El Telégrafo* (Oct. 16, 1833). According to the Constitution of 1824, Title III, article 14, a Territory with a population of more than 40,000 could have a deputy in the Chamber with voice and vote. A contemporary estimate of the population of California by Father J. M. Guzmán was 30,000, one-fourth white, three-fourths Indian (Guzmán, *Breve Noticia,* p. 4). Recent estimates of the number of Indians on the missions in the 1830s run from about 15,000 (J. N. Bowman, "The Resident Neophytes [Existentes] of the California Missions," Historical Society of Southern California *Quarterly, 15* [1958], 144) to about 17,000 (Cook, *Conflict, 1,* p. 5). Professor Cook has estimated a population of some 81,000 non-Christian Indians outside the missions. Bandini, in accord with the sentiment of the day, undoubtedly was counting all Indians, mission and pagan, in his estimation of the population of the Territory.

189

The government is authorized to use every means to assure the colonization, and make effective the secularization of the missions of Upper and Lower California, being able to this effect to use in the manner most convenient the estates belonging to the pious funds of the said territories so as to provide resources for the commission and families going to them who are in this capital.

It is likely that the government itself, perhaps spurred on by Híjar, the new governor, was behind this bill, which showed the difficulty of obtaining funds for the colonizing expedition. It may be noted in passing that the language of the bill was not precise: did Bandini mean that the government was authorized to use every means to assure the colonization of the missions of the Californias and their secularization? Or did he mean that the government was to assure the colonization of the Californias and put secularization of their missions into effect? Bearing in mind the legislation introduced by the Farías government secularizing and colonizing the missions, it is likely that this was what Bandini's bill was designed to do, but it could also be interpreted as simply giving the government the power to colonize the Californias, not the missions. As will be seen, this was how Governor Figueroa chose to interpret it. The government nonetheless needed this bill if it was to go ahead with its colonization plans, for its own detailed and carefully worked out bill had not yet been passed and might not be made into law. The Chamber dispensed with a second reading for the bill and passed it to the joint committees on colonization and the district. But Bandini requested that the bill be immediately considered, without going to committee or being held up in any way. What reasons he used are not known, but they are likely to have been urgent recommendations by the government that this be done. The Chamber agreed to take the bill up without further delay and the next day, November 8, discussed and approved it by a vote of thirty-one to thirteen. It went to the Senate on Saturday, November 9, where Senator Solana asked that it be immediately discussed and voted on without going through the usual channels. The Senate agreed and passed it without opposition. On Monday, November 11, the Senate returned the bill, duly approved, to the deputies, who in turn sent it on to the government. On November 26 it was signed into law by Santa Anna, who was at that time occupying the presidency.[15]

In all probability the main reason for the whirlwind speed with which this bill was approved and made into law was the fact that the special powers under which Farías was acting were to come to an end on November 30. It was urgent that funds be provided at once for the colonizing expedition, and the government had no funds. In fact, in a report to the vice-president, the senior official in the Treasury Department said that it was living in "a continuous state of bankruptcy" and that "a year's revenue is consumed in six months." The law secularizing the missions, which had been passed on August 17, stated that the government was to meet the expenses involved in the law by using the resources of the Pious Fund; and the colonization bill, which had not been passed by the Senate, also levied heavily on the Pious Fund, as well as upon certain revenue which would become available in the Californias themselves and was to go into a California Development Fund. But until this fund was able to operate, the government was charged with meeting the expenses of the colonization bill by using money it owed the Pious Fund. It is likely that the slender resources of the Pious Fund had been almost liquidated by the payments Híjar was authorized to receive from it in August, while the government had no money to pay back into the Pious Fund because of the expenses of the civil war and the drop in receipts from the maritime customs houses, which were almost the only sources of

15. *El Telégrafo* (Oct. 21, Nov. 12, Dec. 3, 6, 8, 1833).

revenue available.[16] A further general law on colonizing the territories was passed by the Congress on November 21, but it merely stated that the government was authorized to spend the "sums necessary on the colonization of the territories," without saying where the money was to come from. Unless funds could be made available, both the secularization of the missions and colonization of their lands would be impossible.

Bandini's bill does not say how the government was to use the estates belonging to the Pious Fund to raise more money than they actually did, but it gave the government the right to use them "in the manner most convenient." This turned out to be by borrowing from a wealthy man who then received the revenue coming in from the estates. It was yet another instance of the unhappy dependence of the government upon financial speculators who fattened upon its miseries.[17]

A further important step in the development of California was taken on October 19, 1833, when a decree was issued giving the government the power to "organize public education in all its branches" in the district and territories. On this same day the University of Mexico was suppressed, and an organization called the General Direction of Public Instruction for the District and Territories set up. Planning for this had been going on since September 20, 1833, by a committee appointed by Farías under the chairmanship of Juan José Espinosa de los Monteros. The new institution had under its control six educational establishments in the district, together with a variety of other cultural assets, including a theater, the national library, a museum, and a printing press. Its funds included those that previously had gone to the university from the treasury, together with revenue from prop-

16. Juan José del Corral, Dec. 21, 1833, to Vice-President. *Dictamen presentado al Exmo Sr. Vice-Presidente en ejercicio del Supremo Poder Ejecutivo por el oficial mayor encargado de la Secretaría de Hacienda* (Mexico, 1834).

17. Dublán y Lozano, *Legislación*, 2, 637; Corral, *Dictamen*.

erty formerly owned by numerous colleges and monastic establishments in Mexico City. Among these was the monastery and church of San Camilo with its urban property, soon to be used as one of the assembly places for the colony to be sent to California.[18]

In his address to the final session of the Congress in December 1833, Farías said that the plans of the new General Direction of Public Instruction were "directed to generalizing among the people the knowledge they need in the various professions and employments in which they are engaged, rather than to showing off a useless erudition not suitable for a new-born society."[19] The Direction of Public Instruction probably selected the teachers who were to go to California with the colony. José Mariano Romero, one of those who went, was appointed to the second chair in Latin in the first of six new "Establishments of Study" in Mexico City.[20] In California, Romero became director of the normal school established in Monterey.

The Direction of Public Instruction met frequently in the course of January, February, and March 1834, but there is no record of its devoting time to California affairs during that period. On April 3, however, the minister of relations requested that it provide the director of colonization of the

18. Dublán y Lozano, *Legislación, 2,* 564, 574; AGN, Instrucción pública, *10,* 136.

19. *Informes y manifiestos de los poderes ejecutivo y legislativo* (2 vols. Mexico, 1905), *1,* 167.

20. *El Telégrafo* (Dec. 22, 1833). Other teachers who went with the colony were Antonio Moreña, who went to the mission of San José; Doña Ignacia Zárate and José Zenón Fernández to Santa Clara; Mariano Bonilla to Los Angeles; Luis Bonilla; Ignacio Coronel, teacher for the colony; Doña Francisca Rosel; Manuel Coronel; Doña Ignacia Paz, teacher for the colony; Alvina Alvarez; José María Oviedo to San Luis Rey; Doña Jesús [sic] Castillo; Carlos Baric to San Diego; Victor Prudon to Santa Barbara; Doña Petra Enríquez; Sabas Fernández; Doña Manuela Fernández; Doña Loreta Fernández; Doña Francisca Fernández; Máximo Fernández; Dionisio Fernández (Híjar, Oct. 29, 1834, BL, Legislative Records, 2, 260).

Californias with "charts according to the Lancaster system, catechisms, elementary books, slates and slate pencils" for elementary schools that were to be established there. The minister offered to pay for these supplies from the California Pious Fund. Two days later, on April 5, the government informed the Direction of Public Instruction that the new schools for California required rather more than 1,100 pesos, but the Direction replied that it could not provide this sum, since it was having difficulty finding money for its own normal expenses.[21]

In spite of the progress that was being made with his plans for colonizing California, by October 1833 Farías was becoming profoundly depressed with the way in which the political situation in Mexico was developing. Santa Anna was to return to the presidency at the end of October, and Farías decided to resign from the vice-presidency at that time. He said he wanted to go to California, but events took a different turn. For reasons that were best known to himself, Santa Anna requested permission to retire to his hacienda at Jalapa shortly after he had returned to the presidency. On November 29 a bill granting him six months' leave "to reestablish his health" was given its first reading in the Senate; the same bill gave the vice-president the executive power in the absence of the president. A decree providing for these changes was issued on December 10, and Santa Anna moved out of Mexico City for Jalapa at dawn on December 16, leaving Farías once more in charge.[22]

Before he left office, Santa Anna removed several members of his cabinet who might be expected to be loyal to Farías and replaced them with his own henchmen. He also directed the minister of war to write Governor Figueroa that he was to remain comandante general in California. This meant that

21. Romero to Minister of Relations, Jan. 17, 1838, BL, Colonización y terrenos baldíos, Secretario de Fomento; AGN, Instrucción pública, 6.

22. José F. Ramírez to Francisco Elorriaga, Oct. 13, 1833, FP; El Telégrafo (Dec. 16, 1833).

Padrés would definitely not be able to take over this position, as Farías had wanted. There were signs of growing opposition to Farías' policies and even threats against his life. Carlos García, who resigned as minister of relations at this time, warned Farías that the opposition was trying to make people think that Santa Anna was really in favor of centralism. If they did not succeed in doing this, he added, they might try to assassinate both Farías and Santa Anna.[23]

Despite the ominous political situation, Farías' address to the Congress at its last session on December 31, 1833, was optimistic. Juan José Espinosa de los Monteros, now president of the Chamber of Deputies, replied to the vice-president's speech and pointed out the many legislative accomplishments of the Congress. These included the law of November 21, which gave the government further power to colonize the federal territories, and the law of November 26 "to assure the colonization of Upper and Lower California and secularize their missions." It was no doubt good for the morale of Congress and the vice-president to take an optimistic view of things at such a time, but in all probability nobody was deceived into thinking that the struggle was won. Farías can hardly have looked upon Bandini's bill, now made into law, as more than a last resort pending completion of his own detailed and carefully studied project for colonizing mission lands. The day following his speech to the closing session of Congress for 1833, Farías again addressed that body on the first day of its sessions for 1834. His theme this time was the all too familiar plea for an organic law for the district and territories. "The well-known activity of the legislators," he said hopefully, would soon complete this urgent work.[24]

While political trouble was in the making, preparations for sending Farías' colony to California were steadily going

23. The Minister of War wrote to Figueroa on Dec. 7, 1833; Figueroa to the Minister of War, Nov. 20, 1834, BL, State Papers, Missions and Colonization, 2, 197; Carlos García to Gómez Farías, Dec. 18, 1833, FP.

24. *El Telégrafo* (Jan. 2, 1834); *Informes y manifiestos, 1,* 172.

forward. Farías had asked Híjar in October 1833 to suggest a suitable person for the position of secretary to the governor of California; Híjar proposed Regino de la Mora, a resident of Guadalajara. Farías accepted this choice, and Regino de la Mora made ready to come to Mexico City with his family. Híjar himself was in Guadalajara in late December 1833 and early January 1834, attending sessions of the congress of the state of Jalisco. In fact he was a candidate for president, and failing that, for vice-president, of the state congress in December 1833. Sometime in February Híjar asked the minister of relations for 2,000 pesos for expenses and sent him a list of 210 persons who had signed up as colonists.[25]

In Mexico City notices began appearing inviting men, women, and families to join the colony that was to settle in California. Adults were to be given four reales and children two reales a day to cover their subsistence during the period of waiting and journey out. José María Padrés, who was being referred to as the "second director" of the colony, was probably responsible for the recruiting of likely emigrants. The colony's headquarters were the former convent of San Camilo and the Hospital de los Naturales. A young French boy of seventeen, Victor Eugene August Janssens, who was interested in joining the colony, recalled that when he went to the convent Padrés talked to him long and enthusiastically about California. Later, when the overland journey reached Tepic and Janssens was thinking of accepting a position offered to him there, Padrés talked him out of it, convincing him that California was the "true land of Promise."[26]

25. Híjar to Minister of Relations, Oct. 14, 1833, AGN; Híjar to Minister of Relations, Nov. 5, 1833, AGN; *Anales de Jalisco* (Guadalajara, Jan. 18, 19, 1834); Lombardo to Presidente de la junta directiva del fondo de Californias, AGN, 20.

26. Carlos María Bustamante, "Voz de la Patria," BL, 9, 4–6; Juan Bautista Esparza, "Vida californiana," BL, p. 7; William H. Ellison and Francis Price, eds., *The Life and Adventures in California of Don Agustín Janssens, 1834–1856* (San Marino, 1953), pp. 7, 15.

On April 13, the Sunday before their departure, the colonists were given a send-off ball at the former convent, which Vice-President Farías attended. He opened the dancing with Doña María de Jesús Ortega, the wife of José Ramírez and daughter of the prominent California rancher José María Ortega of Santa Barbara. According to the recollections of Florencio Serrano, one of the young colonists who wrote down his memoirs for Bancroft in 1877, Farías spoke to the group on this occasion saying that they were but the first of a succession of proposed colonizing expeditions. Farías said he wanted to go with the expedition to California, but although he undoubtedly was thinking of leaving Mexico, there is no evidence that he was seriously planning to go to California. Nor is there any corroborating evidence for Serrano's assertion that the expedition had political motives.[27]

Among those present at the ball was Deputy Juan Bandini, whose name is mentioned prominently on a fifty-nine-page prospectus for a commercial venture in California to be called the Cosmopolitan Company. This prospectus was approved on April 1, 1834, and regulations for the company were drawn up and published. Bandini signed the regulations and prospectus as president and José María Herrera as secretary.[28]

Mexican interest in the use of a colonization company to

27. Florencio Serrano, "Apuntes para la historia de la Alta California," BL, pp. 24–26; Ellison and Price, *Life*, p. 8, n. 5. Another former colonist, José Abrego, makes a similar assertion about California providing a haven for ousted politicians but it would appear to be groundless. Prominent "outs" in Mexico generally left the country completely. Minor figures often did not have to move. (José Abrego to Enrique Cerruti, BL, *31*, pt. 2, p. 414.)

28. *Reglamento para la Compañía Cosmopolitana* (Mexico, 1834). The reglamento was also printed in *El Fénix de la Libertad* in its issues of May 13–18, 1834. Keld J. Reynolds discusses the reglamento and translates it into English in "The Reglamento for the Híjar and Padrés Colony of 1834," Historical Society of Southern California *Quarterly*, *28* (1946), 142–75.

develop the Californias may be traced back to 1825, when Francisco de Paula Tamariz wrote a series of letters to Minister of Relations Lucas Alamán on the subject. In December 1825, Tamariz and Pedro Dionisio Cárdenas, a fellow member of the Commission on the Californias who had independently thought of the same idea, jointly signed a statement proposing a trading company to be known as the Asiatic-Mexican Company. Inspired by the Spanish Philippine Company, it was to have a monopoly on trade with Asiatic countries dealing in such commodities as otter skins, pearls, and fishing. Tamariz' ideas went beyond the stimulation of commerce between California and the Far East, however, to peaceful trading with the non-Christian Indians, which he thought would be more effective in civilizing them than putting them into missions. He considered that the future great prosperity of his company would in turn develop the Californias and help to populate them.[29] He and Pedro Dionisio Cárdenas drew up a set of regulations for their company in sixty-four articles, outlining every conceivable reason why the government should support the venture and giving details of the organization they had in mind. One of their points was that the company would promote colonization in the Californias and help to develop their agriculture and industry. Lucas Alamán, President Victoria, and the Commission on the Development of the Californias expressed considerable interest in the Asiatic-Mexican Company, and its ideas became known in California, but nothing ever came of it.[30] At about the time that Tamariz and Cárdenas were working on their colonization company, a long article on the British East India Company came out in one of the Mexico

29. "Plan político mercantil para el más pronto fomento de las Californias" (Mexico, 1827), "Proyecto para el establecimiento de una compañía a de comercio directo con el Asia y mar pacífico" (Mexico, 1827).

30. "Proyecto de reglamento en grande para el establecimiento de la compañía asiático-mexicana"; all part of *Colección de los principales trabajos en que se ha ocupada la junta;* Reynolds, "The Junta de Fomento," p. 183.

City papers. The idea of stock companies for undertaking public works, such as the road to Veracruz from Mexico City, was present in Mexico in 1826, and there was some sign of continuing Mexican interest in trade with China. The Tamariz project was published in 1827; he himself disappears from sight in 1828.[31]

The idea of a company to colonize and develop the Californias was taken up again by Tadeo Ortiz, who wrote a letter to President Bustamante from Bordeaux, where he was Mexican consul, on October 31, 1830, and another on November 30, both on this subject. He suggested that the Mexican government should sponsor the formation in Europe of colonization companies which, in return for such monopoly privileges as hunting sea otter, bear, and deer, pearl diving, and other concessions, should help to colonize the Californias and other areas. Mexico was definitely company conscious at the time these letters were written; indeed, on October 16, 1830, an important law had been passed creating a Bank of Avío to provide government loans for companies interested in promoting textile and other industries. One of the companies slated to receive a loan through the Bank of Avío was the San Luis Potosí Company, which was planned to develop the industry, agriculture, and mining of the state of San Luis Potosí and which issued its prospectus in 1831. In April 1833 a proposal was drawn up to create a tax-exempt company to promote schools, to be known as the Mexican Scientific-Industrial Company.[32] Bandini's Cosmopolitan Company was but one of many that were being proposed at the time for a number of different projects.

Tadeo Ortiz' two letters on colonization companies were

31. *Gaceta diaria de México* (Oct. 1 and 2, 1825); Bustamante, "Diario," Apr. 29, Dec. 1, 1826, ZAC; *El Sol* (May 11, 1828). When Tamariz died is not known.

32. Tadeo Ortiz, *México considerado*, 2, 186–87, 206–07; Robert A. Potash, *El Banco de avío de México* (Mexico, 1959), p. 243; *Informe y cuentas que el Banco de Avío presenta*, in Alamán, *Memoria* (Mexico, 1832), document no. 2, p. 20; Instrucción pública, AGN, 8, expediente 13.

printed in his book, *Mexico Considered as an Independent and Free Country,* which was available in Mexico City in 1833. Ortiz was himself friendly with Farías, who appointed him director of colonization for Texas—the equivalent of Híjar's position in California—in August 1833.[33] It is likely, therefore, that the ideas behind the Cosmopolitan Company were those of Ortiz. The company was designed to develop California agriculture and manufacturing and promote the export of its products to world markets. Its capital was to come from the sale of shares at the initial price of two hundred pesos each and also from Bank of Avío loans and loans either in cash or goods from private individuals. A board of stockholders was to elect a president and vice-president and a secretary and substitute secretary. The agricultural, commercial, and manufacturing divisions of the company were to be run by three boards of directors of five men each, proposed by a three-man executive called the General Inspection and elected by the stockholders. The first man appointed to one of these boards was to be its president, the last its secretary. The men on the board of directors dealing with agriculture were responsible for what the prospectus called the "scientific part of agriculture" and management of the crops and cattle. They would appoint the administrators of the farms, subject to the approval of the General Inspection, and also those in charge of the stores for selling farm produce. The administrators of the farms, who were to be their actual managers, would look after the cattle, grains, and fruit and execute the orders of the agricultural board of directors. Under the administrators there would be majordomos, head cowboys, captains, and hands according to the regulations to be drawn up for administrators of farms. The administrators were to sell cattle on the hoof when ordered to do so by the directors of agriculture; the crops, fruit, and parts of the cattle, such as fat and skins, were to be sent to the farm stores,

33. Gómez Farías to Ministro de Hacienda, legajo 51–7–57–11, MN.

where they were to be sold at the best price possible. The fruit and wheat were to go to these stores only when they had been processed into commodities which could be kept, such as flour and *aguardiente,* or wine. The hands who were to work these farms are referred to in the prospectus as *gente de servicio,* or service people. They were to be paid for their work and also provided with food, which was to be raised by the farms themselves. The company founders were probably thinking of the mission Indians as gente de servicio.

In control of the commercial or trading activities of the Cosmopolitan Company there was to be a similar five-man board of directors, one of whose duties was to get in touch with as many of the peoples of the world as possible and obtain information on trade in all countries and the causes of its prosperity or failure. They were to find out what export products each country had, what they consumed, and what the normal prices were. Also they were to investigate the manners and customs of the various peoples in order to ship them the things they would be most likely to want. It is presumably from these proposed international activities of the company that it derived its name, "Cosmopolitan." The commercial side of the business would be centered in a trading station to be erected where the stockholders decided; it was to be run by a factor, a treasurer, and a secretary-accountant. This trading station was to supply merchants with up to four thousand pesos worth of goods each for retail trade in the interior of California. The trading station was also to furnish the data on international trade, which the directors of the commercial activities of the company were to accumulate. The third and last division of the company, the manufacturing department, was, like the other two, to be run by a five-man board of directors. Under this board there was to be a business agent *(agente factor),* who was to buy and store the raw material used in manufacturing and to sell the products under instructions from the trading station. Also under the board, there would be an administrator in charge of building and repairing the factory shops, repairing the machinery, and hiring and paying the workers. Shop managers, or *directores*, were to be in charge of the manufacturing. They were to be "scientific" or expert at their work and could fire unsatisfactory workmen.

One of the services that the Cosmopolitan Company was to perform for California was the improvement of transportation. Stopping places were to be built every fifteen miles along the main roads. These were to serve as inns for travelers, as well as buildings for farms, commercial houses, and paper or textile factories or manufacturing plants of some other kind, according to the possibilities of the place and time. They were to have on hand a sufficient number of carriages and mounts so that farmers and anybody else who wanted to travel with his freight could do so either night or day, fast or slow, as he wanted. This was to keep things from slowing down and to maintain production. The transportation section of the company was to be associated with the agricultural division but separately run by a manager whose objective was to provide swift, comfortable, and economical transportation for passengers and goods.

Until March 31, 1836, the profits made by the company were to be divided among the shareholders according to the amount of time or money they invested in the company. The shareholders were to receive new stock as their portion of the profits during that time. Shares were to be offered in 1834 for one-third less than they were to cost in 1836, those in 1835 were to be one-sixth less. After March 31, 1836, profits were to be split with half going to the shareholders and the other half divided into five parts. The first part was to be used for public works such as roads, canals, bridges, and aqueducts for bringing irrigation water to company land. The second portion was to be used to "attract the Indians to the social order by means of a constant system of presents" and to help poor families come as colonists. The third part was for the establishment of a bank, whose funds were to aid the government, so that when the colonists' privileges and exemptions from taxes ceased, the people of California would not be overwhelmed with taxes. The remaining two parts were to be used for development of the company.

Those who owned shares in the company, or employees of the company who had put in working time equivalent to the value of the share they wished to buy, were to be considered associates of the company. If an associate was ever elected to an office in the territory, he was to serve in his elective office rather than continue working with the company. But his salary was to continue to come from the company, and if the office was a salaried one, this money was to be used by the territorial government for useful public projects.

According to Bandini the men associated with the company were well-to-do; among them he mentioned General Juan Pablo Anaya, who was at the time postmaster general and was to be president of the company, while he, Bandini, was vice-president. This has caused some confusion, because in the prospectus issued in the *Fénix* in May, Bandini signed himself as president. It is possible that when the shareholders met to elect the officers of the company Anaya was elected in place of Bandini, who was given a position in the California customs service. Among the associates or shareholders of the company, Bandini mentioned Híjar, Padrés, Luis de Castillo Negrete, and José María Herrera, who was secretary of the company and sub-commissary in the territory. He refers also to other "persons of character" in the business circles of Mexico City as shareholders.[34] Alexander Forbes, a Scottish merchant at Tepic who scoffed at both the com-

---

34. Juan Bandini, "Historia de la alta California," BL, pp. 163–64. Florencio Serrano mentions ("Apuntes," BL, p. 26) that the following were also shareholders although there is no further evidence to confirm the fact: Gómez Farías, Francisco Berdusco, José Mariano Romero, Francisco Javier de Castillo Negrete, José Abrego, Mariano Bonilla. A search for further information on the company in the Archivo General de Notarías in Mexico City has been made without result.

pany and the colony in his *History of California,* some of
which was written in 1835, mentions that about eight thousand dollars was subscribed in shares. Precisely what connection there was between this development company and
the colony that was preparing to go to California is difficult
to say. The company was not a colonization company, although its prospectus stated that a small portion of its eventual profits was to be used for helping impecunious future
colonists. On the other hand, General Anaya, Lieutenant
Colonel José María Padrés, and Deputy Juan Bandini, all
closely connected with the company, were given permission
by Vice-President Farías to buy a brigantine of 185 tons
called the *Natalia.* Formerly Peruvian, this vessel was later
alleged by a French captain who visited California to be the
former *Inconstant,* the ship that Napoleon used for his escape from Elba in 1815.[35] This story, like a good many
others traditionally connected with the colony, is untrue.
The *Inconstant,* a brigantine in the French navy, was disarmed at Brest in 1842 and probably dismantled there at a
later date. The *Natalia's* owner, Miguel Palacios, was to receive 14,400 pesos for his vessel but not in cash, which, as
usual, was hard to get.[36] Palacios demanded that Pascual
Villar, a wealthy capitalist, be responsible for guaranteeing
the sale, so that presumably if Palacios was not paid by the

35. Alexander Forbes, *A History of California* (London, 1839), p. 144;
Bancroft, *California, 3,* 268, n. 52.

36. *Triton* (supplement to *Neptunia*), fascicle 52, 1ᵉʳ trimestre (1960),
p. 16; information supplied by Captain J. Vichot in a letter to the author
of Oct. 4, 1965. The legend that the *Natalia* was originally the *Inconstant*
was given a new lease on life in 1864 by Alexander S. Taylor in an
article entitled "Byron, Nelson and Napoleon in California," *Pacific
Monthly* (1864), p. 648. Two years later it appeared again in Franklin
Tuthill's *History of California* (San Francisco, 1866), p. 136, and thereafter became an established, if at times suspect, part of California history. *El Telégrafo* (August 2, 1834); Minister of Relations to General
Joaquín Parres, Apr. 1, 1834, AGN, Californias, *20.* Junta de Californias
to anon., Jan. 17, 1837, AGN, Californias, *20,* no. 25. Minister of Relations to Parres, Apr. 1, 1834, AGN, Californias, *20.*

three buyers, Villar would see that he did not lose his money. In his turn Villar wanted security, and Vice-President Farías gave orders that one of the haciendas belonging to the Pious Fund of the Californias—Ciénaga del Pastor, near Guadalajara and under the charge of General Joaquín Parres—be turned over to a representative of Villar until Palacios was paid for his ship. During the time that Villar had charge of the hacienda, he was presumably to take any profits that it made. Palacios duly sold his ship at Acapulco on June 21 to Bandini and other members of the Cosmopolitan Company and received in return a draft for 7,200 arrobas (90 short tons) of tallow payable in California.[37] Palacios selected José Noriega, supercargo of the vessel, to represent his interests. That Palacios and Villar were properly cautious in the deal is evident from the eventual upshot, which was the wrecking of the *Natalia* in the harbor of Monterey in December 1834. Bandini says that Palacios was paid his money, but not in tallow, by some of the company associates. The only remaining question in this tortuous piece of financial dickering, probably typical of those into which the government was forced because of its lack of funds, is the way in which the government was to be paid by the company for its help in providing security for the purchase of the *Natalia*. Bandini explains that the company made a contract with the government by which it was to transport the colonists to California on the *Natalia* and provide their board during the voyage at its own expense. This was presumably the company's contribution to the cost of sending the colony to California, in return for which the government assisted it in buying the ship.[38]

37. Pascual Villar was also being paid the rent of one of the town houses owned by the Pious Fund of the Californias which Vice-President Farías and his family themselves rented. In June, July, and August of 1834 Farías paid his fifty pesos a month rent to a representative of Pascual Villar; Bancroft, *California, 3,* 263, n. 43.

38. Bandini, "Historia," pp. 153, 165. The writer follows Bandini's detailed account in preference to the vague references on the subject made by Janssens (Ellison and Price, *Life,* p. 10).

What further connection there might have been between the Cosmopolitan Company and the government's colonization scheme can only be conjectured, since the wrecking of the *Natalia* caused the dissolution of the company, presumably because of the losses involved to the associates, who had to pay for the ship.[39] Nonetheless the company's description in its prospectus of projected agricultural undertakings, with large farms under administrators looking after cattle, grain, and fruit such as grapes, and a labor force which was paid and also fed by the farms, was perhaps the way in which men like Híjar proposed to keep the productive power of the mission haciendas going and thus preserve their economic benefits while doing away with the missions themselves.[40]

While Vice-President Farías, who is described by Bandini as possessing a "particular good will" toward California, was actively working to get the colony under way, relations between President Santa Anna and himself were steadily deteriorating. Already by the middle of March 1834, Santa Anna was writing to Farías complaining openly that he was not being informed of what was going on in the government. By mid-April it was evident that a break between the two men was imminent, and Farías strongly urged Santa Anna to come up to Mexico City and take over the presidency. Farías

39. Bandini, "Historia," p. 165. In his introduction to his translation of the Cosmopolitan Company's prospectus, Keld J. Reynolds suggests that the company was the "legal agency created to support the Mexican California colonization venture of 1834" (Historical Society of Southern California *Quarterly*, *28* [1946], 143) and labels the company's prospectus as the reglamento, or regulations, of the Híjar and Padrés colony. It is difficult to see how this can be maintained, since the prospectus never mentions the colony nor does it have anything to do with the settlement of a colony. The legislation on which the colonization settlement was based is given in the official documents as the laws of Nov. 21 and 26, 1833 (Junta to Gen. Joaquín Parres, Apr. 1, 1834, AGN, Californias, *20*), which have already been discussed.

40. That this was the view of the colonists themselves is mentioned by Alfred Robinson in his *Life in California*, p. 163.

pointed out that fluctuation in power between two men who "do not look at persons or things in the same way" was preventing the government from taking firm measures, since it alternately encouraged and repressed their respective followers and led to a general lack of confidence. Farías, in short, insisted that Santa Anna take over.[41]

This letter apparently convinced Santa Anna that he must return, and he began to prepare to do so. It was at this time, when Farías was petitioning Congress to grant him permission to leave the country for one year, that the colony to which he had devoted so much attention finally left Mexico City on its long journey to California. On Monday, April 14, three of the men, Juan Bandini, José Abrego, and a French pilot named Olivier Delusques, left for Acapulco to receive the *Natalia*. Early the following morning three billeting officers rode out with instructions to find quarters for the colony at the town of Tlalnepantla, nine miles from Mexico City. Later that same morning of April 15 a long line of canvas-covered wagons carrying the rest of the approximately three hundred colonists rumbled through the streets. Some bore the women and children, others carried the luggage and provisions. Somewhere in the wagon train, perhaps, were the ten Merino sheep and five Tibetan goats that the Bank of Avío had given Híjar to take to California. The men went on horseback, organized into a kind of militia unit with officers elected by themselves, and armed with rifles, a small sword or bayonet, and provided with ammunition.[42] In the towns they passed through the mounted men kept in formation on each side of the wagons. It was a gala day, one that would have filled the long line of Spanish viceroys and Spanish and

41. Bandini, "Historia," p. 151; Santa Anna to Gómez Farías, Mar. 12, 1834, FP; Lombardo to Santa Anna, Apr. 16, 1834, FP.

42. Gómez Farías to person unnamed, Sept. 2, 1834, FP; *Informe y cuentas que el Banco de Avío presenta* (Mexico, 1835), p. 27; Abrego to Enrique Cerruti, Nov. 15, 1875, "Memoirs," BL, *31*, pt. 2, 414–18; Florencio Serrano, Apuntes," BL, p. 2; Ellison and Price, *Life*, p. 9.

Mexican governors who had labored to colonize California with joy.

It did awaken unusual interest in Mexico City, as the following notice in *El Telégrafo* attests:

> The novelty of the sight attracted the curiosity of a large crowd, and the streets through which they passed were thronged with people filled with admiration and enthusiasm for the settlers, who had overcome the disinclination of their upbringing and the laziness left us by the Spaniards, and had decided to leave behind the comforts of the capital and set out to guard the remotest regions of the Republic, [and found] new towns which are perhaps destined one day to change the face of this continent and direct the attention of the civilized world to places now entirely unknown. Eternal glory to a government that has been able to promote such useful establishments in the midst of the greatest difficulties.[43]

As they began their journey, an incident occurred which the government newspaper did not mention. Perhaps because of the armed mounted men who surrounded the wagons, the rumor began to go around among the watching *léperos,* the Mexico City mob who lived by their wits, that the colonists were being forcibly exiled to California. They tried to rescue them from such a horrible fate by removing the traces from the wagons. The léperos were finally calmed down by the authorities, who explained what was happening, and the unfamiliar line of wagons slowly continued on its way out of the city.[44]

43. *El Telégrafo* (Apr. 15, 1834).
44. Ellison and Price, *Life,* p. 11; Bustamante, in his "Voz de la Patria," says that the mob attacked the colonists because they thought them lazy good-for-nothings who would cause the loss of California. Such an interpretation is extremely unlikely on the face of it, and when it is remembered that Bustamante had been a member of the Commission on the Californias, which had been working assiduously to pro-

The leader of the expedition, as it moved across country to Querétaro, Celaya, Lagos, and Guadalajara, seems at first to have been Colonel Padrés, for Híjar had not received his instructions when the colony left Mexico City. When these were finally drawn up they were extremely brief, vague, and apparently hastily composed. It was, of course, of the greatest importance that Híjar, the new governor of California and director of the colony, should arrive in California provided with the clearest instructions for his important task of secularizing the missions and dividing up their lands. The law which would have provided him with the necessary detail for dividing up the mission lands had not been passed, and for reasons which are not clear, he received only vague and brief orders which could not be expected to satisfy the Californians, as indeed they did not. Possibly a major cause of this serious error was the fact that Farías and his supporters were in a hurry to leave themselves. The news arrived in Mexico City on Monday, April 21, that Santa Anna was on his way to take over the presidency and was expected to reach the capital the following day. Actually, Santa Anna was delayed and did not reach Mexico City until the evening of Thursday, April 24. Híjar's instructions, however, were not ready until April 23, when they were presumably either handed or sent to him. Farías had insisted on April 16 that Santa Anna take over the presidency, and it is likely that from that time on he was busy trying to clear up all outstanding matters, including Híjar's instructions, before the president arrived.

Later, in California, Padrés admitted that the instructions were "very brief and in a style which could not help but give rise to various doubts," but he attributed this to the "excessive confidence" that Vice-President Farías had in Híjar and

---

mote the colonization of California, it may be realized how bitter Bustamante had become toward the Farías government (Bustamante, "Voz de la Patria," BL, *9*, 4–6).

himself, as evident in the fact that he gave them by word of mouth "the other orders and instructions of great interest which they were to put into effect."[45] Unfortunately, neither Híjar nor Padrés put down on paper what these oral instructions were. The written instructions, which were to cause so much trouble in California, read as follows:

> Article 1: You will begin by occupying all the property belonging to the missions of both Californias and the Military Commandant, on his responsibility, will provide, whenever it is required, the necessary assistance for the occupation.

> Article 2: For one year, to be counted from the day that the colonists reach the place that they are to occupy, they are to be given 4 reales each a day if they are over four years old, and 2 reales a day if they are younger.

> Article 3: The expenses of the voyage by sea and by land will be met by the Federation, and the colonists are to be given as their own property the saddles they buy or have bought for their transportation.[46]

> Article 4: Towns will be formed by bringing together the number of families sufficient to live together in security, by selecting sites that are appropriate for the quality of the soil, abundance and healthfulness of the water and goodness of the winds.

45. Bustamante, "Diario," Apr. 21, 1834, ZAC; *El Telégrafo* (Apr. 25, 1834); José Figueroa, *Manifiesto a la república mexicana* (Monterey, 1835), p. 95.

46. The wording of this article appears to contradict the arrangement made by the government with the Cosmopolitan Company, which was itself to pay for the sea transportation of the colony. This may be because the company did not purchase the *Natalia* at Acapulco until June 21, so that the government could not have known on June 23 whether this had taken place. That there was no reference to the arrangement with the company here is another instance of the inadequacy of the instructions.

Article 5: As soon as possible you will endeavor to colonize frontier areas.

Article 6: Topographical maps will be drawn on which there are to be marked the blocks which are to form the town. The length of each side of a block is to be 100 yards (100 varas) and all sides are to be equal. The width of the street is to be 20 yards (20 varas) and there are to be no alleys. There are to be squares at least after each ten streets, besides the main square, which is to be in the center of the town.

Article 7: Especial care will be taken to bring the Indians into the towns, mixing them with the other inhabitants and [a town] composed only of Indians will not be allowed.

Article 8: In each of the blocks in the towns, house lots will be given to families, so that they may build their houses, but they will not be permitted to do so outside the line traced to form the streets.

Article 9: Outside the towns, every family of colonists will be given full and complete ownership of 423 acres (4 caballerías) of land if it is irrigable, 846 acres (8 caballerías) if it is nonirrigable crop land and about 1,692 acres (16 caballerías) if it is only suitable for raising cattle. Each family will also be given four cows, two yokes of oxen or two bulls, two tame horses, four colts, four fillies, four head of sheep, two female and two male, and also two good plows.

Article 10: Between individual lots of land one parcel of land equivalent to two lots will be kept unsold. The government will be able to sell the land in this parcel when it wishes to do so and the Director of the Colonies will give preference in this case, other circumstances being equal, to the neighboring colonists.

Article 11: When the moveable property of the missions

of California has been distributed, up to half of what is left of this property will be sold in the most advantageous manner.

Article 12: Not more than 200 head of cattle of one kind may be sold to a single family.

Article 13: Half of the remaining moveable property or cattle will be kept to the account of the general government and will be applied to the expenses of religious worship and for stipends for the missionaries, for salaries for the elementary schoolmasters, for supplies for the children of both sexes in the schools, and for the purchase of farm equipment which is to be given free to the colonists.

Article 14: The Political Chief [Governor] and Director of Colonization will prepare at this time and annually thereafter a detailed account of the worth of the mission property, and of how he invests what remains in existence after the division of moveable property and cattle amongst the colonists has been done.

Article 15: He will also report at least once each year on the state of the colonists, the reasons for backwardness, if there is any, and the ways by which they may be made to progress.[47]

It will be noticed that these instructions, which were signed by Francisco M. Lombardo, minister of relations, do not provide for a division of mission lands and property between the various classes of people in California such as the Indians, the resident Californians, the military, or the colonists, as the bill sponsored by the Farías administration did. Instead they appear to give all the mission property to be disposed of to the colonists. The fact that native Californians, either whites or Indians, could qualify as colonists did not

47. Copy made by Agustín V. Zamorano, Nov. 4, 1834, BL, State Papers, 2, 182.

make the instructions look any better in California. This was to prove one of the major obstacles to the success of the colony.

As the colony moved west through mountainous terrain, Farías' position in Mexico City became more and more precarious. Santa Anna returned to Mexico City and the presidency at 8:00 P.M. on April 24 amid serenades by military bands, bursting rockets, and the pealing of bells. Although the government paper mentioned that Santa Anna was received by, among others, many liberal deputies and senators "who are united in sincere friendship with the illustrious president," it was obvious that Farías and the liberals were on the way out. In a foolish attempt to provide against the possibility of General Santa Anna's making himself into a dictator, the Congress decided to halt its sessions on May 15, a week before they were due to end, so that they might reconvene later if Santa Anna semed to be involved in some sinister plot. Two days before they halted their sessions, on May 13, the Chamber of Deputies gave Vice-President Farías the permission he had asked for a few days previously—to leave the country with a year's salary. There followed on May 16 a pronunciamiento at Jalapa calling on Santa Anna to protect the Roman Catholic religion and initiate in the Congress a law to revoke all decrees against it.[48] On May 25 the more important plan of Cuernavaca was announced, which attacked the laws of religious reform and the Masons. All laws passed by both the state and the national congresses contrary to their constitutions must be declared null and void. It called on Santa Anna to protect the just aspirations of the people. After the announcement of the Plan of Cuernavaca, the Congress in Mexico City decided to reconvene, but when the deputies tried to do so on May 31 they found the doors of their chamber locked and the keys removed, while armed guards prevented them from breaking in. Santa Anna, in a

48. *El Telégrafo* (Apr. 25, May 23, 1834); *El Fénix de la Libertad* (May 14, 1834).

speech the following day, justified his actions by saying that the Congress had been planning to conspire against the government.[49] Although he said that he would continue to observe the federal pact, it was to be only a matter of time before this, too, went its way. The overthrow of the federal reform-minded Congress on May 31, 1834, marked the end of the first genuine reform movement in Mexico since the winning of independence.

Farías' enemies bitterly attacked him in June so that a guard had to be posted at his house to protect him and his family. Plots to assassinate him failed, but he was anxious to leave Mexico City as soon as he could get an escort. Early in July the rumor went around that Santa Anna was getting ready to send Farías to a prison ship in Veracruz harbor or let him, as Bustamante sarcastically put it, "visit his dear colony of California." After months of waiting in vain for his passport and his salary, which he needed to permit him to travel to New Orleans, Farías and his wife, who was pregnant, together with their three small children, finally left Mexico City on September 8, 1834, with two carriages, a wagon, and mules to carry them to Zacatecas on the first lap of their journey.[50]

While Farías was still struggling to leave Mexico City, the colony moved slowly and uneventfully to Querétaro, where it was warmly received with baskets of food and wine and where it stayed over a day at the invitation of the inhabitants. A similar welcome took place at Celaya, the next stop, where another day was spent. On May 21, when it was at Guadalajara, Híjar's home town, he wrote Minister of Relations Lombardo telling him that he had only been given sufficient funds

49. The Plan of Cuernavaca is printed in Enrique Olavarría y Ferrari, *México independiente, 1821–1855, 4,* 341–42, in Vícente Riva Palacio, ed., *México a través de los siglos* (5 vols. Mexico and Barcelona, 1888–89).

50. Bocanegra, *Memorias,* 2, 598; Gómez Farías to anon. n.d., FP; Bustamante, "Diario," July 9, 1834, ZAC; *La Lima de Vulcano* (Sept. 9, 1834), cited in Olavarría y Ferrari, *México independiente,* p. 347.

for twenty days of travel, and they had then been on the road thirty-seven days. He had no money with which to go on, and he was afraid that the expedition would break up; he said he needed 6,457 pesos, 4 reales as soon as possible. Lombardo passed the matter on to the committee looking after the Pious Fund, which may have sent Híjar what he needed. In any case, after some delay in Guadalajara, the expedition continued on its way. The roads were too bad for the wagons from then on, so that these were disposed of, and the women rode horses, the younger children being suspended in baskets between the animals.[51] They probably reached Tepic about the end of June and waited there until information reached them that the *Natalia* had arrived at the port of San Blas on July 2, having probably left Acapulco on June 25. It carried seven other colonists as well as Juan Bandini and an Italian by the name of Oliver Delangner. It had a crew of fourteen and was under the command of Captain Juan Gómez. Word then came that the *Morelos* was in, and a part of the colony set out from Tepic on July 20, reaching San Blas late on July 22. After an uncomfortable night on the beach, during which mosquitos took their toll, the colonists boarded the *Natalia*. The *Morelos* needed repairs, and supplies had to be loaded while the impatient colonists waited. Finally, about July 31, Padrés and the rest of the colony arrived and went on board the *Morelos*. The ships left for California on August 1.[52]

51. Ellison and Price, *Life,* pp. 12–13; Lombardo to President of Junta de Californias, June 3, 1834, AGN, Californias, *20.*

52. Agustín Janssens, "Libro de lo que me a pasado en mi vida," Huntington Library, San Marino, California, pp. 39–40, 41; *El Telégrafo* (Aug. 2, 1834); Ellison and Price, *Life,* p. 15; Bandini, "Historia," p. 152.

Chapter Six

Governor Figueroa and the Missions

Governor Figueroa reached Monterey about the middle of January 1833. A little over two months later he wrote the minister of war that he had succeeded in pacifying the territory. He attributed his success to the laws of amnesty he had published and to the measures he had taken to disband the faction that had attacked the authority of former Governor Victoria. Figueroa had taken sides with the northern men who wanted to keep the capital at Monterey. He showed his northern sympathies in his confidential note to the minister of relations stating that Juan Bandini, the California representative in the Mexican Congress, was the head of a group plotting to separate California from Mexico. In Figueroa's view, the desire of this group to remove the military command from the governor was simply a way of achieving secession. He also disapproved of their desire to give the governorship to a Californian, for he did not think there were any Californians sufficiently qualified to undertake it.[1]

That Figueroa's quick success in bringing order to California was not done without some hard work on his part is perhaps implied in his petition to the minister at this same

1. Figueroa to Ministro de Guerra, Mar. 25, 1833, BL, Departmental State Papers, 3, 1831-34; Tays, "Revolutionary California," p. 289.

time to be relieved from his duties. The California climate did not agree with him, he thought, and he suffered from "apoplectic attacks and rheumatism," which prevented him from attending to "intellectual" tasks. There is no reason to think that this was not a genuine health problem, for he seemed at this time to be in sympathy with the reform-minded government of Gómez Farías and Santa Anna and opposed to what he called "the exasperated efforts of the aristocracy, who see the power with which they want to tie us to their ominous chariots slipping through their hands."[2]

The new government in Mexico, caught up in an interminable series of revolts and staggered by a devastating cholera epidemic, was too busy to do anything about Figueroa's petition. In the meantime his health improved, and he began to come to grips with some of the long-term problems of the territory. The first to claim his attention was the foreign danger. The minister of war had written him, shortly after he arrived in California, to beware of "the movements of the North Americans." About the middle of March, Father José de Jesús María Gutiérrez of the mission of San Francisco Solano, who was at Sonoma, wrote him the first of three letters about the foreign danger on the northern frontier. At the end of March, Ensign Mariano Guadalupe Vallejo, then stationed at San Francisco, wrote Figueroa that he had information that Baron Wrangel, governor of Sitka, was going to pay a visit to the Russian settlement at Ross. This news apparently made Figueroa decide to take action to protect the northern frontier from possible Russian expansion. Recalling the orders given to Echeandía in 1827 to build a fort in this frontier region (Echeandía had been unable to do more than design one), he told Vallejo that he was going to begin the construction of an outpost to protect settlers who might like to colonize the region. Just a few days before, at

2. Figueroa to Ministro de Guerra, Mar. 25, 1833, BL, Departmental State Papers, 3; Figueroa to M. G. Vallejo, May 21, 1833, BL, Cowan.

his inauguration in Mexico City, Vice-President Farías had referred to the urgent need of protecting the "almost deserted frontiers" of Mexico by colonization, so that Figueroa was acting in full accord with the plans of the new administration.[3]

Figueroa's plan was to have Vallejo make a quick reconnaissance of the Russian settlements and report back to him the best site for the outpost, bearing in mind several requirements. These included military defense, convenience for settlers, and the need of "advancing our establishments and occupying as much land as possible, not forgetting the port of Bodega, because of the importance of possessing it." Vallejo was also to try to find some families willing to colonize the frontier region, and he was authorized to offer them their own land to farm (rather than land with restricted ownership rights, as was customary in California) as an incentive. Figueroa sent with Vallejo letters of greeting to Baron Wrangel and Peter Kostromitinov in which, after expressing cordiality and a desire for closer trade relations, he urged that they use their influence to persuade the Russian government to recognize Mexican independence. Whether he had been instructed to make this suggestion by the Mexican government is not known, but as has been noted, Baron Wrangel took the matter up, although without success. Figueroa's flattery of the Russians was just his way of obtaining their good will. In a letter to his own government, written two days after this, he referred to the Russians as intruders on Mexican soil who were planning further encroachments. Figueroa told Vallejo confidentially that he would have to pretend that they had received word that Baron Wrangel was actually at Ross. This would be the excuse for the expedition. In his typically thoroughgoing

3. Secretary of War to Figueroa, Feb. 22, 1833, BL, Archivo de Guerra transcripts; Hittell, *History*, 2, 171–72; Figueroa to Mariano G. Vallejo, Apr. 10, 1833, BL, Cowan; Diputación, Monterey, Session of May 1, 1834, BL, Legislative Records, 2; *El Telégrafo* (Apr. 2, 1833).

fashion, Figueroa also prepared a secret set of instructions for Vallejo, which have come to light since Bancroft's time, giving him detailed questions to answer. For example, Vallejo was to reconnoiter the land around Santa Rosa and the port of Bodega, noting its agricultural capacity, what Indian tribes lived on it, and its suitability for founding a town or building a fort for defense against attack, either from inland or from the sea. Figueroa instructed Vallejo that he was to treat the non-Christian Indians whose lands he passed through with the greatest tact and care, in order to win them over by friendly means. He was to assure them that they would not be molested or disturbed if they remained at peace. He was particularly to make every effort to win the friendship of the tribes living near Ross and to invite them to visit him in San Francisco and Figueroa at Monterey. When Vallejo got in touch with the Russians he was to find out what their purposes were in developing their American colonies, appraise their success, calculate their strength in men and resources, and observe how they treated the Indians. He was to report on the ability and education of the Russian officials, mentioning whether they were military men or civilians. He was to do all this without letting them know that he was gathering information, and he was not to mention Governor Figueroa's plan to erect a fort unless absolutely necessary. If he did mention it, he was to say that the governor was unwilling to build one and that he (Vallejo) was simply preparing a report on whether such a fort was necessary or not. He was to give the impression that it was something they were vaguely thinking about for some time in the remote future.[4] In all this Figueroa reveals something of his craftiness. Vallejo duly received his instructions on April 19 and set out about April 21 on his journey. He left Ross on April 28 for Bodega and was back in San Francisco by May 5, when

4. Figueroa to Vallejo, Apr. 10, 12, 14, 1833, BL, Cowan; Bancroft, *California, 4,* 161, n. 7, 162.

he submitted his report. The Russian commandant, Peter Kostromitinov, gave him numerous statistics about the Russian colonies, which he duly reported to Figueroa. When it came to the crucial region of Ross, Vallejo, acting as innocent and unconcerned as he could, learned that the Russians had founded it for catching sea otter and seals. Later they farmed the land around it to support the population, which then amounted to some three hundred persons, men, women, and children. Of these, seventy were Russians, most of the remainder being either mestizos of Russian and Kodiak or Californian Indian origin. There was no military force there, Vallejo said; everyone was a merchant, and the site was not well fortified. But if his report revealed that there was no particular cause for alarm at the Russian colony of Ross, it also showed that the pagan Indians in this frontier region were strongly hostile to Mexico. An Indian captain named Tuitinje had told Vallejo about the treacheries of the soldiers, and "indeed I can see," Vallejo went on,

> that [the Indians] have been vexed and deceived both by the troops and by the missionaries because of their detestable and ill-advised system of reducing the unfortunate Indians to Christianity by removing them forcibly from their homes and taking them to foreign lands where they are baptized in the same way.

As a result of these methods, Vallejo continued, the region of Santa Rosa and Jaquiyomí, which he would recommend for the foundation of a new settlement, was heavily populated by Indians who deeply distrusted the Mexicans. In fact, they were now in a state of "alarming hostility," and he could understand why. The reasons for this situation, he felt, were "the great violence and injustice committed against the unhappy Indians by those charged with the administration of civil justice and, even more so, of spiritual justice." These men, he continued, had made a mockery of "our true religion," and he thought the Indians were entirely justified in banding together in large numbers to oppose the Mexicans. The trouble, he concluded more specifically, was directly due to the "bad faith, ill-treatment and cruelty of the missionaries and of the sanguinary system that they introduced, while trying to persuade people that these were the methods and example of Jesus Christ."[5] It is possible that Vallejo's sympathy for the pagan Indians was due as much to his dislike of the missionaries for withholding supplies for his troops as to the sad state of the frontier tribes. When he learned, later in the year, that the federal government had passed a law secularizing the missions, Vallejo rejoiced "that those poor men are being freed from the clutches of the missionaries, who will now at last finally lose their swarms of people and pesos."[6]

Figueroa was highly pleased with Vallejo's report, which he said he would send on to the government in Mexico with a recommendation for Vallejo. He agreed with Vallejo that a further reconnaissance of the terrain was advisable before deciding on the site of a new town. He did not comment on Vallejo's outburst against the missionaries, but in later communications, when he was assuring Vallejo that he was doing his best to persuade Father García Diego, prefect of the Zacatecan missionaries and then in charge in the north, to help provide the necessary supplies, he showed that he did not disagree with him. "While this system of missions lasts," Figueroa remarked, "we shall run into the same difficulties; I am endeavoring to get rid of them, but this cannot be done in a moment. They must be tolerated while some reforms that I think are indispensable are made." What these reforms were he did not say, but in a later letter to Vallejo he implied that one of them would be to deny the missionaries the use

5. "Vallejo Informe," San Francisco, May 5, 1833, BL, State Papers, 2, 98, 101, 104, 105, 107, 109–11; Figueroa to Vallejo, May 15, 1833, BL, Cowan.

6. Figueroa to Vallejo, June 16, 1833, BL, Cowan; Vallejo to Figueroa, Oct. 3, 1833, BL, State Papers, 2, 232.

of troops in making converts among the pagan Indians. It may be recalled that this reform was emphasized in the proposals for dealing with the missions drawn up by the Committee on the Californias in 1825.[7]

At about this same time Indian difficulties were becoming apparent in the San Diego region, where Echeandía had begun his secularization project. Father Durán was there and wrote a letter to Figueroa on conditions at Los Angeles. He was very much distressed by what he saw. He found some two to three hundred emancipated Indians in the town and close to it, "subject to a white commissioner." "Beyond comparison," he wrote Figueroa on July 3,

> they live far more wretched and oppressed than those in the missions. There is not one who has a garden of his own, or a yoke of oxen, a horse, or a house fit for a rational being. The equality with the white people, which is preached to them, consists in this: that these Indians are subject to a white comisionado, but they are the only ones who do the menial work. I saw with mine [own] eyes on Corpus Christi Day (May 31) the poor Indians sweeping the street through which the procession wended its way; and I was told they do the same for their livelihood. For offences which the white people consider small, or as nothing among themselves, those Indians are placed over a cannon and given one hundred blows on the naked body. . . . All in reality are slaves, or servants of white men, who know well the manner of securing their services by binding them a whole year for an advanced trifle. This abuse the natural frailty of the Indian makes possible, because he looks not beyond the present. If he wants to free himself from future servitude

7. Figueroa to Vallejo, May 15, June 16, Aug. 17, 1833, BL, Cowan; "Plan para el arreglo de las misiones de los territorios de la alta y de la baja California," in *Colección de los principales trabajos,* pp. 8–10, items 1 and 10.

by flight or in any other way, he experiences the full rigor of the law.

Here indeed was a whole new set of problems. Was the Indian to be emancipated from the missions only to become a peon, bound in debt servitude to the whites? Would he not be better off under the paternalism of the missionaries? Father Durán was himself convinced that the Indian could never become a landowner independent of the white man. "The benevolent ideas of the Government," he continued in his letter to Figueroa,

> with regard to the plan that the poor Indians should be proprietors and independent of white people, will never be realized, because the Indian evinces no other ambition than to possess a little more savage license, even though it involved a thousand oppressions of servitude. I have seen that the Indians of said pueblo are in far worse condition than the neophytes of the missions, in exchange for a little more freedom to lead vicious and irrational lives.[8]

There is no reason to suppose that this is not an accurate picture of the situation, but it does not necessarily imply that the answer to the problem was to keep things just as they were. In fact, the Indian disturbances which obliged Figueroa to leave Monterey about June 26 for San Diego were caused by Indians on the missions, not by those who had been emancipated. In another letter of July 19 to Figueroa about conditions on Mission San Luis Rey, Father Durán reported:

> I see with mine own eyes the insubordination of these Indians with regard to such work as belongs to them. Half the people do not want to go to the fisheries. Yesterday half of the men, who were to take the tallow to the port, were missing. The reason for all this is the want of proper punishment. Don Pablo [Portilla, Captain of

8. Engelhardt, *Missions, 3,* 477–79.

San Diego presidio] neither works nor permits work, so that the Father is a real slave and servant of all. Said Father is afraid of the Indians, and therefore permits them to do anything. I confess that I would not have charge of the temporalities under these circumstances; for the whole year round, from Indian and non-Indian it is: "Father, give me, Father, give me"; but to find the Indian not willing and no one able of forcing him to work for want of a suitable and paternal chastisement, is nothing but a state of things which is apt to consume the health and patience of a saint.[9]

When he reached San Diego, Governor Figueroa caused a half-dozen of the Indian leaders in the movement to be arrested, and the whole conspiracy, if it was a conspiracy, came to an end. On looking more closely into the cause of the trouble, Figueroa came to the conclusion that the Indians were discontented because Echeandía had promised them liberty and had not given it to them. After a number of conferences with Father Durán, Figueroa worked out what he called "Provisional Steps for the Emancipation of Mission Indians," which he issued on July 15. These "Provisional Steps" went right back to Governor Echeandía's first secularization experiment in 1826, by which selected mission Indians who met certain conditions were to be permitted to leave their missions. Under Echeandía's scheme the Indians selected had to be married and able to earn their living, and they had to have been Christians for fifteen years. Figueroa's plan provided the same conditions, except that the Indians had to have been Christians for only twelve years and must be willing to work. According to Figueroa's scheme, the Indians to be freed were to be chosen by a commissioner, appointed by the governor of the territory, working with the missionary at his mission. For his first year outside the mission, the freed

9. Figueroa to Vallejo, June 23, 1833, BL, Cowan; Engelhardt, *Missions*, 3, 479–80.

Indian was to be given mission food, but he was to help the mission at planting and harvest time and at other determined times. The governor was to decide how many Indians were to be freed at any mission and when this was to be done. If a sufficient number of Indian families left the missions, they were to be given lots in a town to be founded at a spot near the coast selected by the commissioners and the missionaries. One of the articles in Figueroa's project stated that as the freed Indians ceased to be minors and entered upon the enjoyment of the rights of citizens, the authorities were to see that they were given equal rights with other people in elections and given the chance to hold municipal offices. To give them an opportunity to learn their civics at firsthand, a magistrate, two city councillors, and a *síndico procurador* (literally, a person who looked after the interests of the town) were to be appointed from their number every year to run the town. They were to do their part in cooperative work undertaken by their town, such as digging ditches, building dams, making corrals, and constructing churches and public buildings.[10] The land they received was to be their own, given in title to them by the governor to be inherited by their children. But they were not allowed to divide it up or transfer it to another person.

Figueroa sent his new mission program off to the minister of relations on July 20 and enclosed with it an unusually frank account of his views on the mission problem. He was anxious, he began, to put into effect the instructions that the government had repeatedly issued to give the mission Indians land of their own, remove them from the influence of the missionaries, and make them into free men. But there were complications. The Indians were still children, more backward than had been thought. And if they were given mission lands, white men, both natives and foreigners, who wanted these lands for themselves would soon get them in exchange

10. Figueroa to Vallejo, Aug. 17, 1833, BL, Cowan; Diputación, May 1, 1834, BL, Legislative Records, 2; Bancroft, *California*, 3, 328–30, n. 50.

for liquor and trinkets. Indeed, the Indians would shortly find themselves either beggars or slaves of the white man. There were many people in California, Figueroa went on, who pretended to be interested in freeing the Indians from the missions, but who were really aiming at seizing both mission lands and mission Indians. He would not be surprised if these men did not try to get what they wanted by force. Furthermore, these same men were hoping to use Indian manpower to fight for the independence of California from Mexico. The idea was absurd, Figueroa said, for they had no resources or population to do this, but nevertheless it was there. They looked upon Mexicans much as Mexicans looked upon the hated Spaniards.

Giving lands wholesale to the Indians, then, would not help them, and it would ruin the missions. Figueroa emphasized the fact that California depended on the missions. Each mission was a valuable hacienda which maintained its mission Indians, the missionaries, and its church and in addition supported the troops and many of the whites. The Mexican government, because of its empty treasury, had been unable to send sufficient funds to cover the expenses of the garrison, which had therefore been dependent to a large extent on the missions. But numerous Californians were also dependent on them. The missions helped many families by making loans to them and giving them other assistance. Some industrious and less dissipated persons even made their fortunes out of the missions. On the other hand, the common whites, who did no work, occupied their time by swindling the mission Indians. They gambled with them at cards, provided liquor for them, and in return took their clothing and their food. They even persuaded the Indians to become robbers and then took what they had stolen. The missions, went on Figueroa, were also hostels where travelers and the poor found food, lodging, and horses or whatever they needed at their disposal free of charge. From all this, he continued, it could be seen that the California missions were the sole source of the prosperity of the territory; all of the inhabitants depended on their preservation.

As far as the missionaries were concerned, Figueroa said that he disapproved of the methods they used in taking care of the temporalities, for they did not keep accounts, but nonetheless the missions were in flourishing condition and many of the missionaries had proved their probity. He thought it would be hard to find laymen as honest to administer the missions. The real danger, as far as the missionaries were concerned, was that so many of them were Spaniards who did not approve of Mexico's independence or her system of government. If an attack came, their influence in the territory was so great that they could persuade many of the people to follow them. If the Spanish missionaries could be replaced with Mexicans, the security of the territory would be strengthened.

It was with these ideas in mind that Figueroa drew up his provisional steps for emancipating the mission Indians. The missions, for the reasons he had stated, would have to be preserved for the time being. He said that he had consulted with Father Durán and had come to an agreement with him. Father Durán concurred with the ideas of the government, and the missionaries were not opposed to the plan. He was going to limit his plan to Indians at the four missions of San Diego, San Luis Rey, San Juan Capistrano, and San Gabriel. As soon as he received the government's approval, he would go ahead with others. Figueroa concluded by saying that he realized the disturbance such a change would make, but it was more important to improve the lot of so many oppressed beings sunk in ignorance who could never escape from their condition unless something was done for them.[11]

If it could be conveniently forgotten that Governor Echeandía's similar plan had failed, Figueroa's new proposal looked practicable enough on paper. He took care of the

11. Figueroa to Minister of Relations, July 20, 1833, Vallejo, "Documentos," BL, *31*, pt. 1.

vexing problem of getting the Indians to make a living on their own by granting freedom to only a select few. The missionaries might be expected to approve of his departure from Echeandía's later method of transforming missions into towns, and they were themselves to have a say as to which Indians might be freed. If they had any doubts about the Indians' ability to perform their part of the bargain, they might take consolation in the stringent provisions for returning delinquent Indians to the missions. On the other hand, Father Durán's description of the peonage into which Echeandía's emancipated Indians had fallen might be avoided by settling the freed Indians in their own towns. As it happened, Father Durán's letter revealing this new problem did not reach Figueroa until his provisional emancipation procedure had already been announced. The day after it was announced, Father Durán penned a criticism of Figueroa's plan. He did not oppose it, but after recommending some minor changes, he repeated in his own words the closing paragraph of the plan:

> If after three or four years it shall be observed that the emancipated Indians depend upon wild fruits for their subsistence; that they allow their live-stock to decrease; that they neglect their planting and other work in a spirit of vagabondage; or that they manifest no zeal or liking for a rational and civilized life; and if, being several times warned, they do not mend, then let them be returned to their missions.

Undoubtedly this is what Father Durán was convinced would happen. In a later communication to Figueroa, Father Durán repeated his doubts about the Indians and added a strong indictment of the white Californians: "The ideas of the Indians and of those who are not Indians and those of the Government are very different," he began;

> The [Government] wants the Indians to be private owners of lands and of other property; this is just. The

Indians, however, want the freedom of vagabonds. The others want the absolute liberation and emancipation of the neophytes without the command to form civilized towns, in order that they may avail themselves of their lands and other property as well as of their persons. I do not see how these opposing interests can be harmonized.[12]

Figueroa remained at San Diego until the latter part of August and was able to see for himself the difficulties involved in the process of secularization. A letter of his to Vallejo on the practical application of his plan showed that all was not smooth sailing. "I have made a beginning in emancipating some natives," he reported, "so that they may form separate towns and be given lands and some other possessions. But these unfortunates are so prejudiced and incapable of thinking that many of them refused to accept the favor." Perhaps, one is tempted to interject at this point, they had heard something about one of the freed Indians being "placed over a cannon and given one hundred blows on the naked body" in Los Angeles some two months before? Whatever the reasons for their reluctance, Governor Figueroa was determined to go ahead with his project. He had begun to establish a town at San Dieguito, he told Vallejo, and he had in mind slowly forming other towns at other missions, keeping the missions going until the Indians were all freed, "for it cannot be done all at once without causing great disorder and harm." In his report to the Territorial Deputation in May 1834, Figueroa stated that he had founded towns at Las Flores and San Juan Capistrano as well as at San Dieguito. "All of them are getting along quite well," he added, "and soon the great difference between emancipated Indians and the neophytes will be apparent. I dare to predict not only their elevation to the dignity of free men, but their better

12. Engelhardt, *Missions, 3,* 479; Durán to Figueroa, July 16, 1833, and Durán to Figueroa, San Gabriel, Aug. 6, 1833, both cited in Engelhardt, *Missions, 3,* 480, 481.

preservation away from the annihilation so evident in the missions." Figueroa's letter to Vallejo of August 16, 1833, shows that he had seen in the newspapers from Mexico (perhaps in the official *El Telégrafo*) the debates in the Chamber of Deputies on the bill to secularize the California missions. He told Vallejo he thought the bill would soon be made into law, but he did not seem too happy about it. "I shall always be of the opinion," he said, "that this affair should be undertaken with the greatest care, for it is very dangerous and if mistakes are made the territory will be ruined." His knowledge that the government in Mexico was working on a secularization law for California missions, together with the multitude of other business that he had to take care of without sufficient staff, caused him to slacken his efforts to put his project into effect elsewhere. Still anxious to hand over his position as governor to a successor, Figueroa made his way back to Monterey about August 23, 1833.[13]

Figueroa had said in his letter to the minister of relations about his new mission program that he would have regulations prepared for the complete secularization of the missions in accordance with his instructions. On August 2 he asked Fathers Durán and García Diego to state what missions were ready for secularization under the law of September 13, 1813, what objections there were to secularization, and how best it should be done. Father García Diego, prefect of the newly arrived Mexican friars from Zacatecas, replied first on September 24. He began by stating that all the missions in the northern district held by the Zacatecans, except San Francisco Solano, were liable to secularization under the law of September 13, 1813, since they had been in existence for more than the required ten years. San Francisco Solano lacked only a few weeks of this time. "But," he added, "I believe that none can be secularized." He proceeded to give his reasons for this opinion:

13. Figueroa to Vallejo, Aug. 17, 1833, BL, Cowan; Diputación, Session of May 1, 1834, BL, Legislative Records, 2.

When the Cortes passed this decree they were not aware of the character, vices, ignorance, frailty, and needs of these wretched natives, otherwise the legislators, two thousand leagues away, would not have enacted the law or included California. The neophytes must be treated with kindness and vigilance as though they were children. The missionary must care for their clothing, their health, food; he must instruct them, put them to work, in short be everything to them. If unhappily they should be emancipated they will go naked. It is about a month since I distributed clothing; only a few have their new clothes still. Then, who will attend them in sickness, unless the missionary takes pity on them? . . . Then there is the passion for gambling, for the sake of which they will not hesitate to steal. . . . They are, moreover, inclined to drunkenness, and then what excesses they commit when intoxicated! I would not write them down. . . . Can such people be allowed to go about at will and to do as they please? If entirely independent of the missions, who will induce them to attend Christian instruction? . . . Even now they attend holy Mass but reluctantly.

In other words, these mission Indians were still completely unable to live according to the fashion of the white man. Indeed, not having adopted the taboos of the whites, and being forbidden to practice their own, they were inclined to adopt without restraint vices such as gambling and drunkenness which they saw around them. Nor were they greatly interested in the white man's religion.

If this sorry state of affairs was not sufficient to deter would-be secularizers, Father García Diego did not let the opportunity slip to point out another serious consequence of suppressing the missions, even if only partially. This was in the sphere of economics, and it would primarily affect the whites in California, military as well as civilians. "The missions," he pointed out, "are communities which are conserved by the labor of those who belong to them. By them the land must be cultivated, mechanical arts fostered, and the herds guarded. If the hands are missing, all must go to ruin." Father García Diego did not answer Figueroa's question about how secularization could best be undertaken. Instead, he asked himself what measures should be taken to raise the mission Indians from their low condition and answered this question by saying that "the means which have been employed by the Fathers will do this in time." On the other hand, he was in favor of doing away with flogging, and he would permit the neophytes to cultivate some fields for themselves.

Father Durán replied to Figueroa's questions on secularization on October 3 in a long and important report. First of all, he suggested the "experimental secularization" of eight missions—San Juan Capistrano, San Buenaventura, Santa Barbara, Purísima, San Antonio, San Carlos, Santa Cruz, and San Francisco. He pointed out that none of these missions had admitted pagan Indians for many years, and therefore the Indians in them were further removed from what he called "the vicious habits of the [pagans]." Also he thought the Indians on these missions somewhat better able to live "by themselves in a civilized manner." For example, he discovered in them "some interest to cultivate their little gardens, which they care for moderately well and raise some produce when conditions are favorable, as when they are given the aid of implements, animals, and other conveniences, though not without the pain of seeing them lose those articles through the vice of drink, which has spread among them horribly." He suggested that when the missions were secularized the mission Indians be given "a certain amount of property which they might enjoy as their own." He felt that the remainder of the property should be put aside into a kind of community fund, administered by the Indians through an Indian majordomo they themselves selected. At first, he thought, the missionaries should have "some kind of authority" over this fund, but this was not to include coercion of the majordomos, who were to be solely responsible to the government for losses incurred through failure to heed the advice of the missionary. This fund would provide the expenses of "Divine Worship, spiritual administration and others that might occur."

When secularization was undertaken, Father Durán felt that the emancipated Indians should be warned that they would be put back into the missions, "whenever it should be discovered that through sloth, preference for wild fruits, or an inclination to vagrancy or other vices, they neglect their property and frustrate the advance of civilization and agriculture, which the government expects of them." In a comment which reveals where he thought the mission Indians were getting their bad habits, he added, "At the same time, the government should see that similar results are observed in the white people, so that the natives may receive practical lessons through the eyes, which is the shortest road to progress." It must be admitted that this last suggestion would have been a good idea, but unfortunately it was not a very practical one.

Father Durán saw two major difficulties confronting secularization. The first was "the indifferent and slothful disposition of the neophytes," which, he said, was "surely notorious and evident, since any one can observe with what little eagerness they do all that pertains to the community, notwithstanding that they know they are working for themselves." Their indolence when working in their own fields and gardens he found "not quite so remarkable." But even here he did not feel hopeful, for when they were on their own they would have to provide their own tools and implements, and he was afraid that they would not "plant or achieve much." He admitted that the mission Indians still craved a return to their old wild habits in which nature provided "the necessaries without personal labor." In spite of the enormous labor of the missionaries "to make men of them," he conceded that "they are barely able to appreciate that which is proper to human beings, except for the faint hope, founded, or unfounded, of being able to enjoy in some degree their former liberty of roving about." After painting the character of the California Indians in these black colors and adding that they were all the same, with "scarcely [a] known single exception," he endeavored to counteract the reaction to such statements over the years by the government:

> Inasmuch . . . as it would not be strange that any one should think that I or the missionaries have an interest in undervaluing the Indians, and emphasizing their in-aptitude and immaturity for emancipation, for the reason that we find ourselves well fixed in the manage-ment of their affairs, in my name as well as in the name of all the missionaries of San Fernando College, I pro-test against such a supposition.[14]

After calling upon Governor Figueroa and the federal gov-ernment to relieve the missionaries of their work in the Cali-fornia missions, he remarked that he thought Echeandía's secularization decree of January 6, 1831, which he had so strongly criticized when it came out, "provided it had been feasible and issued in good faith, was for us incomparably more advantageous than the system proposed." It is not clear what he meant by "the system proposed," but perhaps it was the bill for general secularization being considered in the Chamber of Deputies in Mexico.

The second major difficulty involved in secularization was the economic one, and Father Durán put it to Governor Figueroa in terms that a military man might readily com-prehend. The missions, he reminded the governor, who did not need to be reminded, "support the troops, whom the gov-ernment does not pay." For twenty-three years the soldiers had not been paid. "Had it not been for the communities of

14. Engelhardt, *Missions,* 3, 486, 487–89, 491–92; Figueroa to Vallejo, San Diego, Aug. 17, 1833, BL, Cowan.

Indians under the management of the missionaries," Durán went on,

> there would not have been any soldiers for internal peace and external defense, because they would have perished from hunger. Consequently, after the missions have been secularized, we can no more rely on them for anything; for, if the Indians notice that they must pay taxes on their private property, they will soon manage to have nothing, will abandon everything, and go off to the wilderness and tulares in order to live on the products of nature, and there will be no possibility of forcing them from their haunts.

Can the government support the military in California without the missions? he asked Figueroa.

Finally, Father Durán made two proposals by which he thought that secularization of all the missions could be undertaken "without destroying what has been planted and reared with so much labor." The first proposal, which Echeandía had himself put forward, was to found a new chain of missions and presidios to the east of the old missions, "leaving it to the neophytes to join the new establishments or to organize civilized pueblos on the sites of the old missions." If this were done, he felt that the danger of the emancipated Indians' dispersing into the wilds of the interior might be prevented, for "the natives near the new missions, as is likely, will attach themselves to them, and those neophytes who remain at the old missions will form civilized pueblos." Also, the Indians "would lose the hope of returning to their nomadic life" and would "insensibly, as it were," be forced to "lead a life of virtue." He remarked that if a general dispersal of mission Indians into the interior did take place, it might prove dangerous for California—supposing, for instance, that in alliance with the pagan Indians, they received arms from foreigners in return for furs.

Since this method would require government aid and

would be expensive, he did not think it practical; but he suggested a second method which would be inexpensive and, he thought, equally effective in preventing the destruction of what had been done, although it would take longer. This was to create a bishopric for California, the bishop to have control of the tithes. With the funds from these, he could establish a seminary for the ecclesiastical education of the sons of decent California families. From this seminary, in due course, would come a surplus of priests who could found a second missionary college which would in turn supply the new missions and old pueblos. When these things were done, and he did not think it would take more than a few years, "then a general secularization of all the missions can be effected without the risk of scattering the newly made Christians," and in a moment of rare optimism, he added, "then with giant strides will the natives advance in civilization; and among the white people will also be banished vagrancy which is the real pest of California society." These ideas that he was putting forward were not new, he said at the close of his report: he had had them almost from the beginning of his service in California, twenty-seven years before.[15]

On October 5, 1833, two days after Father Durán wrote his report on secularization of the missions, Governor Figueroa sent further comments of his own to the government in Mexico on the subject. Anxious as he was, he began, to put into effect the benevolent views of the government on the secularization of the missions "as a justification to afflicted humanity," he had been assiduously collecting information on the state of civilization of the neophytes, in accordance with his instructions. After consulting those persons most likely to have this information, he was planning to send in a report to the government. But he had heard that the Congress was discussing a bill secularizing all of the missions and distributing their land and property. He was therefore

15. BL, State Papers, 2, 90; Engelhardt, *Missions, 3,* 492–94.

hastening to send in the two reports by Fathers Durán and García Diego which, he said, "will inform you of the difficulties which can be detected in this [method of] putting into practice the said Law and of the disagreeable consequences that may result." It is not certain from Figueroa's vague language whether Fathers Durán and García Diego wrote their reports with knowledge of the debates going on in the Congress, but this is possible. While he himself, went on Figueroa, did not entirely agree with the reports, he did think that general secularization was premature. He felt that it should be done "partially and with restraint, insensibly substituting for the mission system a government analogous to the character and circumstances of our natives." If this were not done, he continued, the work of many years would be destroyed in one blow, and "these Citizens, whom it is proposed to benefit, would run the risk of an unhappy fate." Furthermore, he said, "an absolute and sudden change will necessarily cause general disorder and ruin."

Having delivered a warning against the bill to secularize all the missions, which he did not know had passed into law on August 17, Figueroa proceeded to back up his views by specific examples. First of all, he emphasized that the Indians were not yet ready for it. "These natives, Sir," he began,

> are close to being domesticated, but they are very little civilized, and most of them are as savage as if they had just left the forests. They are as innocent as children and it is necessary to lead them by the hand to civilization. By all means make whatever reforms are desired to improve their civil and religious education and to teach them the right to own land, but do not destroy the missions all at once, for such a cure is worse than the disease.

He reminded the minister that when he had drawn up his own provisional emancipation plan, he had opposed general secularization, and now that he had had some experience in the matter, he remained convinced that he was right. He himself had selected more than sixty families for emancipation at the mission of San Diego and more than one hundred at San Luis Rey. He had founded separate towns for them, giving them land and water for irrigation, as well as cattle and everything else they needed to establish themselves. He had called them together to exhort them, explaining the advantages they would have and the liberty they would enjoy, but it was all in vain: "I was grieved to hear them renounce everything so as to remain in the servitude in which they lived." Finally, unable to persuade them, he decided to go ahead and emancipate the few who agreed to leave the missions, in the hope that the others would change their minds. But, he added, "a great deal of patience and constancy are necessary, and this is the most conclusive proof of their ignorance and the little aptitude they have for being able to govern themselves." The end result was that ten families out of the sixty selected at San Diego left the mission, and four out of the hundred from San Luis Rey.

In spite of these setbacks, Figueroa advised the minister that he was going to make the experiment of emancipating all the Indians on the mission of San Juan Capistrano because they seemed to be the most civilized. He would inform him in due course how this experiment turned out. As for the other missions, Figueroa felt that the eight missions listed by Father Durán could be secularized, along with some others in similar circumstances, under certain conditions necessary to protect the lands and property distributed to the Indians.

In the final portion of his letter to the minister of relations, Figueroa attacked what he called the law on mission property which, as has been seen, did not actually become a law. His criticisms of it are revealing and provide the key to his bitter opposition to the coming of the Farías colony to California. As will be recalled, the first article of the bill distributed mission lands and other publicly owned lands to the following groups in the order named: the California Indians, the military who were in arrears in their pay, settlers in California who did not own land or who owned less than the bill provided, Mexicans who emigrated to California, and foreigners who emigrated there. The minister should bear in mind, Figueroa began his criticism of this article, that

> all cattle, goods and chattels, and real estate are the exclusive fruit of the neophytes' work. They alone have been sacrificed for the acquisition of this property. It is used to give aid and succor to every traveller, it has been used for many years to provide part of the maintenance of the troops in the Territory, it is used to sustain the Church and its Ministers, it is used to build churches, walls, and all kinds of buildings, in fact, in different ways the inhabitants of California are supported by it.

The property which does this, Figueroa went on, belongs exclusively to the neophytes, "whose labor has provided it and preserved it." It would therefore be very much to the point to make an inquiry into the motives for despoiling them of it and to investigate by what right strangers may take it who have had to pay nothing for it.

Figueroa presented one other criticism of this article distributing mission property. He objected to what he called the "preference" that the bill gave to foreigners over nationals in the acquisition of land and property. The bill actually placed foreigners after the Indians, the military, California residents, and Mexican immigrants, but it specified that the military, to be eligible, were those whose pay was in arrears, and the California residents were to be those without land or those who had less land than the bill provided. The bill did not impose any conditions on Mexican immigrants that would give foreigners a preference over them, but there is some reason to believe, as will be seen later, that Figueroa, like some residents of California, looked upon Mexican immigrants with less approval than foreign immigrants. Figueroa's specific complaint was that "the military, who maintain the rights of the Fatherland with their blood" could not obtain lands unless they were in arrears in their pay—a predicament from which, presumably, Figueroa did not suffer. Figueroa also did not see why foreigners should be allowed to obtain land that had already been settled when so many Mexicans needed it, although he did not object to their having virgin lands to colonize.

The governor ended his letter by saying that he was making these comments solely to call the attention of the government to a law which had perhaps been made without bearing in mind the topography of California, "the character of the men to whom it is directed," their state of civilization or barbarism, the general customs of its inhabitants, and "the connections, dependence and relationship between the missions and the other foundations of the country"—a law, he concluded abruptly, which had been made "without the least practical recognition of local circumstances." Perhaps aware of the role that Vice-President Farías had played in formulating the law dealing with mission property, Figueroa asked the minister to put his letter before President Santa Anna.[16]

It was probably not long after he had written this letter protesting against the bill secularizing all the missions that Governor Figueroa learned it had been passed into law on August 17, 1833. His reaction to this news was to put a temporary halt to his own provisional measures in the same direction. Furthermore, when the Territorial Deputation finally met on May 1, 1834 (it had originally been called to meet on October 1, 1833, but for some reason did not do so), he did his best to dissuade it from at once going ahead with

16. Figueroa to Minister of Relations, Oct. 5, 1833, BL, State Papers, 2, 70. Figueroa mistakenly refers to one bill secularizing and distributing property when, as has been noted in chapter 4, pp. 161–67, two bills were involved. The translator believes that a *no*, which should directly precede the words *"lo poblado y seguro,"* has been omitted from the copy of Figueroa's letter, and he has inserted it in making the above translation relating to foreign settlers.

a secularization measure of its own. "Out of delicacy," he later said in his *Manifiesto,* "and because he hoped that his successor would bring with him regulations for the law [of August 17], he opposed the opinion of the Deputation and held up for more than six months the formation of the Regulation."[17]

In his opening address to the Deputation, of which he was ex officio the president, he called the mission problem "one of the very greatest objectives entrusted to our zeal." In the missions, he went on, "for many years monastic despotism has been entrenched under the double investiture of spiritual and temporal administration," and they "imperiously call for salutary reform adequate for our present system [of government]." The federal government, "anxious to improve the fate of our unfortunate natives," he continued, had given his predecessors the necessary powers to change "insensibly" their situation so that they might "perceive the advantages of our independence." But unfortunately nothing had been done, and the missions remained the same as they had been when they were founded. Governor Echeandía, he conceded, had tried to put his instructions into effect, but he managed to do very little, and unfortunately "far from producing favorable results, symptoms of disorganization appeared because of the not very prudent fashion in which he inculcated in the neophytes the idea of liberty without carrying it into effect." It was because of this, he went on, and for humanitarian reasons, that he had drawn up and put into practice his own secularization plan. Designed to conciliate "diverse heterogeneous interests," he expected it would "bring about after a few years a political change that would reintegrate that unfortunate group of people into the enjoyment of their imprescriptible rights." The federal government, however,

17. Figueroa, *Manifiesto,* pp. 64–65. Since the Deputation did not meet until May 1, and its secularization regulations were issued on August 9—a little over three months later—Figueroa may even have delayed the time of the original meeting of the Deputation.

had now passed a general secularization law, and his own plan was held up because he was waiting for instructions from Mexico. In the meantime, he was anxious to put the new law into effect, and he submitted it to the Territorial Deputation on May 14, asking that it be considered by a committee. He wanted to know whether it might be put into effect at once, and if so how this should be done.[18]

Figueroa had divided his six-man deputation into eleven committees of three. One of these, the Committee on Missions, examined the governor's questions. The records do not give the names of the three men on this committee, but from other evidence it is clear that Carlos Antonio Carrillo was a member of it and probably its chairman. The committee reported on May 24 that it did not consider that Figueroa had sufficient powers to put the secularization law of August 17, 1833, into effect until he received "orders and instructions" from the government. In debate on June 3, Carlos Antonio Carrillo said that the power to secularize the missions was granted only to the president of the republic. He also mentioned that it was "positively known" that a special commission was on its way to California to put the law into effect. Figueroa agreed with the committee and said that he had "meditated" a great deal on the secularization law since he had seen it, and in his view only the federal government was empowered to put it into effect. His reason for coming to this conclusion was that the law "passes over in silence everything relating to measurements of land and distribution of property."[19] Any further doubt about the matter, Figueroa considered, was cleared up by the more recent law passed on November 26 authorizing the federal government to "use every means to assure the colonization and make effective the secularization of the missions of Upper and Lower Cali-

18. Diputación, May 1 and 15, 1834, BL, Legislative Records, 2, 47, 73.

19. Ibid., pp. 36, 93, 96, 100, 101. The six men on the Deputation were Carlos Antonio Carrillo, José Joaquín Ortega, José Antonio Estudillo, José Antonio Carrillo, Francisco de Haro, José Castro.

fornia." It will be recalled that according to the second paragraph of this law, which had been proposed by Bandini, the rural estates belonging to the Pious Fund were to provide resources for the commission and families waiting in Mexico City to come to California. Figueroa published the law in Monterey on May 20, 1834. This may have been the first news he received that a colony was preparing to come north. At all events, Figueroa felt this act made it quite clear that he did not have the power to deal with secularization. In order to justify himself for the preliminary steps he had taken toward secularization of the missions in the southern part of the territory, he mentioned that his instructions from the government authorized him to do this, but he had now suspended his own attempts because of the federal law secularizing all the missions. One of the members of the Deputation, José Castro, said he was in agreement with the committee's views, but he thought it would be "convenient" to add to their proposed article a statement providing that in case circumstances demanded it they might take some action on the matter. Figueroa replied that he had happened by chance to see a letter stating that former governor José María Echeandía had been appointed to take charge of colonization in the territory and was being given a secretary to assist him. This was proof, Figueroa thought, that Echeandía was completely prepared to put the law into effect, and it would be unnecessary to make an addition such as José Castro had suggested. In any case, he went on, if something urgent arose before secularization took place, the Deputation and the political chief were empowered by law to take action. Figueroa concluded by asking that the article proposed by the committee be approved. The record states that after the matter was "sufficiently discussed," the vote was taken and it was unanimously approved. The article was the first of three proposed by the committee and ran as follows: "The Political Chief is not considered sufficiently empowered to execute the provisions of the law of August 17 of last year until he receives orders and instructions from the Supreme Government." In article two the committee proposed that the Deputation petition the government that the new towns to be formed from the missions should be given cattle, orchards, vineyards, and land for cultivation and pasturage, the revenue from which would pay the priests and teachers if they were not paid by the government. This was approved. The third article proposed that the government should be asked to begin secularization promptly, even though the secular priests who were to take over the former missions were delayed. The missionaries, the committee suggested, could take over in the interim as parish priests. This article was also approved.[20]

Governor Figueroa's reluctance to undertake the practical application of the secularization law did not mean, of course, that either he or the Territorial Deputation opposed the idea of secularization as such. Figueroa remarked himself, "Everybody is convinced of the advantages that the law of secularization is going to bring about, nobody has denied this truth." He even went on to say that he had been the first to praise it. On the other hand, he felt that the government had given itself excessive powers in both the law of August 17, 1833, and the law of November 26, 1833.[21] The real problem, however, was not secularization but how mission lands and property would be divided up after secularization had been decided upon. At this point, both Figueroa and the Deputation, and presumably everybody else in California, knew that legislation was being prepared which would divide mission lands for the first time among the Indians, the military, the white settlers, Mexican immigrants, and foreign immigrants. This legislation annulled the law of September 13, 1813, which had been considered valid up to that time and which had provided for division of mission lands among the

20. BL, Departmental State Papers, Monterey, 2, 81; BL, Legislative Records, 2, 95, 101–02, 105.

21. Remark made at the Deputation session of July 31, 1834. BL, Legislative Records, 2, 21–22.

Indians living on the missions. Figueroa still believed on June 12 that José María Híjar, the new governor, would bring with him instructions to divide mission lands in accordance with this legislation, which he thought had passed into law.[22] Figueroa had already put himself on record as opposed to this division because the military could not obtain land unless they were in arrears in their pay and because foreigners were given undue preference over Mexicans. What the members of the Territorial Deputation thought of the methods of distributing land is not known, but it is not to be expected that they would approve of a bill which granted lands to white California residents only if they were landless or had less than fifty-two acres (five hundred varas square). Furthermore, they could not be expected to welcome the fact that they would have to share the available lands with several other claimants from Mexico and abroad. What legislation there had been on the matter in recent years had perhaps given them the hope that they would have to share these lands only with the Indians. Three of the white Californians, in their memoirs prepared for Bancroft, confirm that they considered they had equal rights with the mission Indians to mission lands. José de Jesús Vallejo stated flatly that Californians born in California had as much right as the Indians to ownership of lands there, while Juan B. Alvarado referred to the threat that the colony later posed to "the property of all Californians." Mariano G. Vallejo felt that in all justice mission lands should have been divided according to agreement between the mission Indians and the white residents.[23]

It is important to bear in mind also that the proposed bill distributing mission property divided up the other vacant

22. BL, Legislative Records, 2, 112.

23. See article 17 of the Reglamento of Nov. 21, 1828, in Maza, *Código*, p. 240; José de Jesús Vallejo, "Reminiscencias históricas," BL, p. 41; Juan B. Alvarado, "Memoirs," BL, 2 (1824–34), 223; Mariano G. Vallejo, "Recuerdos históricos," BL, 2, 309.

lands in the Californias among the same groups who were to receive mission lands, keeping the same priorities. It was perhaps because of this, and because of the great interest displayed by Governor Figueroa in making grants of vacant lands with full title (unlike his predecessors) that the sessions of the Deputation were frequently interrupted to obtain their approval of land grants. Figueroa strongly pushed his new program, which was warmly welcomed by the Deputation. It soon became apparent, however, that since the mission lands were not properly surveyed, there would be differences of opinion as to where their boundaries were. This might at times benefit the missions as, for example, when the missionary at San Francisco Solano attempted to claim the land at Petaluma and Santa Rosa which Vallejo was planning to use for a northern colony. On the other hand, if mission lands were to be distributed, it would be essential to have them surveyed. These matters were brought up by José Antonio Carrillo and José Castro at the meetings of the Deputation. José Antonio Carrillo suggested that all mission boundaries be surveyed, but his brother Carlos Antonio Carrillo argued that even if this were done it might be overruled by new regulations that Híjar would supposedly bring with him. Carlos Antonio Carrillo was of the opinion "that there should be no attempt to interfere with these lands that are said to belong to the missions." Figueroa agreed with him and said that for this reason he had suspended his final decision on the claims of several individuals to lands adjoining the missions until the new governor arrived. José Castro in his turn put forward a three-point proposal. First, he suggested that Governor Figueroa assign to the missions the lands "they judge they need" for the preservation and increase of their property (probably meaning cattle). Secondly, he proposed that vacant lands and land left over after his previous suggestion had been acted upon should be distributed in accordance with "the laws cited." He probably meant by this the colonization law of August 18, 1824, and the *Reglamento* of November

21, 1828, both of which had been previously mentioned in connection with the granting of lands. Thirdly, he called attention once again to a matter he had previously brought before the Deputation, namely the wastage that was going on in some of the missions. He suggested that Governor Figueroa should take executive steps to prevent "the large slaughter of cattle that is being done and is planned in several missions." The governor should not issue a permit for this, he felt, unless it could be certified that it was necessary.

The Committee on Missions made these suggestions of José Castro's their own and presented them again, somewhat rephrased, about three weeks after Castro had submitted them. They changed his first article to read that Governor Figueroa should assign to the missions the lands "he considers necessary" for the increase of their herds. This change was made, Carlos Antonio Carrillo explained, because of the difficulty the committee had in talking about precise measurements in mission lands, which were unsurveyed. The committee had therefore left it up to the governor to assign the missions the lands they could occupy with their cattle, so that those remaining vacant might be cultivated. It would appear that both José Castro and the Committee on Missions expected that the result of Governor Figueroa's assignment of pasture lands would be to make more land available for general distribution. In other words, in their view, mission land claims were exaggerated, and they would like to see land granted to the missions on the basis of the number of their cattle. They did not mention mission lands under cultivation, but these were probably not involved.

As might have been expected, Governor Figueroa immediately objected to this article on the ground that he supposed that José María Híjar, the next governor, would bring with him instructions for dividing up mission lands based on a law proposed by "Sr. G." (Gómez Farías) that he had seen in the newspapers. He recommended that the article be voted down. José Castro said he was convinced by what

Governor Figueroa had said, and he agreed that the article should be disapproved. He suggested sending it back to the committee to be amended, but the committee rejected this and called for a vote, whereupon the article was defeated.

What is remarkable about the discussions is that the members of the Deputation did not strongly object to meddling with mission lands at this stage. The records present no impassioned appeals about the sanctity of Indian claims to these lands. Even Governor Figueroa, who had made just such an appeal to the minister of relations a few months before, appears to have been willing to await the coming of his successor with full instructions for dividing up mission property. All this was to change abruptly when Híjar and his colony did appear.

The Deputation next proceeded to discuss the second article of the Committee on Missions' proposal. After the defeat of article one, the committee amended article two to read as follows: "Mission vacant lands will be distributed according to the law of colonization." Unfortunately the records do not say what these vacant lands were; nor do they give any further indication as to which law of colonization. The article, however, was duly approved. Discussion then took place on the third article, which stated that the governor would suspend the large slaughter of cattle taking place in the missions and would only permit it if it were certified to be urgent. Carlos Antonio Carrillo made the following statement on the matter: "The disorder which is being permitted on the missions by the slaughter of cattle is well known, and it will necessarily bring about both the complete destruction of the value of those establishments as well as be prejudicial to public health in them."[24] The article was duly approved.

A heated argument has developed over this slaughter of

24. BL, Legislative Records, 2, 45–46, 84–85, 87, 94, 110–13; Bancroft, *California, 3,* 255.

mission cattle, some arguing that the missionaries ordered it so they would be able to leave the country with mission funds in cash when secularization finally came, and others denying the story as anti-missionary propaganda. In considering this controversial matter it should first be noted that many contemporaries in California in 1834 and 1835 said they had seen large numbers of cattle bones lying on the ground. In a letter to Figueroa from San Luis Rey, written on December 20, 1834, Portilla said that the fields were covered with the remains of cattle. Robinson in his *Life in California* said he passed through a valley covered with the skulls and bones of cattle killed in 1835. Many others, both friendly to the missionaries and unfriendly toward them, confirm that large slaughters of cattle took place at about this time.[25] Mission cattle were generally rounded up and killed in July and August each year. The hides and tallow were then traded with foreign ship owners for clothing and other essentials for the missions. The point at issue here, however, is that the missionaries were said to be killing an unusually large number of their cattle at this time. The available evidence does point to such an occurrence, but it is by no means so clear that there was anything reprehensible about it or that the missionaries were responsible for all the killing that took place. Those who deny that the missionaries were doing anything wrong admit that cattle were killed at this time in large numbers at San Gabriel and San Luis Rey. Father Vicente Pascual Oliva of San Luis Rey stated that he had ordered a large slaughter in order to pay for badly needed clothing for the mission Indians, which Governor Figueroa at length permitted. The reason for the large slaughtering at San Gabriel is not known

25. Robinson, *Life in California*, p. 204. Cf. Sir George Simpson, *An Overland Journey Round the World During the Years 1841 and 1842* (Philadelphia, 1847), p. 170; Guerra Ord, *Occurrences*, p. 32; Padrés to Minister of War, June 3, 1835, FP; Forbes, *California*, p. 283; José Fernández, "Cosas de California," BL, p. 73; J. de J. Vallejo, "Reminiscencias," BL, pp. 54–55.

but may have been the same. There is no specific evidence for similar killings at the other missions, but it is known that recalcitrant mission Indians were stealing cattle and slaughtering them for their hides in large numbers elsewhere. Perhaps the combination of this loss at the hands of the Indians with the slaughter known to have been done at San Gabriel and San Luis Rey has helped to cause misunderstanding and controversy. It should be pointed out that at the time some of these slaughters were carried out, it was not yet known who was going to inherit the mission lands. The bill dividing up mission lands—which Governor Figueroa and other Californians, no doubt including the missionaries, thought had been passed into law—gave the mission Indians twice the number of cattle as the whites. Furthermore, while each Indian family was to be given a specific number of animals, the whites were simply to share whatever surplus cattle remained. Is it possible that some of the missionaries decided to convert these surplus cattle into hides and tallow, which could be sold for the benefit of the Indians, so that the whites would find that there was nothing left for them? While it is difficult, with the evidence available, to come to a definite conclusion on this matter, it is unlikely that there was any concerted move by the missionaries to slaughter mission cattle for their own advantage.[26]

Up until about the middle of June 1834, Governor Figueroa's attitude in the debates of the Deputation toward distribution of mission property was consistently that this should be left to the next governor, who would come out with full instructions. But within the next month he changed his mind. This came about principally, it appears, because of a proposal made by José Antonio and his brother Carlos

---

26. Engelhardt, *Missions*, 3, 658–59; *Northwest Coast of America and California: 1832* (Los Angeles, 1959), pp. 7, 15. Cases against the missionaries are presented by Bancroft, *California*, 3, 348–49, and Hittell, *History*, 2, 207–08. A defense of the missionaries is presented by Engelhardt, *Missions*, 3, 556–59, 654–63.

Antonio Carrillo that administrators should be appointed to take over the management of the mission temporalities; in other words, that the missionaries should no longer have control over the crop raising and other commercial activities of the missions and should be limited to the purely religious aspects of their work. This proposal went to the Committee on Missions, of which Carlos Antonio Carrillo was a member. The committee, after a week's deliberations, expanded the original suggestion by the Carrillos into a full set of provisional regulations for secularization of the missions. The records of the debates in the Deputation are unfortunately too scanty to give a definite indication of how this important change came about, but some actions by Governor Figueroa shed light on what took place.

First of all, the governor strongly opposed a move by Carlos Antonio Carrillo to speed up the Deputation's debates on the proposal for administrators in the missions. His opposition to immediate consideration of the proposal by the Deputation won in a close vote (four to three) over those who wanted the usual procedures to be bypassed. A week went by (July 22–29, 1834) before the Committee on Missions presented its revision of the original motion, which changed it completely into a provisional set of regulations for secularization.[27] Although there is no information on what happened during this week, it seems likely that the extensive modifications in the proposal were made in consultation with Governor Figueroa. According to his own account of the affair, the governor changed his views from opposition to reluctant support of a secularization plan because he felt that the government in Mexico had already done great damage by passing the secularization law, and he was forced to obey the law and put it into effect. According to Father Durán, on the other hand, the Territorial Deputation threatened to rebel, and Figueroa weakly gave in against

27. BL, Legislative Records, 2, 12, 14–15.

his better judgment. Yet another circumstance should be mentioned. On June 30, 1834, some three weeks before Governor Figueroa changed his mind on the secularization proposal, he bought the Los Alamitos ranch near Los Angeles from Juan José Nieto. He paid five hundred pesos for its 26,000 acres—an incredibly small sum even in those days. There is no evidence to connect this transaction, which has been assumed to be a favor or bribe by Nieto, with Governor Figueroa's change of mind over secularization. But even if, in fact, there was no connection, it is clear that by taking over a vast ranch Governor Figueroa was acquiring the same vested interests as the Californians and would perhaps be less likely to oppose their desire for more land.[28]

Whatever the truth of the matter may be, at one point in the Deputation's debates on the provisional secularization regulations, Figueroa rose to stress the fact that the Carrillo brothers had simply proposed that the missionaries should cease to administer the mission temporalities, while he himself had insisted that the Indians be granted the "liberty which has been given them [by the secularization law of August 17, 1833]" and that "a part of [the mission] property should be distributed to them in spite of the fact that he lacked insrtuctions which the Supreme Government had given to the Director of Colonization." The Carrillos' proposal, he went on, far from improving the Indians' condition, would "reduce them to a worse situation by giving them new masters." If Governor Figueroa is responsible for enlarging the original proposal, it is also evident that he was reluctant to go ahead with secularization proposals without authorization from the government. Every time he spoke on the matter he listed several good reasons why he should not do so, but he always closed by saying that in spite of this he was going to support the committee's proposals. Figueroa's

28. Figueroa, *Manifiesto*, p. 65; Father Durán to Father Hidalgo, Sept. 25, 1837, cited in Engelhardt, *Missions, 4*, 109, n. 41. For an account of the Los Alamitos ranch affair, see pp. 377–78.

difficulty was that although in his view the secularization law had made the mission Indians into Mexican citizens, it had done nothing to free them from the material domination of the missionaries. He was aware, as has been seen, of the bill sent to Congress by Gómez Farías which was designed to distribute mission property, but it had disappeared from sight, and in any case, Figueroa opposed its provisions on the ground that mission property should be given only to the Indians.

Figueroa was, then, fully conscious of the fact that both he and the Deputation were exceeding their powers in going ahead with secularization, and he did not hesitate to say he could foresee that they would both be criticized for doing so. On the other hand, he felt that the federal government in its turn had gone beyond its powers in passing the laws of August 17 and November 26, 1833. More to the point, although the law of August 17 had been promulgated almost a year before, the government had done nothing to put it into effect. The result of this, he said, was that mission funds were being "misapplied" or squandered and that he was "convinced of the necessity of taking steps to prevent the total ruin of the missions." He is presumably referring here to the slaughtering of mission cattle, which the Deputation had previously given him instructions to curb. If the missions were put under administrators, the missionaries would no longer have the right to decide upon such matters. But the Carrillos had suggested this, and as has been seen, Figueroa argued that this action by itself would put the Indians in a worse position than before. Out of this difficulty came Figueroa's decision to support the committee's provisional secularization plan. While it is not possible to corroborate or reject Figueroa's opinion that the situation in the missions required immediate action, this was not the only reason why he decided to go along with the committee. From the very first Figueroa had been under pressure from the Territorial Deputation to do something about secularization. After he had managed to avoid putting the law of August 17, 1833, into effect on the ground that he did not have the power to do so, he had to oppose a move to survey mission lands and an attempt to get him to assign lands to the missions. The objective of these proposals was perhaps to open up lands still claimed by the missions as their own to Californians, who were now actively interested in petitioning for land since Governor Figueroa granted it with full title. Presumably the Californians realized that if they waited for the new governor, Híjar, to distribute the mission lands, they would have to share them with Mexican immigrants and foreigners, as well as with the Indians and the military. There was nothing they could do to stop this, but if boundaries could be set for mission lands, then the Californians might perhaps get in ahead of the other eligible claimants in securing vacant land that had been claimed by the missions but was now considered not to belong to them. Governor Figueroa had defeated these moves, although the pressure behind them was still there. In an indirect way he admitted as much when on one occasion he gave as an additional reason for going along with the committee the fact that he knew "public demands and the anxiety with which the change from missions to towns is awaited."[29]

If the Californians had indeed hoped that Figueroa and the Territorial Deputation would produce a secularization decree that would delimit mission boundaries or give them

29. BL, Legislative Records, 2, 16–17, 22–23. In his discussion of this matter, Bancroft was unaware of the bill sponsored by Gómez Farías to distribute mission property, so that Figueroa's actions seemed to him to be based merely on a desire to take action before his successor arrived. (Bancroft, *California, 3,* 341). Bancroft is dubious about Figueroa's sincerity in holding off secularization and considers his final action a "trick." Engelhardt follows Bancroft *(Missions, 3,* 522–23). Hittell, without producing the necessary evidence, says that Figueroa "prepared and passed through the legislature his plan of secularization" *(History, 2,* 190). Figueroa, however, was at pains to deny that it was his plan of secularization when Híjar referred to it in this way (Figueroa, *Manifiesto,* p. 77).

equal chances with mission Indians to obtain mission lands, they must have been disappointed with the provisional secularization regulation that the Deputation produced. This regulation owed something to Figueroa's "Provisional Steps for the Emancipation of the Mission Indians," which he had begun in the south, and it also owed something to the *Plan for the Regulation of the Missions* which had been prepared by the Committee on the Californias in 1825. On the other hand, as its first article indicated, it was drawn up "according to the spirit of the law of August 17 of last year [1833]" and in accordance with Figueroa's instructions from the government. It went back to Echeandía's plans of 1828 and 1831 and stated that the governor, acting in accord with the missionaries, would "partially convert into towns" ten missions, beginning in August, and would follow with the rest in succession.[30] Presumably, if Figueroa had not felt impelled to act in accordance with the new secularization law, he would have preferred to avoid this kind of wholesale secularization. In three further articles in what may be termed its first section, the regulation removed the missionaries from control of mission temporalities and limited them to their religious duties until parish priests were provided. It said that the territorial government would "reassume" administration of the mission temporalities and would seek for quick approval of the regulation by the Mexican government.[31] Articles five through thirteen are listed under the title "Distribution of Property and Lands" and are designed to take the place of Gómez Farías' bill distributing mission property. Article five declares that "each individual head of a family" and all

30. BL, Legislative Records, 2, 25; Engelhardt has a complete translation of the plan *(Missions, 3, 523–30)*. Bancroft *(California, 3, 342–44, n. 4)* has a synopsis of the decree.

31. The use of the word "reassume" in article 3, which Engelhardt criticizes *(Missions, 3, 524, n. 24)*, is taken from article 9 of the program proposed in the *Plan for the Regulation of the Missions* of the Committee on the Californias *(Plan para el arreglo de las misiones, p.10)*.

others over age twenty, even though they have no family, will receive not more than about thirty-three acres (four hundred varas) nor less than about two acres (one hundred varas) of either irrigable or nonirrigable crop land from the mission. The article continues by granting in common enough land for them to pasture their stock and assigning *ejidos,* or commons, for each town. It concludes by stating that revenue-producing town land will also be granted in due course. Article six provides that the governor see that half of the livestock be proportionately divided among the same persons on the basis of the latest estimates submitted by the missionaries, while article seven divides up half or less than half of the tools and seeds available, which are "indispensable for cultivating the soil." Article eight provides that all surplus lands, real estate, cattle, and other property "remain in the care of and under the responsibility of a majordomo or employee appointed by the Governor." Article nine declares that this property be used to provide the stipends of the missionaries, the salary of the majordomo and other servants, and the expenses of worship, schools, and other objectives such as good government and beautification. Article ten gives the governor, who was to have control over mission temporalities, the power to determine and authorize all expenses required to put the secularization regulations into effect and to preserve and increase former mission property. Articles eleven and twelve allow the missionary to choose his rooms in the former mission and put the library, sacred vestments, and certain other ecclesiastical property under his care. Article thirteen calls for general inventories of mission property.

The great difference between this important section of the Deputation's provisional secularization plan and Farías' bill for the distribution of missionary property is that under the former regulations, it must be assumed that only mission Indians were to benefit. The Deputation's wording in article five is curiously vague in this respect, but the regulation as a whole leaves little doubt that this was the meaning intended. When Híjar arrived with the colony, both Figueroa and the Deputation particularly stressed the point that mission lands must be given only to mission Indians. The amount of land granted under the Farías bill was considerably larger than that allotted by the Deputation.[32] The system of distributing livestock in the Farías bill was by head, with the Indians to be given precedence over the whites and granted twice as many animals as the latter. Another difference between the two methods of distributing property was that the Farías bill did not set aside half the livestock, half the tools and seeds, and all surplus land under a majordomo. If "any property should be surplus," ran article ten of the Farías bill, it was to form part of a fund to be used for the development of the Californias.

When Híjar arrived in California and learned of the Deputation's provisional secularization regulations, he angered Figueroa by sarcastically remarking, "If it is believed that mission lands belong to the Indians, how is it that by your Regulation they are only to receive a little square of 400 varas a side (about 33 acres) as a maximum and this small amount of pasture in common?" After remarking that Híjar's "satire ill-became him," Figueroa went on to say that the Indians had at first been granted this small acreage because "they are not considered capable of cultivating a larger amount." He also said that the Deputation was endeavoring to distribute the land in proportion to the number of persons who were believed to have a right to it, "leaving the door open so that it may be given to industrious persons who de-

32. By the Farías bill each family was to receive full property rights to not less than about 52 acres (500 varas square) nor more than about 2,169 acres (*medio sitio de ganado mayor*) of irrigable crop land. If the land was nonirrigable but suitable for crops they were to get not less than about 826 acres (2,000 varas square) and not more than about 4,388 acres (sitio de ganado mayor). If the land was only fit for cattle raising they were to get not less than about 1,856 acres (3,000 varas square) and not more than 8,676 acres (2 sitios de ganado mayor).

vote themselves to its cultivation with greater activity." As for Híjar's comment on the small amount of common pasture land they were to receive, Figueroa pointed out that the regulation did not mention any specific amount of pasture but left the matter up to the commissioners, who could add to it or cut it down depending on the number of cattle and the amount of land belonging to each mission. Figueroa also reminded Híjar that each town was to have an ejido and revenue-producing land of its own.[33]

Articles fourteen through seventeen are grouped together under the heading, "Political Government of the Towns." The first two concern the setting up of town councils and are self explanatory. Article sixteen, however, is of importance, since it gave the governor the power to force emancipated Indians to do their share of work in the vineyards, orchards, and crop lands still undistributed. Since this meant, according to article eight, that the freed Indians would be obliged, in fact, to continue to do forced labor on all mission lands that remained after distribution of their individual lots, it was a key article, probably designed to prevent the collapse of the missions as income-producing farms. The uses to which the income from this land were to be put, according to article nine, as has been noted, were sufficiently vague to cover anything that might be considered to contribute toward "good government," including support for the garrison. By article seventeen the emancipated Indians were to continue to provide free personal service for the missionaries.[34]

It would appear from these provisions of the new regulation that although the former mission Indians were to receive lots to cultivate for themselves, they were still to be forced to work on remaining lands that had formerly belonged to the missions, at the discretion of the governor. Governor Figueroa had opposed the attempts of some mem-

33. Figueroa, *Manifiesto,* pp. 73, 77–78.
34. This article was abrogated by instructions issued by Figueroa on Nov. 4, 1834 (Engelhardt, *Missions, 3,* 532).

bers of the Deputation to turn over the farming and commercial work of the missions to lay administrators on the ground that this would simply put the Indians under new masters, but it is to be noted that he did not oppose such a procedure when he himself became the new boss.

Articles eighteen and nineteen, grouped together under the title "Restrictions," provided that the Indians could not sell or otherwise dispose of their new property. Anyone who attempted to buy it would lose his money. These were the usual paternalistic precautions designed to protect innocent Indians from the wiles of the white man. Some contemporaries, such as José María Luis Mora, disliked the clear implication that the Indians were inferior to the whites, but other supporters of the Indians felt they were necessary. In view of his own attitude toward the California Indians, Governor Figueroa went along with those who felt these limitations on the freedom of the Indians were essential. There is, however, a more significant point to be noted in these two articles. Article eighteen provided that the government would recover the former mission property which had been distributed to the Indians from anyone who tried to buy it, and it would be considered as "belonging to the nation." According to article nineteen, if an owner of these lands died without heir, the lands "would return to the power of the nation." In other words, according to these articles, mission lands belonged to the nation, which was granting them to the former mission Indians and could get them back under certain conditions. This point became a matter of the utmost importance when Híjar arrived with his colony and demanded custody of the mission lands in the name of the nation. As will be seen, Figueroa and the Deputation rejected his demands on the ground that the nation had no right to mission property, which belonged solely to the Indians.[35]

35. Figueroa, *Manifiesto*, p. 119; Padrés to Minister of War, June 3, 1835, FP.

The last four articles of the regulation, which are given the title of "General Rules," provided that the governor was to appoint the commissioners who would put the secularization plan into effect (article twenty) and that he was to settle any doubts or other affairs which came up relating to the execution of the regulation (article twenty-one). Article twenty-two prohibited the missionaries from undertaking any extensive slaughter of cattle, other than the usual amounts customarily made for the subsistence of the neophytes, until the regulation was put into effect. Article twenty-three, the last item in the regulation itself, provided that mission debts were to be paid preferably out of the income from former mission property remaining under the control of the majordomo after the Indians had received their lots. The governor was to say when and how this was to be done.

It is interesting that except for its first article, over which there was some debate on the time element in putting the regulation into practice, it was passed article by article apparently without any discussion. This makes it seem more likely that Governor Figueroa, who was at first reluctant to agree to any general secularization provision, discussed the regulation with the members of the Deputation at unofficial meetings of that body. The regulation gave the governor virtually complete control over secularization and left no power to the Deputation, which is credited with drawing it up. Whether this was a tactful self-depriving move on the part of the Deputation or whether Governor Figueroa politely insisted on taking the dominant role in the regulation can only be conjectured.

Governor Figueroa officially proclaimed the new secularization regulations on August 9, 1834, and issued along with them some twelve additional articles of instructions for putting them into practice. These articles require only brief general comment. They provided that the commissioners were to proceed to their missions as soon as they were appointed and to take immediate possession of the former missions' account books. They were to administer an inventory of mission property. It was to be explained to the mission Indians at once that the missions would be made into towns and that the missionaries would have no authority over them except in religious matters. Each commissioner was to tell the Indians that they were to receive land and other property and to own the houses in which they lived. In return for these things, the Indians were to be informed that "they have to subject themselves to what is ordered in this reglamento and these regulations." Since this, in fact, meant forced labor on remaining land formerly belonging to the missions, it probably took all the "sweetness and patience" the commissioners were instructed to use to make explanations satisfactory to the Indians.[36]

While Governor Figueroa spent more time on the complicated problem of secularizing the missions than on anything else, he did not lose sight of the need to colonize the northern area of California against possible Russian encroachment from Ross. Figueroa had sent Ensign Vallejo north in April 1833 to make an investigation of suitable terrain for founding a new town, but after receiving Vallejo's report, he decided that further reconnaissance of the area must be made before a site was finally selected. Figueroa then became deeply involved in mission questions in the San Diego area and, after he returned to Monterey, with the Deputation's general secularization regulation. From time to time, however, he dealt with urgent matters on the northern frontier, which he had left under the general charge of Vallejo.

Vallejo was busy during the fall of 1833 establishing small settlements at Petaluma and Santa Rosa, when the pagan Indians in the area became greatly excited over the killing of twenty-one of their number by a force sent out by Father

36. Engelhardt, *Missions, 3,* 527–30.

Mercado of San Rafael, following an alleged robbery by the Indians.[37] Vallejo's report on his trip to Ross had stressed the ill will of the pagan Indians toward the Mexicans, and Figueroa was particularly anxious to be on good terms with the frontier tribes so that the new settlement would not have difficulty with them. He also wanted to prevent the pagan Indians from going over to the Russians. The governor was, as has been noted, particularly opposed to the use of troops by the missionaries when dealing with non-Christian Indians. On the other hand, he had to bear in mind that Vallejo's men were almost completely dependent on the missions for their subsistence.[38]

In this instance, Figueroa ordered Vallejo to free the Indian prisoners taken by Father Mercado's men if they were not guilty of the robbery and to march immediately to Mission San Francisco Solano or farther on. He was to return all Father Mercado's prisoners (presumably Figueroa did not think they were guilty) and explain to the Indians that they had been attacked without knowledge of the government, and the missionary was being punished. He was to tell them that they could settle at Santa Rosa or anywhere they liked and would be left in peace so long as they did not go on the warpath. He gave Vallejo verbal instructions that under no circumstances was he to cause the Indians the slightest injury or annoyance; he was to use weapons only in self-defense, when it was absolutely necessary to do so. The objective of his expedition, Figueroa concluded, was to "reestablish confidence" among the pagan Indians. In another letter, Figueroa told Vallejo to confer with the missionary at San Francisco Solano on how the settlers at Santa Rosa might be established at Petaluma. This was to be done so that the Indians at Santa Rosa might be left in peace. Since there were also Indians at

37. Bancroft, *California*, *3*, 255, 323–24.
38. Figueroa to Vallejo, Aug. 17, 1833, BL, Cowan; Figueroa to Agustín Zamorano, Dec. 2, 1833, BL, Departmental State Papers, *1*, 189–91.

Petaluma, Vallejo was to try to arrange that the settlers went to a site called the Lagoon of San Antonio, to be out of the way of the Indians. The settlers were to be warned that these locations were temporary ones for them until the new town was founded, when they would be notified. They could have no claim on the lands they temporarily occupied at Petaluma.[39]

In his address to the Deputation at its opening session on May 1, 1834, Figueroa referred to the government's orders to found a strong military post on the other side of San Francisco Bay near Ross. "I am determined to carry this out," Figueroa said, and he briefly mentioned that he "made some small preparations" for it, adding that lack of resources would "naturally place a thousand difficulties in the way of the undertaking." It was probably shortly after this that Figueroa received the law of November 26, 1833, designed to assure the colonization and make effective the secularization of the missions of the Californias, which in its second paragraph brought the information that some families were waiting in Mexico City to come out with Híjar as colonists. Figueroa later mentioned in his *Manifiesto* that he had learned about "a multitude of colonizing families" coming with Híjar "extraofficially," by which he presumably meant that the government did not inform him directly that the colony was coming. Although, Figueroa went on misleadingly, neither the government nor Híjar was counting on the local authorities to aid the colony, he thought it would be "prudent to make some preparations for its settlement." The preparations he had in mind were to locate the colony in the new town he was planning to found north of San Francisco Bay. This idea, for which Figueroa takes the credit, was of course precisely what the government in Mexico had in mind in sending out the colony.[40]

39. Figueroa to Vallejo, Dec. 9, 11, 1833, BL, Cowan.
40. BL, Legislative Records, 2, 50; Figueroa, *Manifiesto*, p. 7.

Governor Figueroa decided to locate the site of the new town himself. He probably set out from Monterey shortly after August 21, 1834, with Captain Agustín Zamorano, an engineer who was to do the surveying. Ensign Vallejo apparently joined the party en route. By August 27 the expedition was investigating the area close to Santa Rosa, and on August 28 the site for the new town was selected. It was on what is now known as Mark West Creek, which runs a few miles north of Santa Rosa. It was to be called Santa Anna and Farías, "in memory of the President and Vice-President of the Republic [who were] the principal supporters of the new foundation under whose government it was established." Reveille was sounded at six the following morning and the men were put to work under the direction of Captain Zamorano on the surveying of the new town. In the time-honored fashion of Spanish colonial founders of towns, Zamorano began by laying out the site of the main plaza or square and the blocks surrounding it. The work continued all day on August 30 and was completed on August 31, when an ash tree was planted at each of the four corners of the square and one in the center. Camp was struck at four o'clock that afternoon, and the expedition marched to Santa Rosa, where it spent the night. The following day, September 1, they marched to Mission San Francisco Solano by way of Petaluma.[41]

It may have been at this point that Figueroa visited Ross, for he did not return to Monterey until September 12. Before returning, however, he left a military post to guard the site of the colony. The commander of this force was probably Ensign Vallejo, who was given orders by Figueroa to continue with the founding of Santa Anna and Farías. On September 11, the day before he got back to Monterey, Figueroa

41. Bancroft, *California*, *3*, 256, n. 30, says that Figueroa was still at Monterey on Aug. 21. Juan B. Alvarado, "Memoirs," BL, 2, 243; *Historical Atlas Map of Sonoma County*, (Oakland, 1877), p. 14; *History of Sonoma County* (San Francisco, 1880), p. 382; "Diary of an Expedition to Fort Ross, August 9–September 12, 1834," BL.

was at San Juan when a messenger reached him with important news. The *Natalia* had landed at San Diego on September 1 with Híjar and 129 members of the colony. The rest of the colony, consisting of more than 100 persons, including José María Padrés, were expected momentarily at Monterey on the *Morelos*. But the most remarkable part of the news was the order from President Santa Anna, which he had sent overland by a special courier named Rafael Amador, a native of Lower California. Amador left Mexico City the night of Saturday, July 26, and handed over his note to Governor Figueroa at San Juan on September 11. "It is the first case on record [of a messenger coming overland]," remarked Figueroa, "and the most notable thing about it is its brevity."[42]

The instructions, dated July 25, that Santa Anna had urgently wanted Figueroa to receive were brief and to the point. Figueroa was ordered not to turn the governorship of the territory over to Híjar but to remain himself at the post. Hardly had the new governor landed with his colony than he was deprived of his powers. The day after he reached Monterey, Figueroa wrote Vallejo about the surprising new situation. According to scattered pieces of news, he said, there had been a revolution in Mexico. President Santa Anna had apparently dissolved the Congress, because it had wanted to destroy the army and had passed laws that caused a great deal of opposition. "I do not know what other causes they give as a pretext," Figueroa wrote, "but the result is that there is no Congress. I am inclined to believe they have attempted a change of persons rather than of system [of government], but whatever it may be the horizon is very dark. As soon as it clears, we shall learn the truth."[43] Figueroa's

42. Figueroa, *Manifiesto*, p. 7; Figueroa to Vallejo, Monterey, Sept. 13, 20, 1834, BL, Cowan; José María Amador says in his "Memorias" (BL, p. 138) that Rafael Amador was his cousin.

43. Figueroa, *Manifiesto*, p. 8; Figueroa to Vallejo, Sept. 13, 1834, BL, Cowan.

hunch about the situation in Mexico was a shrewd one; most revolts at that time and later were simply changes of personnel in the government without any change in policy. This one, however, was different: most of the personnel cynically stayed on, but the federal system of government gave way to the centralist.

Chapter Seven

Colonists and Californians

Governor Figueroa was at Monterey making preparations to march down to Santa Barbara to meet Híjar when the naval corvette *Morelos,* Captain Lucas F. Manso, finally arrived the night of Wednesday, September 24, 1834. On board were 120 more colonists and Colonel José María Padrés, vice-director of colonization. (For a list of the colonists, see Appendix D.) On September 26 Padrés wrote Figueroa of his arrival with the colonists, whom, he stated, the government had arranged to send north of the port of San Francisco, "with the interesting objective of making it secure." Since, he went on, the colony "momentarily did not have sufficient resources to maintain itself," he was counting on "the well-known good will"of Figueroa to order the sub-commissary to provide him with the necessary provisions. As soon as the affairs of the commission consisting of himself and Híjar as directors of colonization had been arranged, he said, he would replace the provisions with identical or equivalent goods. It should be noted that Padrés said nothing about Híjar's position as governor of California, which Santa Anna had canceled by special courier. Padrés had perhaps learned of this and was careful not to mention the matter until Híjar himself arrived from San Diego.[1]

1. Figueroa to Vallejo, Sept. 20, 1834, BL, Cowan; Figueroa to José R. González, Oct. 2, 1834, BL, Departmental State Papers, p. 256.

Figueroa reported to Vallejo on September 28 that all the colonists had disembarked from the *Morelos* because "they were dying of hunger." Figueroa's first impressions of the colony were unfavorable. There were fewer colonists than he had expected; nor were they such good farmers as were needed, most of them being artisans from the city. Some of them were dissatisfied, went on Figueroa, and he did not think they would be willing to reembark for the remainder of their journey north. On the other hand, they would be useful settled in the new town that he and Vallejo were founding, and they could go on by land if Vice-Director Padrés were willing to make any decisions on his own. Híjar, with the rest of the colony, was still at San Diego, unable to do anything. Foreseeing "disagreeable consequences for those who command and for those who obey" from the confusion this situation could cause, Figueroa said that he wanted to get the colonists to come to some agreement as to what they should do. Meanwhile he was irritated because his device of agreeing with everybody was producing a general paralysis in affairs.[2]

Governor Figueroa's initial disappointment with the colony led by Híjar and Padrés was destined to change in the course of a few months to bitter enmity toward Híjar, Padrés, and several of the colonists. It led to Figueroa's publication of his self-justificatory *Manifiesto a la República Mejicana (Manifesto to the Mexican Republic)*, which he completed on September 4, 1835, a little over three weeks before he himself died. This *Manifiesto* contains much of the correspondence that passed between Figueroa and Híjar, and for lack of any similar published statement by Híjar, it has colored the circumstances of this cause célèbre of Mexican California to an extraordinary degree; Governor Figueroa's pen has undoubtedly done more for his reputation than his sword. In the course of a letter dated October 23, 1834, which

2. Figueroa to Vallejo, Sept. 28, 1834, BL, Cowan.

Figueroa includes in his *Manifiesto*, Híjar wrote, "One day the whole of this affair will see the public light: all men will become acquainted with the reasons of each party; they will form a comparative opinion and render their verdict." Figueroa's comment on this is to say that the day Híjar was talking about had come—in other words, the public could decide by reading his *Manifiesto* who was right.[3] Yet it should not be forgotten that Figueroa wrote his *Manifiesto* to justify his conduct, and although he gives an impression of impartiality, the *Manifiesto* remains simply an able but one-sided account of a famous controversy.

Many of Figueroa's contemporaries seem to have made up their minds that Figueroa was indeed right, and most later historians have done the same.[4] A notable exception to this

3. The *Manifiesto a la República Mejicana* was printed on the newly arrived press of Agustín Zamorano at Monterey in 1835 and has become a valuable collector's item. In San Francisco in 1855 it appeared in an English translation, which was reprinted in 1952 (Oakland, California); Figueroa, *Manifiesto,* p. 86.

4. A number of Spanish-speaking residents of California have left memoirs, many of them written at the request of H. H. Bancroft. Among those who are highly critical of the colony, as most of them were, are the following: Juan B. Alvarado, Mariano G. Vallejo, José Fernández, Antonio María Osío, José de Jesús Vallejo, Vicente P. Gómez, and Manuel Castro. Dr. John Marsh, an American early resident of California, had nothing good to say of the colony when writing a summary of interesting facts about California for Commodore Thomas ap Catesby Jones in 1842 (BL). Among the critical accounts of the colony by foreign travelers the most significant is that by Alexander Forbes in his *California: A History of Upper and Lower California* (London, 1839), much of which may have been supplied by Abel Stearns. Many later writers did little more than take Forbes' word for it that the colonization project was "ill-concerted" and "foolish." Other critical accounts of the expedition occur in Abel du Petit-Thouars, *Voyage autour du monde* (2 vols. Paris, 1841) *2,* 88–89; Duflot de Mofras, *Travels on the Pacific Coast* (2 vols. Santa Ana, 1937), *1,* 150; Charles Wilkes, *Narrative of the United States Exploring Expedition* (5 vols. Philadelphia, 1845), *5,* 163; Alfred Robinson, *Life in California* (New York, 1846), pp. 159–67. An unfavorable comment by a contemporary in Mexico may be found in Carlos María Bustamante, "Voz de la patria," BL, *10,* 29.

attitude is Hubert Howe Bancroft, who instructed Thomas Savage to interview Híjar's nephew, Carlos N. Híjar, at San José in May 1877 and to try to bring back Híjar's entire version of his differences with General Figueroa." In his treatment of the colony episode, Bancroft is constantly reminding the reader that there is insufficient evidence to condemn Híjar and Padrés. On the other hand, he gives Híjar and Padrés the major role in organizing the colony, whereas the evidence indicates, as has been seen, that it was Farías who planned the colony and selected its leaders.[5] Bancroft's contemporary, Theodore Hittell, who also used the Spanish archives of California before they were destroyed in the San Francisco fire of 1906, is more typical of later historians in his view of the colony leaders as unprincipled adventurers, scheming to make their fortunes out of mission lands.[6] Except, in fact, for favorable statements by some of the colonists, such as

5. "California en 1834, recuerdos de Carlos N. Híjar," BL; Bancroft, *California, 3*, 259–61, 262, 264, 265, 286, 290.

6. Hittell, *History, 2*, 191–92. A brief summary of the views of other historians on the colony would run as follows. Engelhardt heads the chapter in which he deals with the colonization attempt "A Sly Scheme and How It Was Foiled." He follows Hittell in his interpretation of the affair (Engelhardt, *Missions, 3*, 501–14). Zoeth Skinner Eldredge is equally unfavorable (Eldredge, ed., *History of California*, 5 vols. New York, 1915), *2*, 228–40. Chapman, in his *History of California. The Spanish Period*, briefly mentions the colony (pp. 464–66), again following the views of Hittell. Others who interpret the affair in the same manner with varying vehemence include Tuthill, Geary, Harding, and Tays. Irving Berdine Richman mentions the colony without saying what he thought about its purposes (*California Under Spain and Mexico*, pp. 250–52). William Wilcox Robinson, in his *Land in California*, puts the cart before the horse by suggesting that the Híjar and Padrés attempt made the Mexican congress take action to colonize California. William Wilcox Robinson, *Land in California* (Berkeley, 1948), p. 29. In his article, "The Reglamento for the Híjar and Padrés Colony of 1834" (Historical Society of Southern California *Quarterly, 28* [1946], 142–75), Keld J. Reynolds simply states that the directors of the colony aroused heated controversy. Margaret Romer, in "The Story of Los Angeles," *Journal of the West, 2* (January 1963), 46, remarks that the "scheme deservedly failed."

Antonio Franco Coronel or José María Híjar's nephew, Carlos N. Híjar, or by Juan Bandini, who was an official in the Cosmopolitan Company (which was more bitterly attacked than the colony), there is an impressive unanimity in opposition to the colony by contemporary Californians, foreign residents of the territory, and later historians. Híjar realized that the evidence against Padrés and himself looked damning in California at the time, and after he was arrested and confined to the Sardinian ship *Rosa*, he wrote to José María Noriega asking him to suspend judgment on the affair until he was returned to Mexico, where he could prove that he was innocent. "I am not able to justify myself in this unfortunate country," he said, "where the laws are trampled under foot [and] I have no other recourse but to beg sensible persons to suspend their judgment on this uproarious affair until its end is in sight."[7] Unfortunately, so far as is known, neither Híjar nor Padrés published a rebuttal to Figueroa's *Manifiesto* or to his previous proclamations against them, so that the entire account of the colony must be reconsidered in some detail.

Governor Figueroa was later to claim that the leaders of the colony had begun to conspire against him from the very moment they landed in California, and although he did not present any evidence that this was so, a number of incidents occurred in the course of the colony's march to the north that aroused his ever-present suspicions. The original plans called

---

A recent textbook account by Andrew F. Rolle does not level any accusations against the colony leaders (*California, A History* [New York, 1963], pp. 154–55). An unpublished doctoral dissertation by Jessie Davies Francis entitled "An Economic and Social History of Mexican California" (University of California, 1935) seems to be alone in openly supporting the colony (pp. 115–16). Woodrow James Hansen appears to support Figueroa and distrust Híjar and Padrés (*The Search for Authority in California*, Oakland, California, 1960, pp. 12–19).

7. Híjar to J. M. Noriega, Apr. 17, 1835, BL, State Papers, Benicia.

for the *Natalia* as well as the *Morelos* to land their colonists at Monterey, but according to his nephew, Híjar was seasick from the very beginning of the month-long voyage to the vicinity of San Diego and ordered the *Natalia* to land there, so that he and the many others who were ill could disembark and continue by land.[8] Híjar left his baggage on board the *Natalia* to be taken to Monterey, but since a great part of the colonists' gear consisted of saddles given them by the government, it was probably landed at San Diego. The colonists were hospitably received by the people of San Diego, who lodged them in their homes, Híjar staying with José Bandini, father of Juan.[9] After recovering from his unpleasant voyage, Híjar wrote to Lieutenant Colonel Nicolás Gutiérrez, the military commander of Southern California who was at Mission San Gabriel, and made arrangements for the colony's march north. This was done by splitting up the colonists into several small groups who were to leave every three or four days, so that the oxcarts borrowed from each mission to carry the heavy baggage to the next mission would have time to return to pick up another load. Some of the colonists rode on top of the baggage in the oxcarts, while some, not liking the rolling motion of these slow-moving wagons, preferred to walk, and others, the lucky ones, rode horseback. A certain amount of discontent seems to have occurred among the

8. Figueroa, *Manifiesto*, p. 135; Híjar, "Recuerdos," BL, p. 4 verso. According to Florencio Serrano, Bandini and Lieutenant Buenaventura Araujo, a Mexican naval officer accompanying the colony, helped to persuade Captain Gómez of the *Natalia* to disobey his original orders and land his ship at San Diego (Serrano, "Apuntes para la historia de la Alta California," BL, pp. 3 verso, 4).

9. Angel Ramírez, "Sobre carga que el Bergantín Nacional Natalia trajo a este territorio," BL, Departmental State Papers, *4*, 79–80; Híjar, "Recuerdos," BL, p. 6. Híjar recounts a story of passionate enmity between Lieutenant Araujo and José Bandini which does not ring true, although conceivably the two might have met when Araujo was fighting the Spaniards in the Peruvian Navy at the siege of Callao in 1825. José Bandini, a Spaniard, had formerly lived in Lima.

colonists on this march because they were not receiving the daily allowance of four reales they had been promised, and some of them, irritated at the slow pace of the march, stopped off at certain of the missions.

When they were at the missions, the colonists went out of their way to make friends with the Indians, with considerable success.[10] In doing so, they were following the instructions of Híjar, who had impressed upon them as soon as they reached San Diego "that they should try to win over the affection of the natives by every possible means of humanity and philanthropy." They were to tell the mission Indians, went on Híjar, "that I had come charged by the Supreme Government to improve their lot; that they were to be given full ownership of lands, some cattle and all possible protection so that they would prosper. Also they were to be paid for their personal work—when this was performed for the missions." Lieutenant Araujo sent on to Híjar from San Gabriel a pagan and a Christian Indian, who had asked him for recommendations. In doing so he explained that he had predisposed them "in our favor by explaining to them as well as I could how well prepared we were philosophically."[11]

As far as anyone who met him knew at this time, Híjar was the new governor of the territory, although Híjar himself mentions that when he traveled north to Monterey, which he did in advance of the colony, arriving there on October 14, there was a suspicion abroad "that the government would not be handed over to me." Florencio Serrano recounts a story that Lieutenant Araujo learned in some way that a courier with Santa Anna's orders not to yield the government to Híjar was to pass by the rancho San Bernardino, near the mission of San Gabriel; the lieutenant seized him as he came

10. Serrano, "Apuntes," BL, p. 6; Híjar, "Recuerdos," BL, pp. 6–7, 59–60.

11. Híjar to Minister of Relations, Jan. 30, 1835, BL, Colonización y terrenos baldíos, Fomento, legajo 6, expediente 173; Araujo to Híjar, Sept. 18, 1834, De la Guerra, "Documentos," BL, *4*, 154.

through but was forced by Híjar to release him. Quite apart from the fact that it is unlikely that anyone could have brought the news in ahead of this courier, who amazed everyone by the speed with which he came, it seems likely that Serrano remembered correctly that Araujo had got into trouble at San Bernardino but forgot the cause of the trouble, which, as will be seen, concerned pagan Indians.[12]

The friendly attitude of the colonists toward the mission Indians, and perhaps their statements about the government's intentions to help them, brought the colonists great popularity among the Indians. When the colonists moved on from one mission to another, the Indians sometimes accompanied them for three or four leagues and wept like children when they finally had to part from them. Some of the mission Indians were even ready to abandon their families and their missions and join the colony, "and they would have done it more than once," Carlos Híjar recorded, if they had not been stopped by the colonists. After his journey north, José María Híjar reported that in general the Indians were enthusiastic about his proposals and that within a few days "delegations of Indians from various missions came to me and told me of their pleasure and gratitude."

Híjar and the colonists were also greeted with enthusiasm by the pagan Indians, who lived in their own villages in the interior. Híjar instructed his colonists to tell the pagan Indians that the Mexican government would protect them, provided they cooperated with the government. "They were also to have lands," he went on, "and these lands and their huts would be respected. They would be free to live where they wanted, without anybody molesting them and we should all form a family of brothers." Híjar reported to the minister of relations that the non-Christian Indians were delighted with these ideas and that the news of them spread "like a flash

12. Figueroa, *Manifiesto*, p. 10; Híjar to Minister of Relations, Jan. 30, 1835, BL, Colonización y terrenos baldíos, Fomento, legajo 6, expediente 173; Serrano, "Apuntes," BL, pp. 8–10.

throughout the territory." From the River Colorado of the Tulares and more than a hundred leagues inland, he reported, came pagan Indians and their captains to meet with him. "I impressed upon them," he said, "the benevolent intentions of the Government and [told] them that the objective of my coming was to bring about their happiness, which they could enjoy by conforming to the social order. They all gladly agreed to unite themselves with the government," Híjar concluded, on the bases he had set forth.[13]

Unfortunately for Híjar and the colonists, these early good relations with both mission and pagan Indians were soon to arouse suspicions in the mind of Governor Figueroa. On October 21, Figueroa wrote identical letters to eight of his commissioners, including Captain Pablo de la Portilla at San Luis Rey, Colonel Gutiérrez at San Gabriel, and Anastasio Carrillo at Santa Barbara. He had learned, he wrote, "that some persons have inspired distrust among the Indians with the object of conspiring against the Government, by making them believe that [the authorities] do not wish to give them their property." Figueroa recommended that the commissioners "persuade the Indians of the falsity of these reports and assure them that they will receive their property and lands, and that no colonist will settle in their towns."[14] It would appear from this letter that some of the colonists, fearful that Híjar was not going to be accepted as the new governor and they were not going to get their lands, were communicating similar fears to the mission Indians. But there is no direct evidence that this was actually happening, and it is

13. Híjar, "Recuerdos," BL, p. 60; Híjar to Minister of Relations, Jan. 30, 1835, BL, Colonización y terrenos baldíos, Fomento, legajo 6.

14. Figueroa to J. Rocha et al., Oct. 21, 1834, BL, Departmental State Papers, 3. It should be noted that this letter is not a verbatim copy of the original from the destroyed California archives, but is a brief résumé by one of Bancroft's copyists of the original. One cannot be sure, therefore, that such key phrases as "conspire against the Government" were actually written by Governor Figueroa, although it is possible they were.

possible that there was some sign of discontent among the Indians which was then interpreted by Governor Figueroa's informant, or by himself, as coming from mischievous propaganda being spread by the colonists. While there is insufficient evidence to come to a definite conclusion on this matter, the governor himself was not satisfied with the information he was getting. Some kind of disturbance had broken out at Mission San Luis Rey, where a group of the colonists were staying, and he wrote Colonel Gutiérrez on October 22 to find out what the causes of the difficulty were, so that those responsible might be arrested. He instructed the colonel to calm the Indians by telling them that the Deputation, which was meeting at that time, was going to protect their interests. The colonists were to be told that the Deputation would attend to their "pretensions," but not at the expense of the Indians. In other words, the colonists were to be put in the position of men seeking to settle on mission lands at the expense of the former mission Indians.

If Governor Figueroa's suspicions were not sufficiently aroused by the happenings at San Luis Rey, which after all had a history of Indian discontent for several years, he was soon to receive information which would quickly confirm his worst fears. Anastasio Carrillo reported to Figueroa from Santa Barbara on October 28 that ever since the colonists had arrived in the territory, he had received news from the south that there were symptoms of revolution there, caused by the colonists' wanting to disturb the existing order among the natives. Carrillo added that he was taking very special precautions to prevent disorder and was prohibiting travelers passing through from speaking to the mission Indians at Santa Barbara.[15] The implication here would appear to be that the Indians in the south were becoming restive because they liked what they heard about Híjar's ideas. And until

15. Figueroa to Nicolás Gutiérrez, Oct. 22, 1834, BL, Departmental State Papers; Anastasio Carrillo to Figueroa, Oct. 28, 1834, BL, State Papers, Missions.

Figueroa announced publicly that Híjar was not going to be the next governor, it was quite in order for the colonists to follow Híjar's instructions and keep on telling the Indians about his plans. Governor Figueroa's instructions to the commissioners to reassure the mission Indians that the colonists would not be permitted to take their lands away from them, whether justified by the facts or not, provided an excellent way of countering the growing popularity of Híjar's new plans.

Governor Figueroa later directly blamed the colonists for the troubles in the southern missions. He put into his *Manifiesto* that Francisco Berduzco, a colonist, had tried, while he was at Mission San Luis Rey, to get the mission Indians to "surprise" a small detachment stationed there, but his plan was discovered and prevented. Berduzco was accused of trying to obtain weapons to arm two companies of colonists, seize the property of the missions, and, after running them for a year or two, leave with the booty before the mission Indians rose in revolt. Berduzco's defense rings truer than the alleged plan of the conspiracy. Figueroa also stated that another colonist, Romualdo Lara, who accompanied Híjar on his journey north, had tried to win over the Indians at several missions to his party. Híjar himself, Figueroa claimed, "delivered speeches to the Indians in the missions along his route, exhorting them to defend liberty, which nobody was attacking."[16]

What little evidence there is about the nature of the trouble at San Luis Rey suggests that the mission Indians knew they were to be freed from the mission and were anxious to get back to their old wild hunting grounds and do no more laboring in the fields. After the colonists had left the mission, on December 20, 1834, commissioner Pablo de la Portilla

16. Figueroa, *Manifiesto*, pp. 106, 107, 155; Berduzco Criminal, BC; Figueroa mentions that a diary that Lara was keeping, which he happened to come across, proves this. The diary has disappeared so that his allegation cannot be checked.

reported in great distress to Governor Figueroa that his Indians "absolutely refuse to work." They had fled in large numbers to the mountains, and he had been unable to get them to return. "We are free, we don't want to obey, we don't want to work," he reported them as saying. The season for planting was coming, he reminded the governor, and nothing could be done for lack of hands. The fields were covered with the bones of cattle the Indians had killed to get their skins. "Everything," he concluded, "predicts the ruin of the country." This draining away of mission manpower, which foretold the end of the productive mission farms, can hardly, however, be blamed on Híjar. In fact, as will be seen, Híjar was appalled at this development and laid the blame for it squarely on Figueroa's secularization policies. One may perhaps conclude that the news of mission Indian restiveness that was reaching Governor Figueroa while the colonists were in the south was due, in large part, to the approach of secularization and not to distrust of the motives of either Figueroa or Híjar.

If this is true for the mission Indians, it may be asked what caused the troubles that arose among the pagan Indians while the colonists were moving north. It will be recalled that Híjar had a message for them as well as for the mission Indians. In the case of the pagan Indians, however, they had to be invited to come hear the message, and this fact by itself might cause trouble, as it did in one instance involving Lieutenant Araujo. Araujo, apparently acting in concert with Híjar, called a meeting of pagan Indians of the Cahuilla tribe while he was at Mission San Gabriel. Four non-Christian captains and some two hundred warriors were on their way to San Gabriel on October 19, 1834, when another Indian captain named Maroma informed Colonel Gutiérrez that they had stolen some horses on their way past the San Bernardino ranch, which belonged to the mission. Araujo had apparently omitted to tell Gutiérrez that he had invited these Indians to meet him, for Gutiérrez immediately sent for Araujo and asked him about the matter. At 8:00 A.M. the following day, October 20, Araujo, Father Tomás Esténaga, the majordomo of San Gabriel, and a cowboy set out to meet the Cahuillas. At two o'clock that same day the majordomo returned breathless to report that he had escaped from the Indians, who were in a hostile mood. They had seized Father Esténaga, who had apparently separated from Araujo, and had stolen the horses he had with him. When the Indians came across Araujo, however, they recognized him, and he was able to get them to free the padre. About four o'clock that same afternoon, four Cahuillas came up to Colonel Gutiérrez mounted on the horses they had taken from Father Esténaga, which they claimed he had given them. Colonel Gutiérrez' answer to this was to take the horses from them and tell them that he would not listen to them until they sent Father Esténaga back. At seven that night Father Esténaga returned. The Indians had taken the two-wheeled cart in which he had been riding, a horse, a silver cup, his hat, a Holy Christ, and a breviary. Araujo returned shortly after the padre, followed by the captain of the band. At this point, Colonel Gutiérrez questioned the captain in front of Araujo. The captain told him that he and his companions had come because Araujo had invited them to do so, whereupon Colonel Gutiérrez told them they had come too soon and must go back to their own country until Señor Híjar returned (if he took over the governorship). Colonel Gutiérrez said that the captain could return the following day with the other captains, if they had anything to tell him. They were to bring with them the things they had taken from the padre and the horses they had removed from San Bernardino. Having got rid of the Indians and given himself some leeway, Colonel Gutiérrez at once sent for reinforcements from Los Angeles, which arrived at ten o'clock that night under Ensign José María Ramírez. The following morning there was no sign of the Indians, and Colonel Gutiérrez sent off Ensign Ramírez at the head of a body of twenty men to pursue them. They eventually caught up with the Indians, who attacked them and were defeated. "Pagan Indians," concluded the colonel, "need to be punished the first time they commit a crime, if not we shall be forever threatened." As for Lieutenant Araujo, Colonel Gutiérrez informed Governor Figueroa that he had told him to prepare to leave for Monterey, and he would depart without fail the next day.[17]

Governor Figueroa replied to Gutiérrez' letter saying that he approved of everything the colonel had done, and he was to take whatever further steps he thought necessary to preserve order. He cautioned Gutiérrez that to begin with he was to use "lenient and prudent" means to bring the Indians to order, and he was to see that they knew of the "falsities and deceits" by which they had been led to commit crimes against society. If they submitted, they were to be pardoned; if not, they were to be pursued and forced to obey and, if they did so, treated with consideration. In another letter to Gutiérrez of the same date, Governor Figueroa instructed him to bring together in a memorandum information on the crimes committed by the Indians, their motives, who had taken part, and their strength. The governor sent three more letters that same day warning the commissioners at Missions La Puríssima Concepción, San Antonio de Padua, and Nuestra Señora de la Soledad that Lieutenant Araujo had "caused disorder among the pagan Indians in the direction of San Bernardino by suggesting subversive ideas to them because of which they have committed great crimes against society." He explained that Araujo had been ordered to proceed to Monterey, and he might try to do the same thing again on his way. They were warned to be on their guard against him. About two weeks later the governor ordered Colonel Gutiérrez to call off the expedition against the Cahuillas until he could get more horses. In the meantime he was to make a peace pro-

17. Portilla to Figueroa, Dec. 20, 1834. BL, State Papers, Missions, *11;* Gutiérrez to Figueroa, Oct. 23, 1834, BL, Departmental State Papers; Figueroa, *Manifiesto,* 106.

posal to them and to offer them a pardon, provided they returned the stolen goods. If they did not, they were to be
threatened that they would be as severely treated as if they
were enemies. According to Governor Figueroa, the Cahuillas, presumably at a later date, made another robbing foray
against San Bernardino and killed some people there, in
addition to carrying off booty. A party of fifty men went after
them and defeated them in a fight which cost some Indian
lives.[18]

Was Governor Figueroa justified in blaming Lieutenant
Araujo for the trouble with the Cahuillas? It would appear
that Araujo was at fault in not letting Colonel Gutiérrez
know that he had invited the Indians to meet with him,
although he may have felt that Gutiérrez would not have
permitted him to do so. But there is no evidence that Araujo
himself caused the Indians to be disorderly or that he suggested subversive ideas to them. In fact, the Cahuillas, who
were in touch with the independent Colorado River tribes,
may have been encouraged by them to start an uprising; or
possibly they were resentful of past injuries at the hands of
the white man. Local circumstances at San Bernardino, however, may perhaps be fairly stated as follows: a band of Cahuillas, invited into the settled area near San Bernardino by
Araujo, was unable to resist taking some horses from the
ranch. Later, when they encountered the padre in his cart
and saw his shining silver cup, his hat, and his book, they
took these, too, and of course any other horses they came
across. These would hardly seem to be what the governor
called "great crimes against society." They are more like the
actions of naughty children than serious crimes, although of
course, as in the case of children, they might deserve punishment.

18. Figueroa to Gutiérrez, Oct. 31, Nov. 13, 1834, BL, Departmental
State Papers; Figueroa to Comisionados, Oct. 31, 1834, BL, Departmental
State Papers; Figueroa, *Manifiesto*, p. 106; Jack D. Forbes, *Warriors
of the Colorado,* pp. 276–77.

Híjar sent to Governor Figueroa a copy of a letter Araujo had written to the minister of relations on the San Bernardino affair. Although Araujo's letter has not come to light, Híjar regarded it as revealing the sufferings of the Cahuillas at the hands of the white Californians.[19] On the other hand, Governor Figueroa regarded the information he was getting about the relations of mission and pagan Indians with Híjar and his colonists in the most serious light. "All these efforts," he wrote in his *Manifiesto*, "inspired the government with the distrust of their authors that it was natural it should have, but it limited itself to dictating some precautionary measures to avoid disorder, without even taking any steps against those responsible, for it believed them capable of listening to the voice of reason and ceasing their activities." Governor Figueroa failed to mention in his *Manifiesto* that some of the colonists at San Gabriel had helped fight the Cahuillas and that he had himself thanked them for their services in the name of the government.[20] If his fears seem exaggerated, from the evidence available, it is possible that he was receiving other more disturbing reports, which he thought too dangerous even to mention. A passage in Híjar's letter of January 30, 1835, to the minister of relations suggests a much more serious threat to Figueroa, which might somehow have come to his attention. In this letter Híjar explained that when he traveled from San Diego to Monterey after disembarking from the *Natalia*, he was regarded as the next governor of California. But it was suspected that Figueroa had received an order from Mexico not to turn the governorship over to him. Because of this, Híjar revealed, "I was offered sufficient funds to take over the command by force [and] a large part of the insignificant garrison

19. Jack D. Forbes, "Indian Horticulture West and Northwest of the Colorado River," *Journal of the West*, 2 (Jan. 1963), 5; Forbes, *Warriors*, pp. 273–75; Híjar to Minister of Relations, Jan. 30, 1835, BL, Colonización y terrenos baldíos, Fomento, legajo 6, expediente 173.

20. Figueroa, *Manifiesto*, p. 107; Nicolás Gutiérrez to Figueroa, Oct. 20, 1834, BL, State Papers, 2, 193.

of this territory, which is very discontented because it has not been paid, likewise put itself at my orders." And later in the same letter Híjar added, "The interior of the country is traversed by parties of North American hunters. I was offered as many as seven hundred of these men, armed with rifles and provided with ammunition, so that I could seize the political government." If any inkling of these offers came to Governor Figueroa's ears, he would have had good reason for taking precautions. He might even have had some difficulty in understanding why Híjar turned them all down. Híjar explained it as follows: "But I, who had come seeking peace and avoiding war, did not want to use any violent measures, and this is why the Territory is at peace."[21]

When Híjar reached Monterey on Tuesday, October 14, Governor Figueroa received him, according to his own account, "with public demonstrations of friendship and respect" and lodged him in his own home. As it happened, the reports from the south about Indian troubles connected with the arrival of the colony do not appear to have reached Figueroa at this date, although within a week he was answering them. The other colonists who had come with Colonel Padrés on the *Morelos* had been in Monterey since September 24, lodged with families who were treating them hospitably. After the greetings were over, Figueroa showed Híjar President Santa Anna's order that he was not to become governor of California, and Figueroa was to remain in that position. According to his own account of what must have been a dramatic private meeting on the night of Wednesday, October 15, Figueroa told Híjar that he would have to enforce this order, although he regretted having to do so. He offered Híjar his services and promised to see whether the Territorial Deputation could persuade the authorities in Mexico to give Híjar back his position as governor. Meanwhile, Híjar could continue to hold his special commission

21. Híjar to Minister of Relations, Jan. 30, 1835, BL, Colonización y terrenos baldíos, Fomento, legajo 6, expediente 173.

as director of the colony. In a final gesture of goodwill, Figueroa says he told Híjar that if he could find any legal way by which he, Figueroa, could turn over the governorship to him without evading his responsibilities, he would gladly do so, for he was not ambitious to keep it.

Híjar gives no indication of what his feelings were on receiving this news, but perhaps it was not too much of a surprise, for he had heard rumors of the kind on his way to Monterey. According to Figueroa, Híjar was satisfied with his position of director of the colony and felt that the governor was amicably disposed toward him. On his part, Governor Figueroa was somewhat doubtful whether Híjar could keep his post as director of the colony since he was not governor of the territory, but he did not think there would be any danger in his doing so and agreed that he could, on condition that the government in Mexico be so informed.[22]

Up to this point relative harmony appears to have reigned at the meeting between Figueroa and Híjar, but it soon became evident that this would not last. Híjar, as director of colonization, asked Figueroa to hand over to him the property of the missions, which he considered went along with this position. Figueroa, who was probably genuinely surprised, replied that he did not know on what basis this assumption rested. Then Híjar showed him his written instructions in fifteen articles, the first of which authorized him to occupy all mission property.[23] "I replied," Figueroa states in his *Manifiesto*, "that for my part these arrangements would be attended to but that in my view it was an injustice to despoil the neophytes of the wealth of the missions, which they regarded as their property." With the prospect of direct disagreement now threatening, the two men broke up their meeting.

Early the following morning, Figueroa received a letter from Híjar, who was staying at Figueroa's home. It stated

22. Figueroa, *Manifiesto*, pp. 10, 11.
23. See pp. 209–13, 309–10 for a discussion of the instructions.

that in the orders and instructions he had received as director of colonization, the first article provided that he was to begin by occupying all the property belonging to the missions, and the military commandant was to give him the necessary assistance in doing so. The letter went on:

It being therefore of the greatest importance that my commission be begun both to avoid the losses that the missions are suffering, and to improve the lot of the natives, as well as establish the colonizing families who have come with me, I beg you to give orders to the commissioners whom you have appointed for secularization so that they may act in accordance with my plans, and so that the military commanders at every point in the Territory provide the assistance that I or my representatives may need for the above object.

In a letter written the same day, Figueroa agreed to do all that Híjar had asked, but he added at the end of his letter, "You will permit me to consult the Territorial Deputation prior to doing so in order to enlist their support and to expedite in a better fashion your duties in this commission."[24]

Híjar answered the following day in a way which showed he suspected that the governor's move in consulting the Deputation was more likely to slow down than expedite his plans. "I beg you," he wrote, after expressing satisfaction at Figueroa's willingness to carry out the government's orders,

that if possible this matter be decided today. The ruinous disorder which many of the missions I passed through were in, the approaching time for planting wheat, which the missionaries seem to have forgotten, assuredly because they are afraid of losing control of the tem-

24. Figueroa, *Manifiesto,* pp. 11–14; Híjar to Figueroa, Oct. 16, 1834, BL, Colonización y terrenos baldíos, Fomento, legajo 6, expediente 162. Also reproduced in Figueroa's *Manifiesto,* pp. 14–15. Figueroa to Híjar, Oct. 16, 1834, BL, Colonización y terrenos baldíos, Fomento, legajo 6, expediente 162. Also in *Manifiesto,* pp. 15–16.

poralities, the clamor of the natives, who up to now have been suffering infinitely, the colony which I cannot establish unless this matter is settled, and the shortness of time remaining to undertake the cultivation that must provide their subsistence for the whole year, everything, everything, my dear General, points to the fact that not a moment must be lost.

In a concluding paragraph, Híjar called upon Figueroa as military commander to give him the assistance his instructions called for, and then he rather tactlessly added, "I should be extremely sorry if you should be made responsible for the disorders and irreparable losses that delay may cause."[25]

When Figueroa wrote his *Manifiesto*, he said that at this point he became suspicious of Híjar's determination to get hold of the property of the missions. At the time, however, he seems to have been spurred to energetic action to a considerable extent by popular interest in the reasons why Híjar had not received the governorship and by public curiosity as to what was to happen to the colony. On October 17, the same day that Híjar wrote him the letter asking him to make a decision about granting him the mission property, Figueroa wrote two letters to the Deputation, which he had called into special session to meet that same day. In the first he referred to the government's accepting his resignation as governor and the appointment of Híjar to the post, followed by the unexpected removal of Híjar by message sent overland at great speed. The order removing Híjar from the governorship had not mentioned Híjar's other position as director of colonization, and Figueroa wanted to have the advice of the Deputation on whether Híjar might act as director of colonization although he was not governor. Figueroa, basing his argument on article three of the law of April 6, 1830, which had given

25. Alexander Forbes (*California*, p. 254) says that the sowing time for corn and other grains began in November. Híjar to Figueroa, Oct. 17, 1834, BL, Colonización y terrenos baldíos, Fomento, legajo 6, expediente 162.

the government the power to appoint commissioners to look after colonization, felt that Híjar should carry out his colonization duties, but he nonetheless wanted the opinion of the Deputation on the matter. Next he asked the Deputation whether Híjar as director of colonization should be given the property of the missions, in accordance with article one of his instructions from the government. Linking mission property with secularization of the missions, Figueroa could not understand how Híjar's position should give him the power to have control over secularization. With the clear indication that Figueroa did not approve of Híjar's being given mission property, the Deputation was asked to advise him what would be the "most just" thing to do.

In his second letter Figueroa, in high-flown, opaque language, offered to resign the civil governorship if public opinion, which he admitted was strongly in favor of separating the military command in California from the civil, backed such a move, in order to preserve California from the disturbances that were plaguing Mexico.[26] What these disturbances were Figueroa explained to the Deputation when he addressed its opening session later that same day. It was known unofficially, he said, that when President Santa Anna took over the government from Vice-President Gómez Farías after having recovered from his illness, there had been a quarrel between the legislature and the executive. There had been trouble in the states of Puebla, Querétaro, San Luis, and Jalisco. Some skirmishing had broken out in Puebla and Jalisco, but it had now ceased. Thus far there was no doubt about this news, although it was all unofficial. Some people believed, went on Figueroa, that there was a move to centralize the republic, although there was no assurance of this; nor was it known that President Santa Anna had openly attacked the federal system.

The connection between the civil disturbances in Mexico and the situation in California, according to Figueroa's

26. Figueroa, *Manifiesto*, pp. 17, 18–22.

Manifiesto which was prepared later, was that the partisans of Híjar were causing trouble by suggesting that the civil governorship and the military command should be divided. This, according to Figueroa, was but a ruse to cover up their idea of making California independent of Mexico. To bring this about, the Indians were being wooed, men's material interests were being engaged, and the rumor was spread that President Santa Anna had done away with the federal system and forcibly destroyed the Congress. All this was being said, continued Figueroa, to try to intimidate him with threats of revolution under various pretexts.

After Figueroa's two letters and the original documents which accompanied them had been read to the Deputation, they were passed on to its Committee on Government and Policy, which was composed of José Antonio Carrillo, Pío Pico, and José J. Ortega. Figueroa then presented Híjar's note of that morning, asking that if possible a decision on his getting the mission property should be made that very day. The governor requested that priority should be given to this matter "because circumstances demanded it."[27] To this the Deputation agreed.

The Deputation met again on the following day, Saturday, October 18, and approved a motion made by Pío Pico to ask Híjar, through Governor Figueroa, that "if it was not inconvenient for him," he might show the Deputation the instructions he had received from the government. Figueroa duly notified Híjar by a letter written on Sunday, October 19 (although Híjar was still staying at his house), and Híjar that same day gave Figueroa his instructions, politely requesting that the originals be returned to him.[28]

The Deputation's committee did not present its report

27. Diputación, Oct. 17, 1834, BL, Legislative Records, p. 193; Figueroa, *Manifiesto*, pp. 22–23.

28. Diputación, Oct. 18, 1834, BL, Legislative Records, p. 198; Híjar to Figueroa, Oct. 19, 1834, BL, Colonización y terrenos baldíos, Fomento, legajo 6, expediente 162.

until Tuesday, October 21. It was a long, able document, consisting of an explanatory preamble followed by eight proposals. The preamble began by seeking to explain how public opinion in California had been misled by Figueroa's action in not permitting Híjar to take over as governor. The committee first of all referred briefly to the political change in Mexico, which it felt had been accurately presented to the public. Next it stated that when the government in Mexico had decided to separate political control in California from the military command, it had given Híjar the political position (it did not mention that Padrés had been made military commander should Figueroa still wish to resign). Then, the committee continued, the government, without stating its reasons, had sent an order saying Híjar was not to take over as governor and that General Figueroa was to continue in the position. This of course meant that the long-desired separation in California of civilian and military power was once more delayed. While the committee admitted that a matter such as this could indeed legitimately alarm Californians, they stated that the public was mistaken in believing that President Santa Anna was thinking of changing the system of government in Mexico and that he had sent the order preventing Híjar from becoming governor as part of his new scheme. In other words, the committee was at pains to deny what it appears the supporters of Híjar were saying, namely that Santa Anna was planning to do away with federalism and that because of this he wanted to preserve military control in California. They suggested that Figueroa enlighten the public by presenting the true facts in the case. The committee itself went on record as being in favor of the separation of civilian from military rule by including such a petition in their seventh proposal following the preamble.

The committee then took up the question of who should be governor and quickly decided that the government's order to Figueroa left no room for doubt on the matter. They noted that Governor Figueroa had spontaneously offered to resign from his civilian position if the peace of the territory demanded it. They were satisfied, however, that he should continue to be governor. As for Híjar, the committee felt that he should be permitted to act as director of colonization, and Governor Figueroa should provide him with the necessary resources for his work from mission revenue but "without prejudice to the natives and to the other obligations connected with the said foundations." Among these other obligations, it should be pointed out, were the vital ones of helping to pay for the troops and the expenses of the California government.

The committee emphasized that mission property was not to be used to pay the expenses of the colony, so if Governor Figueroa was to help out the colony with mission funds, he would have to repay these funds later. But where, then, was the money to come from? According to the committee's interpretation of the law of November 26, 1833, the government was authorized to use the Pious Fund of the Californias for colonization expenses.[29] On the other hand, it will be seen that this law, which had been presented as a bill by Bandini, was so vaguely drawn up that it could be interpreted in several other ways. Perhaps because of this, the committee had recourse to the law of April 6, 1830, which stated in its article seven that Mexican families voluntarily wishing to be colonists were to be assisted by the government on their journey and "maintained for a year," as well as given lands and farming tools. This law, however, had provided in earlier articles for customs duties on cotton cloth to provide a fund for such expenditures. The committee did not stop to inquire whether any such fund actually existed.

The mission Indians, whom the committee referred to as "our unfortunate compatriots" and "this unhappy class of our brethren," had, they said, labored like slaves for a century on the missions, and all mission property was theirs

29. Figueroa, *Manifiesto*, p. 27. For the text of the law of Nov. 26, 1833, see pp. 189–90.

alone.[30] The president must have been deceived by un-scrupulous courtiers into thinking that he was acting for the good of the Indians by agreeing to such measures as Híjar's instructions, which would bring about their ruin and "surround them with misery." The committee felt that it was the duty of Governor Figueroa, who was charged with look-ing after the Indians and promoting their happiness, to de-fend their rights. Men had come together in societies, the committee went on, to protect their lives and property, and they could not be deprived of even the least part of these without breaking the pact and the common law of nations. Based on these principles the committee felt that those parts of Híjar's instructions which called for taking over mission property, distributing it, and selling it, should be suspended, and that the government should be asked to revoke them. The government should also be asked to provide for the dis-tribution of mission property to the mission Indians and "for objects beneficial to them," since they alone owned it. And while the colonists might be assisted by using some mission funds, it was to be on condition that the Pious Fund or the federal treasury repay the owners.

Returning to Híjar's role, the committee pointed out that the duties of a director of colonization were not outlined in any law, and in their view the government had sent its in-structions to Híjar as governor of California, not as director of colonization. Nonetheless, they agreed that he might per-form the latter office, provided he did so as a subordinate of Governor Figueroa, who would decide where the colony was to settle. On the other hand, the committee stated that the government's promises to the colonists would be kept and they would be treated as brothers. "Californians," they said, "are hospitable people and will gladly share their fortune with all who approach their homes." The committee con-cluded its preamble by recommending that its report and the final resolution of the Deputation on the matter should be

30. By "a century" they no doubt simply meant a long time.

published, in order to avoid possible unfortunate results due to public misconceptions.

The committee thereupon presented its eight propositions to the Deputation. First, Híjar was not to be made governor. Second, Híjar, "if he wishes," was to undertake the special commission of director of colonization under the orders of the government of the territory. Third, Híjar was not to have anything to do with secularizing the missions, nor was he to be given mission property. Fourth, while the government decided what it was going to do, the provisional regulations for secularization agreed on by the Deputation were to be continued, and the Indians were to be put in possession of their property and lands. Fifth, when the colonists reached the place where they were to settle, the governor was to provide them with implements and other assistance, according to the government's instructions, using mission property in such a way that the missions bore the burden equally. Each colonist, on an individual basis, was to be given seed, meat, and what was essential for his upkeep. The director of colonization was to be subject to the governor and was to hand him a detailed list of the number of colonists and an estimate of how much was to be paid them each month. The Indians owned mission lands and no colony was to settle on them. Sixth, the governor was to keep the originals of Híjar's instructions and give him copies of them if he needed them. Seventh, the government was to be notified of this report and what was agreed to, so that it might give its assent. It was to be asked to revoke those parts of Híjar's instructions which dispossessed the Indians of their property. And a respectful petition was to be sent to the government asking it for the separation of civil and military government and presenting the names of three persons considered competent to hold office. Finally, the committee's report and the decision of the Deputation should be published and circulated as soon as possible.

According to Figueroa, while the committee was preparing

its report, a great deal of unsuccessful behind-the-scenes intrigue was going on to try to influence it. Meanwhile the public became avidly interested in the matter, and when the Deputation made its public announcement on October 22 accepting its committee's report, there was considerable excitement. This was the time, remarks Figueroa, when men revealed how greedily they coveted mission property. It was then, he says, that the plans for the Cosmopolitan Company were announced, revealing that it was to have a monopoly on both the domestic and foreign trade of California. There was to be an agency of the company at each mission or town, and its ships were to bring in both Mexican and foreign goods as well as take out California's products. Writing his comments in his *Manifiesto* at a later date, when he had become convinced of the nefarious activities of the colony's leaders, Figueroa asserted that the real objective of the expedition was to set up the Cosmopolitan Company. This, he said sarcastically, was what Señor Padrés (stripping the colonel of his military rank) was working for while he praised his own efforts ad nauseam as being "inspired by the most eminent patriotism." Nonetheless, continued Figueroa, the public realized an attack was being planned on mission properties, and it could see the bankruptcy which "threatened the only capital which provides public wealth and the ruinous monopoly which is aimed at." And so, concluded the governor, the pretensions of Híjar and Padrés conflicted openly with public opinion, "and this is the origin of the ill feeling that was later shown towards them."[31]

It is interesting that Figueroa makes no mention of the mission Indians in this outburst. It appears he is saying that public opinion was exercised because people were afraid that Híjar and Padrés were threatening mission property, which was the only capital providing for public funds. If this is so, then perhaps the ill feeling against the colony and

31. Figueroa, *Manifiesto*, pp. 23, 28, 29–31, 33–35.

its leaders was caused not so much by their seeking to dispossess the mission Indians of the property of the missions—which Figueroa and the Deputation were at such pains to persuade Híjar and Padrés that they alone owned—as by fear on the part of the white Californians and the foreign merchants that their own livelihood was at stake.[32]

How widespread in California this feeling of opposition to the colony and the Cosmopolitan Company was it is difficult to say. It is likely, however, that public opinion in Monterey would be strongly opposed to any enterprise in which Bandini played a part because of his continuous attempts to push his own southern section of the territory at the expense of the Monterey area. Bandini was also a prominent member of the Cosmopolitan Company and an opponent of Governor Figueroa. It is unlikely also that the foreign merchants and the captains of American and English ships, which provided most of the coastwise trade as well as the bulk of the import and export trade of the territory, would view with equanimity an approaching monopoly of this commerce by the Cosmopolitan Company. The Yankee traders were even opposed to secularization of the missions because of its unsettling effect on business. The impression in Monterey, according to Figueroa, was that the Cosmopolitan Company's capital was to be made up entirely of mission property, although, as has been seen, this was not in fact true.

In the course of his critical remarks on the discussions aroused by the publication of the Deputation's report, Figueroa notes with disapproval that much ado was made of

32. Some of the white Californians alleged that twenty-one Mexican administrators for the former missions came along with the colony, and admitted that they opposed it for this reason, since they wanted these positions themselves. There is no evidence, however, that any such body of Mexican administrators came with the colony or by themselves (Bancroft, *California, 3*, 274). It is possible that the Californians thought that the school teachers who went to the missions were actually administrators.

the fact that the government—or rather, he adds, Gómez Farías—had mortgaged one of the rural estates of the Pious Fund as a security for the sale of the *Natalia*.[33] Yet the Deputation's report itself mentions the law of November 26, 1833, which specifically stated that the estates of the Pious Funds could be used by the government to provide for transportation of the colony to California. Figueroa also mentions that the *Natalia* was to be actually paid for with tallow from the missions, although he implies that the tallow was simply to be taken from the missions, whereas Bandini states in his "Historia" that the owner was paid, but not in tallow.[34]

Acting in strict accordance with the Deputation's request that its report be published and circulated without delay, Governor Figueroa sent out a letter on October 22, the same day that the report was issued, to the Alcalde of Los Angeles and probably to other bodies, stating that political control was not to be turned over to Híjar and mission property was not to be given to him.[35] He also sent a note to Híjar the same day containing a copy of the government's order to him not to turn the governorship over to Híjar, a speech of his own to the Deputation on the difficulties that might be caused by putting the government's order into effect because of the desire in the country to separate political and military government, and the eight propositions of the Deputation.[36]

According to Figueroa, Híjar was highly offended by the Deputation's propositions, and the following day, October 23, he sent a long statement to Figueroa which the latter characterized as being "full of gratuitous imputations." Along with this statement Híjar sent some further scornful remarks that appear to have enraged Figueroa. On Friday, October 24,

33. Morison, *Maritime History*, p. 267; Figueroa, *Manifiesto*, p. 34.

34. Bandini, "Historia," p. 165.

35.Figueroa to Alcalde de Los Angeles, Oct. 22, 1834, BL, Departmental State Papers.

36. This statement does not appear to be available. Híjar to Figueroa, Oct. 23, 1834, FP. Also in Figueroa, *Manifiesto*, p. 35.

Híjar moved out of Figueroa's house to that of José Joaquín Gómez. Apparently making an effort to swallow his pride Figueroa went to call on Híjar at his new lodgings and asked for a conference with him to discuss the matter. Figueroa offered to show Híjar the orders and regulations upon which the Deputation based its report and said if Híjar could show that they had been annulled, the resolution would be changed. Híjar agreed to this, and on Saturday and Sunday, October 25 and 26, Híjar and Padrés met with Figueroa and José Antonio Carrillo, Pío Pico, José Castro, District Judge Luis del Castillo Negrete, and Licenciado Rafael Gómez. The conference opened with Híjar's reading the statement he had written on October 23. He later sent copies to numerous persons whom he wanted to convince of the rightness of his case, including Father Narciso Durán and Gómez Farías. According to Figueroa, Colonel Padrés later read this letter, with long comments of his own, to the colonists at San Francisco Solano every day to arouse their anger.

Híjar's angry reply to the Territorial Deputation's eight points (he apparently did not see their preamble until he had almost completed his reply) and Governor Figueroa's equally indignant refutation take up more than fifty pages of print in Figueroa's *Manifiesto,* Híjar's replies being interspersed with Figueroa's rebuttals in the manner of the Mexican pamphleteers of the day. On the Deputation's first point, that he was not to be made governor, Híjar limited himself to saying that he was surprised the government had not said anything to him on the matter, so that he might know whether the order was permanent or not. In his comments on the Deputation's second proposition, that he could act as director of colonization, Híjar commented on the proviso that the director would have to keep to the Deputation's regulations on the matter. The Deputation, Híjar said, had no legal right to make any such regulations, which could be drawn up only by the federal government. He would obey only the federal regulations and, indeed, if the regulations could be changed in this way, colonists would not be willing to come to California. In an important statement, which Governor Figueroa apparently did not at once understand, Híjar said, "Take into consideration that I am a Director of Colonization and not merely of the colony that has arrived. Consequently natives of the country, and foreigners who wish to do so, have a right to colonize. But if the regulations change they will all withdraw for lack of security and the damage done will be to the Territory which so badly needs useful hands."[37] Híjar was particularly indignant at the Deputation's third proposition not permitting him to occupy mission property. According to him, the Deputation was here openly disobeying the federal law of November 26, 1833, which he interpreted as giving him the right to use mission property in the way the federal government thought fit.[38] As far as the Deputation's prohibition that he intervene in the process of secularization, Híjar said that he had never attempted to do so, and he did not know what the purpose of this was. Híjar apparently meant that he had not taken any part in the process of converting the missions into towns and providing for parish priests to replace missionary friars.

The Deputation's fourth proposal; that the Provisional Regulations for secularization drawn up by the Deputation were to be put into effect while the federal government was continuing to consider the matter, drew bitter criticism from Híjar, which must have been most painful to Figueroa, both because he was sensitive to criticism and because he knew

37. Figueroa, *Manifiesto*, pp. 35–37, 39, 88, 92, 114, 155.

38. Híjar's interpretation of this poorly drawn law, which, it should be remembered, was signed by Santa Anna and not by Farías, is presumably the interpretation that Bandini and the government authorities put on it when it was sent to the Congress. The first sentence of the law reads: "The government is authorized to use *every means* [italics the writer's] to assure the colonization, and make effective the secularization of the missions." In other words it gives the government complete power to do what it wants in the matter.

very well on what shaky ground the Deputation was in making the regulations. "I cannot conceive," said Híjar, "how so respectable a corporation can persist in such a way not only in disobeying the orders of the general government but in thwarting them." He leveled his objections to the regulations first at their provisions for disposing of mission property. Neither the Deputation nor Governor Figueroa, he pointed out, had any right to make grants of mission lands or property, since they did not own them. Supposing their regulation was overruled by the government, he went on, there would be serious trouble if the recipients of mission properties were forced to give them back. Secondly, he was critical of the way in which political institutions were to be set up in the new Indian towns, whose inhabitants could not be expected to know how to run them. He also pointed out that the regulations continued to put the mission Indians in a position of servitude. He unfortunately did not give the evidence for this last statement, which Figueroa later questioned him about in his rebuttal. Evidently what he had in mind, however, was the provision in article sixteen that Indians could be forced to work on the land and the stipulation in article seventeen that they were to continue to provide free personal service for the missionaries. That Figueroa did know what Híjar meant may be inferred from the fact that he abrogated the less vital article seventeen on November 4, 1834, not long after his discussions with Híjar.

Híjar's comments on the Deputation's fifth proposition were limited to those parts of it which stated that the director of colonization was to obey the instructions of the governor and that no colony was to settle on mission lands, since the mission Indians owned them. For his part, said Híjar, he was going to obey the instructions issued to him by the federal government, and he remarked with cutting sarcasm that he obeyed laws, not personal whims or arbitrary actions. On the matter of Indian ownership of mission lands, Híjar wanted to know, if this was so, why the Deputation's regulation had not given them more land than it did. "It would seem," he said, "that an attempt is being made to delude the unfortunate natives by taking advantage of their simplicity."[39] He concluded his brief remarks on this matter by saying he did not think this was the place, or he was the person, who should investigate by what right the Indians were being taught that they owned mission lands, to the exclusion of the government's right of eminent domain over them. He unfortunately failed to bolster his case by reminding Figueroa that articles eighteen and nineteen of the Deputation's regulation provided that under certain circumstances mission lands would return to the nation, which, it must therefore be presumed, had original title to them.[40]

In the Deputation's sixth proposition, Governor Figueroa was authorized to keep the original copies of Híjar's instructions. Híjar said that he was amazed at this and could not see any reason for it. The government had not taken his position of director of colonization away from him, and he would like to have his instructions returned. Figueroa must have agreed with him on this point, for they were returned. Híjar's comments on the seventh proposition were limited to the Deputation's provision that the government should be asked to revoke those parts of his instructions which dispossessed the mission Indians of their property.

> I believe it is my duty to point out that this idea could only originate in some error or through the different conception we have formed of mission property. The Government, far from taking away from the natives, orders me to make them proprietors and give them possessions that they have not had up to now. They were to benefit from real genuine property the moment that I was in a position to discharge my duties. But Your Excellency and the Very Excellent Deputation have not

39. Figueroa, *Manifiesto*, pp. 59, 66–67, 72–73.
40. See p. 259.

judged this to be convenient. Consequently the responsibility will not be mine.

The Deputation's eighth and final proposal was that its decision should be published. Híjar did not object to this, but he regretted that some of the facts had been distorted in such a way that it would result in discredit to the federal government. He added that some day the whole story would come out, and men could judge for themselves. Winding up his comments, Híjar said he would like to know how it came about that the Deputation had linked together the decision by the federal government not to turn the governorship over to him with his special commission on colonization. He could have corrected any errors in this matter, if they had told him how this came about. There must have been some mistake made, he felt, for otherwise he could not understand how measures so "anarchical, obstreperous, and of such far reaching importance to the social order" could have been passed.

Híjar then remarked that in view of what he had said, he hoped Figueroa would change his mind on the affair and would let him have his final decision. As he was writing his concluding remarks, Híjar saw the published version of the Deputation's report, together with its preamble. His final paragraphs had become more moderate in tone, for he had said what he wanted to say, but his anger boiled over again when he read the preamble. According to it, he said, the government's instructions were sent to him in his capacity as governor and not in his capacity as director of colonization. Since his position as governor had been removed, the Deputation had considered that his instructions did not now apply. To refute this, Híjar referred to the letter which he had received at the time that Vice-President Farías had sent him his instructions. He had shown Governor Figueroa this letter, and Figueroa had returned it to him. The letter said that enclosed with it were "the instructions with which you must conform in carrying out your commission relative to the colo-

nization of California." "Ask school children," Híjar angrily
demanded, "whether these instructions were addressed to
someone other than the Director of Colonization." Then he
pointed out that his colonization commission also extended
to Lower California, where he was given no political power.
"It seems then," he concluded, "beyond any doubt that the
special commission was given to me as Director and not as
governor."[41]

In his long refutation of Híjar's point of view, Figueroa
marshaled every constitutional and legal argument that he
could find to defeat his opponent. So ably did he defend himself that his contemporaries and later historians have almost
all been convinced that he was right. Nonetheless he is not
always convincing, and at times he is clearly in the wrong.
He begins by pointing out that the government's order to
him preventing Híjar from becoming governor is clear. Then
he refers to the federal decree on colonization in the states,
passed on February 4, 1834, which in article nine provided
that colonies were to be sent out under the person or persons
appointed by the government, and in article ten stated that
colonies would remain under the chief or political chiefs that
the government designated. Figueroa interpreted this law to
mean that since Híjar had ceased to be the federal government's appointed political chief (governor), then the colony
would necessarily be subject to himself as governor. But in
actual fact this law was designed for state governments, and
as it turned out, there was a printer's error in article ten of
the law when it first appeared. According to the corrected version, which was issued on April 11, 1834, article ten stated
that colonies were to remain under the chief or political chiefs
that the government of the state designated.[42] Clearly this
law had no reference to the territory of California.

Figueroa's reply to Híjar's challenge as to where the Terri-

41. Figueroa, *Manifiesto*, pp. 81, 84–85, 87–89.
42. Maza, *Código*, p. 266; Figueroa, *Manifiesto*, p. 37.

torial Deputation got the right to pass colonization laws was to say that neither he nor the Deputation was thinking of making general regulations, but simply regulations for colonization in California. In support of his view that he and the Deputation had ample power to do this, he cited the Spanish Constitution of 1812 which, he said, "is the one in effect in this territory." That Figueroa meant what he said in this instance is shown by the fact that he cited the Spanish Constitution of 1812 on two other occasions in support of his views. Actually, of course, the Mexican Constitution of 1824 was in effect in California, and it is interesting to note that when it was convenient for him to do so, Figueroa did not hesitate to cite it, too. It should be added that neither the Spanish Constitution of 1812 nor the law of June 23, 1813, gave the Territorial Deputation or the political chief (governor) specific authority to make local colonization regulations. That Figueroa did not think the Deputation's case was tenable in this instance is revealed by his amendment of the Deputation's second proposition after the conferences with Híjar. According to the original second proposition, Híjar was to be director of colonization under the orders of the territorial government. Figueroa added the words, "and the laws and regulations made on the subject," so that the Deputation would not appear to be ignoring previous federal colonization regulations. This amendment was approved by the Deputation.

Figueroa next touched upon the position of director of colonization, which he and the Deputation were going to permit Híjar to hold in California. He admitted that he did not know what the functions of the job were; in fact he did not think it really was a genuine position. He correctly traced it, however, to the mission colonization bill of April 16, 1833. There is no question that the position existed in its own right, even if Figueroa was correct in thinking that it was not outlined in a law.[43] The Farías government appointed a direc-

43. Figueroa, *Manifiesto*, pp. 37, 39–41, 53, 61, 69, 97–98.

tor of colonization for Texas in 1833, and Figueroa himself later sent a Mexico City newspaper containing an article in praise of directors of colonization to Mariano Vallejo to amuse him. Furthermore, Figueroa appointed Vallejo director of colonization on the northern frontier after the colony had gone. In support of his own right to control the colony that Híjar had brought out, however, Figueroa continued to lean on the law of February 4, 1834, which he frequently cited, although it is evident that it could give him no support.

Governor Figueroa's rebuttal to Híjar's comments on the Deputation's third proposal, preventing him from intervening in the process of secularization and from occupying mission property, is more solidly based than his previous comments. It reveals what would appear to be genuine differences of opinion between the two men, caused by different interpretations of a vaguely worded law and lack of precision in discussing the word "secularization." Híjar felt that he had not taken any part in the process of secularization, but Figueroa pointed out that assuming control of mission property was, in fact, part of that process.[44] In Figueroa's view, the law of November 26, 1833, which Híjar cited as giving him the necessary authority to take control of mission lands, did not give any such authority. The governor's interpretation of this law, which he said was held by others who had thought about it, was that it simply gave the government the right to make the secularization of the missions effective. He did not see how it could possibly permit the taking over of mission property. The only specific authority it granted, he pointed out, was to use the estates of the California Pious Fund to provide resources for the commission and families in Mexico City who were preparing to go to California.[45] And the California Pious Fund estates were not mission property.

44. Figueroa to Vallejo, June 24, 1835, BL, Cowan; Hittell, *History*, 2, 201; Figueroa, *Manifiesto*, pp. 43–44.

45. Figueroa, *Manifiesto*, pp. 45–46.

As far as he went, Governor Figueroa would seem to be making a valid point here. Yet he failed to mention the most important section of the law from Híjar's point of view: its granting of all powers to the government to "assure the colonization" of the missions as well as to make their secularization effective. As Figueroa pointed out, the law of August 17, 1833, provided the rule by which secularization was to be put into effect. But as has been seen, the important complementary bill, which would have provided for the division of former mission property, failed to become law. The haste in passing Bandini's makeshift legislation of November 26, 1833, can be blamed for much of the trouble that arose over the settling of the colony. Híjar interpreted this law to mean that the government had provided him with full power to assure the colonization of all available public land in California, including mission lands, and this naturally included taking mission property. That the government of Vice-President Farías interpreted the law to mean this is evident from the written instructions it gave Híjar, which started by ordering him to occupy all mission property.

Governor Figueroa next examined Híjar's instructions to see what he was supposed to do with the mission property he was authorized to occupy. Figueroa did not comment on the dividing up of mission land among the colonists, but he did question what was to become of some of the movable property or cattle. According to Híjar's instructions, mission movable property or cattle was to be distributed to the colonists, each family receiving a specific amount of stock and farm equipment.[46] It was assumed that there would be a good number of cattle left over after each family had received its share. Up to half of the remaining herds were to be sold for the best price they would fetch, while the other half were to be kept as government property. The revenue from these government-owned herds was to be used for the ex-

46. For the text of Híjar's instructions see above pp. 210–12.

penses of religious worship, stipends for the missionaries, salaries for the teachers, school supplies, and the purchase of farm equipment for the colonists. In his comments on these provisions, Governor Figueroa first wanted to know what was to be done with the money obtained from the sale of the first half remaining after the colonists had received their share. "Only Señor Híjar knows," he remarked, "for the instructions do not say."[47] It is indeed true that Híjar's instructions did not say what was to be done with this money, but it is also true that there was to be no secrecy about it, for the instructions stated that the political chief and director of colonization was to report to the government how he invested it; annual reports were to be made thereafter.

Figueroa also questioned by what right the government could use revenue from the other half of the undistributed cattle. He pointed out that the admittedly worthy objectives for which these funds were to be used had in most cases already been taken care of by the secularization law of August 17, 1833, which levied upon the Pious Fund of the Californias. He could also find no law, he said, which would permit the government to invest California mission property in colonization. Figueroa's first objection may be readily met by considering the heavy expense involved in paying the numerous teachers who had come out with the colony, bearing in mind that the Pious Fund was probably at a low ebb. As for his inability to find a law that would permit a transfer of this kind, it is true that past colonization laws, which he cited, did not do so, but the wide powers attributed to the law of November 26, 1833, would have taken care of the matter.

Figueroa's reply to Híjar's attack against him and the Deputation for their insistence on putting their own secularization regulations into effect was that the Deputation was well within its rights in doing so. In support of this conten-

47. Figueroa, *Manifiesto,* p. 57.

tion he listed a long string of laws, all of them dating back to Spanish colonial days, including the Spanish Constitution of 1812.[48] Perhaps the most interesting aspect of his reply, however, is the paternalism he showed toward the Indians. "The mission Indians," said Figueroa, "have not yet come out of the abject state in which nature placed them, and being children in the pursuit of civilization, not making use of their reason nor knowing their true interests, the government must play the part of common father to them and provide them with every kind of protection." The Deputation, he later stated in a revealing passage, "has only taken care to maintain the natives in the precise and indispensable amount of dependence, which will preserve good order and subordination among them, in order to avoid the excesses and weaknesses to which they are inclined, because of their stupid ignorance: it has also been careful not to attack their liberty or violate the social guarantees." In Figueroa's view, the mission Indians were clearly not the equals of the white man, although they were now citizens along with the other residents of the republic. Figueroa cannot be said to be anti-Indian (it will be recalled that he was of Indian blood himself), but like Rodríguez Puebla (also of Indian blood) and other prominent men, he thought they should continue to receive the special protection that the Laws of the Indies had provided. On the other hand, he felt they should have the same rights to own property as other men and should be given preference in assistance to obtain it. Figueroa's insistence on a policy of paternalism for the mission Indians does not appear to conceal a desire to keep them in their current underprivileged status, for when pressed by Híjar about setting up town governments that the Indians could not manage, Figueroa countered that some would be able to rise to the challenge.

48. Ibid., pp. 58–59, 61–62. Figueroa cites the following laws: of June 23, 1813, *Recopilación de Indias*, law 9, title 3, book 6; law 14, title 4, book 6; laws 5, 7, and 9, title 12, book 6; of Mar. 13, 1811, Nov. 9, 1812, Jan. 4, 1813, Sept. 13, 1813.

The effort should be made, he said, "not only to convert them from pupils into proprietors but to educate them and make them industrious, and if this is not undertaken, they will never leave the wretched class of slaves." He maintained, however, that the Indians should not be left to themselves but should be protected and put under special regulations and laws, as they were in Spanish colonial days.[49]

This protective attitude toward the Indians had been attacked by men like José María Luis Mora as indicating a belief that the Indians were actually inferior to the whites,[50] and the whole matter had been discussed in the debates on the mission colonization bill of April 16, 1833. This Farías-supported measure, however, had in fact given the mission Indians preference in obtaining land and protection against others in holding onto it. The difference, then, between the new egalitarian attitude toward the Indians held by Farías (and probably Híjar) and that held by men like Figueroa was not so complete as might be assumed from their attacks on each other. Figueroa accused the Farías government, for example, of trying to deprive the mission Indians "of even the property they have acquired by their personal labor." And although Híjar insisted that the government wanted him to make the Indians landowners, Figueroa did not hesitate to assert that Híjar had told him at a meeting that the Indians were not worthy of possessing property and should not be given any. Figueroa did concede that under Híjar the Indians were to be given the chance to be colonists like other persons and given land in the same way, but he rejected this idea because they were already landowners, and for other reasons that he claimed would take too long to explain.

It is at this point in his *Manifiesto* that Governor Figueroa begins the personal attacks on Híjar and Colonel Padrés that later become its dominant theme. Commenting on Híjar's statement that the Deputation's secularization rules would

49. Figueroa, *Manifiesto*, pp. 63, 67, 70–71.
50. See above p. 170.

ruin the territory, Figueroa sarcastically asks whether this might be because Híjar would not be able to enjoy the wealth of the neophytes. He then accuses Híjar and Padrés of agitating in Mexico for the passage of the law of August 17, 1833, secularizing the missions, "which was to make them rich." After scoffing at Híjar's attitude toward the Indians, he says, "It must be repeated that the fate of the natives is of little or no concern to him and that the sole motive for his ill-digested discourse is that he sees the abundant wealth over which he claimed exclusive control as a speculator, ostensibly for colonization, escaping from his hands." These passages reflect the bitterness that was to come over Figueroa after the discovery of the alleged revolt at Los Angeles in March 1835.

Many of the comments by Figueroa on Híjar's criticisms of the Deputation's fifth proposition are merely elaborations of points that he had previously made in the debate with Híjar and need no further discussion. Two comments of Figueroa's, however, require some notice. One of these is his justification for the Deputation's statement that no colony was to settle on mission lands. He found support for this view in the colonization law of August 18, 1824, which eliminated from colonization lands belonging to individuals or corporations or towns, and in article seventeen of the regulation for the colonization of the territories of November 21, 1828. This regulation stated that in those territories containing missions, mission lands could not be colonized at that time or "until it is determined whether they are to be considered as the property of the mission neophytes and Mexican settlers." The Farías colonization bill of April 16, 1833, had provided that the missions were to be colonized; but since this bill had not become law, Híjar's legal basis for attempting to colonize mission lands would have to rest upon the all-inclusive but vague power granted by the law of November 26, 1833, which Figueroa rejected. Figueroa also discusses the government's right of eminent domain over mission lands, which Híjar had brought forward. He says he does not know what "eminent domain" can be and refers to his previous demonstration that the Mexican Constitution of 1824, in item three of article 112, listing restrictions on the power of the president, provides that the president may not occupy the property of a person or corporation.[51] The article continues that if it is necessary for the government to take such property for reasons of the general welfare, it must first obtain the consent of the Senate, or if it is in recess, of the Council of Government, and the former owner must be indemnified. Figueroa's able argument in this instance, however, is seriously weakened by the fact that in the secularization provisions of the Deputation, worked out with him, the nation is implied as the original owner of mission lands.[52]

Figueroa's further comments on the matter of returning Híjar's instructions need no discussion, but his exclamation of amazement that Híjar should claim that he was going to give land to the Indians is of interest. "Is it not true," he asks, "that the instructions do not say a single word in favor of the neophytes?" Is it not true, he continues, that article one of the instructions, ordering Híjar to occupy all mission property, authorizes seizure of property that the neophytes have acquired by their own labor, whose possession they are peacefully enjoying? Will Señor Híjar deny, he goes on, that on the different occasions on which he discussed this matter with him, Híjar maintained that to make the neophytes happy it was enough to give them their freedom, and in future to pay the daily wages of those who worked for the missions? At the most, Figueroa alleges, Híjar was willing to think of Indians who wanted land as colonists.

Taking up Figueroa's first point, it is indeed remarkable, at first sight, that Híjar's instructions say so little about the mission Indians. The only reference to them is in article seven, which prohibits the founding of purely Indian towns

51. Figueroa, *Manifiesto*, pp. 53, 62, 66, 68–72.
52. See p. 259.

and provides for integrating Indians with whites in the new towns. Presumably Governor Figueroa did not think this a favor to the Indians. Although he does not mention it, Governor Figueroa undoubtedly noticed that the white California residents were not mentioned at all in Híjar's instructions. Híjar made clear, however, that both the Indians and the Californians could become colonists. He referred to them both as "natives of the country." If, in fact, the Farías government was anxious to do away with the old racial distinction between Indians and whites, it was logical not to mention such distinctions in preparing Híjar's instructions. Figueroa either did not fully understand this point of view or, perhaps more likely, rejected it.

The rest of Governor Figueroa's criticisms of what he calls "Señor Híjar's libel" do not require further discussion because they are reiterations in different language of points he had previously made. At the close of his remarks, he says that he asked Híjar to inform him which of the laws, orders, and regulations that the Deputation used to back up its views had been repealed, but he did not receive the "satisfactory answer" that he was looking for. He does not say, however, what kind of an answer would have been satisfactory to him. Figueroa adds that everyone who attended the first day's conference, at which it must be presumed the gist of the above debate occurred, agreed with him that Híjar's answers were unsatisfactory. The two lawyers who were present, Luis del Castillo Negrete and Rafael Gómez, added further arguments and cited additional laws (which are not mentioned by Figueroa) in support of the Deputation's decision. Then, remarks Figueroa, Híjar and Padrés, "either pretending to be surprised or because they really were surprised," asked for time to think the matter over so they could either prepare a satisfactory answer or admit that they were convinced. This was agreed to, and it was decided to continue the conference on the following day, October 26.

Before the meeting began again the next day, however, a

remarkable incident took place. From his new rooms in José Joaquín Gómez' house, Híjar sent a friendly note to Figueroa asking him to meet for a secret interview before the conference. Figueroa walked over, and a private discussion took place between the two men. Padrés knew about it but was not present. According to Figueroa, Híjar made the following proposition to him:

> If I handed over to him the property of the missions he would protect my private interests with the same mission property, with assets that he had in Mexico City and Guadalajara, and with his credit and connections that he would apply in my favor in the way that would be most advantageous for my affairs. And finally, he would put at my disposal a note for twenty thousand pesos or more that he would ask for from Mexico or Jalisco if I wished, provided the missions were handed over to him.

Figueroa adds that Híjar was sure the Deputation would be willing to do whatever Figueroa wanted and that the governor had it in his power to make the fortunes of all of them.

It is interesting that although Figueroa introduces his account of this proposed transaction with an exclamation of pious horror ("Oh fatal moment how I should like to obliterate you from time") he refers to it as an accommodation rather than as attempted bribery. Furthermore, if Híjar did attempt to bribe Figueroa in this fashion, Figueroa reacts in a curiously matter-of-fact way to an offer that should surely have touched him where he appeared to be most sensitive—his honor. The governor does not appear to feel that Híjar insulted him by making such an offer, although he had been quick to resent real or fancied insults to him in Híjar's letter of October 23. Figueroa says he told Híjar that only considerations of justice would make him change his mind on mission property. And he added, "Interest is not a legal and decent consideration, nor one which would induce me to be base enough to sell the property of some innocent persons which I believed myself obliged to defend and which I would only hand over to him by express order of the Supreme Government after I had pointed out to it the injury which would be inflicted on the neophytes." After that, according to Figueroa, the subject was dropped, and the two men went on to discuss other matters.

It is remarkable that Governor Figueroa makes no further use of this incident in his lengthy polemic against Híjar and Padrés. Although, as will be seen, he constantly accuses them of robbing the missions and of a variety of other crimes, he does not mention that Híjar tried to bribe him. In fact, the only other reference to the matter in the *Manifiesto* is on the next to the last page, where the governor says, "There is one point in this manifesto so devoid of direct and conclusive proof that only the individual opinion that each person privately holds of me and of Señor Híjar can weigh in the balance of opinion."[53] Such a statement does little to lend credence to the affair. In a letter to Vallejo about a month later, Figueroa makes an interesting reference either to another similar incident or to the same incident but with a different protagonist. Speaking of Padrés, he says,

> He has made a mistake in thinking that, like him, I want to make my fortune at the expense of my fellows. He knows from experience now that I am not bought so easily as he tried to do when, thinking me capable of such baseness, someone proposed to me, on his advice, that I should take part in his business affairs on condition that I handed over to them the property of the missions.[54]

This presumably refers to an offer made by some person through Padrés for Figueroa's participation in the Cosmo-

53. Figueroa, *Manifiesto*, pp. 85, 90–94, 176.
54. Figueroa to Vallejo, Dec. 30, 1834, BL, Cowan.

politan Company. In his "Reminiscences," José de Jesús Vallejo says that at a secret interview Híjar and Padrés offered Figueroa a tenth of the shares of the Cosmopolitan Company if he would turn over the governorship to Híjar. What Vallejo meant by this, however, is by no means clear, since the company had not issued a fixed number of shares but was simply offering shares to subscribers who paid for them. Presumably he is accusing the directors of offering Figueroa shares in the company without having to pay for them. Since Figueroa had no intention of letting the company obtain mission property, these shares would be worth so little that it is unlikely they would be of any interest to Figueroa or to anyone else. There were also allegations that José Joaquín Ortega was offered a share of the company's profits if he would persuade the Deputation to go against Governor Figueroa and that the Deputation was offered a similar bribe to allow Híjar to take mission property. None of these accusations, however, is supported by any tangible evidence, and it is likely that they are based on little more than attempts by associates of the company to sell shares to Californians.[55] Unfortunately neither Híjar nor Padrés commented on Figueroa's accusation against Híjar which, in fact, they may not have seen, for Figueroa's *Manifiesto* was not published until after they had left California.

After the mysterious affair of the "accommodation," Figueroa's secret interview with Híjar continued with a long discussion on the right of the mission Indians to mission land and property. According to Figueroa, Híjar argued that they had no such right, and the government could dispose of mission lands as it saw fit, while Figueroa put forward the contrary view. Figueroa apparently thought he was on the point of convincing Híjar, but he felt that Híjar was swayed by Colonel Padrés' "chimerical projects," Padrés being a

55. José de Jesús Vallejo, "Reminiscencias históricas," BL, pp. 50–51; José Fernández, "Cosas de California," BL, p. 76; J. B. Alvarado, "Memoirs," BL, 2, 237.

man, in his opinion, "who did not even take care of his own reputation." It is strange, in view of his recent alleged experiences with Híjar, that he has no such harsh statement to make about him, unless he thought that Híjar was acting on the advice of Padrés. In the end, Híjar made a final proposal to Figueroa: he suggested that Figueroa hand over to him the property of the missions (presumably he is referring to movable property or cattle) on the understanding that he, Híjar, would not sell any of it until the federal government made a decision on the matter. Híjar offered to make ·a formal guarantee that he would keep this pledge if Figueroa accepted the offer. After considerable discussion, Figueroa told Híjar that if the Deputation agreed to his proposal, he would not oppose it, provided the property of the neophytes was not alienated; on the other hand, he would not support it.

After Híjar's secret meeting with Figueroa, the formal conference of Híjar, Padrés, the two lawyers, and the three members of the Deputation met for the second day's discussions. Híjar began by putting before the group the proposal that he had just made to Figueroa at the secret meeting. But they opposed it, whereupon Híjar and Padrés, according to Figueroa, agreed that the Deputation was within its rights. Híjar also conceded that his instructions were neither so clearly expressed as was necessary to remove all doubts, nor did they now have sufficient validity because of the government's action in dismissing him from the governorship. As a result of this, Híjar did not insist on making his former demands. On the other hand, he was determined to lead the colony to Lower California, where he would continue to be director of colonization. Padrés agreed to this, and likewise admitted that their instructions were inadequate. Figueroa reported him as saying, "It was certain that their instructions were very brief and [written] in a style which necessarily gave rise to various doubts; but that this came about because of the excessive confidence they merited in the eyes of the Vice-

President [Gómez Farías], who verbally gave them other orders and instructions of great interest, which they were to put into effect."

The remainder of the second day's conference was taken up with persuading Híjar and Padrés to stay on in California and not to attempt to lead the colony to Lower California. Figueroa reported that they told them there were no ships or funds to provide for the transportation of the colony. They mentioned the political consequences that might occur because of the failure of the expedition, which the government had sent out primarily to settle in California. Also they pointed out that Lower California was arid country and there would be no land on which to settle, nor did the missions there possess more than a very few cattle, which did not produce even enough support for the clergy, let alone for a colony.[56] "We begged [Híjar]," reported Figueroa, "to put aside his resentment and stay with us in good harmony." He could establish the colony and be paid the four thousand pesos that the government had assigned him. Figueroa also told him that they would give him effective help in carrying out his undertaking. Híjar agreed, concluded Figueroa, with all the proposals they had made and decided to go ahead with his project in California.[57]

56. Figueroa, *Manifiesto,* pp. 93–96.

57. It will be recalled that Híjar's salary as Governor was 3,000 pesos, the remainder being for his duties as Director of Colonization, so that Figueroa was either being very generous or attempting to bribe him. Figueroa, *Manifiesto,* p. 96.

Chapter Eight

A Colony of Artisans

On October 29, 1834, Governor Figueroa sent the Deputation
Híjar's letter of October 23 and a statement of what he and
Híjar had agreed upon after two days of conferences; the
Deputation referred these documents to its Committee on
Government. The committee, like Figueroa, took a poor view
of Híjar's letter, which it considered highly insulting to the
Deputation. In the interests of harmony the committee
waived its right, as Figueroa had done, to refute in detail all
of Híjar's errors. Asserting that Híjar had tried to deny the
authority of the Deputation, the committee said that after
the conferences with Governor Figueroa, Híjar realized his
error and stated that he would obey the Deputation. Among
the committee's specific proposals was one that the original
wording of the Deputation's second proposition of October 22
regarding colonization in California should be changed, and
another that Híjar should be asked to indicate in writing
whether or not he agreed with all the statements made by
the Deputation. If he did agree, the governor was to authorize
that he be paid a salary of 4,000 pesos, which the federal
government was to be asked to approve.[1] The committee's

1. Figueroa, *Manifiesto,* pp. 99–101. For the original wording and
changes made to the Deputation's October 22 proposition see above,
pp. 296, 302.

decision could not be considered by the Deputation until it met on Monday, November 3, the final day of its sessions. Meanwhile, at 8 P.M. on Saturday, November 1, a ball was given in honor of the directors of colonization "and their estimable travelling companions" at Governor Figueroa's residence.

At its meeting on the following Monday, the Deputation duly approved the committee's report, and on Tuesday Figueroa sent the Deputation's statement to Híjar.[2] He suggested that if Híjar was doubtful about anything, or if there was anything he did not agree with, that he and Híjar should have another conference about the matter at issue. On the other hand, if Híjar did not disagree with the report, he would like him to write to this effect. Híjar replied to Figueroa on November 6. There were several matters in the Deputation's report that Híjar disagreed with, but he did not accept Figueroa's invitation to have another conference because, as he said, "I consider any further argument on the matters we have discussed useless, since we do not see things in the same light." In spite of this, Híjar did set down in writing the various points in the Deputation's report to which he objected. First of all, he said that he had not tried to deny the authority of the Deputation, but simply its right to put itself above the law. Secondly, in a vague but interesting reference to the conferences he had had with Figueroa, Híjar said that when Figueroa spoke about the Indians he put forward "only reasons of utility, convenience, philanthropy, and humanity toward the natives but not a specific power to act in the way that was decided upon." He went on to say there was no law in existence that would give Figueroa and his supporters the right to act in the way they did. Some Spanish laws had been cited, he went on, but "these are annulled by our laws since they conflict with the system of government."

2. BL, State Papers, Sacramento, p. 241; Figueroa to Vallejo, Nov. 5, 1834, BL, Cowan; Figueroa, *Manifiesto,* p. 101.

Híjar took particular exception to the Deputation's requirement that he state in writing whether he agreed or disagreed with what had been done by the territorial government, with the proviso that if he did agree he was to be paid a salary of 4,000 pesos. "I am very sorry," Híjar said, "that the Very Excellent Deputation should have formed such a low opinion of me and that it should perhaps believe that money would make me defer to everything that has been decided. No Sir, not only am I not in agreement with but I protest against what you have determined to do at every point that it is against the laws and orders of the general government, as I have demonstrated in my letter of [October] 23."[3] Híjar was more sensitive about this rather indirect attempt to persuade him to come to terms, it will be noted, than Figueroa was about what he describes in such a way that it looks like open bribery. It is interesting that in spite of Híjar's open disavowal of the terms of the Deputation, Figueroa authorized the payment of his salary of 4,000 pesos two days after Híjar wrote this letter.[4]

The remainder of Híjar's reply to Figueroa and the Deputation was taken up with the affairs of the colony. He said that he was determined to go ahead and establish it where the government wanted him to put it for a number of reasons. First, the families in the colony had decided to follow him, and he could not abandon them without doing them harm. Secondly, if the colony failed it would be a blow to the federal government, for people would think it was incapable of carrying out undertakings of this kind, and it would never again be able to persuade people to go out and colonize. Thirdly, the important northern frontier area threatened by the Russians and the Anglo-Americans would be left unprotected, and the government would lose the large sums that it had spent on the colony. These considerations,

3. Figueroa, *Manifiesto*, pp. 101–03.
4. Figueroa to José María Herrera, Nov. 8, 1834, BL, Departmental State Papers, *I*, 226.

said Híjar, had made him decide to subordinate his own resentment and hurt pride and make every sacrifice "even though the ungrateful government, which has acted so outrageously toward me without any motive, should not repay me."

Híjar concluded his letter by hoping that Figueroa, in his turn, would keep his pledge that the colonists should be given everything the federal government had promised them. He was sure, he said, that Figueroa's integrity would see to it that everything was provided at the right time. After remarking that Híjar kept insisting on making several mistakes which he had already pointed out, Figueroa limited himself to the comment that it could be seen from this letter that Híjar always understood things differently from anyone else.

With this last interchange of letters, it began to look as if Híjar and Figueroa would be able to work out their problems satisfactorily and jointly establish the colony somewhere near San Francisco Solano. Figueroa, for his part, recounts that the "Territorial government," which probably meant himself, was pleased at having brought the negotiations to a friendly conclusion, and he publicly congratulated Híjar on the event.[5] Even before Híjar had written his letter of November 6, active preparations were being made to send the colonists at Monterey and their equipment north to San Francisco. Híjar informed Figueroa on November 5 that a brigantine, the *Granmare,* was about to sail for San Francisco and suggested that fifty or sixty bundles of the colony's baggage be put aboard it. This was apparently arranged, and it was decided that the colonists in Monterey would leave by land for San Francisco in a week's time. Figueroa advised Vallejo of the coming of the colonists and asked him to have the mission boats from San Rafael and San Francisco ready to transport the colonists and their baggage from either Yerbabuena or the estuary of Santa Clara to San Francisco Solano. During this time the other half of the colony was at

5. Figueroa, *Manifiesto,* pp. 103–05.

San Gabriel and San Luis Rey, far to the south, and unexpected troubles developed in transporting them north. Figueroa had planned to have the *Morelos,* which was still at Monterey, go down to San Diego and bring them back; but the day it was to leave, its captain reported that the foremast was damaged and it could not sail. Figueroa ordered a new mast to be stepped in, but since he calculated that this would take a month, he thought that the colonists in the south might come north in the *Natalia,* which was still at San Diego. When the *Natalia* left San Diego about November 21, however, it did not have the colonists on board. It arrived in Monterey on December 4.

In order to speed up transportation arrangements in the south, two of the colonists at Monterey, José Abrego and Romualdo Lara, were sent down to hurry the southern group along. They apparently did not have much success, for Francisco Torres, the physician from Guadalajara, was also sent down on November 20 to try to get them going.[6] Meanwhile Mariano Vallejo reported to Figueroa on November 7 that he was on his way to San Francisco Solano, where the colonists were to stay until the new settlement could be made. Figueroa wrote him on November 20 warning that if the colonists tried to make use of Indian labor they were to be allowed to have the services of those who volunteered to work for them on a paid basis, but they were not to be allowed to use force. Considering the care with which the colony's leaders had impressed upon them the need of making friends with the Indians, Figueroa's warning would seem unnecessary, but it reveals the kind of temptation to which white settlers in the California of that day might be expected to succumb.

While Governor Figueroa was helping to get the colony on its way to San Francisco Solano, Híjar was preparing estimates of colony expenses to submit to the governor. Híjar

6. Figueroa to Herrera, Nov. 5, 1834, BL, Departmental State Papers, Benicia Military, *79,* 62, 133; Figueroa to Vallejo, Monterey, Nov. 5 and 20, 1834, BL, Cowan.

informed Figueroa that the colony consisted of 204 persons—99 men, 55 women, and 50 children. Of these, 182 persons were over four years of age and were entitled to 4 reales a day, while 22 were under four and were entitled to 2 reales a day. On this basis the expenses of the colony for a month of thirty days amounted to 2,895 pesos, and for a year 35,222 pesos, 4 reales. The federal government had also said that the colonists would receive a certain amount of stock and farm equipment. Híjar stated that the colony had 42 families and 54 single men, each of whom (both single men and heads of families) was to receive four cows, two yoke of oxen, two broken-in horses, four colts, four fillies, four sheep, and two plows in working order.[7] The cost for the distribution to the total of 96 individuals of this stock and the plows, Híjar estimated, would be 9,984 pesos.[8] Adding the totals for the stock and plows to the daily maintenance for a year, Híjar calculated that the colony would require 45,206 pesos, 4 reales. Híjar was aware, however, that the territory was short of currency, so he asked Governor Figueroa to supply the colony with stores in place of the daily sum they were supposed to receive. These stores included corn, wheat, beans, chickpeas, lard, soap, sugar, tallow, lamb, beef, pork, salt, and candlewicks. Híjar also wanted axes, shovels, hoes, mason's hammers, pickaxes, bucksaws, hand saws, steel, tin plate, and iron.[9]

7. State Papers, BL, Missions and Colonization, 2, 187–89, 192. There were 8 reales to the peso.

8. Híjar estimated the prices of the various items as follows: a cow at 5 pesos; a yoke of oxen at 5 pesos; a broken-in horse at 4 pesos 4 reales; 4 colts at 5 pesos the lot; 4 fillies at 30 pesos the lot; 4 sheep at 6 reales the lot; a plow at 2 pesos 4 reales. There would appear to be slight arithmetical errors in the last two items, perhaps caused by a copyist's mistakes.

9. Híjar to Figueroa, Nov. 9, 1834, BL, State Papers, Missions and Colonization, 11, 189, 192. For a period of forty weeks, with an allowance of about 14 quarts (2 almudes) per person, Híjar calculated the amounts the colony would need as follows: 3,339 bushels (1,333 fanegas) of corn;

Governor Figueroa does not appear to have argued with Híjar over his estimates, for a few days after receiving them he sent out instructions to the commissioners of ten of the missions to provide the necessary supplies on a pro-rata basis. Requests were also sent to four other missions for the farming tools, which were to be sent to Híjar at the port of San Francisco. Governor Figueroa gave orders that the cattle and grain for the colony were to be sent to the Strait of Carquinez, and the missions of San Rafael and San Francisco were to provide the use of their boats to take the cargo across the bay to wherever Híjar ordered.[10]

Governor Figueroa also seems to have had no hesitation in busying himself with the placement of the twenty-two teachers who had come with Híjar as part of the colony. A brief four months before the arrival of Híjar, Figueroa had reported to the federal government that there were only three elementary schools for boys in the territory, and they were poorly endowed and staffed with incompetent teachers. The schools in Monterey and Los Angeles were supported by municipal funds; the one in Santa Barbara was supported partly by municipal funds and partly by a fund raised by the local military company. Figueroa reported that there were

---

1,718 bushels (666 fanegas) of wheat; 859 bushels (333 fanegas) of beans; 52 bushels (20 fanegas) of chickpeas; 12,680 lbs. (500 arrobas) of lard; 12,680 lbs. (500 arrobas) of soap; 1,522 lbs. (60 arrobas) of sugar; 7,101 lbs. (280 arrobas) of tallow; 122 lbs. (120 *libras*) of lamb; 284 lbs. (280 libras) of beef; 31 lbs. of pork (30 libras); 761 lbs. (30 arrobas) of salt; 122 lbs. (120 libras) of candle wicks. For the farm tools he suggested 40 axes, 40 shovels, 40 hoes, 10 mason's hammers, 10 pickaxes, 4 bucksaws, 8 handsaws, 304 lbs. (12 arrobas) of steel; 2 cases of tin plate, and 203 lbs. (20 *quintals*) of iron.

10. Nov. 12, 1834, BL, Departmental State Papers, *3*. The ten missions were Santa Clara, San José, San Francisco, San Francisco Solano, San Rafael, San Juan Bautista, Santa Cruz, Soledad, San Antonio, San Miguel. Nov. 12, 1834, BL, State Papers, Missions and Colonization, *11*, 193–94. The four missions were San Gabriel, San Luis Rey, San Fernando, San Buenaventura.

no schools for girls in the territory, and no attempt had ever been made to provide a good education for girls.[11]

Híjar had no written instructions with him about the teachers, but he had been told by the authorities in Mexico (perhaps by Vice-President Gómez Farías, who was particularly interested in elementary education) what they should be paid and where they should go. Híjar therefore made a list of the teachers, with suggested salaries and places where they might have their schools, and sent it to the Deputation. Figueroa called their attention to the question in a letter, and the Deputation passed the matter to its Commitee on Public Education. The Deputation finally decided that the teachers should receive the salaries mentioned by Híjar, which should be paid out of municipal funds and from the common cattle herds of the former missions in cash or produce or other articles at current prices. It appears, from a note by Híjar, that some of the teachers were to teach in the colony.[12] In addition to the elementary schools, a normal school for training elementary school teachers was to be set up at Monterey. Híjar was himself made the first master of it, but he was probably replaced shortly by Mariano Romero, one of the teachers who had come out with him. By November 5 the teacher question had been settled, by November 9 the teachers were asking for money to help them get to their destinations, and by November 20 they had all left Monterey for their posts.[13] Critics of the colony and its leaders have seldom if ever mentioned the work of the teachers who came with them. That life was not always easy for them is revealed by a letter to Figueroa dated June 25, 1835, from Florencio Serrano at the mission of San Antonio, where he seems to have

11. Figueroa to Secretario de Estado, May 23, 1834, BL, Departmental State Papers, 3.

12. Figueroa, *Manifiesto*, p. 98; Diputación, Oct. 30, 31, Nov. 3, 5, 1834, BL, Legislative Records, 2, 201, 260, 263.

13. Nov. 7, 1834, BL, Legislative Records, 2, 262–63; Figueroa to Vallejo, Nov. 20, 1834, BL, Cowan.

taught in the new pueblo established by the secularization program. He reported that there had been disorder in the pueblo, and his elementary school had no students. He had tried treating the children "in a friendly fashion so as to inspire in them a love for school," but it was no use. He also tried stiff punishments of spankings and keeping them in, but these did not work, either. Then he went to see the parents, and he found that they were working their children too hard for their age and even hid them when he came looking for them. As the years went by, however, the good effect of the teachers slowly became evident. In 1845 Manuel Castañares, deputy in the Mexican Congress from California, wrote "The young men who today occupy public offices in that country [California] were taught by these unhappy colonists." And in 1877 one of the sons of the former teachers, Antonio Franco Coronel, reported to Thomas Savage, who had been sent by Hubert Howe Bancroft to interview him: "Many sons of the country who today are men of importance and have been important, owe to them [the colony's teachers] the little education and knowledge they possess."[14]

By the middle of November 1834, the educational aspects of the colony's overall program had been launched, thanks to a new-found spirit of cooperation on the part of Governor Figueroa. Just at this point, however, when, according to Figueroa, the territorial government was enthusiastically going ahead with its plans for settling the colony itself, disquieting news began to come in from the south. Sometime during the last week of October, Figueroa learned of the trouble with the Cahuilla Indians at San Bernardino and of the alleged part of Lieutenant Buenaventura Araujo in the affair. Araujo was not a member of the colony, but he was one of two naval officers (the other was Juan Bautista Leigh-

14. Serrano to Figueroa, June 25, 1835, BL, State Papers, Missions, *11*, 309; Manuel Castañares, *Colección de documentos relativos al departmento de Californias* (Mexico, 1845), p. 40; Antonio Franco Coronel, "Cosas de California," BL, p. 18.

ton) who were being sent, along with a number of naval artisans from San Blas, to work on a proposed naval base in San Francisco Bay at the orders of the governor. Immediately following the trouble at San Bernardino, Araujo was sent to Monterey, where Governor Figueroa kept an eye on him. Meanwhile Figueroa reported to the minister of war and marine that he had been given no instructions by the government about the duties of Araujo and Leighton and did not know what to do with them. Until he heard from the government, he planned to use them in inspecting the ports and coastal fortifications and in some other duties.[15] Araujo must have continued to arouse suspicion in Governor Figueroa, for he wrote to the government in Mexico about him again (perhaps early in December), saying that he suspected the lieutenant of involvement in revolutionary activities and requesting his transfer. On January 27, President Santa Anna authorized Figueroa to remove Araujo from the territory; but Araujo did not actually depart until May 1835, when he left California with the colony's leaders, who were being removed by Figueroa. Figueroa sent a statement to the Ministry of War regarding Araujo's revolutionary activities, but its naval board returned the statement to Figueroa as being "imperfect." Leighton, the other naval officer sent to California, was still there in October 1835, but it does not appear that the government's plans for strengthening Mexico's naval hold on California were ever put into effect.[16]

Governor Figueroa's immediate reaction to the news about the incident involving the Cahuillas was mild. At the time he reported to Vallejo that there had been a little trouble with pagan Indians, that it had been necessary to use force

15. Figueroa, *Manifiesto*, p. 106; Buenaventura Araujo, Service Record in AD. Statement dated Feb. 19, 1834; Figueroa to Minister of War, Nov. 12, 1834, in Araujo, Service Record, AD.

16. Tornel to Figueroa, Jan. 27, 1835, BL, Superior Government State Papers, *11*, 106; Araujo, Service Record, AD; Nicolás Gutiérrez to Patricio Estrada, Oct. 26, 1835, Berduzco Criminal, BC.

on them, and that he thought this would be sufficient to persuade them to return to their previous peaceful pursuits. In his *Manifiesto,* however, Figueroa also mentions that it was at this time that he learned of subversive activities by two of the members of the colony: Francisco Berduzco at San Luis Rey, and Romualdo Lara at various missions on his way north with Híjar from San Diego. Although, Figueroa adds, the territorial government felt naturally suspicious of these men, it merely took a few precautionary steps without making any move against the men themselves, because it thought they would listen to reason and desist.[17]

If Governor Figueroa appeared tolerant toward the alleged conspiratorial activities of Berduzco and Lara, he adopted an entirely different attitude toward Colonel Padrés, whose career in California had been brought to his attention in a highly unfavorable fashion by former Governor Victoria. Padrés landed from the *Morelos* the night of September 24, 1834, with his brother Rafael, five ladies (two of whom may have been the wives of Colonel Padrés and his brother), five children, and a servant. Padrés was instructed to take over from Figueroa as comandante general, if General Figueroa "should continue to be ill and wish to resign." According to Figueroa, Padrés wanted him to surrender the office of comandante general as soon as he landed from the *Morelos.* Figueroa told him that his health was better, he did not now wish to give up his position, and in any case President Santa Anna had sent instructions through the minister of war on December 7, 1833, that he was to continue to be comandante general.[18] When Padrés informed the governor that he was

17. Figueroa to Vallejo, Nov. 5, 1834, BL, Cowan; Figueroa, *Manifiesto,* pp. 106–07.

18. Padrés to Figueroa, Apr. 14, 1835, BL, Departmental State Papers, *4,* 28; José J. de Herrera to Figueroa, July 12, 1833, BL, State Papers, Missions and Colonization, *2;* Figueroa, *Manifiesto,* p. 107; Figueroa to Minister of War, Nov. 20, 1834, BL, State Papers, Missions and Colonization, *2,* 197.

sub-director of the colony as well as still holding the position of assistant inspector of California, Figueroa replied that the military companies in California needed a complete reorganization and military discipline required that Padrés devote himself to being assistant inspector. In his own account of this affair, Padrés states that he had not come to California to take up actively his position of assistant inspector, which he describes as "laborious" and incompatible with the continued poor state of his health. He thought that since he could not take over as comandante general, he was free to return to Mexico. On the other hand, he felt that he had to stay with the colony until the government decided what he should do. He told Figueroa that he wanted to be sub-director of the colony and not assistant inspector.

Governor Figueroa's account of his meeting with Padrés provides a different interpretation of Padrés' reasons for not wanting to be assistant inspector. According to the governor, who obviously wanted Padrés to take up his military career —perhaps to keep him under his immediate orders as his military subordinate—Padrés did not want to be under the control of Figueroa as comandante general. Also, he looked upon his position of sub-director of the colony as being incompatible with that of assistant inspector. Figueroa, at all events, regarded Padrés' determination to march north with the colony as another proof that he wanted to avoid his military duties. What is more, Figueroa said that Padrés, before he left with part of the colony, probably about mid-November, asked him for the position of military commander of the northern frontier, with the rank of second-in-command of the military forces of the territory. If, in fact, Figueroa is accurate in saying that Padrés did not want to be under his military command, there is some justification for Figueroa's considering this request to be contradictory. At any rate, Figueroa's suspicions were aroused: "Signs of ambition and disorder show through his mysterious conduct," he reported to the minister of war. He refused to give Padrés the position he asked for and wrote to Vallejo that he had better be on his guard.[19]

After Padrés had reached the frontier with the colonists, Figueroa began to hear alarming stories about him. He received confidential information from persons whose names he did not disclose that Padrés was "secretly spreading subversive ideas" and that his main preoccupation was "arousing public hatred against me so as to loosen in this way the bonds of obedience." In a confidential letter to the minister of war, Figueroa reported that Padrés had "made up the most atrocious calumnies" about him, that he was using every possible slander to abuse Figueroa's honor, and that he was biding his time to form a party to support him. Figueroa thought that Padrés was resentful because the governor had prevented him from getting hold of mission property, and he felt that Padrés would now seek vengeance against him and the people of California. Padrés even had a grudge against the federal government, Figueroa suggested, because it had not permitted Híjar to take over as governor. Figueroa continued his letter by saying that it was "an absolute necessity" that Padrés be removed to another position outside the territory. Undoubtedly recalling Governor Victoria's view of Padrés' former activities, Figueroa said that past experience of his "turbulent character" showed that if he stayed in California he would cause trouble. He warned that although there had been no disturbances so far, he was afraid the Californians might be taken advantage of by "his rivals" (presumably Híjar and Padrés) or that the colony led by Padrés might commit some illegal act that he would have to punish.[20]

In his *Manifiesto* Figueroa provided a further long cata-

19. Figueroa to Padrés, Nov. 8, 1834, Padrés to Figueroa, Nov. 9, 1834, and Figueroa to Minister of War, Nov. 20, 1834, BL, State Papers, Missions and Colonization, 2, 182, 191, 197; Padrés to Minister of War, Feb. 2, 1835, AD; Figueroa to Vallejo, Nov. 20, 1834, BL, Cowan.

20. Figueroa to Minister of War, Dec. 8, 1834, BL, State Papers, Missions and Colonization, 2, 202.

log of the sins of Padrés. He had boasted, according to Figueroa, that he had come to California at the head of an armed people. And while everyone knew that he had with him two hundred rifles and a considerable amount of ammunition, he failed to mention these facts to the governor and had even tried to hide them from him. Padrés had given orders that no member of the colony was to come to see the governor or deal with the governor in any way, but only with Padrés. He had observed, continued Figueroa, that Padrés had a great deal of influence on Híjar, and it became clear to him that Padrés was the man behind all the conspiracies, the man he must watch.[21]

During the course of December 1834, Governor Figueroa became more and more irritated with what he heard about Padrés. Vallejo, who was previously on friendly terms with Padrés, wrote that he was impugning Figueroa's patriotism, calling him a "little king," and alleging that Figueroa was going to benefit from secularizing the missions. Figueroa replied to Vallejo that his patriotism was so well known in the republic that he did not need to defend it against Padrés' aspersions, and he had already sent in his resignation from his civil position as governor, so that he would be only comandante general and unable to be a "little king" or derive any benefit from secularization. In spite of a valiant attempt to appear aloof to Padrés' reported criticisms, it is evident that Figueroa deeply resented them. "I am angry," he concluded his letter to Vallejo at the end of December, "and I shall not be happy while I am in command, for I have agreed to resign and slanderous attacks always make me burn." In spite of his secret report to the minister of war, however, the government did not give him permission to remove Padrés from California. There is no doubt that Governor Figueroa was genuinely afraid that Colonel Padrés might succeed in winning over some of his garrison, whose salaries were far in

21. Figueroa, *Manifiesto*, p. 108.

arrears.[22] This may have led the governor to describe Padrés in his *Manifiesto* as a kind of evil genius who was leading Híjar astray.

About the third prominent figure in the colonization movement, the Californian Juan Bandini, Figueroa, despite his obvious mistrust of him, has very little to say. Bandini's interests were mercantile, he was one of the top officers in the Cosmopolitan Company, and in addition he had been given the post of visitador of customs of the Californias. On December 7, 1834, a few days after the *Natalia* arrived in Monterey from San Diego, Bandini presented himself to Angel Ramírez, the administrator of maritime customs. Ramírez was apparently a friend of Gómez Farías and had been appointed to his post, with a salary of 2,000 pesos, in July 1833. Two members of the colony later provided two very differing views of Angel Ramírez. José Abrego, writing in 1875, said that Ramírez was an intimate friend of Gómez Farías and that through him Farías and his party would be able to seek asylum in California when they wished to do so. Coronel, on the other hand, writing in 1877, pointed to Ramírez as the mainspring of opposition to the colony. Coronel is clearly more accurate in this matter than Abrego. Bandini showed Ramírez the official order appointing him to his post, but Ramírez expressed amazement, complained that the government had said nothing to him about the matter, professed that Bandini's arguments "did not convince him," and refused to allow him to take his post.[23] After informing the government in December 1834 that he regretted not having

22. Figueroa to Vallejo, Dec. 30, 1834, BL, Cowan; Tornel to Figueroa, Jan. 27, 1835, BL, Superior Government State Papers, *11*, 106; Figueroa to Minister of War, Dec. 8, 1834, BL, State Papers, Missions and Colonization, *2*, 201.

23. Mendoza to Sub-Comisario de Alta California, BL, Departmental State Papers, *1*, 235; Coronel, "Cosas de California," BL, p. 15; José Abrego, "Documentos," BL, *21*; Angel Ramírez to Director General de Rentas, Dec. 12, 1834, BL, Departmental State Papers, *1*.

been able to "fulfill completely" the government's orders which he said he respected so highly, Ramírez heard from various people, whose names he does not mention, that when Bandini arrived with the colony he had landed goods on which he did not pay duty at San Diego. The customs receiver at San Diego, Santiago E. Argüello, had said nothing about the matter, but Ramírez started an inquiry at which various persons who had been on the vessel reported whether they thought Bandini had landed contraband. It would appear from the evidence given by some of the witnesses that Bandini may have landed goods without paying duty on them, but some of the witnesses seem to have done the same. Ramírez' attempt to blacken Bandini's name before the federal government would carry more weight if he himself had a reputation for probity in such matters, but Agustín Janssens, one of the colonists, reported that while he was living at Ramírez' house, he had a little shop where he sold merchandise belonging to Ramírez, "though he did not appear as owner." Ramírez was still administrator of customs and forbidden to engage in trade. The fact of the matter was, as Ramírez himself admits, smuggling was common because there were insufficient men in the customs service.[24]

After his rebuff at Monterey, Bandini went back to San Diego. He had apparently been given permission by the federal government to make San Diego and San Francisco into maritime customs houses but was opposed in this by both Ramírez and Governor Figueroa. In his valuable report on commercial matters in California, Figueroa said that he opposed the permission that Governor Echeandía had given for foreign ships to unload their cargoes at San Diego as well as at Monterey. He restricted such unloading to Monterey because it was the capital, with the only existing customs house, and the governing authorities could keep close watch

24. Mar. 21, 1835, BL, Departmental State Papers, *4*, 72; Ellison and Price, *Life and Adventures of Janssens*, p. 49; Angel Ramírez, BL, Departmental State Papers, *1*, 215.

over proceedings there. He also said it was one of the best and safest ports, where shipping could stay "without any danger at all." He did not say, but undoubtedly he had in mind, that by concentrating all imports at Monterey, he also concentrated all the customs revenue at the same port, so that there would be no danger of any opposition group in San Diego or any other port getting hold of customs funds to provoke a rebellion in the way that Santa Anna had frequently done at Veracruz. As has been mentioned above, Figueroa was particularly suspicious of the efforts of Bandini and other residents of San Diego in their attempts to promote their own region.

While he was not in favor of allowing foreign or Mexican owned ships to land their cargoes at any port other than Monterey, Governor Figueroa did not favor doing away with foreign control of the coastal trade, at any rate for the time being. He explained his views reasonably enough to the government. The goods provided by the foreign ships were necessities which the few Mexican ships could not provide; the towns and missions where the business was were a long way from Monterey; there were no wagons, mules were little used, and the people did not know how to manage them. Furthermore, foreign ships could not dispose of their goods at the one port where they unloaded because the population was too small to buy them all, and there were no wholesale merchants who could purchase from them in bulk. Nor was there a way of transporting the merchandise on land, and there were no Mexican ships which plied in the coastwise trade. Figueroa admitted that it was illegal to allow foreign ships to engage in this trade and to sell at retail in each port, but he insisted that if he stopped it he would run into strong opposition from the Californians, who depended on it for their needs and for disposing of their own products of ranch and farm. In his November 1834 report he recommended that it be continued for another five years. He also suggested that the ports of San Francisco, Santa Barbara, San Pedro, and San Diego be legally opened to the coastwise trade.[25]

It can be seen from Figueroa's report, which is confirmed by other sources, that California commerce was hampered by two main problems: not enough Mexican shipping to take away the products of the country, and inadequate land transportation to bring the goods to port.[26] Aside from its cumbersome administrative structure, it is clear that the Cosmopolitan Company was designed to provide solutions for both of these major problems. Using paid former mission Indians, the major part of the former missions' lands were apparently to be highly developed by means of the latest agricultural methods. Foreign markets for California products were to be sought out and shipping provided to transport the goods to them. In California itself, particular attention was to be given to the problems of transportation. In addition, there was to be a beginning of manufacturing.

Along the lines of the Caracas Company in eighteenth-century Venezuela or the British East India Company, the Cosmopolitan Company was to be given certain concessions by the government and encouraged to make a profit that would both benefit its shareholders and help to develop California. Governor Figueroa became its determined foe and did his utmost to discredit it. He spoke of "the grandiose speculations of the pompous mercantile Cosmopolitan Company." He referred to the "picturesque and ridiculous creation of the Cosmopolitan Company, which smacks more of tortilla makers, merchants and monopolists than of patriots." In yet another scornful reference, he spoke of it as the "boastful mercantile Cosmopolitan Company, as short of funds as it was full of hopes and notable for the pedantry of its name."[27] Bandini later stated that Figueroa had tried to

25. Ramírez to Director de Rentas, Apr. 5, 1835, BL, Departmental State Papers, *1*, 221; Figueroa to Secretario de Hacienda, Nov. 28, 1834, BL, Departmental State Papers, *3*, 198–200, 203.

26. BL, Departmental State Papers, Benicia Military, *79*, 118.

27. Figueroa, *Manifiesto*, pp. 17, 167, 174.

discredit everything connected with the colony, and his base slander of the Cosmopolitan Company was part of this procedure. Whether or not the company would have been able to succeed, even with the support of Governor Figueroa, is by no means certain. With the governor's opposition it did not stand a chance. What is more, public opinion in California became aroused against the company. The public, wrote Ramírez, quickly understood Bandini's intention to "reduce commerce to a system that would benefit only the Company called Cosmopolitan." And in a reference to the "ruinous monopoly" which was the company's alleged aim, Figueroa mentioned that public opinion in California became directly opposed to the leaders of the colony. A final and crushing blow to the Cosmopolitan Company occurred on December 21, 1834. The *Natalia,* which belonged to the company, was anchored at Monterey when a strong north wind arose with a rough sea. At about 3:30 P.M. both of the cables holding the ship gave way, and at about 5:15 it ran ashore some two miles off and became a total wreck. Three crew members were drowned.[28] Bandini partly blamed the captain for the wreck, a judgment which is confirmed by Richard Henry Dana, who speaks of the "carelessness or ignorance of the Captain." Bandini also remarks that the loss of the *Natalia* made it difficult for the directors of colonization to communicate with the government in Mexico. Governor Figueroa duly reported the incident to Vallejo, ending his account with what must have been to him the satisfactory conclusion: "With this it seems to me that the great Cosmopolitan Company has come to its end."[29]

28. Bandini, "Historia," BL, pp. 160–61; Ramírez to Director de Rentas, Apr. 5, 1835, BL, Departmental State Papers, *1,* 222; Figueroa, *Manifiesto,* p. 35; BL, Departmental State Papers, Benicia Military, *79,* 73 (old numbering).

29. Richard Henry Dana, Jr., *Two Years Before the Mast* (Boston, 1929), p. 102. Dana does not mention the *Natalia* by name, but it is likely that his references are to it. Bandini, "Historia," BL, pp. 164–65; Figueroa to Vallejo, Dec. 30, 1834, BL., Cowan.

By the end of December 1834, the colonists who had arrived at Monterey on the *Morelos* were at the mission of San Francisco Solano. According to one of them, Antonio Franco Coronel, they left Monterey on horseback or in oxcarts, crossing the bay at the Strait of Carquinez in launches handled by mission Indians from San José. At the mission of San Francisco Solano at Sonoma they were lodged in the mission itself. Alongside them, occupying most of the mission, were Ensign Mariano G. Vallejo and his troops.[30]

Híjar spent the winter quietly at Monterey, perhaps waiting until the colonists who had landed with him on the *Natalia* at San Diego and who were now scattered out along the length of California, staying at various missions, reached Monterey. Some of them arrived at the end of December. Híjar also busied himself writing to the government in Mexico presenting his view of the colony's situation. That Híjar's thoughts were not of the most cheerful can be seen from his letter of resignation sent to the government at the end of January 1835:

> When the colonization plan for California was conceived in Mexico a large scale plan was projected. It had as its aim human kind in general. If it had come from the hands of the Supreme Government as it should have come, then it would need a Director; but reduced to nullity as it is now, I believe my position of Director is useless and my salary onerous to the public treasury. In view of this, if the Supreme Government has nothing else more useful for me to do, I beg that you permit me to retire to a place where I can be employed with more advantage to my country and my fellows.

Híjar went on to suggest that Colonel Padrés, sub-director of the colony, could take over control of the colony without

30. Coronel, "Cosas de California," BL., p. 11.

additional salary.[31] That Híjar's step was taken with the knowledge of Colonel Padrés is likely. At any rate, two days later Padrés wrote from San Francisco Solano to the minister of war pointing out that he had asked for his retirement from the army three years before and that his ill health had become worse since then. Furthermore, since he had become a lieutenant colonel of cavalry in April 1834, the problem which had delayed his previous retirement—the question of his rank—no longer existed. Although he asked once more for his retirement from the army, Padrés stated that he would stay in California long enough to establish the colony on the northern frontier, if the president wished him to do so. Otherwise he would leave whenever the minister gave him the order.

It is difficult to fathom what Governor Figueroa's real feelings about the colony were at this period. In his *Manifiesto* he says that he received two communications from different persons at the mission of San Antonio that a conspiracy was afoot. He also states that several members of the colony secretly told him about plans that were being made for disorder, while other members of the colony wanted to leave it on various pretexts. One of those who wanted to leave the colony, it may be noted, was Florencio Serrano, who says that he was dissatisfied because the government was not keeping its maintenance promises. He reports that Governor Figueroa made him a clerk at the former mission of San Antonio, with a salary of twenty-five pesos a month and his board. He was also to be the elementary school master for the children of the district. According to Figueroa, sedition was everywhere and especially dangerous at Monterey itself, although he says that Híjar was "passive" and showed a "simulated indifference" which kept suspicion away from

31. Florencio Serrano, "Apuntes," BL, pp. 11–12. Híjar to Ministro de Relaciones, Jan. 2, 1835, BL, Colonización y terrenos baldíos, Fomento, legajo 6, expediente 162. Híjar to Ministro de Relaciones, Jan. 31, 1835, BL, Colonización y terrenos baldíos, Fomento, expediente 175.

him. He immediately adds, however, that "the principal agents of the revolution" called on Híjar, had conferences with him, and were high in his confidence. "It is almost impossible," surmises Figueroa, "that he should have been ignorant of the plans they were to put into effect under his auspices and in his name."[32] It is important to bear in mind, however, that when he wrote these words Figueroa was putting forward the idea that he was aware in advance of the plotting that was eventually to lead to the revolt at Los Angeles. Actually, as will be seen, there is little evidence that he had any such prior knowledge, although he wrote on February 22, 1835, about rumors that Berduzco wanted to arm the colonists and put them under the orders of Colonel Padrés. But the governor never produces any concrete evidence to substantiate his accusations.

Toward the end of February, Híjar, along with Romualdo Lara, Francisco Berduzco, and Buenaventura Araujo, started for the mission of San Francisco de Asís, from which they would travel on the last lap of their journey to San Francisco Solano to meet the colonists under Padrés.[33] Governor Figueroa also left for San Francisco, apparently traveling apart from the colonists, although his objective was to keep them under observation and try to find out what their plans were. At the mission of San Francisco, Figueroa met them again and had a conference with Híjar. According to the governor, he told Híjar that his friends were plotting against the territorial government and especially against himself, the governor. He told him who the leaders of the plot were and urged him to put an end to it, promising that if there was no outbreak he would keep the whole affair silent. But Híjar paid no attention to his warnings, treating him, remarks Figueroa, with the "same coldness and indifference with

32. Padrés to Minister of War, Feb. 2, 1835, AD; Figueroa, *Manifiesto,* p. 110; Florencio Serrano, "Apuntes," BL, p. 13.

33. Figueroa to Bernardo Navarrete, Feb. 22, 1835, Berduzco Criminal, BC; Figueroa, *Manifiesto,* p. 116.

which he is accustomed to deal with important affairs." It is unfortunate that Híjar has left no statement about his conferences with Figueroa, except to say that Figueroa told him in the course of several meetings that it would be impossible to provide the colonists with all that the government had promised them when they had contracted to come to California.

It was on this subject that Híjar and Figueroa exchanged a series of letters during the first few days of March, just before Híjar left San Francisco for Sonoma. In the first letter, dated March 1, Híjar said that he was on the point of going to San Francisco Solano to select the site where the colony was to be established, but he wanted Figueroa to tell him definitely, one way or the other, whether the government would honor its obligations toward the colony. If Figueroa was going to provide the support that had been offered, Híjar said, he would go ahead with his plans to settle the colony. But if not, he would inform the colonists so they might decide what they wished to do. Híjar reminded the governor that the federal government had put a great deal of money and effort into the colony, and if it should fail it would affect the government adversely. In his previous meetings with Figueroa, Híjar had apparently told him that most of the supplies that Figueroa had ordered for the colony had not materialized.

Figueroa replied to Híjar in a long letter the following day. After saying that the federal government had not sent him any advance warning about the colony (although, as has been noted, Figueroa had read about it in the newspapers) and repeating that Híjar's instructions to take over mission property were unconstitutional—since they conflicted with article 112, restriction three of the Mexican Constitution of 1824, which prohibited the president from taking property from a private individual or a corporation—Figueroa went on to state at length why the missions could not provide the supplies that the colony needed. The missions, he said, were well known to be in a bad state: they were loaded with debt, the mission Indians were being freed and had to be given mission property so they could live, and there were a number of new officials—such as ministers, teachers, majordomos, and others—whose positions had previously not existed and who had to be paid from mission funds. The men who worked the former mission farms also had to be given their daily wages. Figueroa said that in spite of these difficulties he would do his best to provide enough supplies for the colony to subsist, but he could not promise to pay its daily expenses punctually. There was no currency, he said, and it would be impossible to provide goods in a short time to the value of over 35,000 pesos, which was what the colony's expenses would amount to in a year.

At this point Figueroa put forward a new suggestion of his own which he said he had already mentioned to Híjar previously: to allow the colony to disband, so that the colonists could go anywhere they liked to earn their living. Several colonists had already asked him for permission to do this, Figueroa said, adding that it was well known that "The majority of the individuals who compose the colony, although very recommendable and useful in various occupations, are not [suitable] for working in the fields, which they have never done before." Governor Figueroa went on to adduce a long string of additional reasons why the colony should be disbanded: six months had gone by and the colony had not established itself or undertaken any useful work; Padrés, without informing him or Híjar, was persuading families and individuals already resident in California to join the colony, which merely added to the expense; transporting the cattle and other movable goods to the other side of San Francisco Bay would be very expensive and slow and there would, in addition, be losses in the course of it; it was very difficult to bring together at one point all the property of the colony; the colonists were already disgruntled, and if their sufferings were made worse this might result in disorder; and finally, and especially, he thought the colony should be disbanded because Híjar had told him that he had written to the government asking for permission to leave the colony and that he was thinking of going to Lower California to await the government's orders.

Figueroa went on to say he thought that if the colonists could establish themselves where they wanted and earn their living as they wished, it would benefit both the territory and the individual colonists. He had thought about this a great deal, and every day his experience convinced him that "there was no more adequate remedy for our circumstances nor one that would better conciliate public and private interests." He closed his letter by saying that he was giving orders that day for necessary goods to the value of 2,000 pesos to be given to the colony.

Híjar began his reply, dated March 3, by saying that permitting the colonists to settle where they wished would not discharge his responsibilities. He thought that if the supreme government could fulfill its part of the bargain, the colonists should proceed to the site that the government had in mind for them. He did not think the government would have spent the large sums it had simply to settle four or five persons in each of the towns in the territory. He felt that Governor Figueroa must be aware that the government was persuaded to make extraordinary sacrifices to send out the colony at a time of extreme want for reasons of state, among them the need to preserve the integrity of the republic's territory. The colonists could have no reason for complaining if they were sent out to unpopulated regions to settle, for they agreed to go where the government wished. Since the fate of the colony now depended entirely on Governor Figueroa, he would be obliged if the governor would tell him definitely whether the supreme government would fulfill its pledges toward the colony. If Governor Figueroa replied that the pledge could not be fulfilled, Híjar would consider that his duty had been done, and the colonists might stay where they wished.

Governor Figueroa knew very well, continued Híjar, that

only a small amount of the supplies he requested of each mission for the colony had actually been provided, and it would be difficult to collect these. Obstacles had arisen on every hand which had delayed establishing the colony and had forced Governor Figueroa to arrange for the colonists to spend the winter scattered at various missions where, since they were transients, they could not begin any kind of farm work. Híjar said he would prefer the governor to say now that the government's agreement with the colonists could not be kept, rather than wait and tell the colonists later. In this way the colonists would be relieved of their painful uncertainty, and he would be free from further responsibility. The colonists had been told in Mexico, he informed Figueroa, that currency was short in California, so they knew they would be paid in goods. As for Padrés' accepting California residents as colonists, this would not increase expenses, for they would only be given land, without any of the other inducements offered to colonists from Mexico. Finally, Híjar said that even if he did leave the colony, this should not affect its future in any way.

Figueroa replied to Híjar the following day, March 4, by reminding him that on repeated occasions he had told him how difficult it was to meet fully the expenses of settling the colony because of a lack of funds. Since Híjar wanted a definite statement he would give it to him: "It is not possible to pay in full all that the government offered the colony because the funds at my disposal are not sufficient. Consequently, I order that the colonists be free to establish themselves at a place agreeable to each individual within the limits of the Territory, where they will be assisted according to the resources available to me."[34]

Farías' dream of a colony that would found a town in northern California close to the Russian settlement at Fort Ross was dead, killed by Figueroa's apparent inability to find

34. Figueroa, *Manifiesto*, pp. 116–18, 120, 122, 124–28.

sufficient funds to pay the colony the full amount the government had promised. It may be conjectured that the governor could have provided more for the colony than he actually did, but it is not possible to prove it. All he said was that he would do the best he could. He made no promises of specific amounts on which Híjar might decide whether the colony could succeed or not. On the other hand, was Híjar being unreasonable in seeming to demand that Figueroa find the exact amount that the government had promised the colony or be responsible for its dissolution? Could Híjar have prepared a minimum budget on which the colony might have subsisted? It is possible that he did so but became convinced that Figueroa was, in any case, thinking of dissolving the colony for reasons not connected with money and supplies. In a letter written to Vallejo some two months before his conferences with Híjar at San Francisco, Figueroa provides some evidence that he was even then thinking of dispersing the colony on the grounds that they would not be able to found a settlement. After counseling Vallejo to be patient with the colonists, who had been irritating him, Figueroa says that the persons who are really to blame are their leaders, who had told them they were coming to a paradise where there would be only joy and no suffering. The colony, continued Figueroa, was composed of people "so delicate that it will not be able to produce a good effect nor will it progress in the way that Señor Padrés has dreamed in his overheated imagination. I am aware of the difficulties they have to overcome and how hard it will be for them to get established, but I want them to become disillusioned themselves. And experience will prove that my prediction is correct: it is that the colonists will make up their minds to spread out over the Territory in order to be able to live more comfortably."[35] According to Figueroa, by the beginning of March some of the colonists had asked him if he would permit them to settle

35. Figueroa to Vallejo, Dec. 30, 1834, BL, Cowan.

where they wanted (it should be noted that they asked
Figueroa to give them this permission, rather than Híjar or
Padrés), but his prediction that the colony would give up as
a whole did not occur. In spite of this, Figueroa, rather than
give the colonists encouragement to found their settlement
near San Francisco Solano under Colonel Padrés, made his
announcement that they were to be free to disperse.

It is interesting that in his *Manifiesto* Figueroa does not
dwell so much on his lack of resources when justifying his
procedure in dispersing the colony, as on the weakness of the
colony itself:

> A people who are going to be founders need to be hard-
> working and to have strong arms. They must be men
> accustomed to work in the fields and used to a frugal,
> simple life. The colony directed by messrs. Híjar and
> Padrés is in its majority composed of delicate persons
> worthy of a better fate. They are families suddenly
> wrenched from the capital where they were born and
> educated in the midst of pleasures and opulence. How-
> ever scanty their fortune was in Mexico, they had estab-
> lished a way of life appropriate to their strength, their
> character, their inclinations, their customs, their tem-
> perament and their taste. In proportion to their industry
> and their connections they enjoyed comforts and plea-
> sures that would be hard to find elsewhere. Many of
> them possess a mechanical or liberal art that in Mexico
> would have provided them with an income but is worth-
> less in California. Let the tinsmiths, the silversmiths, the
> makers of trimmings, the embroiderers, the painters, etc.
> testify to this. Compare the difference between using one
> of the instruments of the arts and handling a plow, a hoe,
> an axe or the other implements used in cultivating the
> fields. Compare the difference between working in your
> house, sheltered from the sun, wind and rain, to laboring
> in the fields exposed to the weather and the hazards of

a life filled with privation, discomfort and danger. Could it be that the fields that these young girls, ladies and delicate young men passed by on the roads they travelled were the first they had ever seen? Would it be possible, I repeat, for these individuals to overcome the fatigue, difficulties, privation, lack of necessities and the accumulation of afflictions and accidents that beset those who undertake to be founders? Let those who are taking part [in the project] answer for me. And impartial men will justify the measures that the Territorial government has taken to put an end to the sufferings of the colonists and free them from the harsh undertaking to which their Directors were committing them to make their destiny more ill-fated.[36]

Governor Figueroa's self-justification for dispersing the colony received almost unanimous approval from his contemporaries and later writers. Of the Californians, Mariano Vallejo, Ignacio del Valle, and Juan B. Alvarado entirely agreed with him. Alvarado even provides an alleged speech by some of the colonists, who told him that in Mexico they had been led to expect that when they arrived in California everything would be prepared for them to live a "comfortable and restful life." Alvarado says at the close of his account, however, that most of the colonists were orderly persons and that after Híjar and Padrés were removed from California they settled down and did well; they had been led astray by their leaders. This interpretation, it will be noticed, takes care of the difficulty of explaining how alleged ne'er-do-wells later turned into solid citizens.[37]

Of the foreigners, the Scots merchant Alexander Forbes, who published his book on California in 1839, takes an even

36. Figueroa, *Manifiesto,* pp. 111–13.

37. Juan B. Alvarado, "Memoirs," BL, 2, 244, and 3, 32–33; Ignacio del Valle, "Lo pasado de California," BL, p. 14; H. H. Bancroft, Unbound Notes, No. 4, BL.

dimmer view of the colonists' abilities than Figueroa himself. "They were of every class of persons except that which could be useful," he began,

> there was not one agriculturist amongst them. They were chiefly from the city of Mexico, and consisted of artizans and idlers who had been made to believe that they would soon enrich themselves in idleness in this happy country. There were to be seen goldsmiths proceeding to a country where no gold or silver existed, blacksmiths to where no horses are shod or iron used, carpenters to where only huts without furniture were erected, shoemakers to where only sandals of raw hide were worn, tailors to where the inhabitants only covered themselves with a blanket, doctors to where no one gets sick; there were also engravers, printers, musicians, gamblers, and other nameless professors, all bound on this hopeful crusade, which their enthusiastic leaders assured them would procure unalloyed felicity and unbounded riches.[38]

Dr. John Marsh, an American who had lived in California for six years, wrote in 1842 that the colonists were "of a description entirely useless in a country like California." He contradicted the other critics, however, by asserting that the uselessness of the colony was due to the fact that there was "not a farmer, blacksmith, carpenter nor any useful artisan among them." Two French travelers, Abel du Petit-Thouars and Duflot de Mofras, are as unflattering in their comments on the colony as the other critics. Petit-Thouars states that it was harmful to California because it was composed of idlers accustomed to live off society, while Duflot de Mofras speaks of it as being composed of musicians, goldsmiths, dancers, plotters, and "adventurers of every character." Only one farm-

38. Forbes, *California*, p. 143.

er came, he laments.[39] As for recent historians, Hittel dismisses the colony as consisting "almost exclusively of the vagabond class; [they] were idle, thriftless and vicious; not much if any superior to the convicts with which California had already been repeatedly cursed." On the other hand, Hubert Howe Bancroft has been favorably disposed. "The truth is," he writes, "that the men were of a class far superior to any that had before been sent as settlers to California."[40] Irving Berdine Richmond also refers to the colonists as "substantial settlers."[41]

The only one of the colony's leaders to comment on the fitness of its members for its intended work is Juan Bandini, who takes exception to the criticisms of Alexander Forbes.

> The persons who came to California as colonists belonged in general to the artisan class so that there were carpenters, farm workers, silver smiths, tailors, shoemakers, hat makers, and others who, in spite of what is said, were to be and have been of service to the country. Mr. Forbes has unjustly found fault with the government's conduct in sending professors of the said trades to California, basing himself on the fact that *carpenters were sent where there was no furniture, tailors where the people do not know how to dress, shoemakers where they do not wear shoes etc.* If Mr. Forbes had been in California he would have learned that the great weak-

39. Dr. John Marsh to Commodore Catesby Jones, Nov. 25, 1842, BL, p. 5; dė Mofras, *Travels, 1*, 150.

40. Hittell, *History*, 2, 191–92; Bancroft, *California, 3*, 262.

41. Richman, *California*, p. 251. Further unfavorable comments on the abilities of the colonists, some of them clearly taken from Figueroa's *Manifiesto* or Forbes' book, may be found in the following: Vicente P. Gómez, "Lo que sabe sobre cosas de California," BL, p. 375; José Fernández, "Cosas de California," BL, p. 82; Alfred A. Green, "Life and Adventures of a 47'er of California," BL, p. 29; Alfred Robinson, *Life in California*, p. 167; Charles Wilkes, *Narrative of the United States Exploring Expedition, 5*, 163.

ness of the Californians, as far as the economy is concerned, is that they spend more on dress than they
should, and speaking respectively and proportionally, I
think that no country in the world will spend as much
on clothes as the Californians do. For the persons who
have some means it would be not merely shameful but
dishonorable to go out with mended or patched trousers,
jacket or any other piece of clothing, and they would
give up their food in order to be well dressed. California
is not, therefore, in the savage state that may be supposed and its inhabitants are, to a superlative degree, interested in [dressing] properly and in good taste.

Bandini also comments upon the fact that Forbes followed
Figueroa's *Manifiesto* "without realizing that [Figueroa] was
talking to vindicate himself and at a place where he alone
had the power."[42]

Actually, Figueroa's criticisms were not leveled at any
moral failings that he observed amongst the colonists. Indeed, he remarks at one point in his *Manifiesto* that although
its members lacked the qualities that would have made it a
good colony, this was "not because of any defect in its individual [members] but because of the ignorance and malice
of its Directors, who only sought in the enterprise a pretext
for enriching themselves at the expense of the neophytes of
the California missions and of the unfortunate colonists,
who allowed themselves to be deceived by the false promises
and fantastic pictures of prosperity with which they deluded
them to make them decide to march to this country."[43]
Many of the colony's later critics, who found the basis for
their comments in Figueroa's *Manifiesto,* went in fact a good
deal further in their unfavorable judgments than he did.

In view of the general criticism of the skills represented in
the membership of the colony, it is necessary to consider the

42. Bandini, "Historia," BL, pp. 148, 160.
43. Figueroa, *Manifiesto,* p. 113.

original report on the subject submitted by Híjar to Figueroa on November 8, 1834. If the trades represented on Híjar's list are classified under workers connected with agriculture and food processing, it will be noted that some 29 percent of the colonists fell into this important category, most of these being listed as farmhands. The second largest group of workers might be classified under the title of garment workers, and they made up over 27 percent of the total. This would be surprising indeed were it not for Bandini's explanation that the Californians were inordinately fond of dressing up. The third most important category in Híjar's list is what might be called today men in the building and allied trades, who constituted about 25 percent of the colony. A fourth category of considerable importance for California is composed of those in the medical arts, who made up nearly 7 percent of the total. The above classifications account for 88 percent of the people mentioned in Híjar's list.[44] The remainder of the group consisted of seven silversmiths, a pilot, a musician, and two printers. The number of silversmiths would seem too high and may have reflected a state of unemployment among the trade in Mexico, rather than a demand for their services in California. The services to be rendered by a pilot do not need further discussion. Nobody, presumably, would object to the inclusion of the musician. Híjar is credited with being a musician himself and may have had something to do with including him. One of the two printers is known to have been Pepe de la Rosa, or more formally José de la Rosa, who came to California with his wife María Dolores. A fellow

44. The list is as follows. In the first category were 19 farmhands, 1 surveyor, 1 horticulturist, 1 vineyard worker, 1 distiller, 1 wine bag maker, 1 pork butcher, 1 candymaker, 1 Italian pasta maker, 2 blacksmiths, 2 saddlemakers. The second category included 8 tailors, 12 seamstresses, 5 shoemakers, 2 hatmakers, 1 trimmings maker, 1 reboso, or shawl, maker. Under the third category were the following: 8 carpenters, 11 painters, 5 tinsmiths, 1 machinist, 1 smelter, 1 carriagemaker. The fourth included: 2 doctors, 1 surgeon, 1 midwife, 1 apothecary, 2 barbers. Censo de población, Nov. 8, 1834, BL, State Papers, 2, 187.

colonist states that José de la Rosa was a printer by profession and also a relative of Colonel Padrés.[45] It is known that José de la Rosa worked in Zamorano's print shop, for he assisted Zamorano in printing Figueroa's *Manifiesto*. It is somewhat ironic that one of the artisans whose skills Figueroa held in such low esteem in California should have helped to print his tirade on the colony. In addition to being a printer, José de la Rosa seems to have had some skill as a musician and a tailor, and in 1844 he and his wife are credited with opening a shop at Sonoma selling wine and liquor. In 1845. he was an alcalde at Sonoma.[46]

While there is no question that the membership of the colony included two printers,[47] there is some question as to whether they brought a printing press with them. After all, it might well be asked, what are printers going to do if they

45. Abrego, "Documentos," Archivo de Mariano G. Vallejo, BL, *31,* 417. That he was a printer by profession is confirmed by Juan B. Alvarado ("Memoirs," BL, 2, 239). It is to be noted that George L. Harding, in his life of Agustín Zamorano, does not mention José de la Rosa. Harding states that Zamorano was not a printer by trade and that there is no indication that he had printing experience before he came to California. (Harding, *Don Agustín V. Zamorano, Statesman, Soldier, Craftsman, and California's First Printer* [Los Angeles, 1934], p. 199). Actually, there is some indication that Zamorano had had some printing experience, for Juan B. Alvarado says that "in his youth he had learned to be a compositor" (Alvarado, "Memoirs," BL, 2, 238). On the other hand there is no indication that Zamorano ever made a profession out of his interest in printing. Perhaps José de la Rosa and his unnamed printer colleague in the colony should be rescued from oblivion and credited with being the first professional printers in California. Zamorano may be given his due by allowing him to assume the titles of California's first amateur printer and first publisher.

46. Alvarado, "Memoirs," BL, p. 239; Juan N. Padilla to José de la Rosa, July 17, 1845, Leidesdorff Papers, Huntington Library, San Marino (cited hereafter as LP); Bancroft, *California, 3,* 263, 289, *5,* 704; Francis, "An Economic and Social History of Mexican California," p. 200.

47. The first mention of the printers is in Alexander Forbes, *California,* p. 143. This book seems to have been completed by Oct. 22, 1835, although it was not printed until 1839.

have no printing press? Using typographical comparisons, Harding has proven that the press on which the first pamphlet was printed in California came from Boston on the *Lagoda* consigned to Zamorano, and it may have arrived at Monterey in June 1834. This press was in operation in July of that year, before the arrival of the colony. Although Harding does not use it, there is evidence from a contemporary, Juan B. Alvarado, which confirms that the press came from Boston and was ordered by Zamorano. On the basis of his findings, Harding disputes the contention of Duflot de Mofras that the printers in the colony brought a small press with them and that this was the first press to be brought to California. If the colony brought along a press it was clearly not the first one to reach California, but can it be demonstrated that they did not bring such a press? Harding does not attempt to do this, although his rejection of Duflot de Mofras' statement is a general one that does not permit any exceptions to be made. The question might perhaps be dismissed entirely if it were not for the fact that a contemporary in California, José Fernández, also says that the colonists brought a small printing press with them.[48] If they did bring such a press, it is not known what happened to it, unless it went down with the *Natalia*.

While it cannot be said how well this colony of printers, agriculturists, builders, garment makers, and others would have fared as pioneers on the northern frontiers of California, it is evident that Governor Figueroa preferred not to let them test their mettle by trying it out. Furthermore, it ill behooves the governor to criticize them for being artisans, when his own instructions from the Mexican government recommended that he take skilled workmen such as hatters, tailors, and shoemakers with him "even though they might be con-

48. Harding, *Zamorano*, pp. 180, 193; Alvarado, "Memoirs," BL, p. 238; de Mofras, *Travels, 1,* 150; José Fernández, "Cosas de California," BL, p. 82.

victs."[49] Finally, as will be pointed out, Figueroa's picture of a colony composed of delicate young men and young girls and women unable to stand the rigors of farm work suddenly changes after he hears about the revolt at Los Angeles on March 7, 1835. From then on the colony is composed of potentially dangerous men, ready to overturn the government by force.

49. Hittell, *History*, 2, 161.

Chapter Nine

The Colony Dispersed

Híjar learned from Governor Figueroa on March 4, 1835, that the colony was to be dispersed, but he stayed a day or two longer in San Francisco before leaving for San Francisco Solano. Figueroa left before him for Santa Clara, on his way back to Monterey. Meanwhile Figueroa had immediately written to Ensign Vallejo at San Francisco Solano about the new developments, letting him know that he had given orders that those colonists who wanted to leave San Francisco Solano should be given assistance and transportation. He added that he was giving 2,000 pesos in effects to Híjar, who was going to distribute them to the colonists. Figueroa reached Santa Clara on March 9 anxious to know, as he admitted to Vallejo, what had happened on Híjar's arrival at San Francisco Solano.

Figueroa told Vallejo that he had no fears of anything occurring, but he wanted to have the colonists peacefully settled there so that the difficulties confronting them could be overcome. He recommended that Vallejo "protect in every way possible those [colonists] who decide to stay [at San Francisco Solano], especially the foreigners and native Californians who have joined the colony. For now that they can see that they are free to select the place where they wish to live, I think many will decide to stay with you." At this point, in other words, Figueroa was hoping that the colonists might remain with Vallejo and make a success of their northern settlement under his auspices. On the other hand, the governor evidently had some doubts about what Colonel Padrés might do, for he asked Vallejo to be sure to tell him how Padrés received the news that the colony was to be dispersed. He also particularly enjoined upon him that if there was anyone who knew about or who would make a declaration about the "subversive projects" planned by Padrés, he was to take down a formal written statement. Such a document would be a protection for both Vallejo and Figueroa, either against the possible threat of danger or against the falsehoods spread by the leaders of the colony who, "when they are unable to seize the government by force, have recourse to calumny to persecute us."[1]

In spite of his closing injunction to Vallejo to "live cautiously," there is nothing in this letter to suggest that he was aware of any widespread conspiracy to remove him from power, or indeed that he was particularly perturbed over the way his plans were working out. He continued on his way to Monterey on March 10, stopping at San Juan Bautista before he reached his destination. It was here, on March 13, that a special messenger reached him with the alarming news that on March 7 a revolt against the territorial government had broken out at Los Angeles in which one of the colonists, a doctor named Francisco Torres, was involved. Torres had been commissioned by Híjar to take important documents to the government in Mexico.[2] He had left Monterey for Los Angeles, probably sometime in February, with a Spanish clerk named Antonio Apalátegui, who had asked Governor Figueroa for a position but had been turned down. Dr. Torres, a young man of twenty-nine, was from Guadalajara,

---

1. Figueroa to Vallejo, Mar. 4, 6, 9, 1835, BL, Cowan.
2. Figueroa, *Manifiesto*, p. 159.

Híjar's home town. The state of Jalisco had made use of his services as a physician in 1831, and he had taught physiology, hygiene, and general pathology at the Institute of Public Instruction of Jalisco. As secretary of this institution, he signed a statement in August 1831 to the effect that a student by the name of Francisco Híjar was moderately proficient in figures. Francisco Híjar may perhaps have been José María Híjar's son. In July 1833 Torres wrote a long letter to the official government paper of Mexico City, El Telégrafo, on precautions that might be taken against Asiatic cholera. It is possible that he was invited to write this letter by Vice-President Gómez Farías, also a physician and likewise from Guadalajara.[3] With connections such as these, it is not surprising that the young physician was recruited for service with the colony.

The first intimation that a revolt might be brewing at Los Angeles and that Torres and some visiting Sonorans were involved in the affair came in a letter dated March 3 from Colonel Gutiérrez at San Gabriel. Gutiérrez assigned a man to keep a watch on Torres and informed Governor Figueroa that if he came across any other information confirming what he already knew, he would arrest Torres and draw up charges against him. For about a week before the revolt began it seems to have been an open secret in Los Angeles that it was brewing.[4]

Early on the morning of Saturday, March 7, sounds of shouting and firing of guns announced the beginning of the revolution, which lasted until about three o'clock that afternoon. A band of some fifty newcomers to California from Sonora, led by Juan Gallardo, a shoemaker and carpenter,

3. *Gaceta del Gobierno del Estado Libre de Jalisco,* Mar. 29, 1831, Sept. 2, 1831; BL, Departmental State Papers, Benicia, 5, 4; *Memoria* of Governor of Jalisco, 1832; *El Telégrafo,* July 7, 1833.

4. Gutiérrez to Figueroa, Mar. 3, 1835, BL, Departmental State Papers, 4, 8; BL, Departmental State Papers, Benicia, 5, Miscellaneous 1821–46, pp. 209, 211, 213, 214, 217.

and Felip Castillo, a cigar maker and merchant, seized some weapons and marched on the town hall. They presented a *plan,* or statement of their grievances, which the hastily summoned city council considered and refused to support, whereupon the Sonorans turned over to the authorities the two men they accused of being responsible for getting them involved, Apalátegui and Torres. The *plan,* which Apalátegui said he wrote down, following the ideas of Gallardo, was principally aimed at the administration of Governor Figueroa, against whom it leveled various accusations.[5] It alleged that he had not put into effect a number of orders sent to him by the federal government to improve the lot of the inhabitants of California; he had exceeded his powers by illegally joining together again the civil and military control of the territory; he had made a scandalous commercial monopoly out of mission products by the secularization law; and he disposed of the soldiers' pay as he wanted, without consulting the revenue officials. In its turn, the Deputation was accused of exceeding its powers by drawing up secularization regulations. As for the missions, they were described as rushing headlong to their ruin because of the steps that had been taken to confine the natives (just what was meant by this is not clear) and to distribute mission property. Finally, some of the commissioners were accused of building up their own interests at the expense of the missions, either because they had no knowledge of how to manage businesses of this kind or because they were dishonest. To right these wrongs, the *plan* set forth six articles. (1) Governor Figueroa was declared to be an officer "unworthy of public confidence" who should be removed. Provisional control of the civil governorship was to be given to the first alcalde of the Monterey City Council, and Captain Pablo de la Portilla, the highest ranking military officer, was to be

5. Figueroa, *Manifiesto,* p. 129; Bancroft, *California, 3,* 281–84; BL, Departmental State Papers, Benicia, *5,* 191, 222.

comandante general. (2) The Deputation's regulations for the administration of the missions were to be made null and void. (3) The missionaries were to take exclusive control of mission temporalities as they had before, and the commissioners were to hand over to them their account books. (4) Article three was not to interfere with the powers of the director of colonization to act in accordance with his instructions from the supreme government. (5) The *plan* was to be subject to approval by the government. (6) The forces who had "pronounced," as the expression in Mexico at that time went, would not lay down their arms until the above articles had been put into effect, and they concluded their rebellious statement by the customary remark that they would safeguard the honest administration of justice and protect the authorities.

This *plan,* which was typical of those all too prevalent in the Mexico of the day, was designed, like modern political platforms, to appeal to as many people as possible. Those who wanted separation of civilian and military power were to have their desires fulfilled. Merchants (presumably foreigners) who disliked the way in which the governor was organizing the sale of mission products were to find redress. Others whose desires were to be taken into consideration were the soldiers, the missionaries, and the director of colonization, who was to be given the power to go ahead with his instructions from the government. In spite of the resentments present in San Diego and other southern California localities against control from Monterey, the *plan* fell through. No one came forward to support it, and the Sonorans, apparently penniless adventurers, quickly backed out and handed over Torres and Apalátegui to the authorities.

The whole affair seems to have been unusually crude and badly managed. The *plan* was filled with inconsistencies, such as returning the temporalities to the missionaries and at the same time giving the director of colonization the right to proceed with his instructions, which would mean taking over all mission property. But Governor Figueroa nonetheless took it very seriously and spent some twelve pages of his *Manifiesto* in a detailed analysis of its defects. The reason for Figueroa's concern, perhaps, was not so much that he was in any great fear of the outbreak's recurring as that he thought it provided him at last with his long-sought proof that the leaders of the colony were conspiring against him. The account of the revolt in Figueroa's *Manifiesto* points to the colonist Dr. Torres as the author of the *plan,* and at one point Figueroa even refers to "Torres' revolution."[6]

The actual workings of the conspiracy that led to the revolt are obscure, and the records of the trial are neither sufficiently ample nor clear enough to provide much light. The Sonorans seem to have been living at the Los Nietos ranch, although there is no indication as to what they were doing. The owner of the ranch (also known as Rancho Santa Gertrudes) was Josefa Cota, widow of Antonio María Nieto, one of the sons of Manuel Nieto, whose vast domain had been divided up by Governor Figueroa in 1833 among his heirs. In this mysterious transaction Juan José Nieto, another son, obtained the lion's share of the original estate, and Governor Figueroa later received from him the 26,000-acre ranch of Los Alamitos for so small a sum that he was considered to have been bribed by Juan José Nieto to arrange the award in his favor. If there was ill feeling within the Nieto family over this transaction, as there may well have been, it is possible the owner of Los Nietos was not out of sympathy with the plotting against Figueroa that was apparently going on in Los Angeles. As a matter of fact, a good deal of the plotting seems to have taken place at Los Nietos.[7] However this may be, one of the Sonorans was arrested for an unspecified reason, and the rumor began to circulate that the alcalde, Fran-

6. Figueroa, *Manifiesto,* pp. 131–33, 134–46.

7. Robert Glass Cleland, *The Cattle on a Thousand Hills: Southern California 1850–1870* (San Marino, 1941), pp. 12–13; BL, Departmental State Papers, Benicia, pp. 204, 214, 223, 229, 232.

cisco Javier Alvarado, had a list of men whom he was going to arrest which included Juan Gallardo. Also said to be included on the alcalde's list of wanted men were Apalátegui and Torres, and this may have given them a fellow feeling for the Sonorans. According to Apalátegui, Gallardo and the Sonorans were opposed to Governor Figueroa's secularization of the missions because after they had been secularized they were unable to obtain provisions from them. It appears that both Apalátegui and the Sonorans thought there would be support forthcoming from the residents of Los Angeles and from the city council for a revolt against Governor Figueroa. There is no question that Apalátegui joined the revolt, although he denied taking a leading part or promoting it. Torres, on the other hand, denied that he had taken part in it. Later, at Monterey, a witness testified that Torres had tried in a guarded fashion to persuade him and others at Los Angeles to join a plot. An attempt was made through this witness to prove that Híjar and others had an understanding with the plotters, but although this failed, Figueroa reported that "nobody in the Territory doubted it, public opinion unanimously affirms it."

On April 16, 1835, while the trial was still going on, the news came that Governor Figueroa had pardoned everyone involved in the case except Apalátegui and Torres. Regino de la Mora, Torres' counsel, who had come to California with the colony to be secretary to Híjar and now resided in Los Angeles, declared in a strong statement that if justice had been done, Torres would be a free man, exonerated from the accusation made against him. "But unfortunately," he added, "on this occasion justice has yielded to circumstances and the law has remained silent."[8]

The available evidence would hardly seem to offer sufficient corroboration for Governor Figueroa's view that Torres was the leading figure in the revolt. Nevertheless, from the

8. BL, Departmental State Papers, Benicia, pp. 191–242, 267; Bancroft, *California*, 3, 285, n. 19; Figueroa, *Manifiesto*, pp. 171–72.

very day that he learned of the revolt and before he had more than a sketchy outline of the movement, Governor Figueroa assumed that Torres was responsible. "At last," he wrote Híjar—almost, it would seem, with a sense of relief —"the revolution that Don Francisco Torres went to promote has broken out." And later he asserted that the evidence showed Torres was the "immediate agent" of the revolt. What was more, because Torres was a member of the colony, the colony's leaders were suspect. Figueroa at once sent a series of orders to Vallejo at San Francisco Solano. "As soon as you receive this," ran one of them, "you will see that the persons of Don Francisco Berduzco and Don Romualdo Lara are secured aboard the Frigate *Rosa,* whose captain and supercargo you will ask for help in the name of the nation, so that they may be transported to Monterey and remain prisoners on board at the disposition of this government." In his letter Figueroa informed Híjar, that he and Padrés were no longer directors of colonization, and they were both to turn over to Vallejo all their weapons, ammunition, property, and everything else they had in their charge. They were to leave immediately, at the orders of Vallejo, to return to Mexico, where they would have to answer for the charges against them as a result of their conduct since they landed in California.[9] In separate instructions, Figueroa told Vallejo not to take action against Híjar and Padrés until he (Vallejo) had collected their arms; then he was to see that they were at once embarked aboard ship, so they would not have time to cause trouble.

Governor Figueroa partly excused the abrupt nature of his actions, based only on suspicion, by alleging that he had long known that such a plot was afoot. He wrote Híjar that he had warned him, in an amicable fashion, that his friends wanted to cause trouble by deceiving the government. Despite

9. Figueroa, *Manifiesto,* pp. 157–58, 162; Figueroa to Vallejo, Mar. 13, 1835, BL, Cowan; Figueroa to Vallejo, San Juan Bautista, Mar. 13, 1835, BL, Cowan.

359

a prior warning of what was going to happen, Figueroa went on, he had kept silent because he did not want to be considered violent.[10] But now that his enemies had revealed themselves, he had acted. Later on, when he wrote his *Manifiesto* (probably during the months of June, July, and August 1835) Figueroa went further. He alleged that when Torres had come to him for a passport to go to Los Angeles, Figueroa had given him one without any objections, although he "knew that the object of his journey was to go to Los Angeles on the pretext of finding a passage on some ship, [but really] to start a revolution there." He knew what the colonists were doing, Figueroa stated elsewhere in his *Manifiesto,* but he was waiting until "they revealed their crime more publicly or backed down." In spite of the good will he showed toward them, however, he was never able to make them recant and he thought that perhaps they took his moderation for weakness.[11] In his own view, Figueroa had been treating the colony leaders with consideration, but now that they had shown their hand in the revolt at Los Angeles, he wrote Vallejo, there would be no more need for patience.[12]

In further justification of his actions in seizing the leaders of the colony on suspicion that they were involved in the Los Angeles revolt, Figueroa alleged that they had been secretly plotting the ruin of the territory ever since they landed. Nor had the failure of the revolt at Los Angeles stopped them: like "advocates of anarchy," he exclaimed, "they do nct cease to preach disorder and I shall not lose sight of their liberticidal plans." The ramifications of the revolt went far beyond Los Angeles, he continued; in fact, the entire idea of establishing a colony was but a pretext. The leaders of the colony "wanted to organize a force with which to support their pretensions. For this reason they

10. Figueroa to Vallejo, Mar. 13, 1835, BL, Cowan; not the same letter as in n. 9 above from San Juan Bautista.

11. Figueroa, *Manifiesto*, pp. 115, 155.

12. Figueroa to Vallejo, Mar. 13, 1835, BL, Cowan.

brought from Mexico a supply of rifles and cartridges which the government gave them." And Híjar's reason for going north to San Francisco Solano, ostensibly to unite the colony, was actually to start a revolt there.

It was perhaps at this point that Figueroa began to think his previous reasons for ordering the dispersal of the colony were not sufficiently convincing. Having demonstrated that the colony was composed of young girls, women, and delicate young men, who because of their "natural incapacity" could not found a new town, he now began to argue that they formed an armed force aiming at taking over the territorial government.[13] Ignoring the obvious contradictions in his new line of reasoning, he explained to the minister of relations at the end of March that he had ordered the colony dispersed because it was too dangerous to unite. "When I ordered this measure," he wrote, "I only proposed to avoid the reuniting of men who wanted to deceive the government. For, as I came to see, they were proposing to cause an alarm at several places on the same day, and San Francisco Solano was to be the headquarters. So it was that I had to issue these orders on [March] 4 and on the 7th the revolt broke out in this town [Los Angeles], which is about 600 miles away from San Francisco Solano. This event proves the foresight with which I acted."[14]

If Governor Figueroa had not previously made such a point of emphasizing the weakness and incapacity of the colonists, over half of whom were women and children, his new argument that they were a potentially dangerous armed force might have been more convincing. One of the colonists revealed another weakness in Figueroa's new theory: "If," he wrote, "the intentions and plans [of the directors of the colony] were hostile, they would have been able to carry out their plans at less cost, and with greater security, if they had

13. Figueroa, *Manifiesto*, pp. 114, 116, 151, 153–54.
14. Figueroa to Ministro de Relaciones, Mar. 31, 1835, BL, Colonización y terrenos baldíos, Fomento, legajo 6, expediente 167.

brought along a force of military men instead of good family men of intelligence with some knowledge of the sciences and the arts."[15]

Neither of Governor Figueroa's arguments for dispersing the colony was convincing, and to make matters worse, they were contradictory. But he was not so much concerned with the colony as a whole—most of the colonists, he admitted, were not involved in the conspiracy—as he was with its leaders.[16] If he could have made a good case for Híjar's involvement in the Los Angeles revolt, he would have gone far to prove his point. His indictment of Híjar, however, while energetically advanced, carries little or no weight. He begins by saying that Híjar "in spite of his apparent modesty, was unable to conceal the part he played in these movements." Unfortunately, he does not say what this part was. He attempts to show that Híjar was very close to Torres. "Who in Monterey," he says, "did not know that Torres was a favorite of Híjar's?" And he continues by asking whether anyone doubted that Torres was one of Híjar's daily counselors. The fact that Híjar had entrusted Torres with letters for Mexico seemed to Figueroa sufficient evidence that he was a close friend of his.

Unable to establish guilt by association, Figueroa tried to get closer to the point:

> Whether Señor Híjar decidedly protected the revolution or whether he served as a blind instrument for its authors, the fact is his adherence to it was sensed, and after I realized, in friendly intercourse and in various ways, his attachment to my enemies, I could have no further confidence in him. For even doing him the favor

15. According to one of Híjar's lists, the makeup of the colony was: 99 men, 55 women, 50 children (Censo de población, Nov. 8, 1834, BL, State Papers, Missions and Colonization, 2, 187); Coronel, "Cosas de California," BL, pp. 17–18.

16. Figueroa to Ministro de Relaciones, Mar. 31, 1835, BL, Colonización y terrenos baldíos, Fomento, legajo 6, expediente 167.

of believing him to be innocent of the scheming of his creatures, he is so insensitive and apathetic that his own existence would be a matter of indifference to him.

In spite of his lack of evidence that Híjar or the other leaders of the colony, except for Torres, were in any way involved in the Los Angeles revolt, Figueroa felt that he could not wait until further evidence was collected against them before he struck. Even when a lawsuit is instituted, he remarks, "it is difficult to prove exactly the secret crimes of revolutionaries," and meanwhile they are waiting for the right moment to strike.[17] For these reasons he acted when he did. It was after he had seized his men that he began to look around eagerly for the necessary evidence to convict them.

After firing off a broadside of peremptory orders to Vallejo at San Francisco Solano as soon as he heard of the disturbances at Los Angeles, Figueroa continued on his way from San Juan Bautista to Monterey. He informed Vallejo that he was going on south himself as soon as he could because he was afraid that Bandini might cause trouble in San Diego. At Monterey on March 16, Figueroa issued a public proclamation to the inhabitants of California, informing them of the revolt at Los Angeles and alleging that the leaders of the colony, "Híjar, Padrés, Torres, Berduzco and others," were responsible. They were trying, he said, to spread to the peaceful shores of California the civil war that had raged in Mexico.[18] He also announced that he had decided to resign from his position of governor, and the Deputation had requested that a successor be sent out. One of the results of Figueroa's proclamation was to scatter the seeds of resentment and hatred of the colony, and indeed of Mexicans in general, throughout California.

As he marched rapidly down the coast to make sure that no further disorder occurred in Los Angeles, Governor

17. Figueroa, *Manifiesto*, pp. 155–57, 171.
18. Figueroa to Vallejo, Mar. 13, 1835, BL, Cowan. Figueroa, *Manifiesto*, pp. 151–54.

Figueroa received a number of letters from Vallejo keeping him informed of events at San Francisco Solano. Vallejo disarmed the colonists on Monday, March 16, at 4 P.M., and the following day escorted Berduzco and Lara on board the Sardinian ship *Rosa*. He did not mention whether he had also sent Híjar and Padrés on board the *Rosa* that day, but in due course they were put on board, where they were considered under arrest. Vallejo picked up some forty-one rifles, three boxes of cartridges, and a few other odds and ends of weapons—surprisingly few to the mind of General Figueroa. Only twenty-five of the rifles were in good working order.

Figueroa, from San Luis Obispo, warned Vallejo not to lose sight of their enemies and reminded him of the saying that "bodily ills, like natural ones, are best cured by plucking them out by the roots." He told him that the revolutionaries were not getting any support from the Californians, who had begun to hate all of them. After ordering Vallejo to be sure that Híjar and Padrés were also placed on board the *Rosa*, Figueroa said that none of the prisoners on the ship was to be allowed to touch land until they reached San Blas. If they wished to embark their families and baggage they were to be permitted to do so. He informed Vallejo that he had asked the captain of the *Rosa* to keep the prisoners on his ship, if he did not want to take them to San Blas, until Figueroa could find another vessel to transport them. Figueroa also ordered Vallejo to send two other men aboard the *Rosa*: Rafael Padrés, Colonel Padrés' brother, and Ignacio Coronel, the schoolmaster. "If in addition to these," Figueroa added, "you know of others who may have decided in favor of revolutionary ideas, have them put on the ship too, so that only those who have conducted themselves with prudence and good sense remain in the Territory."[19]

Figueroa pushed on to Los Angeles, which he reached on

19. Figueroa to Vallejo, Mar. 21, Apr. 4, 1835, BL, Cowan; Bancroft, *California*, 3, 287; Mariano Vallejo, "Documentos para la historia de California," BL, 23, documento 4.

March 28, and found everything peaceful. On March 27 Vallejo wrote him that all of the men were on board the *Rosa* except Ignacio Coronel, who had started off for Monterey by land. It was apparently at Los Angeles that Figueroa received a letter from Híjar, written the day following the disarming of the colonists. In bitter tones, Híjar told Figueroa that the revolt at Los Angeles seemed to him purely imaginary. "I shall never be able to persuade myself," he began, "that Señor Torres, who was travelling with important documents for the Supreme Government, would undertake to start a revolution, without any object, in a country where he has no connections or acquaintances." "I see in all this," he went on, "nothing more than a mystery that time will clear up. If the mask has been pulled off for you it is still obscure enough for me. But I hope that it will soon be torn aside, that things will appear as they actually are and that everything will be revealed as clearly as the light of day." Híjar presented his own theory about the revolt. "I must suppose," he said, "that some hot-headed and justly resentful colonists may have wanted to revolt; but I do not see why this should have anything to do with me, as if I had urged them on or taken part in the revolution." By trying to stain his reputation, went on Híjar, Figueroa had wounded him to the quick. "You have tried to make me appear guilty of crimes or faults I have certainly never committed," he wrote, "but I solemnly swear that I shall drag my persecutor, whoever he may be, before the competent courts where I shall demand due satisfaction." He reminded Figueroa that he had only stayed on in California because Figueroa himself, the Deputation, and other persons had repeatedly begged him to do so. Figueroa also knew, Híjar continued, that he was to leave the territory within a few days and therefore had no interest in continuing to direct the colony. He was saying this, Híjar added, so that Figueroa should understand that he was not distressed because he was no longer to be in charge of the colony, but because of the insulting manner in which he was being removed.

He had been proud of the fact that he had served several governments to their satisfaction and was well known for his services in the interior of Mexico. "If I did not expect to vindicate myself," he said, "I would rather shoot myself than drag out a life of disgrace, an object of scorn in the eyes of my fellows."

Híjar concluded his letter by attacking the methods Figueroa had used in dealing with him and the other colonists. Figueroa had no power to suspend him from his position, he declared, and the colonists had suffered "unheard-of outrages." They had been treated scandalously, worse than if they had been a band of outlaws. The imprescriptible rights of man, guaranteed by the Constitution, had been violently attacked. If Señor Vallejo had asked him for the weapons and ammunition, he would have given them up without there being any need to push anybody around. But in his opinion these arbitrary methods had been used on purpose, and the colonists had been treated like fugitives from justice rather than Mexicans.

At the time that he received this letter, Figueroa limited himself to saying that he would like to reply to Híjar in the courts. He also instructed Vallejo to be sure to collect a good dossier of information on the revolutionary preparations that had been made at San Francisco Solano. "Otherwise," he said, "they will slander me by calling me a despot." Also, he pointed out, it was essential to provide support for the reason he gave for suspending their positions. Later, when he came to write his *Manifiesto,* in which he printed Híjar's letter, he commented on it at greater length. After dismissing part of it as hypocrisy, Figueroa remarked that Híjar would never be able to persuade the Californians that he had not taken part in the revolt at Los Angeles. He then stated that the judges of the court could hardly be other than favorable to the man (Governor Figueroa) who had "saved the integrity of the Republic." He denied that Híjar had been asked to stay in California, although earlier in the

Manifiesto he stated the opposite. In a curious reference to what he termed Híjar's "anglomania," Figueroa called Híjar's threat to shoot himself a cowardly action.[20]

It would appear from Híjar's letter that he assumed that he, Padrés, Lara, and Berduzco were being removed from San Francisco Solano because of their alleged complicity in the revolt at Los Angeles. Figueroa apparently felt, however, that the center of conspiracy was where these men happened to be, namely San Francisco Solano. His action in having them quickly put on board the *Rosa* was a preventive one to make sure that nothing happened in the north. Indeed, if Figueroa and Vallejo had had clear evidence that a plot was being hatched at San Francisco Solano, their position would have been strengthened.

In considering this question, it may be noted first of all that when Figueroa instructed Vallejo to disarm the colonists on March 13, he also told him to move on with his men to San Francisco as soon as he had taken care of the four leaders —Híjar, Padrés, Berduzco, and Lara—because "there will be nothing to fear at San Francisco Solano after having secured [these] individuals." Later, when these men were arrested aboard the *Rosa*, Figueroa urged Vallejo to gather, in legal fashion, all the evidence he could find against them at San Francisco Solano, especially "the preparations they were observed to be making and the sedition they tried to spread among the Indians." Figueroa was still writing to Vallejo in April, May, and June asking him to get this evidence down in the correct legal form.[21]

Documents on the alleged conspiracy in the north are

20. Figueroa to Vallejo, Los Angeles, Mar. 30, Apr. 4, 1835, BL, Cowan; Híjar to Figueroa, Mar. 17, 1835, De la Guerra, "Documentos," BL, 5, 107; Figueroa, *Manifiesto,* pp. 159, 161, 163–64. His statement *(Manifiesto,* p. 96) was, "We begged [Híjar] to put aside his resentment and stay with us in good harmony."

21. Figueroa to Vallejo, Mar. 13, 31, Apr. 5, May 22, June 12, 1835, BL, Cowan.

scanty, but according to Vallejo there was no doubt about its existence. He wrote in his memoirs that Figueroa's accusation that Híjar was involved in attempts to disturb the peace was "abundantly proved," for he himself, in his official capacity, had managed to intercept some secret correspondence of a highly suspicious nature [22] Unfortunately, he did not produce this correspondence or reveal anything more about it. On the other hand, he did not hesitate to make strong accusations against the colonists and their leaders. He said that the arrival at San Francisco Solano of Híjar, Berduzco, and Lara had caused great excitement and brought more open talk about seizing the garrison. He had himself heard such a plan discussed. On March 5, Lara, Berduzco, and some of the other colonists (Híjar had not yet arrived) met in Padrés' house at 11 P.M. to agree upon a way of overcoming the guard. After a long discussion, which Vallejo claims to have heard, it was decided to strike through the church. Vallejo thereupon put his men on the alert and took what precautions he could against such an attack. He waited for nine days and then received Figueroa's special message about the revolt at Los Angeles. According to Vallejo, the coming of the messenger made the conspirators decide to take action. They were handing out their weapons on March 16 when he surprised them and disarmed them. Vallejo added an unusual touch to his story by saying that Padrés' wife had exclaimed she was glad that Vallejo had caught them before they had done anything, and perhaps they would now calm down. Vallejo also stated that the colonists at San Francisco Solano had spent their time plotting and trying to win over the Indians instead of getting to work. Lara and Berduzco, he declared, had spent the 2,000 pesos the colony had received from Figueroa on presents for the Indians.[23]

22. Vallejo, "Recuerdos," p. 350.
23. Vallejo to Figueroa, Apr. 15, 1835, BL, Cowan; Vallejo, "Documentos para la historia de California," BL, 3, pt. 1, no. 28; Bancroft, *California, 3,* 289, n. 28.

Vallejo did not say how he managed to overhear the conspirators making their plans at Padrés' house, and his account of this crucial affair is so brief it seems to lack authenticity. Another version of the uncovering of the alleged plot at Sonoma related by Charles Brown, the American who joined the colony and was at Sonoma with them for a few days, is that two of the colonists, Antonio Ortega, and the printer José de la Rosa, informed Vallejo of what was afoot. Brown describes Ortega as a rough, boisterous fellow whom Vallejo "could have got to kill a man for a trifle. He was a tool of Vallejo to the last day of his life." If Ortega was indeed the source of the information, further corroborative evidence would appear to be imperative. Vallejo himself declared that José de la Rosa had not told him about the plot.[24]

How accurate Vallejo's statements are it is hard to say. Certainly they require more confirmation before they can be given much weight. It must also be remembered that they are contradicted flatly by statements made by two of the colonists at San Francisco Solano, Agustín Janssens and Antonio Franco Coronel. Coronel was a young lad of sixteen at the time; his father, Ignacio Coronel, was the schoolteacher whom Figueroa ordered sent on board the *Rosa,* presumably because he believed him connected with the conspiracy. After stating that because of his father's prominent position with the colony, he had an opportunity to know everything that was going on, Antonio Coronel denied that there was a conspiracy. "I am well satisfied," he declared, "that such a conspiracy did not exist." The colonists, he said, had all been busily engaged with their work and anxious to establish themselves on their land. Some of the principal members of the colony used to meet at his father's house at night, including Colonel Padrés, an old friend of his family, to amuse themselves by singing together and also to talk over their

24. Charles Brown, "Statement of Recollections," BL, pp. 9–10; Bancroft, *California, 3,* 289, n. 28.

plans for the colony. "Never," he stated, "was there any talk about conspiracy, nor indeed were the elements for such a thing present." Janssens, a young man of seventeen in 1834, left San Francisco Solano just before Vallejo disarmed the colonists. He related in his memoirs that he had spent three months there "without hope of progress, as the colonists were continually accused of plotting revolution (plots which I believe existed only in the fevered brains of their accusers)." In Janssens' view the conspiracy was between Governor Figueroa and Vallejo: "It seemed that there had been some plotting between Gen. Figueroa and Vallejo, all undercover and mysterious. Híjar and Padrés bore everything with patience." Whether some of the colonists were actually involved in a conspiracy at San Francisco Solano or were simply complaining out loud cannot be definitely established. The colonists had no great desire to stay there after their leaders had been expelled; seventeen of them left about March 20 for various places, including Santa Clara, San Juan Bautista, and Carmelo.[25]

Meanwhile the *Rosa,* with Híjar, Padrés, Berduzco, and Lara and their families—in all some twenty-five persons— was sailing down the coast. It was at Monterey on April 12 when Híjar wrote a letter to the first alcalde there. "Finding myself pursued, slandered, and deprived of my liberty against the constitution and laws," he said, he would like the alcalde to provide him with a written statement "according to the testimony of your conscience" of his public conduct during the time he lived in Monterey. He would like him to say in it whether he had heard that he (Híjar) had any revolutionary ideas. "The dark road of conspiracies," went on Híjar, "is not the path to glory, and I must justify myself against the slanders of which I have been accused. Life itself is despicable for me unless I can preserve my reputation untarnished, as

25. Coronel, "Cosas de California," BL, p. 12; Ellison and Price, *Life and Adventures of Janssens,* pp. 35, 37–38; BL, Departmental State Papers, Benicia Military, *79, 74.*

I have done with much effort for forty-two years." The *Rosa*
sailed on to Santa Barbara, which it reached on April 16.[26]
There the passengers were permitted to disembark but had
to stay within the limits of the town. It was there that final
testimony was taken from Berduzco on April 23. The *Rosa*
passengers probably remained at Santa Barbara until about
April 30, when they were put on board the *Loriot,* an American brigantine which Governor Figueroa had arranged
should take them to San Blas, stopping on the way at the port
of San Pedro, near Los Angeles, to pick up Apalátegui and
Torres. Lieutenant Buenaventura Araujo and the schoolteacher Mariano Bonilla were also to leave on the *Loriot,*
although Bonilla apparently did not go. The cost of sending
these men and their families back to Mexico was 4,000 pesos,
earmarked by Figueroa to "extraordinary expenses."[27]

The *Loriot* probably left Santa Barbara on May 1 and was
at San Pedro on May 9 when a final flurry arose. Figueroa
had ordered Colonel Nicolás Gutiérrez to obtain confessions
from some of the departing colonists on board the ship. A
legal statement of Padrés' crimes had arrived, and it required
signature by other persons and a confession by him. Gutiérrez made some arrangement with the captain by which those
who were to make their depositions might disembark in order
to do so with greater speed (the port was not a safe one).
Among these was Colonel Padrés. Several letters passed between Gutiérrez and Padrés, whereupon Gutiérrez wrote to
Figueroa that he did not think he would get a reply to his
last one, and he would have to send armed forces aboard,
presumably to oblige Padrés to disembark. Whether Padrés
did actually go ashore to make his statement is not revealed.

26. Híjar to Alcalde Primero Constitucional, Monterey, Apr. 12, 1835,
Huntington Library, MR191; Juan María Ibarra to Figueroa, Apr. 19,
1835, BL, Departmental State Papers, *4, 27.*

27. Berduzco Criminal, BC; agreement between Figueroa and A. B.
Thompson, Figueroa to Administrador de la Aduana, San Gabriel,
Apr. 11, 1835, both in BL, Departmental State Papers, *4, 25.*

In all probability Padrés, remembering Guerrero's fate, was actually in fear for his life. On May 8, the day before his difficulty with Gutiérrez, Padrés wrote a last letter to Governor Figueroa from aboard the *Loriot*. He had planned to write him from Monterey, protesting the illegality of the governor's action in deporting him and the scandalous way in which the colonists had been treated at San Francisco Solano; but when he was at the Dolores mission and saw Figueroa's "incendiary" proclamation to the people of California, he thought he had better not say anything. He kept quiet because in his view the proclamation, by making atrocious statements—such as the one that the supreme government had sent the colony to rob the Indians of their property —"arouses the hatred of the people against us and incites [them to] assassination by tacitly authorizing it." It would not have surprised him if some wretch had been paid to murder them, since no one had taken the hint from the proclamation. For this reason, he had said nothing while he was in California, but now that his ship was about to sail, he felt free from the imminent danger that had threatened him.

After solemnly protesting against Figueroa's proceedings, he said that they would still be illegal, despite the fact that Figueroa had informed him of the crime and told him who his accusers were, if the governor did not follow the prescribed legal methods in everything else. If he had committed a crime, went on Padrés, why had he not been given a trial, so that the appropriate punishment could be meted out to him? Also, why was no proper evidence collected? By what right was he being deprived of the special and important commission entrusted to him by the supreme government, and deported from the country in which he was supposed to exercise it? Or was it that they merely wanted to make him appear to be suspect, or dangerous to the public peace, by imagining the evidence? These considerations made Padrés feel it was clear that Figueroa had been determined to destroy the colony from the very first. His motives for this, Padrés went on, were "not as clear as day but nor were they as dark as night," and they were in any case extraordinarily harmful to the nation. Padrés pointed to the unfortunate colonists as victims of Figueroa, scattered and homeless. He concluded his letter by declaring that Figueroa had deliberately failed to provide funds to assist the transportation of his family; the colonel refused to accept the excuse that Figueroa had made to him in a recent communication.[28]

The *Loriot,* with its downhearted and disillusioned group of would-be colonists, left from San Pedro for San Blas about May 10. When they reached San Blas is not clear, but it may have been about May 25. It is likely they did not stay long in San Blas, which had a bad reputation from the health point of view. Híjar, at any rate, was in the better situated Tepic on his way to Mexico City when he wrote to the minister of relations. He included with his letter documents showing how the colony he had led to California was dissolved by General Figueroa.[29] As a result of this, he pointed out, the government's plan to protect the northern frontier had also come to naught. The colonists, he said, were in a desperate situation. They had not been able to settle down because of the hatred aroused against them by Governor Figueroa. They had shown unexpected patience and steadiness in their sufferings. Most of the families had reached the frontier close to the Russian establishments and to the Columbia River, but when it became apparent that the Governor was going to wage war against them, they decided to leave. Grief-stricken, they all left San Francisco Solano, abandoning the agricultural work they had begun there. Some of them even went on foot. Their condition when they reached Monterey was miserable, and all this was because of a revolt against Gov-

28. Gutiérrez to Figueroa, May 8, 9, 1835, and Padrés to Figueroa, on board the *Loriot,* May 8, 1835, BL, Departmental State Papers, *4,* pp. 33–34, 37, 39.

29. The documents, apparently copies of letters, are not available.

ernor Figueroa that had broken out six hundred miles away in which he was sure that none of them was involved to the slightest degree. He was particularly upset, he went on, "to see the distinction made between 7 or 8 foreigners who had joined the colony at San Francisco Solano, and the group of long-suffering and estimable Mexicans. The foreigners were allowed to keep their arms and were given all the consideration due to free men, whereas the Mexicans were forcibly disarmed and disgracefully insulted." If they distrusted the colony, went on Híjar indignantly, why did they not disarm everyone equally? Governor Figueroa, he said, had unleashed an unjust and inconceivable hatred against the Mexicans, and he had endeavored to make this hatred take root in the hearts of the Californians. He ended his letter by saying that he would soon be in Mexico City and would personally give the minister more details about the colony and the bad conduct of General Figueroa, who was, he concluded, "the sole origin of all the misfortunes of [the colony] and of the country's ills."[30]

What Híjar's reception was in Mexico City is not known, but the times were not propitious for a federalist and a supporter of Gómez Farías, at that time hiding for his life in Monclova while on his way to exile in New Orleans. Acting as interim president, while Santa Anna was at his estate of Manga de Clavo, was the honest and kindly General Miguel Barragán. But behind the scenes, Santa Anna continued to run the country, which was proceeding steadily toward centralism and the dominance of a wealthy aristocratic group in alliance with the upper clergy. Presumably Híjar made his way back to his home at Guadalajara, where he disappeared from sight until June 1845. At this time he came to Santa Barbara as a commissioner to give the blessing of the Mexican government to the new governor of California, Pío Pico, who

30. Híjar to Ministro de Relaciones, Tepic, May 27, 1835, BL, Colonización y terrenos baldíos, Fomento, legajo 6, expediente 171.

had been anything but friendly to him in 1834 or 1835. All was forgotten in 1845, however, and indeed Híjar had only been in California a few months when he died at Los Angeles on December 19, 1845. In his report on the matter to the government, Governor Pío Pico remarked that Los Angeles had striven to provide a dignified and stately funeral that would match the services that "so good a citizen" had rendered his country during his lifetime.[31]

When Híjar arrived at Tepic sometime in May 1835, he was undoubtedly bitter and disillusioned, but he did not seem to be in the financial difficulties that faced his colleague Colonel Padrés, who had his large family with him. Padrés was six months in arrears in his pay, and Figueroa had not paid for his return to Mexico. Before going to Guadalajara (where he managed to obtain one payment on his salary, which he used to continue on to Mexico City) Padrés wrote a long and bitter letter to the minister of war. Governor Figueroa, he alleged, had not only acted unconstitutionally, he was making money in California. After referring in general to weaknesses in Figueroa's secularization regulations, he pointed out how certain provisions in the taking of an inventory of mission property left the door open for abuse. Although cattle, he said, were the main source of wealth of the missions, Figueroa's instructions were that the number of cattle at each mission was simply to be estimated by two intelligent and honest persons because of a lack of horses and because of the large herds involved, which would make it difficult to count their numbers.[32] Padrés labeled this as an excuse, and said that there were more than enough horses; for example, there was no lack of horses for slaughtering the herds, which required much more work. It was because of this inaccuracy in estimating the number of cattle on the missions, he surmised, that Governor Figueroa had acquired his wealth.

31. Pío Pico to Minister of Relations, Dec. 20, 1845, BL, Departmental State Papers, 6, 136.

32. Article 2 of rules for carrying out the secularization regulations.

Padrés pointed out that when Figueroa arrived in California some two years before, he had lost part of his baggage because of the revolt that had occurred on his ship. But now Governor Figueroa owned a hacienda named Los Alamitos, near the mission of San Gabriel, which had more than five thousand head of cattle on it and many horses, and another rancho near Monterey. Also he had a shop in Monterey where he stored and sold the wine and liquors from almost all the missions. He was the only man in the territory, Padrés went on, who was known to have silver and ready money, and this at a time when the officers and men of the garrison were in arrears in their pay for considerable sums. All this Governor Figueroa had amassed in two years. On the other hand, some of the commissioners and majordomos had visibly improved their own positions during the time they had been in office. The ones who had done the best, he said, were those whose lands were close to or bounded upon the missions to which they had been appointed. This was the case with Ensign Mariano Vallejo, whose ranch house was only six miles from the mission of San Francisco Solano and whose property was divided from that of the mission by a stream. It may be noted at this point that the French traveler Duflot de Mofras said of Vallejo that he pillaged the mission "even to the point of demolishing the church in order to build a house out of the materials."

Turning to the missions, Padrés said that they were "almost in the last stages of their destruction, except for four which had not been secularized." The number of Indians in the missions had "notably" diminished because they had gone off into the wilds. Those that had remained on the missions had become extremely corrupt, having been led astray by some of the commissioners. This had happened, he said, at San Gabriel, San Juan Bautista, and other missions, "where the day is passed in vices." He recommended recourse to the missionaries of the College of San Fernando for further information about the missions.

In California, Padrés continued, it was said in public that Governor Figueroa had had his share of the customs and treasury receipts before the present employees arrived. As an example of this, he cited the case of the brig *Dorotea* which had come from China; it should have produced more than thirty thousand pesos in revenues but only brought in a little over three thousand. Other similar cases were known in California, he said, and attention there had been particularly attracted to the information provided by a group of Sonorans (perhaps those who took part in the revolt at Los Angeles), who talked about the governor's deals in that area. Bearing in mind what he had said, concluded Padrés, the minister of war might infer how Figueroa had dealt with the colony and its directors, "whom he especially needed to remove from the country so that they should not see or know [anything]."[33]

Padrés' letter is almost the only example of an attack on Governor Figueroa which cites specific acts and cases, and it must be admitted that some of his allegations can be corroborated from other sources. Governor Figueroa, as has been mentioned, did own the Los Alamitos ranch near Los Angeles which at the time of his death in 1835 was estimated to have on it five thousand head of cattle, twenty-five gentle horses, ten mules, fifty mares, and a large number of colts. This stock did not all belong to Figueroa, however, for in 1833 he had entered into partnership with his brother-in-law Colonel Nicolás Gutiérrez and Roberto Pardo to run the ranch. The partners called their enterprise the Agriculture Company. Figueroa and Gutiérrez both contributed a thousand head of cattle, while Pardo provided six hundred cows and a band of mares which, by agreement, raised his investment to the same value as the other two. Here again, however, appearances were deceptive. Figueroa did not own the thou-

33. De Mofras, *Travels*, *1*, 167; Padrés to Minister of War, Tepic, June 3, 1835, Folder 45, FP; Padrés to Minister of War, June 3, 1835, FP.

sand cattle he contributed to the Agriculture Company but had them on loan for five years from the missions of San Luis Rey, San Gabriel, San Fernando, and La Purísima. And before the five years were up he had to return them. One of the remaining questions on this matter is how Figueroa, who arrived in California apparently without a penny, and indeed seriously in debt, could buy Los Alamitos with its 26,000 acres (six square leagues) of land.

The records show that the transaction occurred in this way: in September 1833, Governor Figueroa divided up among the Nieto family a vast tract of land near Los Angeles, Juan José Nieto receiving for part of his share the Los Alamitos ranch. Then on June 30, 1834, Nieto sold Los Alamitos to Figueroa for five hundred pesos, an incredibly small sum even in those days. The deed contains the following statement by Nieto: "He declares that the just price and true value of the said land is 500 dollars [pesos]; that it is not worth more nor could he find anybody who would give him so much for it, and if it is or may be worth more, he makes in favor of the purchaser and his heir and successor a full, perfect and irrevocable gift and donation of the excess, whether it be a small or large sum, which he does in sound mind." The one additional item in the affair that is not clear is what Governor Figueroa did for Nieto to make it worth Nieto's while to reward him so handsomely. Perhaps, as has been alleged, Nieto simply bribed the governor so that he would get the largest portion of the family domain.[34] Padrés' other accusations against Governor Figueroa cannot be proven one way or the other, but it is not unlikely that, as in the case of Los Alamitos, there was some truth to them.

After writing this letter, which presumably eventually reached Gómez Farías—for it ended up in his papers—Colonel Padrés went on his way to Guadalajara and then to

34. Rancho Los Alamitos, Court Case 290, BL, transcript no. 404; Francisco Figueroa to Manuel Requena, Dec. 27, 1853 and Court Case 208, Box 84, SP; Cleland, *The Cattle*, pp. 252–56.

Mexico City, where he arrived on July 12. He wrote to the minister of war again on August 4 in great distress. He was in prison in the old Inquisition building as a result, he said, of the "tricks of an individual who became my enemy as soon as he had enough proof to make him believe that I would have nothing to do with his depraved projects." Who this was or what the circumstances were are unknown. Also, although he had managed to get one of his back payments of salary in Guadalajara, it had all been spent on travel to Mexico City and on lodging there for some three weeks. In addition he had sent some of it to Tepic, where his large family was living in extreme want. As if all this were not enough, he said that he was supporting two companions in distress, who had no resources at all; they were all exhausted after the long journey and sick because of the change of climate. He asked the minister to get him two or three of his back payments out of the seven he was still owed. In a marginal note on Padrés' letter dated August 10, General Gabriel Valencia recommended that his request be granted, and on August 11 the colonel was given two payments on the authority of President Barragán. As in the case of Híjar, there is no information as to how Padrés' story of his experiences in California was received by the authorities. In fact, after writing a routine letter to the minister of war on October 21, 1835, from Mexico City, he disappears from view.[35]

Back in California, Governor Figueroa stayed at San Gabriel until May 22, when he started his return journey to Monterey. He told Vallejo that the colonists who had departed were very angry at both him and Vallejo and had sworn vengeance. He reported that they were saying that he, Figueroa, had started the revolution at Los Angeles in order to have a pretext for removing them. He was indignant at such an idea, but he thought it would make Vallejo realize

---

35. Padrés to Minister of War, Mexico, Aug. 4, Oct. 21, 1835, Service Record, AD.

how depraved those lying politicians were. He urged Vallejo then, as he was to urge him frequently thereafter, to have the indictments against Padrés drawn up in correct legal form. Having arrived in Monterey, he wrote Vallejo again on June 12, saying that he had received and returned to him the evidence collected against Padrés and his men at San Francisco Solano, so that Vallejo could continue in accordance with the required formalities. Then he added an interesting general remark:

> If all the inhabitants of California are persuaded, as you are, of the necessity of living at peace, they will make any sacrifice whatever to achieve it. I do not doubt that this truth is within the reach of many people and that only the madly ambitious will promote disorder. The wealth of the missions will be the object of misunderstandings and mutual attacks for some time. The government will also begin to be a motive of envy. These passions will begin to unfold now and the clash of heterogeneous interests will start.[36]

Deporting the leaders of the colony, it appeared, was not going to be a panacea for the ills of California.

It is ironic that Governor Figueroa, having just successfully removed the colony from San Francisco Solano and banished its leaders, on his return to Monterey should at once busy himself again with promoting colonization north of San Francisco Bay. Yet on June 24 he wrote to Vallejo—now a lieutenant—whom he had appointed military commander and director of colonization on the northern frontier, ordering him to found a town in the Sonoma area near San Francisco Solano instead of Santa Rosa. He authorized him to select families to come as colonists from anywhere in the republic, and he could make grants of land provisionally to them which would be confirmed on application by the ter-

36. Figueroa to Vallejo, May 22, June 12, 1835, BL, Cowan.

ritorial government. In another letter to Vallejo a week later, Figueroa said, "It is necessary to think about increasing the population and protecting it in various ways, so that our enemies do not throw it in our faces that we destroyed the colony for personal reasons. Draw up a plan and write me about it."

Vallejo pushed ahead with his plans for a settlement, but in view of the reception of the Farías colony it is not surprising to learn that the settlers bore such names as James Black, Edward M. McIntosh, James Dawson, and Mark West. Híjar had complained that Figueroa discriminated against Mexicans, and there is certainly some evidence that he favored men like John Cooper, William Forbes, and Charles Brown.[37] Actually there is no reason to think that he was in general biased against his own countrymen. It is more likely that he favored these foreigners with grants of land because there were no eligible Mexicans available. And it was natural, after the way he had treated the colony from Mexico, that it would be hard to persuade another group to come.

By permitting Anglo-Americans to take up land along the northern frontier, Figueroa and Vallejo were no doubt putting further obstacles in the way of the desires of the Russian-American Company to acquire the land between Ross and the north shore of San Francisco Bay. But as it happened, the tsar's imperial government gave only lukewarm support to expansion into this area. Its answer to Governor Figueroa's letter of April 10, 1833, asking Baron Wrangel to try to obtain Russian recognition of Mexican independence, was a polite no. On the other hand, Baron Wrangel was permitted to plan his journey home to Russia in 1836 by way of Mexico, so that he might see whether the Mexican government would be willing to exchange recognition by Russia for land in northern California. Wrangel's mission to Mexico was a com-

37. Hittell, *History*, 2, 201, 280; Figueroa to Vallejo, Mar. 9, June 16, July 1, 1835, BL, Cowan.

plete failure, however, and as a result the Russian-American Company decided to abandon Ross. Mexico's fear of a Russian threat, which had been one of the major reasons for sending the Farías colony, was gone. The threat from the Americans, on the other hand, was considerably greater than it had been. And the policies of Figueroa allowing Anglo-Americans to take up lands that might have gone to Mexicans helped to make it worse.

Governor Figueroa summed up his views about the colony in his famous *Manifiesto,* most of which he probably wrote during July and August 1835. He thought the affair transcended local interest, and he wrote his account of it for the nation, which largely ignored it. There is no evidence that Governor Figueroa opposed the idea of a colony as such. On the contrary, he was interested in founding one himself. Colonization had long been approved by Spain and by the Mexican Republic. Figueroa allegedly opposed the Farías colony because he felt that the resources of the territorial government were insufficient to support it. It was in fact true that foreigners were willing to settle in out-of-the-way places without asking the government for anything except land. These men had the knowledge and the resources to make a success of pioneering by themselves. But the Mexican government, knowing that the territory needed artisans who would have to be helped financially if they were going to reach their destination, sent them along with farmers and others at the expense of the state and the territory. In California the colonists were to be given the best agricultural lands available—lands that were being worked by the mission Indians, the sale of whose grain and cattle supported the territorial government and its garrison. Because of the inadequate and misleading instructions which the Farías government finally gave Híjar, it appeared that no one was to benefit from the new and radical land policies of the government but the colonists, and Figueroa either rejected the idea that the word "colonists" meant Indians, Californians, and foreigners, or failed to understand its full significance. He staked his main opposition to the Híjar colony, however, on the ground that its leaders were unscrupulous adventurers who had tricked the government into providing them with unconstitutional instructions with which to rob the Indians of the mission lands.[38] He hammered at this theme all the way through his *Manifiesto*.

Figueroa's vehemence in putting forward his views has made writers such as Bancroft suspect him. Some of the governor's contemporaries, among them Colonel Padrés, disliked him and seem to have been mystified by his attitude: all that Padrés could say, when he was discussing Figueroa's motives for destroying the colony, was that his reasons were "not as clear as day but nor were they as dark as night." Híjar's reaction to Figueroa's accusation that he and the colonists were involved in the Los Angeles revolt was, "I see in all this nothing more than a mystery that time will clear up." Even some of the Californians who were friendly with him were sometimes at a loss to explain his actions. In his "Reminiscences," set down in 1874 for H. H. Bancroft, José de Jesús Vallejo says at one point:

> I and many others who knew that General Figueroa was in favor of secularization of the missions, could not help wondering why he put up such a strong resistance to Híjar's pretensions. We asked His Excellency about this through José Castro. In his reply [Castro] said the following: "I have spoken with the Governor, he wants the missions secularized but he wishes it to be done in a worthy and just fashion and not in the iniquitous way that Híjar and Padrés have in mind."[39]

38. Minister of Finance to Headquarters, January 1835, p. 165, RRAC; Bancroft, *California*, *4*, 169; Figueroa, *Manifiesto*, pp. 167, 172.

39. Bancroft, *California*, *3*, 290; Padrés to Figueroa, May 8, 1835, BL, Departmental State Papers, *4*, 33–34; Híjar to Figueroa, Mar. 17, 1835, BL, De la Guerra, "Documentos," *5*, 107; José de Jesús Vallejo, "Reminiscencias," BL, p. 51.

The question of Governor Figueroa's motive in opposing Híjar and Padrés is still one that requires attention. A simple answer to the problem, of course, is to suppose that Figueroa was dishonest and that he was feathering his own nest at the expense of the Indians, while at the same time posing as their protector. This was apparently Padrés' view of him, and it was subscribed to by others. Perhaps the most plausible statement of this position is by Antonio Franco Coronel, who attacked Figueroa's *Manifiesto* as follows:

The philanthropy that was supposed to be applied in favor of the natives in the missions in order to moralize them, educate them, and grant them the property that they considered they owned, was contradicted by facts that everyone knows. The missions passed into the hands of the administrators, most of whom were the same men who were members of the Provincial Deputation and had constituted themselves as the attorneys for the natives and the defenders of their interests. The result was the complete abandonment of the unhappy neophytes, the protection of their vices, and their total neglect, even in some of the simpler branches of doctrinal education which they did at least give them during the time of the missionary Fathers. [The result was also] to cause the destruction of those hands (more than 20,000 of them)[40] who would have been useful for the progress of the country, [it resulted in] the destruction of the *fincas* which were then the sole fountain of wealth. And most of the administrators who had begun work at their posts as poor men came out owning the most valuable ranches, covered with cattle and horses, that had belonged to those same missions, while the missions remained poor. Because of this I consider that castle in the air, that vast cloud of theories in the said *Manifiesto* of

40. This figure was the number commonly mentioned by Californians when speaking of the mission Indians. A more recent estimate is about 17,000.

the late General Figueroa and the members of the Junta of that day destroyed. The present generation and posterity will judge impartially what were the causes by the results it has seen.[41]

While much of what Coronel says may be granted, and perhaps Figueroa may be blamed for starting the destruction, the fact remains that he died before the main damage was done. It is true that the plan of the Los Angeles pronunciamiento accused some of the mission commissioners of benefiting at the expense of the missions, but without producing any proof. Governor Figueroa replied by saying that it was slander, and the commissioners would prove themselves "by the results and it is not yet time to analyze them." It must also be remembered that there were heated denials that the commissioners in the early days did anything wrong.

The question at issue, however, is not whether the commissioners yielded to be the obvious temptations that came their way, but whether Governor Figueroa planned his secularization law so that he and the Californians, with whom he associated, might benefit at the expense of the mission Indians, and in fact did so benefit. The fact that the Californians spoke in the highest terms of Figueroa's integrity, using such terms as "the public recognizes his honesty, his probity and considers him an eminent patriot and well deserving son of the fatherland," is not sufficient to absolve him in this case, since his defenders had to defend him to clear themselves.[42]

It must be admitted that very few came forward to accuse Governor Figueroa of peculation. Colonel Padrés, on the basis of hearsay, accused him of appropriating some of the customs revenues and pointed the finger of suspicion at him because in the course of two years he had made a lot of money.

41. Coronel, "Cosas de California," BL, pp. 16–17.
42. Figueroa, *Manifiesto*, pp. 140, 179; Pío Pico to person unnamed, July 1, 1836, BL, State Papers, Missions, *11*, 332.

It does appear that Figueroa accepted the Los Alamitos ranch as a bribe, but Padrés' other accusations are unproved. Híjar, who had every reason to feel aggrieved at Figueroa, did not accuse him of dishonesty, although he considered him a tyrant. The French traveler Duflot de Mofras later alleged that Figueroa "made a pretense of distributing land and a few head of cattle among the Indians," insinuating, in other words, that the whole secularization procedure was a trick.[43] But Duflot de Mofras did not produce any direct evidence to back up his views. While it is all too easy to find holes in Governor Figueroa's accusations against Híjar and Padrés, it can hardly be reasoned that because Figueroa's arguments are weak and at times positively misleading, he is therefore to be accused of making money at the expense of the mission Indians. If he did not attempt to crush the colony because he wanted to cover his own tracks, however, he must have done so because he disagreed completely with the views of the colony's leaders, as he himself said he did.

In one of his letters to Figueroa, Híjar cut off further discussion with him because, he said, "we are not in agreement on the way we see things." On nothing, perhaps, were they so far apart as in their attitudes toward the Indians, who were a central issue in the whole long conflict over the colony. Híjar's attitude toward the Indians was that reflected in the laws of the new Republic of Mexico—egalitarian as well as humanitarian. Although he found the mission Indians "degraded and demoralized to the extent that they will prostitute their daughters and wives," he considered that they and the pagan Indians in the interior had "wonderful natural talent." He thought that the California Indians were quicker than those in the interior of Mexico in adopting foreign ways and clothing. "It may well be inferred from this last information," he stated optimistically, "that they possess elements which would help them toward civilization, in

43. De Mofras, *Travels, 1*, 151.

which they would make great progress with a policy different from the one used up until now by the three dominating classes [missionaries, soldiers, whites] whom they hate."[44] Híjar's rather optimistic view of the potential of the California Indians contrasts with Figueroa's much less favorable estimate of their abilities. Commenting on Híjar's egalitarianism at one point, Figueroa said, "He claimed that the Indian, still ignorant, needy, and half wild, should be absolutely and identically equal in the exercise of political rights with other citizens." Perhaps, commented Figueroa, this would make it easier to get the better of the Indian. But as an idea it was ridiculous: "According to these principles we should erase from our codes the laws that regulate the control of parents over children, or those that provide for the dominance of husband over wife in marriage, those that discuss guardianship and tutelage of minors, fools, the insane, wastrels and several others. Carried to such an extreme, legal equality would unhinge society."[45]

Figueroa's attitude toward the Indian, then, was paternalistic, although probably no less humanitarian in its objectives than Híjar's views. When he was finally obliged to start a general secularization of the missions, Figueroa sponsored a regulation that provided small amounts of land for the mission Indians, who were to continue to do forced labor on undistributed mission property. Híjar's egalitarian principles led him to propose that the mission Indians receive land of their own and be paid their daily wages for the work they were to do on former mission lands, presumably for the new Cosmopolitan Company.[46] Governor Figueroa would have undoubtedly joined the experienced missionaries in

44. Figueroa, *Manifiesto*, p. 102; Híjar to Minister of Relations, Jan. 30, 1835, BL, Colonización y terrenos baldíos, Fomento, legajo 6, expediente 173.

45. Figueroa, *Manifiesto*, p. 169.

46. Híjar to Minister of Relations, Jan. 30, 1835, BL, Colonización y terrenos baldíos, Fomento, legajo 6, expediente 173.

attacking this plan as impractical, since the major problem that had so long baffled those who wanted to make the Indian into a landowner or farmhand was that the Indian was not interested in working the land even if it were his own. What was more, Governor Figueroa seems to have realized that if the Indian refused to work for some new lay master he would in all probability be forced to do so. On the other hand, it does not seem to have occurred to Figueroa that someone less humanitarian than he considered himself might succeed him as governor and be in control of the partly emancipated mission Indians, who still had to do forced labor. Híjar had only been in California four months, and he appears to have been overly optimistic that the Indians would be able to make themselves into good Mexican farmers overnight. Figueroa's plan, however, although it seemed more practical, actually did not work out for the good of the Indians, who in time lost both their land and finally their very lives when they were faced by the more aggressive white settlers from the United States.

Divided as they were in their attitudes toward the Indians, Governor Figueroa and Híjar were no less far apart in the equally crucial problem of deciding who owned the mission lands, which the Farías government had decided to distribute among several groups. Híjar and Padrés, probably taking their views from José María Luis Mora's famous *Dissertation on the Nature and Application of Ecclesiastical Income and Property*, which first appeared in 1833, argued that the missions were "moral bodies" which could have no rights over their property. Mora's argument was that "moral bodies," the name he gave to such institutions as hospitals, colleges, orphan asylums, cathedral chapters, and similar organizations, were, strictly speaking, "merely administrators of the funds in their charge, which belong to the public and are consequently subject to the authority which represents [the public]." Since the federal government represented the public or people of the nation, according to Mora the gov-

ernment could dispose of mission lands in the way it thought
fit. Perhaps in order to make their case even stronger, Híjar
and Padrés made use of the idea of eminent domain, the
right of the state to appropriate property for public use after
providing reasonable compensation.

Governor Figueroa's answer to these arguments was to
admit that he did not know what eminent domain was and
to pour scorn over the idea that the missions were moral
bodies who could not keep control over their lands. "What
sublime philosophy, what illusory theories the revolutionaries use to seize other peoples' property," he said, continuing,
"more cowardly than bandits they use sophistry, high-sound-
ing and hollow words, and they have on a mask of patriotism
and religiosity when they abuse their country and mock
their religion."

Perhaps it should be asked at this point why the Californians supported Figueroa in reserving mission lands for
the Indians. It is obvious, of course, that the Californians disliked the idea of allowing Mexicans from the interior and
foreigners to get hold of mission lands, which were the best
in the territory. But Governor Figueroa had not assented to
their eager demands that he survey mission property so that
they could take some of the surplus before Híjar arrived with
full government instructions. When Híjar did arrive it is not
difficult to see why they backed Figueroa against him, for it
appeared that these rich lands were to be given to the colonists alone—not even divided among the Indians, the military, and others, as the original Farías bill had proposed.
Even the Farías bill automatically excluded Californians who
already possessed fifty-two acres of land, which the leading
figures in the territory undoubtedly did. So the Californians
had nothing to lose by publicly supporting Figueroa's views
that the Indians owned these lands. Since the Californians
had a poor opinion of the Indians, they may well have
thought that backing Indian ownership of mission lands
would be the best way to ward off outsiders until circum-

stances changed for the better. At any rate, it was clear to them and to Figueroa that the Indians would not be capable for a long time of working these lands for themselves. It would also have been quite possible for them to have subscribed to Mora's view that the missions were "moral bodies," but that the public which owned their property was the people of California, rather than the people of Mexico in general. This is, in fact, probably the way they did feel about mission lands. If Governor Figueroa was sympathetic with this point of view, he could not act upon it without the strong probability of causing serious trouble with the missionary fathers, the Indians—who would presumably be expected to continue working the mission estates—and the Mexican government. But Figueroa prided himself on the way in which he managed to please everyone; and in the difficult question of deciding who owned mission lands, the easiest way to avoid trouble was to assign them to the Indians. This would keep matters quiet for the time being, although he well knew that it could not be a permanent solution to the problem.

Evidently, there is no need to assume that Governor Figueroa opposed the colony from sinister motives, for his ideas and principles were completely opposed to those of Híjar and Padrés. He realized that the new ideas of these men might cause dangerous Indian trouble and even prompt his ill-paid troops to revolt. He fought back against the threat with clever propaganda that the colonists were bringing to California political unrest, the "genius of evil" which, like the cholera epidemic, was causing havoc in the interior. At best, men like Híjar and Padrés were meant to be "bad poets, writers of romances and novels"; at worst, their names "were known only in the annals of fratricidal warfare, in civil discord, in the farce of the anarchists, that ominous sect, hated in America and in Europe, which is the disgrace of our century." [47] In the exuberance of his name-calling, Figueroa

47. Figueroa, *Manifiesto*, pp. 79, 151, 168, 175–76; Mora, *Obras sueltas*, *1*, 223–24.

revealed how the "genius of evil," which was affecting Mexico at the time, had permeated his own political conscience. The colony's leaders were not simply men who had honest differences of opinion with him, they were men whose wickedness ranged all the way from robbers of innocent Indians to anarchists, the Communists of the day. Figueroa created a kind of black legend for the colony which has remained with it ever since.

Governor Figueroa did not outlive the colony by many months. Worn out by his feverish activity and increasingly ill, he informed the Mexican government in May 1835 that he would be obliged to surrender his civil office of governor to José Castro, the senior member present in the Territorial Deputation in 1835. Figueroa intended to turn over his post temporarily to Castro in June but did not do so until August 29, after the Deputation had assembled. He was apparently thinking of going farther south to Santa Barbara, where the climate was warmer and he could avoid the north winds which bothered him at Monterey. But he became so weak that on September 6 he took to his bed and on September 22 resigned both his civil and military duties, the latter going to Lieutenant-Colonel Nicolás Gutiérrez, the ranking officer in the territory. Figueroa died at Monterey, as the result of what was called an apoplectic attack, on September 29, 1835, at the age of forty-three. His coffin was put in the crypt of the church at the mission of Santa Barbara on October 29, where it was found by Father Engelhardt in 1911.[48] Juan Bautista Alvarado suggested in an oration praising Governor Figueroa that his portrait be placed in the hall in which the Deputation met and that underneath the portrait the words "Benefactor of the Territory of Upper California" should be inscribed. He also suggested that a monument to the general be raised at some suitable place in Monterey with an ap-

48. Engelhardt, *Missions, 3,* 599, 601–02; Bancroft, *California, 3,* 295; Hittell, *History, 2,* 213. Hittell is in error in stating that Figueroa died at San Juan Bautista.

propriate inscription. The Territorial Deputation duly approved of these motions and even composed the inscription for the monument, but this is apparently all that it ever did. No monuments or portraits have been forthcoming for Figueroa since that time, but the number of streets in California cities that bear his name, not to mention the mountain near Santa Barbara, show that he is not entirely forgotten.[49]

49. Figueroa, *Manifiesto*, pp. 178–83. The proposed inscription for the monument is on the last page (unnumbered) of Figueroa's *Manifiesto*.

Chapter Ten

The California Frontier

On the eve of what the Mexicans were to call the War of the American Invasion, Manuel Payno, the distinguished writer and statesman, looked despairingly at California and asked, "Is it not probable that the Californias will have the same fate as Texas? Is there no remedy that can be applied? Shall we resign ourselves to lose those fertile and spacious lands without getting even the slightest benefit from them?" It was not that Payno did not know what Mexico should do; he had seen American settlers moving west in the United States in their long trains of covered wagons, and in his view Mexicans should do likewise. Finding nothing of this kind in recent Mexican annals except the Farías colony, which he duly saluted, he came to a depressing conclusion: "It is an unquestionable truth that the honorable man who wishes to work makes his fortune, but the Mexican character is not fitted for colonization."[1]

There is a striking contrast between the relative inability of Spain and Mexico to colonize California and the inexorable westward movement of the American frontiersmen, who were finally to overwhelm it. Payno's theory that Mexi-

1. Manuel Payno, "Alta California," *Revista científica y literaria de Méjico, I* (1845), 83, 84.

cans were prevented by some national characteristic from being colonizers is belied by their Spanish forebears and is, in any case, too vague a statement for useful discussion; but a consideration of what may perhaps be called the California frontier, in the sense that Frederick Jackson Turner used the term, may serve to bring together some of the views previously put forward in this study.

Certain differences between the California frontier and the American westward movement are sufficiently obvious: the drive to colonize California was not due to any pressure of population on Mexico, which was itself badly in need of more settlers, but to the Spanish and Mexican fears of encroachment from Russia and the United States. Since California was, in effect, an overseas colony of Mexico after the closing of overland communication in 1781—even in 1834 traveling from California to Mexico was sometimes referred to as returning "to the continent"—the expense of going there was too great for the poverty-stricken individual even if he had wanted to go.[2] Successive Spanish and Mexican governments, spurred on by fear of Russian aggression, were willing to recruit colonists and give them free passage to California, together with promises of free land, free farm animals, and free farming tools. In spite of these inducements, only a trickle came forward. Both governments then took to sending what Adam Smith picturesquely calls "felons and strumpets" to California, with equally poor results.

Colonization of California, it will be noted, was promoted and paid for by the state, as under the Romans, and not a matter of individual initiative, as on the American frontier. Even the Farías colony, sponsored by the egalitarian government of the time, was paternally controlled by its directors of colonization. Its major difference from previous colonization programs was that it planned to colonize mission lands and to permit Indians to be colonists on an equal basis with the whites.

2. Buenaventura Araujo, Service Record, AD.

Interest in making colonists out of the Indians, however, was not a new idea. It is evident that the Spanish government's support for the missions in California was due, among other considerations, to the fact that there simply were not enough Spaniards available to settle it, let alone cultivate it. Yet according to the highly esteemed Swiss arbiter of eighteenth-century international law, Emmerich von Vattel, a nation must actually populate a country which it takes as its own, and its settlers should preferably not merely run cattle in it but cultivate it. Vattel also disapproved of nations that took more land than they needed. Missions solved these problems by turning the Indians into civilized beings and setting them to cultivate the land. Also, the fact that they made Christians out of pagans and protected their proselytes against the white man would help to offset Spain's vulnerability, from Vattel's point of view, as a country that was engrossing a "much greater extent of territory than it is able to people or cultivate."[3] But trying to convert Indians into Spanish farmers proved a baffling and frustrating experience. While they were willing to accept the presents the missionaries gave them and would even labor in the fields for their food and clothing, Indians always seemed to want to return to their old primitive way of life. As time went by and ideas of the equality of man began to spread, opinion about the worth of the missions changed. The intellectual capacity of the Indians became a subject for debate rather than a cause for the shaking of heads. Observers began to criticize the missionaries for their slowness in civilizing their Indians, and some advanced the idea that segregating the Indians from society in missions was a poor way of making them into members of that society. The attempts of the Mexican government to secularize the missions and integrate the Indians with the other inhabitants of California, however, came to

3. Bolton, "The Mission as a Frontier Institution," *American Historical Review, 23* (1917), 52; Emmerich von Vattel, *The Law of Nations* (Philadelphia, 1849), items 208, 209.

grief. The Indians who were freed from the missions were at the mercy of the whites, who wanted to make use of their labor and take their land.

One of the keys to the problem of the difference between the Hispanic frontier in California and the American frontier lies in this question of land. The dynamic force behind Turner's concept of the moving frontier is free land, and Adam Smith's eighteenth-century prescription for successful colonies was "plenty of good land." Although the Spanish and Mexican governments talked about granting land to colonists, remarkably few settlers seem to have acquired full rights to their land in California. Land was not generally surveyed, and it was often granted in enormous acreages to single individuals. By the time Governor Manuel Victoria came to California in 1830, all the best coastal land had been engrossed by the missions, who spread their cattle domains around them as if to protect themselves from undesirable settlers in the few existing towns. Before the country was populated by more than a handful of people, therefore, there was little land left, unless the settler moved into pagan Indian country. This was where the Farías colony went for strategic reasons; but although the colonists were provided with weapons, which they might have used against Indians if they were attacked, Governor Figueroa saw a threat to himself in these arms and ordered them removed. Only the experienced, independent American frontiersmen in California seem to have been in a position to take exposed lands.

The magnet of free land in California hardly existed as far as Mexico was concerned, and when the Farías government attempted to divide mission lands among the mission Indians and various groups of white men, both Californians and Mexicans, it provoked defiance on the part of Governor Figueroa and his Territorial Deputation. The Californians were unwilling to see the best lands of their territory go to newly arrived immigrants from Mexico; they worked out a secularization plan for the missions which kept them going as productive haciendas—on which most people in California depended—while reserving some land for selected mission Indians. If their experience with freed Indians was to be repeated, the whites might confidently expect that in due course they would fall heir to Indian owned land, if they could not share it on the ground that they, too, were natives of California. Thus the neophytes, who supposedly owned the mission lands they worked, were eventually to lose them.

If "plenty of good land," the most essential ingredient for a movement to the frontier, was lacking in California under Mexico, what about the other requirement put forward by Adam Smith for a successful colony: "liberty to manage their own affairs their own way"?[4] There is no doubt that Mexico neglected California. In spite of constant reminders by successive ministers of relations, the Mexican Congress failed to provide a code of laws for the territory, which was forced to guide its affairs by reference to parts of Spanish laws, Mexican laws, the Spanish Constitution of 1812, and the Mexican Constitution of 1824. On the other hand, neglect by the government in Mexico meant more power for the governor and Territorial Deputation in Monterey. When Mexico did nothing, Monterey had to act, if only provisionally. Governor Figueroa, in the crisis over mission land policy, even went further than this and invoked the traditional, "I obey but I do not comply" of the colonial viceroys when faced with unacceptable legislation made in Spain.

Can it be said that these signs of autonomy were in any sense due to a burgeoning of democracy on the California frontier? There would seem to be little evidence for such an idea. In one of his speeches to the Territorial Deputation, Governor Figueroa lauds the virtues of democracy, by which he seems to mean freeing the governor from the petty affairs of government, which should be taken care of by lower

4. Adam Smith, *An Inquiry into the Nature and Causes of the Wealth of Nations* (New York, 1937), p. 538.

officials.[5] But Figueroa himself acted more like a caudillo than a representative of the people, and in their turns, the other military commanders in California's outlying regions behaved like lesser caudillos. The attempts of many Californians to have the military command separated from the civilian governorship went unheeded until the Farías administration made a vain attempt to inaugurate it. Their demands for more democracy were made to look like treason.

Adam Smith put forward a frontier thesis which provides insight into the situation in California and other Latin American areas. "The absolute governments of Spain, Portugal, and France," he says, "take place in their colonies; and the discretionary powers which such governments commonly delegate to all their inferior officers are, on account of the great distance, naturally exercised there with more than ordinary violence. Under all absolute governments there is more liberty in the capital than in any other part of the country."[6] While a Paraguayan living in Asunción with Dr. Francia might not have entirely agreed with this, perhaps it may be modified to read that life on the frontier, under a dictatorship, is likely to be just as dictatorial, or even at times more dictatorial, than it is at the seat of government. The frontier, in this case, simply gives more free rein to the local official, who becomes a petty despot. In turn, the subordinates of the petty despot, far removed from his eyes, tend to become lesser tyrants. In other words, the frontier reproduces, in somewhat more visible fashion, what is already present in the homeland from which the settlers came. Turner's thesis that the American frontier promoted democracy follows this idea, and it seems to fit the situation in Hispanic California. Híjar and Padrés, at any rate, regarded the actions of Governor Figueroa and Ensign Vallejo in this light. They went back to Mexico City with the intention of revealing to the

5. BL, Legislative Records, 2, 39.
6. Smith, *Wealth of Nations,* p. 552.

government how these men, protected by the distance of the frontier, had overstepped their authority. By the time they reached the capital, however, the Farías government had been removed and Santa Anna had taken over; dictatorship was to be firmly seated at Mexico City itself.

At this point, perhaps, one further question may be raised. Were the liberals in Mexico at this time trying to promote their ideas on the frontier, far from the power of orthodox conservative opinion in Mexico City? More precisely, were they consciously trying to make the frontier a seedbed for their democratic views? There were those at the time who thought that this was their intention and that it accounted for Santa Anna's actions against the Farías colony. But if this was so, it will be noted that Mexico City was the source of the democratic moves, not the California frontier.

If the California frontier reveals little sign of promoting democracy, which Turner held to be the most important effect of the frontier on the United States, it also shows little evidence of other attributes commonly associated with the American frontier. For example, the Californians, sufficiently provided with Indian labor, did little or no work themselves. Commodore Charles Wilkes, on his visit to California in 1841, reported that he had heard a story about a Californian "who had been known to dispense with his dinner, although the food was but a few yards off, because the Indian was not at hand to bring it to him." The Californians are not credited with such frontier virtues as independence or resourcefulness, and they were not self-sufficient. In fact they may be compared with planters in the Old South, if hides and tallow are substituted for cotton and mission Indians for Negro slaves.[7]

While California under Mexico does not appear to have been a frontier in the same sense that Turner used the word,

7. Wilkes, *Narrative*, 5, 176; Carey McWilliams, *Southern California Country: An Island on the Land* (New York, 1946), p. 52.

it does shed some light on the confused political scene in Mexico at the time. Life in Mexican California was relatively simple compared with its counterpart in Mexico proper, and some of the major problems in California are clearer reflections of more complex situations in the metropolis. Take, for example, the division in the ranks of the liberal federalists on Indian policy. The Farías government's policy of integrating Indians into the rest of the population, as opposed to older segregation ideas, is revealed in its program for the missions. Its egalitarianism, as opposed to the paternalism of Figueroa on Indian matters, brings to light a difference of opinion that José María Mora saw as beginning a split in the ranks of the liberal party itself. That President Santa Anna did his best to undo many of the projects set on foot by Farías is dramatically shown by his secretly dispatching a special courier overland to prevent Híjar from taking over the governorship from Figueroa. Mora called Santa Anna the "Attila of Mexican civilization"; it is in his hands, certainly, that most of the responsibility for the failure of the Farías colonization project must be placed.[8]

The repeated failure of the Mexican Congress to draw up an organic code of laws for California, or even to pass adequate colonization laws for the territory, reveals a fundamental weakness in contemporary Mexican life that automatically led to the rise of dictatorship under men like Santa Anna. It was not that the Congress was indifferent to the problem or had not endeavored to do something about it. It was simply that the congressmen were inexperienced, and the problems they faced were overwhelming in both numbers and urgency. The decisive actions of a caudillo could provide escape from such harassments.

The long struggle to secularize the California missions may also be helpful in deciphering the Mexican scene. The main difficulty here was not the decision to reduce the mis-

---

8. Mora, "Revista política," in *Obras sueltas, 1,* ccxxii, cclxiii–cclxiv.

sions to parishes, but the question of how to divide up mission lands and Indian labor. No final decision on this matter was made in legislation in 1824 or 1828; but the Farías government, which was bent on a more equable division of landed property, took the necessary steps to divide and colonize the missions. The missionaries, who opposed secularization, believed that the mission Indians would eventually lose everything they had if they were prematurely freed from the missions without effective protection. At the same time it should be remembered that the Indians were rapidly proceeding toward extinction because of uncontrollable disease in the missions. The mission problem, however, like the church-state struggle going on in Mexico at this time, may be better understood as a conflict over land and labor than simply as a religious question.

If Mexican California in certain respects is a microcosm of Mexico proper, it also reveals how Mexico continued to evolve Spanish policies in dealing with California problems. Inheriting Spain's long fear of Russian encroachments on California, Mexico at once pushed colonization and reconstituted the original Spanish Commission on the Californias —even using some of the same personnel—to determine how best to deal with the complicated problems presented by the missions and their Indians. The Farías government's decision to treat the mission Indians on a basis of equality with the white man put into effect ideas that go back to Bishop Abad y Queipo in New Spain, to the eighteenth-century Enlightenment in Spain, and before that to Bartolomé de Las Casas. These ideas did not spring out of the Mexican movement for independence from Spain, although their application may have been hastened to a certain extent by it. In view of recent suggestions by anthropologists that "rapid change is not only possible, but may actually be very desirable," perhaps the wholesale changes that Híjar and Padrés were instructed to make—including the organizing of the much criticized Cosmopolitan Company—would in the end have been successful if Governor Figueroa and the whites in California had encouraged them. Perhaps, also, the successive failures of Echeandía and Figueroa in their secularization programs were due in part to their reluctance to give the Indians more than token integration into California society. To paraphrase Margaret Mead, if the whites were grudging and selective in their giving, the Indians, in their turn, were grudging and selective receivers.[9]

Like Spain, Mexico did not succeed in her efforts to protect California by peopling it; but also like Spain, Mexico did not give up trying to do so. Writing in 1835, Ignacio Zúñiga, a military officer who had formerly been stationed in Sonora, warned that California, New Mexico, and Sonora must be protected from the advance of the United States and Russia, "two great colossuses who will seize them if they are left in their present abandonment." Again, in the midst of the Texas troubles of 1836, a Mexico City newspaper came to the conclusion that if war began between the United States and Mexico, Russia would seize California. A few years later, when fears of the Russian menace to California had given way to fears of the American threat, Mariano Guadalupe Vallejo sent in a petition to the government for "a large colony of Mexicans composed principally of artisans and farmers."[10] The cycle seemed ready to begin again. Perhaps also like Spain, Mexico suffered defeat at the hands of her own people.

9. Margaret Mead, *New Lives for Old*, pp. 443, 445. The idea of selective giving and receiving is further analyzed in George M. Foster, *Culture and Conquest: America's Spanish Heritage* (Chicago, 1960).

10. Zúñiga, *Rápida ojeada*, p. 60; *El Cosmopolita*, Dec. 28, 1836; George Tays, "Mariano Guadalupe Vallejo and Sonoma—A Biography and a History," California Historical Society *Quarterly, 17* (1938), 59.

Appendix A

FROM *LA GAZETTE DE LEYDE,* MARCH 21, 1775*

From Mexico, November 26, 1774. A Royal frigate [the *Santiago*] which left the port of Monterey on June 13 last with provisions for a year has arrived at San Blas. The objective of its mission has been to explore the coasts of America to the highest possible latitude. This frigate, having reached 56 degrees North, sailed towards the coast, which it discovered at 55 degrees 43 minutes. The Captain [Juan José Pérez Hernández] and the crew first saw a tribe of white and blond Indians who came toward the frigate in more than thirty canoes. These Indians, far from showing any fear, motioned to the Spaniards in a lively fashion to try to get them to land on the beach. They even gave them, in exchange for some sailor's clothing, some kinds of knitted garments in which they were clad. Three of these garments have been sent to the King. They are artistically made of fine wool. It is not known, however, whether these heavy cloths have been brought to these peoples by some foreign nation or whether they make them themselves. Nor is it known whether the wool, which is what the material is made of, is a product of the country in view of the fact that sheep are not known in the regions of the Indies discovered up to the present.

*It was apparently through this account of the Pérez expedition that the Russians learned the extent of Spanish explorations on the northwest coast in 1775.

Night having come, the Indians went back to land and the frigate began to tack, with the intention of continuing to explore the coast on the following day. But a wind arose and forced the ship to draw away from the shore. This coast is the same one that Krascheninnikov† discovered on his first voyage from Kamchatka.

The frigate sighted the coast again at 49 degrees. At this place it encountered Indians who were naked and who also appeared in canoes. The Captain had the anchor cast in order to send out his long boat to explore the land closer in when a new gale forced him to stand out to sea. He discovered land again a third time between 39 and 40 degrees but the large number of sick men he had on board made him decide to sail for Monterey, where he took on provisions. This expedition is the first that the Spaniards have made in the South Sea to such a high north latitude. It opens the way for others which will be able to provide us with interesting information. There are at present seven naval officers here on their way to the port of San Blas.

†Stepan Petrovich Krascheninnikov wrote a history of Kamchatka and the Kurilski Islands which was published in St. Petersburg in 1755. An abridged translation appeared in London in 1764, and a complete French edition was published in 1770 in Amsterdam. As has been seen, it was Chirikov, not Krascheninnikov, who discovered this coast.

Appendix B

From the *Gazeta de Madrid*, March 19, 1776, pp. 103–04*

The Catholic zeal of the King, desirous of propagating the light of the Gospel among the wretched Indians who inhabit his most remote Dominions of the coast and lands of the *North* of *California* sunk in the obscure darkness of paganism, and as a consequence of the happy progress of the two expeditions made by sea and land in the years 1769 and 1770, the former from *Cape San Lucas* with the packetboats *San Carlos* and *San Antonio* under the command of their Pilot Commanders Don Vicente Vila, and Don Juan Pérez, and the latter from the Presidio of *Loreto* under the command of Captain of Dragoons Don Gaspar Portolá, on which the Port of Monte-Rey was examined at latitude 36 degrees 40 minutes, and a mission and a presidio founded dedicated to *San Carlos*. Another expedition was made in 1774 with the Frigate *Santiago* by Frigate Ensign Don Juan Pérez, who sailed up to latitude 55 degrees 49 minutes and, approaching different parts of the coast, found *Indians* of great docility, friendly manner, with pleasing appearance and clean clothing. Because of these favorable results, His Majesty ordered Naval Officers sent to the Port of *San Blas* in the

*By publishing these two accounts of its explorations on the northwest coast the Spanish government departed from its previous policy of secrecy, presumably hoping that if its claims were made public it would be better able to establish them.

Nueva Galicia to advance as much as possible these voyages and discoveries, and with this objective Battleship Lieutenant Don Bruno de Eceta sailed at the beginning of 1775 on the Frigate *Santiago* and Frigate Lieutenant Don Juan Francisco de la Bodega on the schooner *Sonora* and at the same time Frigate Lieutenant Don Juan de Ayala left on the Packetboat *San Carlos* bound for Monte-Rey. Don Bruno de Eceta, the first of these officers, reached latitude 50 degrees, the second, Don Juan Francisco de la Bodega, reached latitude 58, and the third, Don Juan de Ayala, latitude 37 degrees 42 minutes. On this voyage the intermediate coast was examined and several places on it, with the great Port of *San Francisco* and various rivers, whose lands are inhabited by many Indians of notable docility. Such happy results and the accomplishment of the favorable effects of these expeditions are due to the accredited zeal and love for the Royal service, in which he has always distinguished himself, of the Very Excellent Knight of the Order of San Juan, Don Antonio María Bucareli, Viceroy of New Spain, and to the skillful carrying out of his timely orders. And His Majesty, taking into account the report the Viceroy made on the performance of his orders on the last expedition by Naval Officers and Pilots, and in order to encourage others, has promoted Lieutenant Don Bruno de Eceta to Frigate Captain, and Frigate Lieutenants Don Juan Manuel de Ayala and Don Juan Francisco de la Bodega to Battleship Lieutenants; Frigate Ensign Don Juan Pérez to Frigate Lieutenant, and Pilots Don Joseph Cañizares and Don Francisco Maurelle to Frigate Ensigns.

FROM THE *GAZETA DE MADRID,* MAY 14, 1776, pp. 175–76

The Very Excellent Viceroy of New Spain, Don Antonio María Bucareli, continuing his reports on the expedition of the Frigate *Santiago,* Schooner *Sonora* and Packetboat *San Carlos,* which under the command of Battleship Lieutenant Don Bruno de Eceta and Frigate Lieutenants Don Juan Francisco de la Bodega and Don Juan de Ayala, who left the Port of San Blas on the *Nueva Galicia,* at the beginning of 1775, to advance as far as possible the voyages and discoveries of the Northern coast of *Californias,* and examine the Port of San Francisco (of whose happy progress news was given in the *Gazeta* of March 19 of the present year) has lately communicated the return of the two first ships to the said Port of San Blas, sending the log books and authentic documents of their respective commanders, in which it is recorded that they examined different Ports on the same coast which they named, and took possession of them as well as of the other territories stretching from the Port of Monte-Rey to latitude 58 degrees, with the consent and satisfaction of their natives. And since the Naval Officers and Pilots made plans and a very exact map of those coasts and *Northern Seas,* His Majesty has decided that they should be Engraved and given to the public, as was done with the results of the last voyage to Monte-Rey.

Appendix C

The Farías Bill to Colonize California*

Speech of Bernardo González Angulo, Minister of Relations, to the Secretaries of the Chamber of Deputies on April 16, 1833.

Your Excellencies: Occupied as is His Excellency the Vice-President in invigorating all the branches of the public administration, one of those matters that has principally attracted his attention has been the missions, especially those in the two Californias, both because of the large sums that have been devoted to their development and because of the fertility and wealth that they both contain, especially Upper California, and also because of the neglect that they have suffered, to a certain extent, not only under the Spanish government but under the national governments in power since we obtained our independence. As a result of this those Mexicans who live there under a happy sky, with fertile soil which abundantly rewards the toil of laboring hands, with good ports, with diving for exquisite pearls, with fishing that can be done for sea otter, seals and whales and notwithstanding that they have other kinds of industry, they have scarcely been able to settle the coasts, and the recently converted neophyte Indians still suffer from the vices of idolatry, without having tasted all the benefits that civilized life provides.

*The sources for the bill and amendments are *El Telégrafo* (Mexico City, Apr. 22 and May 15–21, 1833).

These evils, and other more serious ones that the present situation of both Californias could bring about, have occupied the attention of the government. As a result of this, information has been sought from persons able to give exact and accurate accounts, and papers, documents, and files relating to the important affairs of the missions of that country have been produced, all of this being done so as to provide enlightenment on a matter which the government believes to be of the greatest importance, and so as to consider permanent and well-thought-out measures that will be capable of completely removing abuses which may be seen in those territories, and to produce advantages which they do not have today only because of the almost total lack of enthusiasm with which, up to a point, that part of the Republic has been regarded. If a little more attention had been given and a little more watchfulness shown in the fulfilment of laws on the giving up of the places where the Indians live in missions and on other matters, it would have been sufficient for the Californias to have considerably increased their population, and for them to have been providing all the benefits that they could for the commerce and industry of the nation. But unfortunately this was not done, and in spite of the action taken by the Spanish Cortes on the secularization of the missionaries, our missions continue under the same system as they did under the colonial administration. And now it can be seen that so long as this practice, which is opposed to reason and justice and in opposition to legal provisions, continues there can be no hope that those regions will be happy or that they will arrive at the state of prosperity that the wealth that they contain promises.

The missions of California had their beginning about 1697, under the care and direction of the regulars of the extinguished Society of Jesus. At the time of their extinction they had fifteen missions in Lower California, which was where they first formed this kind of establishment. And despite the fact that the fertility of its soil is not comparable with that of Upper California, it produces corn and wheat, dates, bananas, olives and other fruits, and these products, together with aguardiente and wine that were made in the time of the Spanish government, and with its dried fruits, used to be sold in Sonora where they were highly regarded and in the Peninsula itself. The east coast of Lower California has wealth in the exquisite pearls that it produces.

New or Upper California, because of its geographic position is superior in every way to Old or Lower California. Its products are more numerous and its climate is so good that in the year 1793, when scarcely 24 years had passed since the oldest mission in that territory was built, those establishments already possessed 24 thousand head of cattle, a large number of sheep, 4,040 with hair [goats?], a little more than 3,000 mares and horses and that year the harvest of wheat amounted to more than 38,700 bushels (15,000 fanegas), 3,612 bushels (1,400 fanegas) of barley, 19,672 bushels (7,625 fanegas) of corn, and 4,434 bushels (1,719 fanegas) of beans, chickpeas and lentils. Other missions have been founded since then, and the population has grown as a result up to the point that in 1831 the number of inhabitants in the territory we are discussing amounted to 27,000 and in Lower California to 15,000 in spite of the fact that venereal disease has taken such a fearful toll.

All these products which I have mentioned, have been in charge of and are still in charge of the religious on their respective missions. On these they have been and still are regarded as spiritual and temporal fathers, and although in both territories the so-called rights of the stole or parochial rights are unknown, each missionary, if he is a Dominican, receives 350 pesos a year in stipends, and if he is a Fernandino 400 pesos, both of them paid from the fund known as the Pious Fund of the Californias. This is made up of several estates and capital which have been set aside, all due to the piety and beneficence of the Marquis of Vilapuente, of Doña Gertrudis de la Peña, his wife, and of Don Juan Caballero, Don Nicolás de Arriaga, to Viceroy Don Luis de Velasco, to the Jesuit Juan María Luyando and to Doña María de Borja, all private individuals who established the fund with their large donations and who have been the real promoters in the establishment of the said missions.

The object of each one of these donors cannot be more noble nor more beneficent; but since the civil domestic administration of the missions is poorly carried out, the entire management of the secular affairs being left in the hands of the religious, it was unavoidable that there would occur what we today see has occurred, and that the influence that each religious has been able to have, according to the greater or lesser wealth that their efforts have caused the mission to produce, has been slowing down or rather has obstructed the development of industry and the benefits that it produces, when an enlightened administration spreads knowledge, encourages industry, and does not put any obstacle in its way. Perhaps these evils could have been remedied if, as soon as the decree of the Cortes of Spain of September 13, 1813, was published, it had been put into effect according to the procedure that it sets forth. But this was not done, although there is no evidence that there was any legal obstacle that might have caused its enactment to be held back. It appears that in this matter too much consideration has been shown, and today that law, which, if it had been applied then might have effectively cured all those evils, now would only cause difficulties and would not provide the fruits that the legislators proposed when they dictated it. Another more positive and more effective remedy is needed now. No sanctuary should be left for greed, bad faith, nor the tricks and schemes that appear and are used when it is desired to avoid compliance with a law. His Excellency the Vice-President is aiming at this, and after having meditated upon what would be most suitable for the happiness and prosperity of both Californias, he instructs me to put forward, as a beginning, the following propositions, which I submit to you so that you may bring them to the attention of the Chamber.

Article 1. Lands belonging to the missions, and remaining vacant lands in both Californias will be divided: first, between the families of the natives of those territories; second, between residents of them who have no property in land, or who, if they do, have less than the minimum assigned by this law to each family; third, between the military who garrison those territories; fourth, between Mexican families who go to take up a new residence there; fifth, between foreign families who go on their own account for this same purpose; six, between *empresarios* [colonizing promoters] and the families they take there; and lastly, between the convicts at the presidios who wish to establish themselves there after their terms are over.

[After debate on May 3 and 4, 1833, article 1 was amended to read as follows: "The lands belonging to the missions, and remaining vacant lands in both Californias will be divided precisely in the following order: first, between the families of natives of those territories. Second, between the military who garrison those territories, and who are in arrears in their pay. Third, between residents of those territories who do not possess any property in land or who, if they do, have less than the minimum assigned by this law to each family. Fourth, between Mexican families who go to take up a new residence there. Fifth, between foreign families who go on their own account for this same purpose, it being understood on missions which are at least ten leagues from the boundaries. Sixth, between empresarios and the families they take there. Seventh, between the convicts at the presidios who wish to establish themselves there after their terms are over, giving the proprietors their titles by the public authority mentioned in article 20, the Indians to get theirs paid by the Pious Funds and the others at cost."]

Article 2.   Lands to be distributed will be considered to be irrigable *(regadio)* if they have permanent water for their irrigation; they will be considered dry or dependent on the weather *(secano o temporal)* if they do not have water for irrigation, although they are good for cultivation, and they will be considered land with watering places *(abrevadero)* if in their present state they are only good for raising cattle.

Article 3.   In dividing the land, the *sitio de ganado mayor* will be used as a basis, it being understood that this means a surface of twenty-five million Mexican square *varas* [4,338.2 acres].

Article 4.   The government will confer, with full property rights, on each of the families mentioned above a piece of irrigable land whose surface is not less than 52 acres (500 varas square or what is the same, 250 thousand square Mexican varas) nor more than 2,169 acres (half a *sitio);* if the land is dry or dependent on the weather they will receive not less than 826 acres (2,000 varas square) nor more than 4,338.2 acres (one sitio); if it is land with watering places they will receive not less than 1,860 acres (3,000 varas square) nor more than 8,676 acres (2 sitios).

Article 5.   The natives are prohibited from transferring the lands granted to them according to this law until after five years, and after this period they may only sell what they have cultivated.

Article 6.   No property in land shall pass into mortmain under any pretext.

Article 7.   For the first and only time each family that receives lands and is not serving an empresario or other persons, will be given free the implements necessary, in the judgment of the Government, for cultivating it.

Article 8. Stock belonging to each mission will be divided between the natives of each of them so that each family will receive two yoke of oxen or steers, two cows which have had calves, four cows for breeding, four sheep, two horses, two mares and a she-mule, he-mule or ass.

[Article 8 was amended on May 4, 1833, so that each family was to get a maximum of twice the number of animals given in the original article, except for cows for breeding, which remained the same. At the end of the amended article the phrase, "maintaining the said natives for a year," was added.]

Article 9. The stock left over after the distribution mentioned in the preceding article will be divided in the same proportion between the residents who do not have property of their own and between the soldiers, convicts in the presidios, and Mexican families who have been granted lands in accordance with this law.

[Article 9 was amended on May 4, 1833, so that those who were to share the surplus stock were to receive half the number granted in Article 8].

Article 10. If surplus stock remains, it will form part of the fund for the development of the said territories.

Article 11. Articles 5, 6, 7, and 11 of the law of April 6, 1830 on the colonization and preservation of Texas are extended to cover the said territories.

[The articles of the law of April 6, 1830, referred to are as follows:

Article 5. The government can send to the colonies that it is establishing convicts destined for Veracruz and other places whom it believes would be useful, paying the transportation of the families who wish to go with them.

Article 6. The convicts shall be put to work on the construction of fortifications, towns and roads that the commissioner believes necessary; and when their terms are up, if they wish to continue as colonists, they will be given land and farm implements, and they will continue to receive their food for the first year.

Article 7. Mexican families who voluntarily wish to be colonists, will be assisted for their journey and given their subsistence for a year and granted lands and farm implements.

Article 11. By use of the power that the general congress reserved to itself in article 7 of the law of August 18, 1824, foreigners are forbidden to colonize boundaries in those states and territories of the Federation that border on their own nations. In consequence, contracts which have not been fulfilled, and which are in conflict with this law will be suspended. (It should be noted that article 11 of the law of April 6, 1830, was annulled on November 21, 1833.)]

Article 12. Mexican or foreign empresarios who at their own expense bring in colonizing families, will be indemnified by lands, if they wish to devote themselves to agriculture, granting them a parcel of land equal to the amount that the families whom they bring to California receive.

Article 13. If the empresario does not wish to devote himself to agriculture he will be granted freedom of the port of San Francisco of Upper California for the period of one year for the same ship, or another of equal size, in which he has brought in one hundred families. Freedom of the port, as far as the time is concerned, will increase or diminish in the same proportion that the families, according to the above basis, increase or diminish. The minimum number for this privilege will be fifty families that may be brought in to San Francisco at one time or in smaller groups; but they will not enjoy the privilege until they have brought in the number of families determined above.

Article 14. Individuals who are physically prevented from devoting themselves to industry shall not be admitted under the class of families mentioned in article 12, and the empresario who brings them in will be forced to re-embark them at his own expense.

Article 15. The empresario who acquires more land than the maximum that this law indicates for each family, will be forced to sell or transfer the excess in the way that he wishes, within fifteen years after he has acquired the property.

Article 16. All foreigners who become colonists in the Californias, observe the constitution and laws of the Republic, will be

414

Mexican citizens as soon as they build their own houses and begin to cultivate their lands.

[It appears from the debates on May 6, 1833, that article 16 as it was approved by the Chamber of Deputies no longer required foreigners to observe the Constitution and laws of the republic, although it is possible that this sentence was omitted in error from the newspaper version of the article.]

Article 17. Families who are brought by empresarios will be given land, provided their contracts give them some free days to work for themselves.

Article 18. Individuals who during the first five years have not cultivated the lands that they have been granted under this law, so as to provide at least for the subsistence of their families, will lose them without fail.

Article 19. Transportation by sea and land, both of Mexican and foreign families, will be paid by the government, making effective use of the sums provided for that object, until the journeys are ended. This offer is made to extend to the empresarios mentioned in article 12 but not to those who are given privileges according to article 13.

Article 20. In each town or mission the first political authority will keep a book in which is recorded the lands and properties that are granted and the persons who receive them, with as many circumstances as are necessary, so that there shall never be any doubt about such matters.

Article 21. An account of each grant or distribution will at once be given to the Governor or Superior Political Chief of the respective territory, so that a book may be kept in which he will order that there be noted down whatever information he receives on those matters; and each month he will prepare a clear and precise statement of them which he will send to the government through the Ministry of Relations.

Article 22. The inhabitants and colonists in both Californias will be exempt from paying tithes for ten years.

[Article 22 was amended on May 8, 1833, to read: "Colonists and inhabitants of the Californias will not in future be forced to pay tithes or first fruits or other equivalent taxes."]

Article 23. For the same period of time they will be free from taxes on the export of their fruits, and on the import of wooden houses, machines and instruments necessary for all kinds of industry or science, foreign food, and cattle, either for breeding or for consumption in the said territory.

Article 24. Since the sea otter and the beaver have become scarce in the harbors, rivers and bays of both Californias, hunting them is absolutely prohibited for the period of two years, counted from the date of publication of this law, and when this period is over, it will be free only to Mexicans.

[Article 24 was amended on May 7, 1833. The amended version omitted the word "beaver" from the first line and added a final phrase as follows: "the same as at present hunting for beavers."]

Article 25. For the distribution of the lands, cattle, and implements mentioned in this law and so that the growth and prosperity of the two Californias may be most effectively promoted, the government will appoint a general Director with subordinate commissioners as it may judge convenient, giving them the necessary instructions and regulations. The Director will receive 4 thousand pesos a year and up to 6 thousand pesos a year will be invested in the subordinates.

Article 26. By means of the above Director there will immediately be established in all towns and missions whose population is more than 200 souls, free schools of primary letters, whose teachers will be paid, according to circumstances and the judgment of the government, from 300 to 600 pesos a year.

Article 27. If the above tutors have to leave the aforesaid territories, the Government will pay their transportation by sea and land and provide them with whatever traveling expenses it judges absolutely necessary.

Article 28. Provided the above tutors wish to devote themselves, by means of their servants, to cultivating the land or raising cattle, they will be granted in the towns or missions where they reside, the amount of lands, implements and cattle mentioned in articles 4, 7, 8, and 9.

Article 29. In order to meet the expenses that must be paid to put this law into effect, and in order to develop the arts, sciences, agriculture, and all kinds of industry in both Californias, a fund will be established which will be made up as follows: first, from the products of the estates, capital, and rent that is known at present as the Pious Fund of the Californias; second, from the surplus property mentioned in article 10; third, from 50 per cent of the liquid products of the maritime customs of both territories and the total of all their interior customs.

Article 30. As soon as the first two sources mentioned in the previous article are sufficient to cover the objects of this law, the products of the third will be returned to the federal treasury.

[On May 9, 1833, the following addition was made to article 30: "and while these products are being used, their total will be credited to the debt that the Federation at present owes the Fund of the Californias."]

Article 31. The development fund of the Californias will be under the direction of the Commission which has controlled what has been called up until now the Pious Fund, and it will provide the government, through the Ministry of Relations, with a general account of its revenues and investments every year.

Article 32. This same Commission will consult with the government on what development is to be undertaken and the means that in its view can and should be adopted.

Article 33. The work to be done by the Director spoken of in article 25, and the advice and proposals that he has to bring to the government's attention, will be done through the directing Commission, which will pass it all along with its own report through the Ministry of Relations.

Article 34. Until the aforesaid fund is organized, the government will provide the necessary sums to carry into effect the projects in this law, taking care to reimburse the public treasury with the products of this same fund.

Article 35. The government shall be able to spend up to 100,000 pesos in sponsoring emigration from foreign countries to develop these colonies.

Article 36. The same government will endeavor, by all means in its power, to attract the tribes of natives to the social order, and it can reward in whatever way it thinks best the chiefs and old men of each tribe, so as to achieve this object. It shall be able to spend for this up to 20 thousand pesos.

Article 37. The Supreme Government is empowered to fulfill all the objectives of this law, overcoming the difficulties which arise, and it is empowered to meet the expenses that it believes necessary for this purpose.

Article 38. The government itself will finally draw up the orders and regulations that are needed so that the present law in all its parts may be put into effect.

Article 39. As a consequence, the decree of the Spanish Cortes of September 13, 1813, is annulled, and other laws which may be in conflict with this one.

Article 40. Likewise article 6 of the law of May 25, 1832, is annulled and the revenues from the fund of the Californias shall be applied to the objectives mentioned in article 29 of this law.

[On May 9, 1833, articles 37–40 were withdrawn, and article 37 was rewritten as follows: "The decree of the Spanish Cortes of September 13, 1813, is annulled and article 6 of the law of May 25, 1832, is annulled, the revenues of the fund of the Californias being assigned to the objectives mentioned in article 29 of this law, and other laws that may be in conflict with this one are annulled." Article 6 of the law of May 25, 1832, provided that revenue from leasing the rural estates belonging to the Pious Fund of the Californias should be deposited in the Mexico City mint, and it was to be used only for the California missions.]

Appendix D

A partial list of members of the Farías colony and others who accompanied them. Where it is possible to do so, approximate age and marital status are given.

Abrego, José. Age 22. Single.
Adrián, Juan Antonio. Single.
Aguilar, José María. Single.
Aguilar, Santiago.
Alanis, Felipe.
Alvarez, Alvina. Teacher.
Andrade, Antonio.
Angela, María (this may not be her full name). Age 12.
Arana, José.
Araujo, Buenaventura. Naval officer.
Ayala, Juan Nepomuceno. Age 20.
Baric, Charles (French). Age 27. Teacher.
Berduzco, Francisco (sometimes spelled Verduzco). Age 22. Merchant.
Bonilla, José Mariano. Age 27. Teacher.
Bonilla, Luis (brother of José Mariano Bonilla). Single. Teacher.
Bonilla, Vicente (brother of José Mariano and Luis Bonilla). Single.
Brown, Charles. Joined the Farías colony in California.
Cabello, Martín S. Revenue officer who came out with the colony.
Camarillo, Juan.

Appendixes

Carranza, Francisco. Age 14. Single.
Castellón, Bárbara.
Castellón, Isidoro. Age 19.
Castillo, Doña Jesús. Teacher.
Castillo Negrete, Francisco Javier. Single.
Castillo Negrete, Luis (brother of F. J. Castillo Negrete). Age 35. Married; 6 children.
Cepeda, Pedro (also spelled Zepeda).
Coronel, Antonio Franco. (son of Ignacio Coronel). Age 16.
Coronel, Guillermo. Teacher.
Coronel, Ignacio. Age 39. Married. Teacher.
Coronel, Josefa. Age 18. Single.
Coronel, Manuel. Age 2.
Coronel, Micaela.
Coronel, Soledad. Age 8.
Cosío, José María.
Covarrubias, José María.
Dávila, Agustín. Age 30. Single. Painter of saints.
Dávila, Antonio (brother of Agustín Dávila).
Desforges, Auguste.
Díaz, Guadalupe (wife of Nicanor Estrada). Age 22.
Díaz Argüello, Benito. Age 20.
Enríquez, Petra. Teacher.
Esparza, Juan Bautista (also known as Victoriano Vega). Age 24.
Espíndola, María Paz.
Estrada, Elena (daughter of Nicanor Estrada). Born on voyage to California in 1834.
Estrada, Nicanor. Age 28.
Estrada, Umesinda (daughter of Nicanor Estrada). Age 7.
Fernández, Dionisio. Teacher.
Fernández, Francisca. Teacher.
Fernández, José Zenón. Teacher.
Fernández, Juan Alonso. Died on voyage from San Blas to San Diego on the *Natalia*.
Fernández, Doña Loreto. Teacher.
Fernández, Manuela. Teacher.
Fernández, Máximo. Teacher.
Fernández, Sabas. Teacher.
Flores, Francisca.

Flores, Gumersindo.
Franco, Encarnación.
García, Francisco.
Gardano, Guadalupe (wife of José de Jesús Noé).
Garraleta, Antonio.
Garraleta, Justa. She is said also to have had a sister with her.
González, José de Jesús. Age 21.
González, Manuel María.
Guerrero y Palomares, Francisco.
Gutiérrez, Anacleto. Single.
Guitérrez, José María.
Híjar, Carlos N. (nephew of José María Híjar). There is also a
    Miguel Híjar listed, which might be another name for Carlos
    N. Híjar.
Híjar, José María.
Janssens, Agustín. Age 17. Single.
Jiménez, Cayetana.
Lara, Romualdo. Single.
Llano, Mariano.
López, José Rosas (known as "el clarín López"). Age 20.
López, Mariano. Single.
Madariaga, Doña María Enciso.
Meneses, Agustín.
Meneses, Florencio. Single.
Montes, José. Single.
Mora, Regino de la.
Morales de Castillo Negrete, Josefa (wife of Luis Castillo Negre-
    te). Age 24.
Muñoz, Juan Antonio. Single.
Noé, José de Jesús.
Noé, Miguel. Infant, 1 year old.
Noreña, Antonio (also spelled Moreña). Teacher.
Ocampo, Francisco. Single.
O'Donoju, Simón. Single.
Olivier, Pierre.
Olvera, Agustín (nephew of Ignacio Coronel). Age 13.
Ortega, Antonio. Single.
Ortez, Hilario. Age 22. Single.
Oviedo, José María. Teacher.

Padilla, Juan de Dios. Widower. Retired army captain.

Padrés, José María.

Padrés, Rafael (brother of José María Padrés).

Paz, Ignacia. Teacher.

Peña, Carmen (daughter of Cosme Peña). Age 10.

Peña, Cesaría (daughter of Cosme Peña). Age 6.

Peña, Cosme.

Pino, Braulis del. Single.

Prudon, Victor. Age 25. Teacher. (He married Teodocia Bojorques.)

Ramírez, Antonio.

Revilla family. 3 women, 2 boys, and Felipe de Revilla. Possibly the latter was the head of the family. His daughter, María Joaquina Revilla, was engaged to be married to Buenaventura Araujo.

Ríos, José. Single.

Rojas, Feliciano. Age 14.

Romero, Balbino.

Romero, Francisca (wife of Ignacio Coronel). Age 35.

Romero, José Mariano. Teacher.

Rosa, José de la.

Rosa, María Dolores de la (wife of José de la Rosa).

Rosas, Daría. A brother of his is also mentioned, whose name is given as Eduwiges.

Rosel, Francisca. Teacher.

Sabici, Matías.

Salgado, Tomás.

Santa María, José. Single.

Serrano, Florencio. Age 25. Teacher. He says he brought with him to California a widowed sister and a child of 5.

Serrano, Rita (wife of Florencio Serrano).

Solis, Juan.

Terán, Miguel.

Torres, Francisco. Age 28.

Valverde, Agustín. Age 22.

Vargas, Francisco.

Vargas Machuca, Miguel. Age 43.

Vidal, Bartolomé.

Zárate, Ignacia. Teacher.

Bibliography

PRIMARY SOURCES

Manuscripts

The richest source of manuscript material on California for this period is the Bancroft Library, which is housed in a wing of the general library of the University of California at Berkeley. Since Hubert Howe Bancroft donated his magnificent collection to the University of California, the Bancroft Library has microfilmed a large number of manuscripts concerning the Hispanic period of California history from repositories in Mexico and Spain. Many of the library's original holdings on the period are also now available on microfilm. It should be mentioned that although the Spanish and Mexican archives of California were destroyed in the San Francisco earthquake and fire of 1906, Bancroft's employees had already copied vast quantities of the original material. These copies are frequently summaries of the original documents, and this must be borne in mind when they are used. In the 1870s Bancroft sent interviewers to take down statements or to encourage the writing of memoirs by old-timers in California. Many of these were Mexicans whose recollections go back to the period of this study. After the passage of some forty years, however, their memories of the past were sometimes inaccurate or influenced by the graft and corruption of the times in which they were living. One of them (José Fernández), for example, states that the corruption of the Farías colony's leaders was only exceeded by the exploits of Ben

Bibliography

Butler. Details of the manuscript holdings of the Bancroft Library are now being made available in a published catalog: *A Guide to the Manuscript Collections of the Bancroft Library, 1*, ed. Dale L. Morgan and George P. Hammond (Berkeley, 1963).

Manuscripts used in the Bancroft Library include items in the following collections (call numbers are not given, at the suggestion of the librarians, because they may be changed at any time): Transcripts from the Archivo histórico militar de defensa nacional; H. H. Bancroft, "Reference Notes on Immigration and Colonization 1773–1833"; Colonización y terrenos baldíos, legajo 2, expediente 52, and legajo 6, from Secretaría de Fomento, Mexico; Departmental Records, *5* and *9;* Departmental State Papers, *1–6;* Departmental State Papers, Benicia, *5;* Departmental State Papers, Benicia Military, *77, 79,* and *81;* Documentos para la historia de California, *3* and *5;* Junta de California, Secretaría de Governación, legajo 1830–1834; Legislative Records, *1* and *2;* Papeles varios; State Papers, *2;* State Papers, Missions *9* and *11;* State Papers, Missions and Colonization, *2;* State Papers, Sacramento; Superior Governmental State Papers, *3, 5, 7, 8,* and *9;* Superior Governmental State Papers, Decrees and Dispatches.

The following is a list of the recollections of the old Mexican residents of California used: José Abrego, "Memoirs," in Mariano G. Vallejo, "Documentos para la historia de California," *31;* José María Amador, "Memorias sobre la historia de California"; Juan B. Alvarado, "Memoirs"; Juan Bandini, "Historia de la Alta California"; Juan Bandini, "Documentos para la historia de California"; Antonio Franco Coronel, "Cosas de California"; Juan Bautista Esparza, "Vida californiana"; José Fernández, "Cosas de California"; Vicente P. Gómez, "Lo que sabe sobre cosas de California"; De la Guerra, "Documentos para la historia de California," *6;* Carlos N. Híjar, "California en 1834, recuerdos de Carlos N. Híjar"; Florencio Serrano, "Apuntes para la historia de la Alta California"; Estevan de la Torre, "Reminiscencias"; Ignacio del Valle, "Lo pasado de California"; José de Jesús Vallejo, "Reminiscencias históricas"; Mariano G. Vallejo, "Recuerdos históricos"; Mariano G. Vallejo, "Documentos para la historia de California," *1, 3, 23,* and *31,* pt. 1.

Other items consulted in the Bancroft Library manuscript collection include: Charles Brown, "Statement of Recollections of Early Events in California"; Carlos María Bustamante, "Medidas para la pacificación de la América mexicana, 1820"; Carlos María Bustamante, "Voz de la Patria," *9* and *10;* the Cowan collection, a valuable set of letters from and to Governor Figueroa; Alfred A. Green, "Life and Adventures of a 47'er of California"; Dr. John Marsh to Commodore Thomas ap Catesby Jones, Nov. 25, 1842; Alphonse Pinart, "Documentos para la historia de Sonora"; Rancho Los Alamitos Court Case no. 290.

Another California manuscript repository which provided material for this study was the Santa Barbara Mission Archives located in the old mission at Santa Barbara, from which documents 390, 630, 697, 735, 765, 827, and 833 were used. The guide to this valuable archive by Father Maynard J. Geiger *(Calendar of Documents in the Santa Barbara Mission Archives* [Washington, D.C., 1947]) does not include some of the more recent manuscript acquisitions. At the Huntington Library, San Marino, the following were consulted: Agustín Janssens, "Libro de lo que me a pasado en mi vida"; Leidesdorff Papers; Stearns Papers, and manuscript MR191. Outside of California a major source of manuscript material is the Western Americana Collection in the Beinecke Rare Book and Manuscript Library at Yale University, New Haven, Connecticut. A number of valuable items for this study were obtained there. Mary C. Withington compiled *A Catalogue of Manuscripts in the Collection of Western Americana founded by William Robertson Coe* (New Haven, 1952), and Jeanne M. Goddard compiled *A Catalogue of the Frederick W. and Carrie S. Beinecke Collection of Western Americana,* edited with an introduction by Archibald Hanna, volume 1 of which appeared in 1965. Manuscripts used from other United States archives: Adams Letterbook, May 1825, reel 147, microfilm of Adams Papers, Alderman Library, University of Virginia; Records of the Russian-American Company, 1802–1867; Letters received by the Governors General, National Archives, Washington, D.C.; The Farías Papers, in the Latin American Collection, University of Texas, Austin, Texas. Material in the possession of the author includes a letter from Captain J. Vichot of Oct. 4, 1965. Manuscripts from Mexican archives: Archivo General de la Nación, Mexico City, Provincias Internas, *23,* Californias, *17, 18, 20, 23* and *45,* Misiones, *24,* Estado *32,* Instrucción pública, *8* and *10;* Archivo de Defensa, Mexico City, service records of Buenaventura Araujo, José María Echeandía, José Figueroa, José María Padrés, Francisco de Paula y Tamariz, Manuel Victoria; Archivo de Hacienda, Mexico City, Consulado, Legajos 426–39; Museo Nacional, Mexico City, Comisión de colonización, 1822; Biblioteca Nacional, Mexico City, manuscript collection items listed in notes; Zacatecas State Library, Zacatecas, Carlos María Bustamante, "Diario." There is a microfilm copy of this "Diario" in the historical collection at Chapultepec Museum, Mexico City.

Manuscripts consulted from Spanish archives: Archivo General de Indias, Estado 20, Estado 25, Estado 28, Estado 31, Estado 32, Estado 33, Estado 40, Estado 43, Estado 86, Guadalajara 416, Guadalajara 417, Guadalajara 492; Archivo General de Simancas, Sección Estado. While this is mostly concerned with Spanish-English relations, it contains valuable material on Russian- Spanish relations. Archivo-Museo Don Alvaro de Bazán, El Viso del Marqués, Ciudad Real, Expediente de nobleza, Francisco de Tamariz y Moure; England, Public Record Office London, F.O. 50/80a, F.O. /84.

The following thesis and dissertations have been consulted: Jessie Davis Francis, "An Economic and Social History of Mexican California" (Ph.D. dissertation, University of California, 1935); Keld John Reynolds, "The Junta de Fomento de Californias, 1824–1827, Analysis and Evaluation of its Work" (Ph.D. dissertation, University of Southern California, 1945); Ruth Staff, "Settlement in Alta California before 1800" (M.A. thesis, University of California, 1931); and George Tays, "Revolutionary California" (Ph.D. dissertation, University of California, 1932).

Printed Materials

LAWS, DEBATES, DOCUMENTS, PAMPHLETS, REPORTS, BROADSIDES

Actas del congreso constituyente mexicano, 4 vols. Mexico, 1822–23.
American State Papers, Miscellaneous, 2, Washington, D.C., 1834.
Butler, Ruth Lapham, "A Statement by Phelipe de Neve," *Hispanic American Historical Review*, 22 (May 1942), 357–60.
Castañares, Manuel, *Colección de documentos relativos al departmento de Californias*, Mexico, 1845.
La Chanfaina se-quita, Mexico, 1820.
Colección de los decretos y órdenes de las cortes de España que se reputan vigentes en la república de los Estados Unidos Mexicanos, Mexico, 1829.
Colección de los principales trabajos en que se ha ocupado la junta

nombrada para meditar y proponer al supremo gobierno los medios más necesarios para promover el progreso de la cultura y civilización de los territorios de la alta y de la baja California, Mexico, 1827.

Corral, Juan José del, *Dictamen presentado al Exmo. Sr. Vice-Presidente en ejercicio del supremo poder ejecutivo,* Mexico, 1834.

Diario de las discusiones y actas de las Cortes, 92 vols. Cádiz, 1810/13–1837.

Diario de las sesiones del congreso de Jalisco, 1, Guadalajara, 1825.

"Dictamen que dió la junta de fomento de Californias al Exmo. Señor Presidente de la República," in *Colección de los principales trabajos en que se ha ocupado la junta,* Mexico, 1827.

Dublán, Manuel, and José María Lozano, *Legislación mexicana,* 52 vols. Mexico, 1876–1910.

Guzmán, José María, *Breve noticia que da al supremo gobierno del actual estado del territorio de la alta California,* Mexico, 1833.

Informe y cuentas que el banco de avío presenta, in Alamán, *Memoria,* Mexico, 1832.

"Informe de las misiones de California, 1826," *Boletín* del archivo general de la nación, *30* (April-June 1959), 233–84.

Informes y manifiestos de los poderes ejecutivo y legislativo de 1821 a 1904, 2 vols. Mexico, 1905.

"Iniciativa de ley que propone la junta para el mejor arreglo del gobierno de los territorios de Californias," in *Colección de los principales trabajos en que se ha ocupado la junta.*

Instrucción reservada que el Conde de Revilla Gigedo dió a su sucesor en el mando el Marqués de Branciforte, Mexico, 1831.

Instrucción reservada que dió el virrey don Miguel José de Azanza a su sucesor don Félix Berenguer de Marquina, Mexico, 1960.

Instrucciones que los virreyes de Nueva España dejaron a sus sucesores, Mexico, 1867.

La Malinche de la constitución, Mexico, 1820.

Mateos, Juan A., *Historia parlamentaria de los congresos mexicanos de 1821 a 1857,* 25 vols. Mexico, 1877–1912.

Maza, Francisco de la, *Código de colonización y terrenos baldíos,* Mexico, 1893.

Memoria del gobernador de Jalisco, Guadalajara, 1832.

Memoria presentada al soberano congreso por el secretario de relaciones, Mexico, 1822.

Bibliography

Memoria que el secretario de estado presenta, Mexico, 1823.

Memoria de la secretaría de estado y de relaciones, Mexico, 1831.

Memoria del secretario de guerra, Mexico, 1825.

Nos el dean y cabildo gobernador de esta santa iglesia metropolitana de Méjico, Mexico, 1833.

Parabién de los indios, Mexico, 1820.

Pastoral que el Illm. Sr. Dr. D. Francisco Pablo Vázquez obispo de la Puebla de los Angeles dirige a sus diocesanos con motivo de la peste que amenaza, Puebla, 1833.

"Plan de colonización estrangera para los territorios de la alta y de la baja California," in *Colección de los principales trabajos en que se ha ocupado la junta.*

"Plan de colonización de nacionales para los territorios de la alta y de la baja California," in *Colección de los principales trabajos en que se ha ocupado la junta.*

"Plan para el arreglo de las misiones de los territorios de la alta y de la baja California," in *Colección de los principales trabajos en que se ha ocupado la junta.*

"Plan político mercantil para el más pronto fomento de las Californias," in *Colección de los principales trabajos en que se ha ocupado la junta.*

Proceedings of the Alaskan Boundary Tribunal, 7 vols. Washington, D.C., 1904.

"Proyecto para el establecimineto de una companía de comercio directo con el Asia y mar Pacífico, cuyo punto céntrico debe ser Monterey, capital de la alta California," in *Colección de los principales trabajos en que se ha ocupado la junta.*

"Proyecto de reglamento en grande para el establecimiento de la companía asiático-mexicana," in *Colección de los principales trabajos en que se ha ocupado la junta.*

Reglamento interior de la secretaría de estado y del despacho de relaciones interiores y exteriores, Mexico, 1826.

Reglamento para la compañía cosmopolitana, Mexico, 1834.

Reglamento para el gobierno de la provincia de Californias, San Francisco, 1929.

Rodríguez de San Miguel, Juan, *Segundo cuaderno de interesantes documentos relativos a los bienes del fondo piadoso de misiones,* Mexico, 1845.

428

San Martín, José, *Memoria y proposiciones sobre las Californias,* Biblioteca aportación histórica, Mexico, 1943.

——, *Memoria y proposiciones sobre las Californias,* trans. Henry R. Wagner, San Francisco, 1945.

Santibañez, Enrique, ed., *La Diplomacia mexicana,* 2 vols. Mexico, 1910–12.

Un siglo de relaciones internacionales de México, Archivo histórico diplomático méxicano, no. 39, Mexico, 1935.

MEMOIRS, TRAVEL ACCOUNTS, LETTERS

Adams, John Quincy, *Memoirs,* ed. Charles Francis Adams, 12 vols. Philadelphia, 1875–77.

Azcárate, Juan Francisco de, *Un programa de política internacional,* Mexico, 1932.

Baegert, Johann Jakob, *Observations in Lower California,* trans. M. M. Brandenburg and Carl L. Baumann, Berkeley, 1952.

Bandini, José, *A Description of California in 1828,* Berkeley, 1951.

Beechey, F. W., *Narrative of a Voyage to the Pacific,* 2 vols. London, 1831.

Beristain de Souza, José Mariano, *Biblioteca hispano-americano septentrional,* 3d ed. 5 vols. Mexico, n.d.

Bocanegra, José María, *Memorias para la historia de México independiente, 1822–1846,* 2 vols. Mexico, 1892.

Bouguer, Pierre, *La Figure de la terre, déterminée par les observations de Messieurs Bouguer et de La Condamine,* Paris, 1749.

Brivazac, Beaumont de, *L'Europe et ses colonies,* 2 vols. Paris, 1822.

Buffon, Georges Louis Leclerc de, *Oeuvres complètes,* 26 vols. Paris, 1828.

Bustamante, Carlos María, *Diario histórico de México, 1822–1823,* Zacatecas, 1896.

Canel Acevedo, Pedro, *Reflexiones críticas sobre la constitución española, cortes nacionales y estado de la presente guerra,* Oviedo, n.d.

Chappe d'Auteroche, Jean, *Voyage en Californie pour l'observation du passage de Vénus sur le disque du sol le 3 juin, 1769,* Paris, 1772.

Condamine, Charles Marie de la, *Viaje a la América meridional,* Buenos Aires, 1942.

Cook, James, and James King, *A Voyage to the Pacific Ocean,* 2d ed. London, 1785.

Coxe, William, *An Account of the Russian Discoveries between Asia and America,* London, 1780.

Dana, Richard Henry, Jr., *Two Years Before the Mast,* Boston and New York, 1929.

Fernández de Navarrete, Martín, *Relación del viage hecho por las goletas Sutil y Mexicana en el año de 1792,* Madrid, 1802.

Figueroa, José, *Manifiesto a la república mejicana,* Monterey, 1835.

————, *The Manifesto to the Mexican Republic,* Foreword by Jos. A. Sullivan, Oakland, 1952.

The First French Expedition to California, La Pérouse in 1786, trans. Charles N. Rudkin, Los Angeles, 1959.

Fleurieu, Charles Pierre Claret de, *A Voyage Round the World performed during the years 1790, 1791, and 1792 by Etienne Marchand,* 2 vols. London, 1801.

Forbes, Alexander, *A History of California,* London, 1839.

Granados y Gálvez, Joseph Joaquín, *Tardes americanas: gobierno gentil y católico; breve y particular noticia de toda la historia indiana,* Mexico, 1778.

Guerra Ord, Angustias de la, *Occurrences in Hispanic California,* trans. and ed. Francis Price and William H. Ellison, Washington, D.C., 1956.

Hardy, R. W. H., *Travels in the Interior of Mexico,* London, 1829.

Humboldt, Alejandro de, *Ensayo político sobre el reino de la Nueva España,* ed. J. A. Ortega y Medina, Mexico, 1966.

Humboldt, Alexander von, *Essai politique sur le royaume de la Nouvelle Espagne,* 5 vols. Paris, 1811.

————, *Political Essay on the Kingdom of New Spain,* trans. John Black, 4 vols. London, 1811.

Iturri, Francisco, *Carta crítica sobre la historia de América del Sr. Don Juan Bautista Muñoz, Puebla,* 1820.

Jefferson, Thomas, *Notes on the State of Virginia,* New York, 1964.

Kenneally, Finbar, *Writings of Fermín Francisco de Lasuén,* 2 vols. Washington, D.C., 1965.

Kotzebue, Otto von, *A Voyage of Discovery into the South Sea and Beering's Straits for the purpose of exploring a North-East Passage undertaken in the years 1815–1818,* 3 vols. London, 1821.

Mahr, August C., *The Visit of the "Rurik" to San Francisco in 1816,*

2, Stanford University Publications, History, Economics, and Political Science, 2, Stanford, 1932.

Manning, William R., ed., *Diplomatic Correspondence of the United States Concerning the Independence of the Latin American Nations*, 3 vols. New York, 1925.

Las misiones de la alta California, 2 vols. Mexico, 1914.

Mofras, Duflot de, *Travels on the Pacific Coast*, trans. and ed. Marguerite Eyer Wilbur, 2 vols. Santa Ana, 1937.

Mora, José María Luis, *Obras sueltas*, 2 vols. Paris, 1837.

Northwest Coast of America and California: 1832; letters from Fort Ross, Monterey, San Pedro and Santa Barbara, by an Intelligent Bostonian, Los Angeles, 1959.

Novo y Colson, Pedro de, *Viaje político-científico alrededor del mundo por las corbetas Descubierta y Atrevida*, 2d ed. Madrid, 1885.

Ortiz de Ayala, Tadeo, *México considerado como nación independiente y libre*, 2 vols. Guadalajara, 1952.

———, *Resumen de la estadística del imperio mexicano*, Mexico, 1822.

Pauw, Cornelis de, *Recherches philosophiques sur les Américains*, 3 vols. London, 1771.

Peña y Peña, Manuel de la, *Lecciones de práctica forense mejicana, escritas a beneficio de la academia nacional de derecho público y privado de Méjico*, 4 vols. Mexico, 1835–39.

Pernety, Antoine Joseph, *Dissertation sur l'Amérique et les Américains contre les recherches philosophiques de M. de P.*, Berlin, 1770.

Petit-Thouars, Abel du, *Voyage autour du monde*, 2 vols. Paris, 1841.

Robertson, William, *Works*, 8 vols. Oxford, 1825.

Robinson, Alfred, *Life in California: During a Residence of Several Years in that Country, by an American*, New York, 1846.

Sales, Luis, *Noticias de la provincia de Californias, 1794*, Madrid, 1960.

Señán, José, *The Letters of José Señán*, ed. Lesley Byrd Simpson, San Francisco, 1962.

Shaler, William, *Journal of a Voyage Between China and the North-Western Coast of America*, Claremont, 1935.

Simpson, Sir George, *An Overland Journey Round the World During the Years 1841 and 1842*, Philadelphia, 1847.

Bibliography

Smith, Adam, *An Inquiry into the Nature and Causes of the Wealth of Nations*, New York, 1937.

Tibesar, Antonine, ed., *Writings of Junípero Serra*, 3 vols. Washington, D.C., 1955–56.

Torrubia, Giuseppe, *I Moscoviti nella California o sia dimostrazione della verita del passo all'America settentrionale*, Rome, 1759.

Ulloa, Antonio de, *Noticias americanas*, Buenos Aires, 1944.

Vancouver, George, *A Voyage of Discovery to the North Pacific Ocean and Round the World*, 3 vols. London, 1798.

Vattel, Emmerich von, *The Law of Nations*, Philadelphia, 1849.

Venegas, Miguel, *Noticia de la California y de su conquista temporal y espiritual*, 3 vols. Mexico, 1944.

Wagner, Henry R., trans., "Journal of Tomás de Suria of his Voyage with Malaspina to the Northwest Coast of America in 1791," *Pacific Historical Review*, 5 (September 1936), 234–76.

Ward, Bernardo, *Proyecto económico*, Madrid, 1787.

Wilkes, Charles, *Narrative of the United States Exploring Expedition*, 5 vols. Philadelphia, 1845.

Zúñiga, Ignacio, *Rápida ojeada al estado de Sonora*, Mexico, 1835.

NEWSPAPERS

El Aguila mexicana, Mexico City, August 1824.

Anales de Jalisco, Guadalajara, January 1834.

La Antorcha, Mexico City, April 1833.

El Cosmopolita, Mexico City, December 1836.

El Fénix de la libertad, Mexico City, May 1834.

Gaceta diaria de México, Mexico City, June, October 1825.

Gaceta extraordinaria del gobierno de México, Mexico City, June 1811.

Gaceta del gobierno del estado libre de Jalisco, Guadalajara, March, September 1831.

Gaceta del gobierno imperial de México, Mexico City, August 1822.

Gazette de Leyde, Leyden, March 1775.

Gazeta de Madrid, Madrid, March, May 1776.

El Indicador de la Federación Mexicana, Mexico City, December 1833.

El Mono, Mexico City, May 1833.

The National Intelligencer, Washington, D.C., 1821.

Bibliography

Niles Weekly Register, Baltimore, January 1818; March, May, December 1819; 1821.
El Sol, Mexico City, 1827, 1828.
El Telégrafo, Mexico City, 1833, 1834.

SECONDARY SOURCES

Books

Amaya, Jesús, *Los conquistadores Fernández de Hijar y Bracamonte,* Guadalajara, 1952.
Andrade, Vicente de P., *Noticias biográficas sobre los ilustrísimos prelados de Sonora, de Sinaloa y de Durango,* 3d ed. Mexico, 1899.
Bancroft, Hubert Howe, *A History of Alaska,* San Francisco, 1886.
———, *History of California,* 7 vols. San Francisco, 1884–90.
Bean, Lowell John, and William Marvin Mason, *The Romero Expeditions, 1823–1826,* Palm Springs, 1962.
Bemis, Samuel Flagg, *John Quincy Adams and the Foundations of American Foreign Policy,* New York, 1949.
Bobb, Bernard E., *The Viceregency of Antonio María Bucareli in New Spain 1771–1779,* Austin, 1962.
Cambre, Manuel, *Gobiernos y gobernantes de Jalisco,* Guadalajara, 1910.
Caso, Alfonso, et al., *Métodos y resultados de la política indigenista en México,* Mexico, 1954.
Caughey, John Walton, *California,* New York, 1940.
Chapman, Charles Edward, *The Founding of Spanish California,* New York, 1916.
———, *A History of California: The Spanish Period,* New York, 1930.
Chávez Orozco, Luis, *Las Instituciones democráticas de los indígenas mexicanos en la época colonial,* Mexico, 1943.
Cleland, Robert Glass, *The Cattle on a Thousand Hills: Southern California 1850–1870,* San Marino, 1941.
Cook, Sherburne F., *The Conflict Between the California Indian and the White Civilization. I. The Indian versus the Spanish Mission,* Ibero-Americana, 21, Berkeley, 1943.
———, *The Extent and Significance of Disease among the Indians of Baja California 1697–1773,* Ibero-Americana, 12, Berkeley, 1937.
Cutter, Donald, *Malaspina in California,* San Francisco, 1960.

Bibliography

Dunne, Peter Masten, S.J., *Black Robes in Lower California,* Berkeley, 1952.

Eldredge, Zoeth Skinner, ed., *History of California,* 5 vols. New York, 1915.

Ellison, William H., and Francis Price, eds., *The Life and Adventures in California of Don Agustin Janssens, 1834–1856,* San Marino, 1953.

Engelhardt, Zephyrin, *The Missions and Missionaries of California,* 4 vols. San Francisco, 1908–15; 2d ed. *1, 2,* Santa Barbara, 1929–30.

Fernández, Justino, *Tomás de Suria y su viaje con Malaspina,* Mexico, 1939.

Folmer, Henry, *Franco-Spanish Rivalry in North America, 1524–1763,* Glendale, 1953.

Forbes, Jack D., *Warriors of the Colorado: The Yumas of the Quechan Nation and their Neighbors,* Norman, Okla., 1965.

Foster, George M., *Culture and Conquest: America's Spanish Heritage,* Chicago, 1960.

Geary, Gerald J., *The Secularization of the California Missions, 1810–1846,* Washington, D.C., 1934.

Geiger, Maynard J., *The Life and Times of Fray Junipero Serra,* 2 vols. Washington, D.C., 1959

Gerbi, Antonello, *La Disputa del nuevo mundo,* Mexico, 1960.

Gleason, John Howes, *The Genesis of Russophobia in Great Britain,* Cambridge, Mass., 1950.

Golder, Frank A., *Bering's Voyages,* 2 vols. New York, 1922, 1925.

———, *Russian Expansion on the Pacific 1641–1850,* Gloucester, Mass., 1960 [1914].

Grant, Campbell, *The Rock Paintings of the Chumash,* Berkeley, 1965.

Greenhow, Robert, *The History of Oregon and California and the Other Territories on the North-West Coast of North America,* Boston, 1844.

Hanke, Lewis, and Manuel Giménez Fernández, *Bartolomé de Las Casas, 1474–1566; bibliografía crítica,* Santiago, Chile, 1954.

Hanke, Lewis, *The Spanish Struggle for Justice in the Conquest of America,* Philadelphia, 1949.

Hansen, Woodrow James, *The Search for Authority in California,* Oakland, 1960.

Harding, George Laban, *Don Agustín V. Zamorano, Statesman, Soldier, Craftsman and California's First Printer,* Los Angeles, 1934.

Hildt, John C., *Early Diplomatic Negotiations of the United States with Russia,* Johns Hopkins University Studies in Historical and Political Science, Series 24, nos. 5–6, Baltimore, 1906.

Historical Atlas Map of Sonoma County, Oakland, 1877.

History of Sonoma County, San Francisco, 1880.

Hittell, Theodore H., *History of California,* 4 vols. San Francisco, 1885–97.

Kroeber, A. L., *Handbook of the Indians of California,* Washington, D.C., 1925.

Lobanov-Rostovsky, Andrei A., *Russia and Europe 1789–1825,* Durham, N.C., 1947.

McWilliams, Carey, *Southern California Country: An Island on the Land,* New York, 1946.

Manning, William Ray, *The Nootka Sound Controversy,* Annual Report of the American Historical Association for 1904 (Washington, D.C., 1905), pp. 279–478.

Mead, Margaret, *New Lives for Old,* New York, 1956.

Mitchell, Mairin, *The Maritime History of Russia 1848–1948,* London, 1949.

Morison, Samuel Eliot, *The Maritime History of Massachusetts,* Boston, 1921.

Müller, Gerhard Friedrich, *Sammlung russischer Geschichte,* 9 vols. St. Petersburg, 1732–64.

Muriel de la Torre, Josefina, *Hospitales de la Nueva España,* 2 vols. Mexico, 1960.

Navarro García, Luis, *Don José de Gálvez y la comandancia general de las Provincias Internas del norte de Nueva España,* Seville, 1964.

Nozikov, N., *Russian Voyages Round the World,* London, 1940.

Ogden, Adele, *The California Sea Otter Trade, 1784–1848,* Berkeley, 1941.

Okun, S. B., *The Russian-American Company,* trans. Carl Ginsburg, Cambridge, Mass., 1951.

Olavarría y Ferrari, Enrique, *México independiente, 1821–1855, 4,* in Vicente Riva Palacio, ed., *México a través de los siglos,* 5 vols. Mexico and Barcelona, 1888–89.

Bibliography

Pérez-Marchand, Monelisa Lina, *Dos etapas ideológicas del siglo XVIII en México,* Mexico, 1945.

Portillo y Diez de Sollano, Alvaro del, *Descubrimientos y exploraciones en las costas de California,* Madrid, 1947.

Potash, Robert A., *El Banco de avío de México,* Mexico, 1959.

Priestley, Herbert Ingram, trans. and ed., *Exposition Addressed to the Chamber of Deputies of the Union by Don Carlos Antonio Carrillo,* San Francisco, 1938.

———, *José de Gálvez, Visitor-General of New Spain (1765–1771),* Berkeley, 1916.

Richman, Irving Berdine, *California Under Spain and Mexico,* Boston, 1911.

Robinson, William Wilcox, *Land in California,* Berkeley, 1948.

Rolle, Andrew F., *California, A History,* New York, 1963.

The Russians in California, San Francisco, 1933.

Sánchez Lamego, Miguel A., *Apuntes para la historia del arma de ingenieros en México,* 5 vols. Mexico, 1943–49.

Saralegui y Medina, Manuel de, *Un negocio escandaloso en tiempos de Fernando VII,* Madrid, 1904.

Simpson, Lesley Byrd, *California in 1792. The Expedition of José Longinos Martínez,* San Marino, 1938.

Spicer, Edward H., *Cycles of Conquest: the Impact of Spain, Mexico, and the United States on the Indians of the Southwest, 1533–1960,* Tucson, 1962.

Suárez y Navarro, Juan, *Historia de México y del General Santa Anna,* 2 vols. Mexico, 1850–51.

Troncoso, Francisco P., *Las Guerras con las tribus Yaqui y Mayo,* Mexico, 1905.

Tuthill, Franklin, *History of California,* San Francisco, 1866.

Wagner, Henry R., *Cartography of the Northwest Coast of America,* 2 vols. Berkeley, 1937.

Williams, Glyndwr, *The British Search for the Northwest Passage in the Eighteenth Century,* London, 1962.

Articles

Andrews, Clarence B., "Russian Plans for American Dominion," *The Washington Historical Quarterly, 18* (April 1927), 83–92.

Baylen, Joseph O., and Dorothy Woodward, "Francisco de Miranda in Russia," *The Americas, 6* (April 1950), 431–49.

Bibliography

Beattie, George William, "Reopening the Anza Road," *Pacific Historical Review, 2* (March 1933), 52–71.

Bolton, Herbert E., "The Iturbide Revolution in the Californias," *Hispanic American Historical Review, 2* (May 1919), 188–242.

———, "The Mission as a Frontier Institution in the Spanish American Colonies," *American Historical Review, 23* (October 1917), 42–61.

Bowman, J. N., "The Resident Neophytes (Existentes) of the California Missions," Historical Society of Southern California *Quarterly, 40* (June 1958), 138–48.

Calderón Quijano, J. A., "Ingenieros militares en Nueva España," *Anuario de Estudios Americanos, 6* (1949), 1–72.

Carrera Stampa, Manuel, "The Evolution of Weights and Measures in New Spain," *Hispanic American Historical Review, 29* (February 1949), 2–24.

Cody, W. F., "An Index to the Periodicals published by José Antonio Alzate y Ramírez," *Hispanic American Historical Review, 33* (August 1953), 442–75.

Edwards, Clinton R., "Wandering Toponyms: El Puerto de la Bodega and Bodega Bay," *Pacific Historical Review, 33* (August 1964), 253–72.

Forbes, Jack D., "Indian Horticulture West and Northwest of the Colorado River," *Journal of the West, 2,* (January 1963), 1–14.

Guest, Florian [Francis], O.F.M. "The Establishment of the Villa de Branciforte," California Historical Society *Quarterly, 41* (March 1962), 29–50.

Hewes, Minna and Gordon, "Indian Life and Customs at Mission San Luis Rey," *The Americas, 9* (July 1952), 87–106.

Hill, Joseph J., "The Old Spanish Trail," *Hispanic American Historical Review, 4* (August 1921), 444–73.

Humphrey, R. A., "Richard Oswald's Plan for an English and Russian Attack on Spanish America 1781–1782," *Hispanic American Historical Review, 18* (February 1938), 95–101.

Hutchinson, C. Alan, "The Asiatic Cholera Epidemic of 1833 in Mexico," *Bulletin of the History of Medicine, 32* (January–February 1958), 1–23, and *32* (March–April 1958), 152–63.

———, "The Mexican Government and the Mission Indians of Upper California," *The Americas, 21* (April 1965), 335–62.

Bibliography

Masterson, James R., and Helen Brower, "Bering's Successors, 1745–1780: Contributions of Peter Simon Pallas to the History of Russian Exploration toward Alaska," *Pacific Northwest Quarterly, 38* (January 1947), 35–83, and *38* (April 1947), 109–55.

Mazour, Anatole G., "Dimitry Zavalishin: Dreamer of a Russian-American Empire," *Pacific Historical Review, 5* (March 1936), 26–37.

———, "The Russian-American Company: Private or Government Enterprise?" *Pacific Historical Review, 13* (June 1944), 168–73.

Ogden, Adele, "Russian Sea-Otter and Seal Hunting on the California Coast, 1803–1841," California Historical Society *Quarterly, 12* (September 1933), 217–39.

Park, Joseph F., "Spanish Indian Policy in Northern Mexico, 1765–1810," *Arizona and the West, 4* (1962), 325–44.

Payno, Manuel, "Alta California," *Revista científica y literaria de Méjico, 1* (1845), 81–84.

Perkins, Dexter, "Russia and the Spanish Colonies, 1817–1818," *American Historical Review, 28* (July 1923), 656–72.

Reynolds, Keld J., "The Reglamento for the Híjar and Padrés Colony of 1834," Historical Society of Southern California *Quarterly, 28* (December 1946), 142–75.

Romer, Margaret, "The Story of Los Angeles," *Journal of the West, 2* (January 1963), 31–65.

Sánchez-Diana, José María, "Relaciones diplomáticas entre Rusia y España en el siglo XVIII,'" *Hispania, 12* (1952), 590–605.

"The Secularization of the Missions," Historical Society of Southern California *Annual* (1934), pp. 66–73.

Servín, Manuel P., "The Secularization of the California Missions: A Reappraisal," *Southern California Quarterly, 47* (June 1965), 133–49.

Sokol, A. E., "Russian Expansion and Exploration in the Pacific," *American Slavic and East European Review, 11* (April 1952), 85–105.

Taylor, Alexander S., "Byron, Nelson and Napoleon in California," *Pacific Monthly, 11* (June 1864), 644–51.

Tays, George, "Mariano Guadalupe Vallejo and Sonoma—a Biography and a History," California Historical Society *Quarterly, 17* (March 1938), 50–73.

Temple, Thomas Workman, Jr., "Se Fundaron un Pueblo de Españoles," *Annual Publications,* Historical Society of Southern California, *15* (1931), 69–98.

Tompkins, Stuart R., and Max L. Moorhead, "Russia's Approach to America," *British Columbia Historical Quarterly,* pt. 1, *13* (April 1949), 55–66; pt. 2, *13* (July–October 1949), 231–55.

Tudisco, Anthony, "The Land, People, and Problems of America in Eighteenth Century Spanish Literature," *The Americas, 12* (April 1956), 363–84.

Triton (supplement to *Neptunia*), fascicle 52, 1ᵉʳ trimestre, 1960.

Winther, Oscar Osburn, "The Story of San José, 1777–1869," California Historical Society *Quarterly, 14* (March 1935), 3–27, and *14* (June 1935), 147–74.

Index

Index

Index

Index

Index

López de Haro, Gonzalo, 14–15, 86, 100

Lorenzo de Antepara, Juan. *See* Antepara, Juan Lorenzo de

Loreto, Lower California, 107, 127, 135, 142, 405

Loriot, brigantine, 371–73 passim

Los Alamitos, ranch, 252, 357, 376–78 passim, 386

Los Angeles: founding, 62, 63; Indians at, 222, 229; revolt at, 308, 351, 353–57, 362–63; school at, 322; mentioned, 151, 295, 364–65

Los Nietos ranch, 357

Lower California, 29, 31, 34, 46, 48, 106, 108, 113, 142, 315, 409, 410

Lozano, Manuel, 163

Luyando, Juan María (Father), 410

McIntosh, Edward M., 381

Malaspina, Alejandro, 65, 70

Manifiesto a la República Mexicana, 268, 269, 313

Manso, Lucas F. (Captain), 267

Margarita, ship, 145

Margil, Antonio (Father), 82

Mark West Creek, California, 264

Maroma (Indian Captain), 278

Marquina, Félix Berenguer de (Viceroy of New Spain), 21, 73, 79

Marsh, Dr. John, 269 n., 345

Martínez, Esteban José, 10, 14, 15

Maurelle, Francisco, 406

Mayo Indians, 154

Mayorga, Martín de (Viceroy of New Spain), 56

Mazatlán, Sinaloa, 157

Mead, Margaret, 402

Mercado, Father, 261–62

Mexican Liberals. *See* Liberals, Mexican

Mexican Scientific-Industrial Company, 199

Mexican-[American] War. *See* War of the American Invasion

Mexico: relations with Spain, 1, 42, 94, 96, 97, 123, 134–36, 140; and Russia, 20, 42, 96, 98, 105, 139, 179, 180, 382; foreign relations of, 98; and Territory of California, 105, 162, 171, 309, 374, 400, 401; Indian status under, 109, 169–71; economic situation, 110, 191; domestic politics, 122, 155, 159, 160, 397; army corps of engineers, 124; senate, 173, 174; church, 175–76; congress, 174, 213

laws and decrees: law of August 18, 1824, 112, 113, 121, 168, 246, 308; *law of November 21, 1828,* 137, 169, 192, 246–47, 308; *law of April 6, 1830,* 171, 286, 290; *bill of April 16, 1833,* 164–73, 307, 308, 408–18; *law of August 17, 1833,* 191, 242, 253, 304; *law of November 26, 1833,* 189–91, 253, 263, 290, 297, 303–04, 308; *decree of Feb. 4, 1834,* 301

Mexico, State of, 154

Mexico City, 153, 175, 176, 178, 196, 263, 379

Middleton, Henry, 100 n.

Mier, Servando Teresa de, 117, 118

Mier y Terán, Manuel de, 115

Muraviev, M. F., 101

Military, in California, 115, 220–21

Miñón, Juan José, 123–24

Minorca, island of, 13

Miranda, Francisco de, 26

Missionaries: and Indians, 75, 78, 81, 84, 126, 220–21; the California economy and, 84, 166; discontented, 89, 106, 128; Spanish, 90–91, 128, 137, 146; and the Mexican government, 91–94, 99, 106, 134, 163; Mexican, 137, 162; and slaughter of cattle, 248–50

Index

Order of St. Francis. *See* Franciscans

Ormaechea, José Ignacio, 117 n.

Ortega, Antonio, 369

Ortega, José Joaquín, 145, 242 n., 288, 313

Ortega, José María, 76, 77–78, 197

Ortega, María de Jesús, 197

Ortiz, María Josefa (La Corregidora), 117 n.

Ortiz de Ayala, Tadeo, 97, 111, 114, 125, 178, 199, 200

Ortiz Monasterio, José María, 156, 157 n.

Osío, Antonio María, 145, 269 n.

Oswald, Richard, 13

Ottoman Empire, 19

Our Lady of Guadalupe, 26

Oviedo, José María, 193 n.

Pacheco, Romualdo, 127, 128

Pacific Ocean, 1, 20

Padrés, José María: relations with Echeandía, 127, 136, 144; early career, 135, 182–84 passim, 349; suspicions against, 144, 145, 337, 353, 363, 368–70, 371; Manuel Victoria and, 144, 148; and the Mexican government, 145, 153, 195, 336; relations with Figueroa, 145, 184, 267, 268, 296, 307, 311–14 passim, 326–29, 372–73, 375–77, 380, 383, 384, 385–86, 398; and the colony, 196, 204, 209–10, 296, 310, 314–15, 329, 335–36, 339, 341, 359; opinions on the missions, 328, 376, 388–89; returns to Mexico, 364, 367, 370, 375, 378, 379; mentioned, 137, 182, 215, 265, 267, 283, 326

Padrés, Rafael (brother of José María Padrés), 326, 364

Palacios, Miguel, 204, 205

Pallas, Peter Simon, 10

Palmerston, Henry John Temple, 3d Viscount, 179

Pardo, Roberto, 377

Paris, Treaty of, 4

Parres, Joaquín, 205

Paul I (Emperor of Russia), 20, 21

Paul III (Pope), 49

Pauw, Cornelis de, 50–51

Payeras, Mariano (Father), 91, 92–94

Payno, Manuel, 393

Paz, Ignacia, 193 n.

Pearls, 111

Pedraza, Manuel Gómez. *See* Gómez Pedraza, Manuel

Peña, Gertrudis de la, 410

Pérez de Tagle, Luis, 78

Pérez Hernández, Juan José, 8, 9–10, 403, 405

Pérouse, La. *See* La Pérouse

Petaluma, California, 246, 261, 262–63

Petit-Thouars, Abel du, 345

Peyri, Antonio (Father), 150

Philippines, 18, 78

Pico, Pío, 145, 150, 151, 288, 296, 374

Pineda, José (Father), 109

Pious Fund of the Californias: origins, 43, 410; and the missions, 163, 168, 172, 191; and the colony, 187, 194, 204, 215, 243, 290, 295, 303; the Mexican government and, 45, 46, 143, 159, 172–73, 187, 205 n., 417

Plan for the Regulation of the Missions, 255

Plan of Cuernavaca, 213

Poinsett, Joel, 139

Polética, Pierre de, 40, 100

Political Chief of California. *See* Governor of California

Portilla, Pablo de la, 223–24, 249, 275, 277–78, 355

452

Index

454

Index

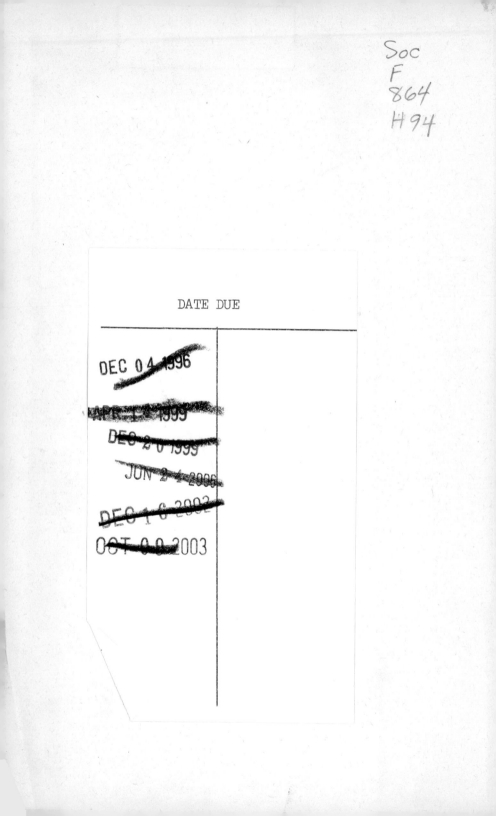

DATE DUE